A TEXT BOOK OF

DISCRETE MATHEMATICS

Mathematics - Paper - VIII

For

B.Sc. Part - II : Semester - IV

According to Revised Syllabus of
Shivaji University, Kolhapur, w.e.f. June 2014

M. D. Bhagat
Ex-Head of Mathematics Deptt.
Tuljaram Chaturchand College,
Baramati (Dist. Pune)

D. R. Hasbe
M. Sc. M. Phil.
Associate Professor,
Head Deptt. of Mathsematics,
Y. C. Institute of Science, Satara

Prof. M. B. Chougule
M. Sc. M. Phil.
Asso. Prof. & Head, Deptt. of Mathematics,
D.K.A.S.C. College,
Ichalkaranji - 416115

N1507

S.Y.B.Sc. DISCRETE MATHEMATICS - PAPER-VIII

Second Edition : January 2016 ISBN 978-93-5164-432-3

© : Author

The text of this publication, or any part thereof, should not be reproduced or transmitted in any form or stored in any computer storage system or device for distribution including photocopy, recording, taping or information retrieval system or reproduced on any disc, tape, perforated media or other information storage device etc., without the written permission of Author with whom the rights are reserved. Breach of this condition is liable for legal action.

Every effort has been made to avoid errors or omissions in this publication. In spite of this, errors may have crept in. Any mistake, error or discrepancy so noted and shall be brought to our notice shall be taken care of in the next edition. It is notified that neither the publisher nor the author or seller shall be responsible for any damage or loss of action to any one, of any kind, in any manner, therefrom.

Published By :
NIRALI PRAKASHAN
Abhyudaya Pragati, 1312 Shivaji Nagar,
Off J.M. Road, PUNE - 411005
Tel - (020) 25512336/37/39. Fax - 25511379
Email : niralipune@pragationline.com

Printed By :
Repro Knowledgecast Limited
Thane

DISTRIBUTION CENTERS

PUNE
Nirali Prakashan
119, Budhwar Peth, Jogeshwari Mandir Lane,
Pune - 411002, Maharashtra.
Tel : (020) 24452044, 66022708
Fax : (020) 2445 1538
Email : bookorder@pragationline.com

MUMBAI
Nirali Prakashan
385, S.V.P. Road, Rasdhara Co-op. Hsg.
Society, Girgaum,
Mumbai - 400004, Maharashtra
Tel : (022) 2385 6339 / 2386 9976,
Fax : (022) 2386 9976
Email : niralimumbai@pragationline.com

RETAIL SHOPS

PUNE
Pragati Book Centre
157, Budhwar Peth, Opp. Ratan Talkies,
Pune – 411002, Maharashtra
Tel : 2445 8887 / 6602 2707

Pragati Book Centre
676/B, Budhwar Peth,
Opp. Jogeshwari Mandir,
Pune – 411002, Maharashtra
Tel. : (020) 6601 7784, 2445 2254

PUNE
Pragati Book Centre
Amber Chamber, 28/A, Budhwar Peth,
Appa Balwant Chowk
Pune : 411002, Maharashtra
Tel : (020) 20240335 / 66281669
Email : pbcpune@pragationline.com

PBC Book Sellers and Stationers
152, Budhwar Peth,
Near Jogeshwari Mandir,
Pune – 411002, Maharashtra
Tel : (020) 6609 2463 / 2445 2254

MUMBAI
Pragati Book Corner
Indira Niwas,
111-A Bhavani Shankar Road,
Dadar (W), **Mumbai** – 400028
Tel : (022) 2422 3525 / 6662 5254
Email : pbcmumbai@pragationline.com

DISTRIBUTION BRANCHES

NAGPUR
Pratibha Book Distributors
Above Maratha Mandir, Shop No. 3, First Floor, Rani Zanshi Square, Sitabuldi,
Nagpur 440012, Maharashtra, Tel : (0712) 254 7129

JALGAON
34, V. V. Golani Market, Navi Peth, Jalgaon 425001, Maharashtra,
Tel : (0257) 222 0395, Mob : 94234 91860

KOLHAPUR
New Mahadvar Road, Kedar Plaza, 1st Floor Opp. IDBI Bank
Kolhapur 416 012, Maharashtra. Mob : 9850046155

www.pragationline.com info@pragationline.com

PREFACE

I am very pleased to present the first edition of the book : Paper VIII, Differential Equations for B.Sc. Part II, Semester IV.

This book is written according to the revised syllabus of Shivaji University, Kolhapur with effect from June 2014.

I have explained all elementary principles and fundamental concepts of mathematics in a simple and lucid language. The worked out examples are very numerous, fully solved and well graded. In exercise also, I have included variety of problems.

In this book, I have included the objective questions with answers and one model question paper which will be benefited to the students.

I am thankful to Mr. D. K. Furia and Mr. Jignesh Furia who took the responsibility to publish this book in time. I am grateful to Mrs. Anagha, Mr. Ilyas Shaikh and Ms. Chaitali Takle for the co-operation they extended. I express my thanks to the staff of Nirali Prakashan who availed this book in short time. I am thankful to our colleagues, friends and well-wishers who supported directly or indirectly to publish this book. Finally, my family to deserve the special thanks for their support, encouragement and tolerance.

I am also thankful to Mr. Virdhawal Shinde (Marketing Executive, Kolhapur) and Mr. Ashok Nanavare (Marketing Executive, Sangli and Mr. Girish Redekar Pune) for the promotion of this Book.

We request our colleagues, teaching Mathematics to offer their criticisms and suggestions, for further improvement in the book.

Author

SYLLABUS

1. **Relations** (10)
   1.1 Product sets, Relations, Inverse relation
   1.2 Pictorial representation of relations
   1.3 Composition of relations and matrices
   1.4 Types of Relation - Reflexive, Symmetric, Anti-symmetric, Transitive and its examples
   1.5 Closure properties and its examples
   1.6 Equivalence relations and partitions
   1.7 Examples on Equivalence relation
   1.8 Partial ordering relations
   1.9 Congruence Relation
      1.9.1 Theorem : (with proof) Let m be a positive integer Then:
         (i) For any integer a, we have $a \equiv a \pmod{m}$
         (ii) If $a \equiv b \pmod{m}$, then $b \equiv a \pmod{m}$
         (iii) If $a \equiv b \pmod{m}$ and $b \equiv c \pmod{m}$, then $a \equiv c \pmod{m}$
      1.9.2 Theorem : (with proof) Let $a \equiv c \pmod{m}$ and $b \equiv d \pmod{m}$. Then :
         (i) $a + b \equiv c + d \pmod{m}$
         (ii) $a.b \equiv c.d \pmod{m}$

2. **Division Algorithm** (12)
   2.1 Division algorithm for positive integers (with proof)
   2.2 Division algorithm for integers (without proof)
   2.3 Basic properties of divisibility
      2.3.1 Theorem : (statement only) Let a, b, c are integers :
         (i) If $a \mid b$ and $b \mid c$, then $a \mid c$
         (ii) If $a \mid b$ then, for any integer x, $a \mid bx$
         (iii) If $a \mid b$ and $a \mid c$, then $a \mid (b + c)$ and $a \mid (b - c)$
         (iv) If $a \mid b$ and $b \neq 0$, then $a = \pm b$ or $|a| < |b|$
         (v) If $a \mid b$ and $b \mid a$, then $|a| = |b|$, i.e., $a = \pm b$
         (vi) If $a \mid 1$, then $a = \pm 1$

- 2.4 G.C.D.
    - 2.4.1 Theorem : (with proof) Let d is the smallest integer of the form ax + by then d = g.c.d. (a, b)
    - 2.4.2 Theorem : (with proof) If d = g.c.d. (a, b) then there exists integers x and y such that d = ax + by
- 2.5 Properties of g.c.d. (with proof)
    - 2.5.1 Theorem : (with proof) A positive integer d = gcd (a, b) if and only if d has following two properties :
        - (i) d divides both a and b
        - (ii) If c divides both a and b, then c | d
    - 2.5.2 Simple properties of the greatest common divisor (with proof)
        - (i) gcd (a, b) = gcd (b, c)
        - (ii) If x > 0, then gcd (ax, bx) = x,gcd (a, b)
        - (iii) If d = gcd (a, b), then gcd (a | d, b | d) = 1
        - (iv) For any integer x, gcd (a, b) = gcd (a, b + ax)
- 2.7 Euclidean algorithm
- 2.8 Examples on Euclidean algorithm
- 2.9 Relatively prime integers
    - 2.9.1 Theorem : (with proof) If g.c.d. (a, b) = 1 and a and b both divides C then ab divides C.
    - 2.9.2 Theorem (with proof) If a | bc and g.c.d (a, b) = 1 then a | c.
    - 2.9.3 Theorem : (with proof) Let a prime p divides a product ab. Then p | a or p | b

3. Logic (10)

- 3.1 Revision
    - 3.1.1 Logical propositions (statements)
    - 3.1.2 Logical connectives
    - 3.1.3 Propositional Form
    - 3.1.4 Truth tables
    - 3.1.5 Tautology and contradiction
    - 3.1.6 Logical Equivalence
- 3.2 Algebra of propositions
- 3.3 Valid Arguments
- 3.4 Rules of inference

- 3.5 Methods of proofs
  - 3.5.1 Direct proof
  - 3.5.2 Indirect proof
- 3.6 Predicates and Quantifiers

4. Graph Theory (13)
- 4.1 Graphs and Multi-graphs
  - 4.2.1 Degree of a vertex
  - 4.2.2 Hand Shaking Lemma - The sum of degree of all vertices of a graph is equal to twice the number of edges
  - 4.2.3 Theorem : An undirected graph has even number of vertices of odd degree
- 4.3 Types of graphs
  - 4.3.1 Complete graph
  - 4.3.2 Regular graph
  - 4.3.3 Bipartite graph
  - 4.3.4 Complete bipartite graph
  - 4.3.5 Complement of a graph
- 4.4 Matrix representation of graph
  - 4.4.1 Adjacency Matrix
  - 4.4.2 Incidence Matrix
- 4.5 Connectivity

CONTENTS

1. **Relations** — 1.1 – 1.86

2. **Division Algorithm** — 2.1 – 2.34

3. **Logic** — 3.1 – 3.70

4. **Graph Theory** — 4.1 – 4.98

CHAPTER 1

RELATIONS

1.1 PRODUCT SETS

1.1.1 Cartesian Product

Consider two sets $A = \{a_1, a_2, ..., a_m\}$ and $B = \{b_1, b_2, ..., b_n\}$ containing m and n elements respectively. Then the Cartesian product of A and B denoted by $A \times B$ consists of all ordered pairs (a_i, b_j); $1 \leq i \leq m$, $1 \leq j \leq n$.

For example, if $A = \{1, 2, 3\}$ and $B = \{a, b, c, d\}$, then

$A \times B = \{(1, a), (1, b), (1, c), (1, d), (2, a), (2, b), (2, c), (2, d),$
$(3, a), (3, b), (3, c), (3, d)\}$

Also, $B \times A = \{(a, 1), (a, 2), (a, 3), (b, 1), (b, 2), (b, 3), (c, 1), (c, 2),$
$(c, 3), (d, 1), (d, 2), (d, 3)\}$

Obviously, if A has m elements and B has n elements then $A \times B$ consist of mn pairs.

The Cartesian product of the set A with itself is possible.

Thus, if $A = \{1, 2, 3\}$

then $A \times A = \{(1, 1), (1, 2), (1, 3), (2, 1), (2, 2), (2, 3), (3, 1), (3, 2),$
$(3, 3)\}$

Obviously see that, $A \times B \neq B \times A$

For three sets A, B, C

where, $A = \{a_1, a_2, ..., a_p\}$
$B = \{b_1, b_2, ..., b_q\}$

and $C = \{c_1, c_2, ..., c_r\}$

The product $A \times B \times C$ consists of all triplets of the type (a_i, b_j, c_k) with $a_i \in A$, $b_j \in B$, $c_k \in C$.

(1.1)

It consists of pqr triplets, we call A × B × C as ternary product.

Likewise the generalization to n sets $A_1, A_2, ..., A_n$ is possible. The n-ary product of n sets is

$$A_1 \times A_2 \times ... \times A_n = \{(a_1, a_2, ..., a_n); a_i \in A_i\}$$

It consists of all possible n-tuples.

Partition of a Set

Consider the set A = {1, 2, 3, 4, 5} and its subsets A_1 = {1, 2}, A_2 = {3, 5}, A_3 = {4}.

We observe that each of A_1, A_2, A_3 is non-empty subset of A. Further these three subsets of A are pairwise disjoint i.e. $A_1 \cap A_2 = \phi$, $A_1 \cap A_3 = \phi$, $A_2 \cap A_3 = \phi$ and their union gives the set A;

$$A = A_1 \cup A_2 \cup A_3$$

We say that the collection P = {A_1, A_2, A_3} is a partition of the set A.

Figuratively, we have

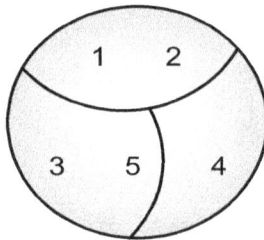

Fig. 1.1

Definition : Let A be non-empty set. Then the collection

$P = \{A_1, A_2, ..., A_r\}$ of subsets of A is called a partition of A if

(i) each A_i is non-empty,

(ii) A_i^s are pairwise disjoint i.e. $A_i \cap j = \phi$ for $i \neq j$, and

(iii) $\bigcup_i A_i = A$.

For the set A = {1, 2, 3, 4, 5, 6}

(a) P_1 = {{1, 3, 5}, {2, 4, 6}} is a partition.

(b) P_2 = {{1, 6}, {2, 4}, {3}, {5}} is a partition.

(c) P_3 = {{1, 2, 3, 4}, {4, 5, 6}} is not a partition since the two sets in P_1 are not disjoint.

(d) P_4 = {{1, 2, 3, 4}, {5}} is not a partition since the union of two sets in P_4 does not give original set A

EXERCISE (1.1)

1. A child has 4 shirts S_1, S_2, S_3, S_4 and 3 trousers t_1, t_2, t_3. Interpret the Cartesian product of these two sets.

2. If A, B, C are three sets, prove :
   (a) $A \times (B \cup C) = (A \times B) \cup (A \times C)$
   (b) $A \times (B \cap C) = (A \times B) \cap (A \times C)$
   Verify the results in (a) and (b) above, by taking
   $A = \{1, 2\}, \ B = \{a, b, c\}, \ C = \{b, d\}$

3. If $A \subseteq B$ and $C \subseteq D$, then prove that $A \times C \subseteq B \times D$. Is the converse true ?

4. Explain why $A \times B \times C \neq (A \times B) \times C$?

5. If $A = \{x; 1 \leq x \leq 2\}$ and $B = \{y; 2 \leq y \leq 3\}$ then show graphically $A \times B$ and $B \times A$.

6. Let $A = \{1, 2\}$ and $P(A)$ be the power set of A (i.e. the set of all subsets of A). Write $P(A) \times A$.

7. List all possible partitions of the set $A = \{a, b, c\}$.

8. A is the set of all positive integers, B is the set of all negative integers. Explain why {A, B} is not a partition of the set Z of all integers.

ANSWERS (1.1)

5.

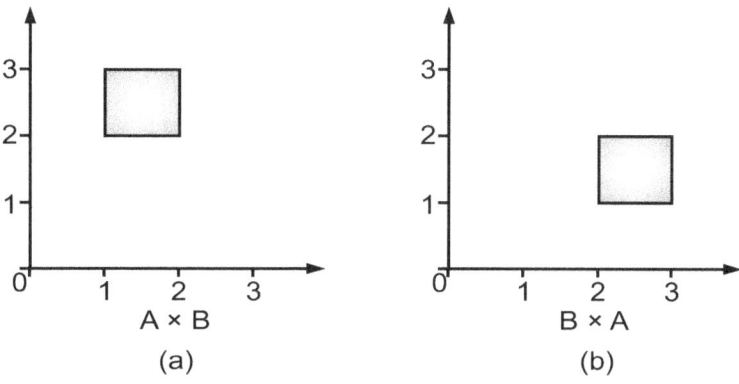

Fig. 1.2

6. {< ϕ, 1>, < ϕ, 2 >, < {1}, 1 >, < {1}, 2 >, < {2}, 1 >, < {2}, 2 >, < {1, 2}, 1>, < {1, 2}, 2 > }.

7. A_1 = {{a}, {b}, {c}}, A_2 = {{a}, {b, c}}, A_3 = {{b}, {a, c}}, A_4 = {{c}, {a, b}}, A_5 = {a, b, c}

8. $A \cup B \neq Z$ because $0 \notin A \cup B$.

1.1.2 Relation

In our everyday life, we always come across with the word relation. For example, 'is brother of' 'is sister of' 'is larger than' 'is smaller than' are some few examples. We now proceed to the precise mathematical idea of a relation.

Consider two sets

A = {2, 4, 5} and B = {1, 2, 3, 4, ..., 10}.

Then the Cartesian product

A × B = {(2, 1), (2, 2) ..., (2, 10), (4, 1), (4, 2), ..., (4, 10), (5, 1), (5, 2) ..., (5, 10)}

It consists of 3 × 10 = 30 ordered pairs.

Now we select the pairs (x, y) from A × B; in which x divides y. These pairs form a subset R of A × B.

R = {(2, 2), (2, 4), (2, 6), (2, 8), (2, 10), (4, 4), (4, 8), (5, 5), (5, 10)}

Definition : If A and B are two non-empty sets, then a subset R of A × B is called a binary relation from A to B.

ILLUSTRATIVE EXAMPLES

Example 1.1 : In the above example find the relations

R_1 = {(a, b); a > b} R_2 = {(a, b); b = 2a + 1}.

Solution : We have A = {2, 4, 5} and B = {1, 2, 3, 4, 5, 6, 7, 8, 9, 10}.

R_1 = {(a, b); a > b}

∴ R_1 = {(2, 1), (4, 1), (4, 2), (4, 3), (5, 1), (5, 2), (5, 3), (5, 4)}

Also, R_2 = {(a, b); b = 2a + 1}

∴ R_2 = {(2, 5), (4, 9)}

In a relation $R \subset A \times B$; when $(a, b) \in R$, we say that $a \in A$ is related to $b \in B$ according to relation R and write aRb. It is also described by saying that 'a is R-related to b'.

If B = A, then a relation R from A to A itself, is called a relation on the set A.

Just like a binary relation $R \subset A \times B$; a subset $R \subset A \times B \times C$ is called a ternary relation. Also, if $A_1, A_2, A_3, ..., A_n$ are n sets, then a subset $R \subset A_1 \times A_2 \times ... \times A_n$ is called n-ary relation.

The case n = 1 corresponds to unary relation.

In our course, we shall deal with binary relations only. As such the word relation we shall mean a binary relation.

A relation R from set A to set B is a subset of $A \times B$. Hence the set of those elements $a \in A$; which appear as first elements in the pairs of R form a subset of A. It is called domain of R.

Likewise the set of those elements $b \in B$ which appear as the second elements in the pairs of R form a subset of B. It is called range of R.

We denote domain of R as Dom (R) and the range of R as Ran (R).

More precisely, if R is a relation from set A to set B, then

Dom (R) = $\{a \in A; (a, b) \in R \text{ for some } b \in B\}$

and   Ran (R) = $\{b \in B; (a, b) \in R \text{ for some } a \in A\}$

Example 1.2 : Let A = {1, 2, 3, 4, 5} and B = {4, 5, 7, 8, 9, 10}.

Define a relation R from A to B as R = {(a, b); a + b is a perfect square}

Find Dom (R) and Ran (R).

Solution : A = {1, 2, 3, 4, 5}   B = {4, 5, 6, 7, 8, 9, 10}

Then   R = {(1, 8), (2, 7), (3, 6) (4, 5), (5, 4)}

Dom (R) = {1, 2, 3, 4, 5}

Ran (R) = {8, 7, 6, 5, 4}

Inverse Relation :

Let R be the relation from set A to set B. Then the inverse relation denoted by R^{-1} is the relation from set B to set A such that,

R^{-1} = {(x, y); (y, x) $\in$ R}

Also the complementary relation denoted by $\bar{R}$ consists of those pairs of elements which do not belong to R.

Thus, $\bar{R} = \{(x, y); (x, y) \notin R\}$

Let $A = \{1, 2, 3, 4\}$ and $B = \{a, b, c\}$

Find the relation, $R = \{(2, a), (2, c), (1, b), (4, a)\}$ is from set A to set B.

Then, $R^{-1} = \{(a, a), (c, 2), (b, 1), (a, 4)\}$

and $\bar{R} = \{(1, a), (1, c), (2, b), (3, a), (3, b), (3, c), (4, b), (4, c)\}$

Illustration : Consider the set, $A = \{2, 4, 5, 7, 8\}$ and the relation R on A defined by $R = \{(x, y); x \text{ divides } y\}$

Then, $R = \{(2, 2), (2, 4), (2, 8), (4, 4), (4, 8), (5, 5), (7, 7), (8, 8)\}$

Then, $R^{-1} = \{(2, 2), (4, 2), (8, 2), (4, 4), (8, 4), (5, 5), (7, 7), (8, 8)\}$

and $\bar{R} = \{(2, 5), (2, 7), (4, 2), (4, 5), (4, 7), (5, 2), (5, 4), (5, 7), (5, 8), (7, 2), (7, 4), (7, 5), (7, 8), (8, 2), (8, 4), (8, 5), (8, 7)\}$

EXERCISE (1.2)

1. Let $A = \{1, 2, 3, 4, ..., 8\}$ and $B = \{1, -1, 2, -2, 3, -3\}$. A relation R from A to B is defined by aRb iff $a = b^2 + 1$.
   State which of the following pairs belong to R :
   (a) (5, −2) (b) (1, −1) (c) (10, 3) (d) (1, 0) (e) (2, 2) (f) (2, 1)

2. A relation R is defined on the set Z^+ of positive integers, as below.
   aRb iff $a = b^k$, where k is some positive integer. State which of the following pairs belong to R.
   (a) (1, 1) (b) (16, 2) (c) (2, 16) (d) (4, 4) (e) (3, 243) (f) (1, 6).

3. Let $A = \{1, 2, 3, 4, 5, 6\}$. A relation R is defined on the set A as below.
   aRb iff a is multiple of b. Find the domain and range of R.

4. A relation R is defined on the set $A = \{2, 3, 5, 6, 7, 8\}$ by $(a, b) \in R$ iff $a + b \geq 12$. Find the domain and range of R.

ANSWERS (1.2)

1. $(5, -2) \in R$ $\qquad \because 5 = (-2)^2 + 1$
   $(1, -1) \notin R$ $\qquad \because 1 \neq (-1)^2 + 1$
   $(10, 3) \notin R$ $\qquad \because 10 \notin A$
   $(1, 0) \notin R$ $\qquad \because 0 \notin B$
   $(2, 2) \notin R$ $\qquad \because 2 \neq (2)^2 + 1$
   $(2, 1) \in R$ $\qquad \because 2 = (1)^2 + 1$

2. $1 \, R \, 1$ $\qquad \because 1 = (1)^1$
   $16 \, R \, 2$ $\qquad \because 16 = (2)^4$
   $2 \, \not{R} \, 16$ $\qquad \because 2 \neq (16)^k$ for any positive integer k
   $4 \, R \, 4$ $\qquad \because 4 = (4)^1$
   $3 \, \not{R} \, 243$ $\qquad \because 3 \neq (243)^k$ for any positive integer k
   $1 \, \not{R} \, 6$ $\qquad \because 1 \neq (6)^k$ for any positive integer k

3. $R = \{(1, 1), (2, 1), (2, 2), (3, 1), (3, 3), (4, 1), (4, 2), (4, 4), (5, 1), (5, 5),$
   $(6, 1), (6, 2), (6, 3), (6, 6)\}$
   Dom R = Ran (R) = A

4. $R = \{(5, 7), (5, 8), (6, 6), (6, 7), (6, 8), (7, 5), (7, 6), (7, 7), (7, 8), (8, 5),$
   $(8, 6), (8, 7), (8, 8)\}$
   Dom $\cdot R$ = $\{5, 6, 7, 8\}$
   Ran $\cdot R$ = $\{5, 6, 7, 8\}$

1.2 PICTORIAL REPRESENTATION OF RELATIONS

Graphical Representation :

Suppose $A = \{a_1, a_2, ..., a_n\}$ is a finite set of n elements. A relation R from A to A itself can be represented pictorially, called directed graph (digraph) of that relation. In a digraph of R each element of the set A is enclosed in a small circle, which is called a vertex in a digraph. Further when $a_i \, R \, a_j$ i.e. the pair $(a_i, a_j) \in R$ we draw an arrowed edge joining the vertices corresponding to a_i and a_j, the arrow being directed from a_i towards a_j.

Consider a relation R defined on the set A = {1, 2, 3, 4}.

R = {(2, 2), (2, 1), (1, 2), (1, 1), (1, 4), (1, 3), (4, 3), (3, 2)}

The digraph of this relation looks as below.

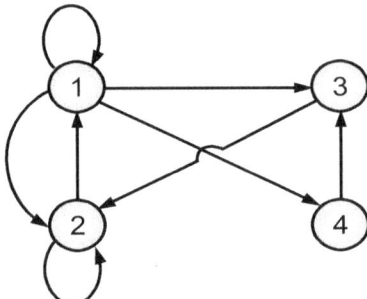

Fig. 1.3

The edges in a digraph are called directed edges or simply diedges.

A diedge whose beginning vertex coincides with the ending vertex, is said to form a loop. In the above digraph, the edges (1, 1) and (2, 2) form a loop at the vertex 1 and 2 respectively.

Consider now the edge corresponding to the pair (4, 3) in the above digraph. This edge leaves the vertex 4 and enters into the vertex 3. We describe this situation by saying that this diedge contributes one out degree at the leaving vertex 4 and one indegree at the entering vertex 3.

In the same manner each edge in a digraph contributes one outdegree at the leaving vertex and one indegree at the entering vertex.

In particular a loop in a digraph contributes one outdegree and one indegree at the same vertex.

ILLUSTRATIVE EXAMPLES

Example 1.3 : Let A = {a, b, c, d} and R be the relation on A, whose matrix is

$$M_R = \begin{bmatrix} 0 & 1 & 1 & 0 \\ 1 & 1 & 1 & 0 \\ 0 & 1 & 0 & 1 \\ 1 & 0 & 1 & 0 \end{bmatrix}$$

Draw the digraph of R, verify that the sum of all indegrees and outdegrees is equal to twice the number of edges.

Solution : $M_R = \begin{bmatrix} 0 & 1 & 1 & 0 \\ 1 & 1 & 1 & 0 \\ 0 & 1 & 0 & 1 \\ 1 & 0 & 1 & 0 \end{bmatrix}$

∴ R = {(a, b), (a, c), (b, a), (b, b), (b, c), (c, b), (c, d), (d, a), (d, c)}

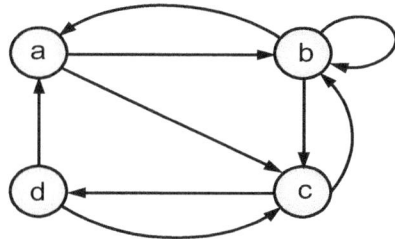

Fig. 1.4

Vertex :	a	b	c	d
Indegree :	2	3	3	1
Outdegree	2	3	2	2

Total indegree = 9

Total outdegree = 9

∴ Total degree = 9 + 9 = 18

which is twice the number of edges.

Example 1.4 : A digraph of a relation R is given as below.

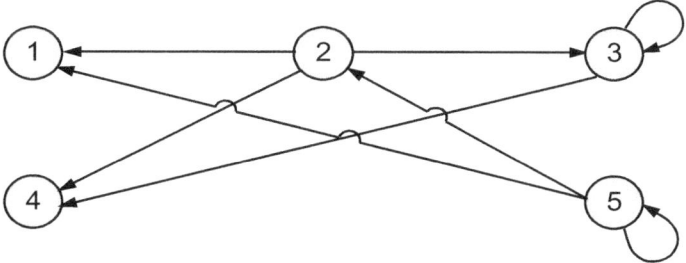

Fig. 1.5

Write the relation R as a set of pairs and write its matrix.

Solution : From the given diagraph

R = {(2, 1), (2, 3), (2, 4), (3, 3), (3, 4), (5, 2), (5, 1), (5, 5)}

$M_R = \begin{bmatrix} 0 & 0 & 0 & 0 & 0 \\ 1 & 0 & 1 & 1 & 0 \\ 0 & 0 & 1 & 1 & 0 \\ 0 & 0 & 0 & 0 & 0 \\ 1 & 1 & 0 & 0 & 1 \end{bmatrix}$

Representation of a Relation

We have already seen that a relation R is represented as a set of ordered pairs (a, b), where a ∈ A and b ∈ B. We now proceed to two other representations of a relation viz. matrix representation and graphical representation. The former is useful in computer programming while the latter gives us the visual display of various properties of the relation.

Matrix Representation :

We begin the matrix representation of a relation with some introductory results about Boolean matrices. An m × n matrix A whose elements are 1 and 0 only, is called a Boolean matrix. For example,

$$A = \begin{bmatrix} 1 & 0 & 1 & 0 \\ 0 & 1 & 1 & 0 \\ 1 & 1 & 0 & 1 \end{bmatrix} \text{ and } B = \begin{bmatrix} 0 & 0 & 1 & 0 \\ 1 & 1 & 1 & 0 \\ 1 & 0 & 1 & 1 \\ 0 & 1 & 0 & 1 \end{bmatrix}$$ are Boolean matrices of order 3 × 4 and 4 × 4 respectively.

Now in a two element Boolean algebra B(0, 1), we have two binary operations, one of them is called 'join' denoted by ∨ and the other is called 'meet' denoted by ∧. Also there is one unary operation i.e. complementation and is denoted by /.

Then in Boolean algebra B(0, 1) we have

$$0 \vee 0 = 0, \ 0 \vee 1 = 1, \ 1 \vee 0 = 1, \ 1 \vee 1 = 1$$

and $\quad 0 \wedge 0 = 0, \ 0 \wedge 1 = 0, \ 1 \wedge 0 = 0, \ 1 \wedge 1 = 1$

Also, $\quad 0' = 1$ and $1' = 0$

For ready reference we represent the above results by composition tables as below.

∨	0	1
0	0	1
1	1	1
Join operation		

∧	0	1
0	0	0
1	0	1
Meet operation		

a	a'
0	1
1	0
Complementation	

Let now $A = [a_{ij}]$ and $B = [b_{ij}]$ be two Boolean matrices of the same order say $m \times n$. Then the join of A and B is a Boolean matrix $C = [c_{ij}]$ of order $m \times n$ such that

$$c_{ij} = a_{ij} \vee b_{ij} \text{ for } i = 1, 2, \ldots, m \text{ and } j = 1, 2, \ldots, n.$$

Similarly, the meet of A and B is a Boolean matrix $D = [d_{ij}]$ of order $m \times n$ such that $d_{ij} = a_{ij} \wedge b_{ij}$ for $i = 1, 2, \ldots, m$ and $j = 1, 2, \ldots, n$.

As an illustration consider

$$A = \begin{bmatrix} 1 & 1 & 0 & 1 \\ 0 & 1 & 1 & 0 \\ 0 & 0 & 1 & 1 \end{bmatrix}_{3 \times 4} \text{ and } B = \begin{bmatrix} 0 & 1 & 1 & 0 \\ 0 & 0 & 1 & 1 \\ 1 & 0 & 1 & 0 \end{bmatrix}_{3 \times 4}$$

Then

$$A \vee B = \begin{bmatrix} 1 \vee 0 & 1 \vee 1 & 0 \vee 1 & 1 \vee 0 \\ 0 \vee 0 & 1 \vee 0 & 1 \vee 1 & 0 \vee 1 \\ 0 \vee 1 & 0 \vee 0 & 1 \vee 1 & 1 \vee 0 \end{bmatrix}$$

$$= \begin{bmatrix} 1 & 1 & 1 & 1 \\ 0 & 1 & 1 & 1 \\ 1 & 0 & 1 & 1 \end{bmatrix}_{3 \times 4} \quad \text{[See table of } \vee \text{]}$$

Also

$$A \wedge B = \begin{bmatrix} 1 \wedge 0 & 1 \wedge 1 & 0 \wedge 1 & 1 \wedge 0 \\ 0 \wedge 0 & 1 \wedge 0 & 1 \wedge 1 & 0 \wedge 1 \\ 0 \wedge 1 & 0 \wedge 0 & 1 \wedge 1 & 1 \wedge 0 \end{bmatrix}$$

$$= \begin{bmatrix} 0 & 1 & 0 & 0 \\ 0 & 0 & 1 & 0 \\ 0 & 0 & 1 & 0 \end{bmatrix} \quad \text{[See table of } \wedge \text{]}$$

We define another binary operation on Boolean matrices, called Boolean multiplication of matrices. It is denoted by $\odot$.

The Boolean product $A \odot B$ of two matrices A and B in this order is defined only when the number of columns in the prefactor A is equal to the number of rows in the post factor B. Thus, if A is $m \times n$ Boolean matrix and B is $n \times p$ Boolean matrix, then $A \odot B$ is $m \times p$ Boolean matrix.

In order to find the $i - j^{th}$ element in $A \odot B$, our left hand finger runs on the ith row of prefactor A, at the same time right hand finger runs on the jth column of B at equal speed. In this way, we find the join of the meets to get $i - j^{th}$ element of $A \odot B$. We illustrate this by an example.

Let $A = \begin{bmatrix} 1 & 1 & 0 \\ 0 & 1 & 1 \end{bmatrix}$ and $B = \begin{bmatrix} 1 & 1 \\ 0 & 1 \\ 1 & 0 \end{bmatrix}$.

Here A is 2×3 and B is 3×2 matrix. Therefore $A \odot B$ is 2×2 matrix.

$C = A \odot B = \begin{bmatrix} C_{11} & C_{12} \\ C_{21} & C_{22} \end{bmatrix}$. To find C_{11}, we consider first row of A and first column of B.

$\therefore \quad C_{11} = (1 \wedge 1) \vee (1 \wedge 0) \vee (0 \wedge 1) = 1 \vee 0 \vee 0 = 1$

Similarly, $\quad C_{12} = (1 \wedge 1) \vee (1 \wedge 1) \vee (0 \wedge 0) = 1 \vee 1 \vee 0 = 1$

$C_{21} = (0 \wedge 1) \vee (1 \wedge 0) (1 \wedge 1) = 0 \vee 0 \vee 1 = 1$

$C_{22} = (0 \wedge 1) \vee (1 \wedge 1) \vee (1 \wedge 0) = 0 \vee 1 \vee 0 = 1$

$\therefore \quad A \odot B = \begin{bmatrix} 1 & 1 \\ 1 & 1 \end{bmatrix}_{2 \times 2}$

For the matrices A and B given above; the product $B \odot A$ is also defined.

We have, $\quad B \odot A = \begin{bmatrix} 1 & 1 \\ 0 & 1 \\ 1 & 0 \end{bmatrix} \odot \begin{bmatrix} 1 & 1 & 0 \\ 0 & 1 & 1 \end{bmatrix}$

$\therefore \quad B \odot A = \begin{bmatrix} 1 & 1 & 1 \\ 0 & 1 & 1 \\ 1 & 1 & 0 \end{bmatrix}_{3 \times 3}$

Let now $A = \{a_1, a_2, ..., a_m\}$ and $B = \{b_1, b_2, ..., b_n\}$ be two finite sets with m and n elements respectively. Let R be the relation defined from A to B. Then a relation R is represented by $m \times n$ matrix $M_R = [m_{ij}]$ such that

$$m_{ij} = \begin{cases} 1; & \text{if } (a_i, b_j) \in R \\ 0; & \text{if } (a_i, b_j) \notin R \end{cases}$$

For example, let $A = \{1, 2, 3, 4\}$, $B = \{1, 2, 3\}$ and relation R from A to B is

$$R = \{(1, 3), (4, 1), (3, 2), (2, 2), (2, 3)\}$$

The matrix M_R associated with this relation is 4×3 matrix and

$M_R = \begin{bmatrix} 0 & 0 & 1 \\ 0 & 1 & 1 \\ 0 & 1 & 0 \\ 1 & 0 & 0 \end{bmatrix}$.

Conversely, if we know m × n Boolean matrix, then we can write the relation R represented by this matrix.

For example, if $M = \begin{bmatrix} 0 & 1 & 1 & 1 \\ 1 & 1 & 0 & 0 \\ 1 & 0 & 0 & 1 \\ 0 & 1 & 1 & 0 \end{bmatrix}$.

It is 4 × 4 matrix. So it represents a relation from the set $A = \{a_1, a_2, a_3, a_4\}$ to the set $B = \{b_1, b_2, b_3, b_4\}$ and $R = \{(a_1, b_2), (a_1, b_3), (a_1, b_4), (a_2, b_1), (a_2, b_2), (a_3, b_1), (a_3, b_4), (a_4, b_2), (a_4, b_3)\}$.

Example 1.5 : Let $A = \{a, b, c, d, e\}$ and $M_R = \begin{bmatrix} 1 & 1 & 0 & 0 & 0 \\ 0 & 0 & 1 & 1 & 0 \\ 0 & 0 & 0 & 1 & 1 \\ 0 & 1 & 1 & 0 & 0 \\ 1 & 0 & 0 & 0 & 0 \end{bmatrix}$.

Find the relation R defined on the set A.

Solution : The entries 1 in the matrix M_R suggest the pairs in the relation R.

∴ $R = \{(a, a), (a, b), (b, c), (b, d), (c, d), (c, e), (d, b), (d, c), (e, a)\}$

1.3 COMPOSITION OF RELATIONS AND MATRICES

The relations from set A to set B or those on the set A are subsets of A × B (A × A). Hence we can find their union, intersection and get the new relations.

(i) The union of two relations R_1 and R_2 is a relation

$$R_1 \cup R_2 = \{(a, b); (a, b) \in R_1 \text{ or } (a, b) \in R_2\}$$

(ii) The intersection of two relations R_1 and R_2 is a relation

$$R_1 \cap R_2 = \{(a, b); (a, b) \in R_1 \text{ and } (a, b) \in R_2\}$$

(iii) The difference $R_1 - R_2$ of two relations is a relation

$$R_1 - R_2 = \{(a, b)\}; (a, b) \in R_1 \text{ but } (a, b) \notin R_2\}$$

(iv) The ring sum of two relations R_1 and R_2 is a relation $R_1 \oplus R_2$ which consists of the pairs in $R_1 \cup R_2$ but not in $R_1 \cap R_2$.

Thus, $R_1 \oplus R_2 = (R_1 \cup R_2) - (R_1 \cap R_2)$

(v) Let R be a relation from set A to set B, then the inverse (also called converse) relation denoted by R^{-1} is a relation from set B to set A as below.

$$R^{-1} = \{(b, a); (a, b) \in R\}.$$

(vi) Let R be a relation from set A to set B. Then the complementary relation denoted by $\overline{R}$ is

$$\overline{R} = \{(a, b); (a, b) \notin R\}$$

It is clear that $\overline{R} = A \times B - R$

Example 1.6 : Let R and S be the relations defined on the set A = {2, 3, 5, 9, 12} as below

$$R = \{(a, b); 3 \text{ divides } a - b\}$$
$$S = \{(a, b); 2 \text{ divides } a - b\}$$

Compute the relations R and S as ordered pairs. Then find $R \cup S$, $R \cap S$, $R \oplus S$, R^{-1}, $\overline{S}$.

Solution : A = {2, 3, 5, 9, 12}

$$R = \{(a, b); 3 \text{ divides } a - b\}$$

$\therefore \quad R = \{(2, 2), (2, 5), (3, 3), (3, 9), (3, 12), (5, 2), (5, 5),$
$\quad (9, 3), (9, 9), (9, 12), (12, 3), (12, 9), (12, 12)\}$

$S = \{(a, b); 2 \text{ divides } a - b\}$

$\therefore \quad S = \{(2, 2), (2, 12), (3, 3), (3, 5), (3, 9), (5, 3), (5, 5),$
$\quad (5, 9), (9, 3), (9, 5), (9, 9), (12, 2), (12, 12)\}$

$R \cup S = \{(2, 2), (2, 5), (3, 3), (3, 9), (3, 12), (5, 2), (5, 5),$
$\quad (9, 3), (9, 9), (9, 12), (12, 3), (12, 9), (12, 12),$
$\quad (2, 12), (3, 5), (5, 3), (5, 9), (9, 5), (12, 2)\}$

$R \cap S = \{(2, 2), (3, 3), (3, 9), (5, 5), (9, 3), (9, 9), (12, 12)\}$

$R \oplus S = \{(2, 5), (3, 12), (5, 2), (9, 12), (12, 3), (12, 9), (2, 12),$
$\quad (3, 5), (5, 3), (5, 9), (9, 5)\}$

$R^{-1} = \{(2, 2), (5, 2), (3, 3), (9, 3), (12, 3), (2, 5), (5, 5),$
$\quad (3, 9), (9, 9), (12, 9), (3, 12), (9, 12), (12, 12)\}$

$\overline{S} = \{(2, 3), (2, 5), (2, 9), (3, 2), (3, 12), (5, 2), (5, 12),$
$\quad (9, 2), (9, 12), (12, 3), (12, 5), (12, 9)\}$

1.3.1 Composition of Two Relations

Let R be a relation from set A to set B and S be a relation from set B to set C.

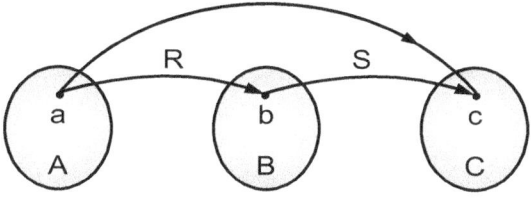

Fig. 1.6

As shown in the above figure a ∈ A, b ∈ B, c ∈ C such that aRb and bSc i.e. (a, b) ∈ R and (b, c) ∈ S. Ultimately then a ∈ A is related to c ∈ C under the relation denoted by SOR from set A to set C. It is called composition of R and S.

For example, let A = {1, 2, 3}, B = {b, p, d} and C = {p, q, r}.

A relation R from A to B is R = {(1, b), (1, d), (3, p), (2, b)}

Also a relation S from B to C is S = {(p, r), (b, q), (d, r)}.

Then the composite relation SOR from set A to set C is SOR = {(1, q), (1, r), (3, r), (2, q)}.

We see that SOR is a relation from set A to set C such that whenever (a, b) ∈ R and (b, c) ∈ S then (a, c) ∈ SOR.

Example 1.7 : Let R be the relation {(1, 2), (1, 3), (2, 3), (2, 4), (3, 1)} and S be the relation {(2, 1), (3, 1), (3, 2), (4, 2)}. Find SOR.

Solution : (1, 2) ∈ R, (2, 1) ∈ S   ∴ (1, 1) ∈ SOR

(1, 3) ∈ R, (3, 1) ∈ S   ∴ (1, 1) ∈ SOR

(1, 3) ∈ R, (3, 2) ∈ S   ∴ (1, 2) ∈ SOR

(2, 3) ∈ R, (3, 1) ∈ S   ∴ (2, 1) ∈ SOR

(2, 3) ∈ R, (3, 2) ∈ S   ∴ (2, 2) ∈ SOR

(2, 4) ∈ R, (4, 2) ∈ S   ∴ (2, 2) ∈ SOR

∴ SOR = {(1, 1), (1, 2), (2, 1), (2, 2)}

Let now R and S be the two relations from set A to set B, where A and B are finite sets. Then $R \cup S$, $R \cap S$, $R \oplus S$ are also relations from set A to set B.

We shall now prove that the matrix of $R \cup S$ is the matrix $M_R \vee M_S$.

Clearly $M_{R \cup S}$, M_R and M_S are $m \times n$ matrices. Let m_{ij}, p_{ij}, q_{ij} denote the $i - j^{th}$ element in $M_{R \cup S}$, M_R and M_S respectively. We have to prove $m_{ij} = p_{ij} \vee q_{ij}$. Suppose $m_{ij} = 1$. Then $a_i \in A$ is related to $b_j \in B$ under the relation $R \cup S$. i.e. $a_i \, R \cup S \, b_j$. This implies that $a_i R b_j$ or $a_i S b_j$ or both.

$\therefore \quad p_{ij} = 1$ or $q_{ij} = 1$ or both

$\therefore \qquad\qquad p_{ij} \vee q_{ij} = 1 \qquad\qquad [\because 1 \vee 0 = 1, \, 0 \vee 1 = 1, \, 1 \vee 1 = 1]$

$\therefore \qquad\qquad m_{ij} = p_{ij} \vee q_{ij}$

Suppose now $m_{ij} = 0$.

Then $a_i \in A$ is not related to $b_j \in B$ under the relation $R \cup S$.

$\therefore \quad (a_i, b_j) \notin R$ and $(a_i, b_j) \notin S$

$\therefore \quad p_{ij} = 0$ and $q_{ij} = 0$

$\therefore \quad p_{ij} \vee q_{ij} = 0 \vee 0 = 0$

In any case, we get

$\qquad m_{ij} = p_{ij} \vee q_{ij}$ for $i = 1, 2, \ldots, m$ and $j = 1, 2, \ldots, n$

Hence, $\qquad M_{R \cup S} = M_R \vee M_S$

On the same lines the proof of following result is straight forward

$$M_{R \cap S} = M_R \wedge M_S$$

Suppose next that the three sets A, B, C have m, n, p elements respectively. Further R is a relation from A to B and S is a relation from B to C so that the composite relation SOR is from set A to set C.

Let M_R, M_S and M_{SOR} be the Boolean matrices of R, S and SOR.

Let $i - j^{th}$ element in M_R be p_{ij}, that in M_S be q_{ij} and in M_{SOR} be m_{ij}.

Now the ordered pair (a_i, c_j) is in SOR if and only if there is an element b_k in B such that $(a_i, b_k) \in R$ and $(b_k, c_j) \in S$.

From this it immediately follows that $m_{ij} = 1$ if and only if $p_{ik} = 1$ and $q_{kj} = 1$, for some k.

Then from the definition of Boolean product, we get

$$M_{SOR} = M_R \odot M_S$$

Example 1.8 : Let A = {1, 2, 3, 4} and R, S be two relations defined on A as below.

$$R = \{(1, 1), (1, 2), (2, 3), (2, 4), (3, 4), (4, 1), (4, 2)\}$$
$$S = \{(2, 3), (4, 4), (3, 1), (1, 1), (1, 4), (2, 4)\}$$

Verify the following results

$$M_{R \cup S} = M_R \vee M_S, \quad M_{R \cap S} = M_R \wedge M_S,$$
$$M_{SOR} = M_R \odot M_S, \quad M_{ROS} = M_S \odot M_R.$$

Solution : We have,

$$R = \{(1, 1), (1, 2), (2, 3), (2, 4), (3, 4), (4, 1), (4, 2)\}$$
$$S = \{(2, 3), (4, 4), (3, 1), (1, 1), (1, 4), (2, 4)\}$$

Then, $M_R = \begin{bmatrix} 1 & 1 & 0 & 0 \\ 0 & 0 & 1 & 1 \\ 0 & 0 & 0 & 1 \\ 1 & 1 & 0 & 0 \end{bmatrix}$, $M_S = \begin{bmatrix} 1 & 0 & 0 & 1 \\ 0 & 0 & 1 & 1 \\ 1 & 0 & 0 & 0 \\ 0 & 0 & 0 & 1 \end{bmatrix}$

Now, $R \cup S = \{(1, 1), (1, 2), (2, 3), (2, 4), (3, 4), (4, 1), (4, 2),$
$(4, 4), (3, 1), (1, 4)\}$

$R \cap S = \{(1, 1), (2, 3), (2, 4)\}$

$SOR = \{(1, 1), (1, 4), (1, 3), (2, 1), (2, 4), (3, 4), (4, 1),$
$(4, 4), (4, 3)\}$

$ROS = \{(2, 4), (4, 1), (4, 2), (3, 1), (3, 2), (1, 1), (1, 2),$
$(2, 1), (2, 2)\}$

(i) $M_{R \cup S} = \begin{bmatrix} 1 & 1 & 0 & 1 \\ 0 & 0 & 1 & 1 \\ 1 & 0 & 0 & 1 \\ 1 & 1 & 0 & 1 \end{bmatrix}$

$M_R \vee M_S = \begin{bmatrix} 1 & 1 & 0 & 0 \\ 0 & 0 & 1 & 1 \\ 0 & 0 & 0 & 1 \\ 1 & 1 & 0 & 0 \end{bmatrix} \vee \begin{bmatrix} 1 & 0 & 0 & 1 \\ 0 & 0 & 1 & 1 \\ 1 & 0 & 0 & 0 \\ 0 & 0 & 0 & 1 \end{bmatrix}$

$= \begin{bmatrix} 1 & 1 & 0 & 1 \\ 0 & 0 & 1 & 1 \\ 1 & 0 & 0 & 1 \\ 1 & 1 & 0 & 1 \end{bmatrix}$

∴ $M_{R \cup S} = M_R \vee M_S$

(ii) $M_{R \cap S} = \begin{bmatrix} 1 & 0 & 0 & 0 \\ 0 & 0 & 1 & 1 \\ 0 & 0 & 0 & 0 \\ 0 & 0 & 0 & 0 \end{bmatrix}$

$M_R \wedge M_S = \begin{bmatrix} 1 & 1 & 0 & 0 \\ 0 & 0 & 1 & 1 \\ 0 & 0 & 0 & 1 \\ 1 & 1 & 0 & 0 \end{bmatrix} \wedge \begin{bmatrix} 1 & 0 & 0 & 1 \\ 0 & 0 & 1 & 1 \\ 1 & 0 & 0 & 0 \\ 0 & 0 & 0 & 1 \end{bmatrix}$

$= \begin{bmatrix} 1 & 0 & 0 & 0 \\ 0 & 0 & 1 & 1 \\ 0 & 0 & 0 & 0 \\ 0 & 0 & 0 & 0 \end{bmatrix}$

$\therefore \quad M_{R \cap S} = M_R \wedge M_S$

$M_{SoR} = \begin{bmatrix} 1 & 0 & 1 & 1 \\ 1 & 0 & 0 & 1 \\ 0 & 0 & 0 & 1 \\ 1 & 0 & 1 & 1 \end{bmatrix}$

$M_R \odot M_S = \begin{bmatrix} 1 & 1 & 0 & 0 \\ 0 & 0 & 1 & 1 \\ 0 & 0 & 0 & 1 \\ 1 & 1 & 0 & 0 \end{bmatrix} \odot \begin{bmatrix} 1 & 0 & 0 & 1 \\ 0 & 0 & 1 & 1 \\ 1 & 0 & 0 & 0 \\ 0 & 0 & 0 & 1 \end{bmatrix}$

$\therefore \quad M_R \odot M_S = \begin{bmatrix} 1 & 0 & 1 & 1 \\ 1 & 0 & 0 & 1 \\ 0 & 0 & 0 & 1 \\ 1 & 0 & 1 & 1 \end{bmatrix}$

$\therefore \quad M_{SoR} = M_R \odot M_S$

(iv) $M_{RoS} = \begin{bmatrix} 1 & 1 & 0 & 0 \\ 1 & 1 & 0 & 1 \\ 1 & 1 & 0 & 0 \\ 1 & 1 & 0 & 0 \end{bmatrix}$

$M_S \odot M_R = \begin{bmatrix} 1 & 0 & 0 & 1 \\ 0 & 0 & 1 & 1 \\ 1 & 0 & 0 & 0 \\ 0 & 0 & 0 & 1 \end{bmatrix} \odot \begin{bmatrix} 1 & 1 & 0 & 0 \\ 0 & 0 & 1 & 1 \\ 0 & 0 & 0 & 1 \\ 1 & 1 & 0 & 0 \end{bmatrix}$

$$= \begin{bmatrix} 1 & 1 & 0 & 0 \\ 1 & 1 & 0 & 1 \\ 1 & 1 & 0 & 0 \\ 1 & 1 & 0 & 0 \end{bmatrix}$$

∴ $M_{ROS} = M_S \odot M_R$

Finally, we consider the matrices of the inverse relation and complementary relation.

We know that if R is a relation from set A to set B, then its inverse R^{-1} is a relation from set B to set A.

The inverse relation of the relation R is denoted by R^{-1}. Thus $bR^{-1}a$ iff aRb.

Let A = {1, 2, 3, 4}

and B = {2, 5, 6, 7, 8}

and R = {(1, 8), (3, 5), (3, 7), (2, 6), (2, 7), (4, 5), (4, 6), (4, 7)}

We have, $M_R = \begin{bmatrix} 0 & 0 & 0 & 0 & 1 \\ 0 & 0 & 1 & 1 & 0 \\ 0 & 1 & 0 & 1 & 0 \\ 0 & 1 & 1 & 1 & 0 \end{bmatrix}$

Now, R^{-1} = {(8, 1), (5, 3), (7, 3), (6, 2), (7, 2), (5, 4), (6, 4), (7, 4)}

$$M_{R^{-1}} = \begin{bmatrix} 0 & 0 & 0 & 0 \\ 0 & 0 & 1 & 1 \\ 0 & 1 & 0 & 1 \\ 0 & 1 & 1 & 1 \\ 1 & 0 & 0 & 0 \end{bmatrix}$$

We observe that the matrix of R^{-1} is the transpose of the matrix of R

$$M_{R^{-1}} = (M_R)^T$$

In the above example the complementary relation $\overline{R}$ defined as

(a, b) ∈ $\overline{R}$ iff (a, b) ∉ R is

$\overline{R}$ = {(1, 2), (1, 5), (1, 6), (1, 7), (2, 2), (2, 5), (2, 8), (3, 2), (3, 6), (3, 8), (4, 2), (4, 8)}

Then $M_{\bar{R}} = \begin{bmatrix} 1 & 1 & 1 & 1 & 0 \\ 1 & 1 & 0 & 0 & 1 \\ 1 & 0 & 1 & 0 & 1 \\ 1 & 0 & 0 & 0 & 1 \end{bmatrix}$

The matrix of $\bar{R}$ can be obtained from the matrix of R; simply by replacing all occurrences of 1 by 0 and all occurrence of 0 by 1.

Example 1.9 : A relation R is defined on the set A = {a, b, c, d, e, f} by

R = {(a, b), (a, f), (b, c), (c, c), (c, d), (d, a), (d, c), (d, e), (f, d)}

(a) Draw the digraph of R.

(b) Find a cycle starting at vertex b.

Solution :

(a)

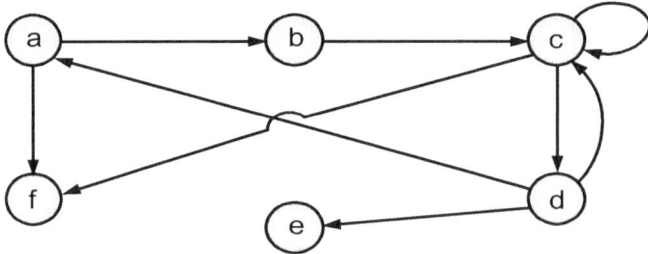

Fig. 1.7

(b) A cycle starting at vertex b is b, c, d, a, b.

Example 1.10 : A relation R on the set A = {1, 2, 3, 4} is as below.

R = {(1, 2), (1, 3), (3, 2), (4, 1), (4, 4)}

(a) Write M_R

(b) Draw the graph of R

(c) Find R^2, R^3 and R^∞.

Solution : R = {(1, 2), (1, 3), (3, 2), (4, 1), (4, 4)}

(a) $M_R = \begin{bmatrix} 0 & 1 & 1 & 0 \\ 0 & 0 & 0 & 0 \\ 0 & 1 & 0 & 0 \\ 1 & 0 & 0 & 1 \end{bmatrix}$

(b)

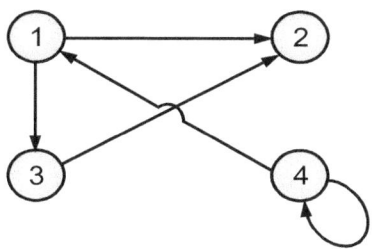

Fig. 1.8

(c) $M_{R^2} = M_R \odot M_R = \begin{bmatrix} 0 & 1 & 1 & 0 \\ 0 & 0 & 0 & 0 \\ 0 & 1 & 0 & 0 \\ 1 & 0 & 0 & 1 \end{bmatrix} \odot \begin{bmatrix} 0 & 1 & 1 & 0 \\ 0 & 0 & 0 & 0 \\ 0 & 1 & 0 & 0 \\ 1 & 0 & 0 & 1 \end{bmatrix} = \begin{bmatrix} 0 & 1 & 0 & 0 \\ 0 & 0 & 0 & 0 \\ 0 & 0 & 0 & 0 \\ 1 & 1 & 1 & 1 \end{bmatrix}$

$M_{R^3} = M_{R^2} \odot M_R = \begin{bmatrix} 0 & 1 & 0 & 0 \\ 0 & 0 & 0 & 0 \\ 0 & 0 & 0 & 0 \\ 1 & 1 & 1 & 1 \end{bmatrix} \odot \begin{bmatrix} 0 & 1 & 1 & 0 \\ 0 & 0 & 0 & 0 \\ 0 & 1 & 0 & 0 \\ 1 & 0 & 0 & 1 \end{bmatrix}$

$= \begin{bmatrix} 0 & 0 & 0 & 0 \\ 0 & 0 & 0 & 0 \\ 0 & 0 & 0 & 0 \\ 1 & 1 & 1 & 1 \end{bmatrix}$

$M_{R^4} = M_{R^3} \odot M_R = \begin{bmatrix} 0 & 0 & 0 & 0 \\ 0 & 0 & 0 & 0 \\ 0 & 0 & 0 & 0 \\ 1 & 1 & 1 & 1 \end{bmatrix} \odot \begin{bmatrix} 0 & 1 & 1 & 0 \\ 0 & 0 & 0 & 0 \\ 0 & 1 & 0 & 0 \\ 1 & 0 & 0 & 1 \end{bmatrix} = \begin{bmatrix} 0 & 0 & 0 & 0 \\ 0 & 0 & 0 & 0 \\ 0 & 0 & 0 & 0 \\ 1 & 1 & 1 & 1 \end{bmatrix}$

Here, $M_{R^4} = M_{R^3}$

∴ $M_{R^\infty} = M_R \vee M_{R^2} \vee M_{R^3}$

$= \begin{bmatrix} 0 & 1 & 1 & 0 \\ 0 & 0 & 0 & 0 \\ 0 & 1 & 0 & 0 \\ 1 & 0 & 0 & 1 \end{bmatrix} \vee \begin{bmatrix} 0 & 1 & 0 & 0 \\ 0 & 0 & 0 & 0 \\ 0 & 0 & 0 & 0 \\ 1 & 1 & 1 & 1 \end{bmatrix} \vee \begin{bmatrix} 0 & 0 & 0 & 0 \\ 0 & 0 & 0 & 0 \\ 0 & 0 & 0 & 0 \\ 1 & 1 & 1 & 1 \end{bmatrix}$

$= \begin{bmatrix} 0 & 1 & 1 & 0 \\ 0 & 0 & 0 & 0 \\ 0 & 1 & 0 & 0 \\ 1 & 1 & 1 & 1 \end{bmatrix}$

Example 1.11 : Let S and R be two relations defined over the set $A = \{1, 2, 3, ..., 29, 30\}$

where, $R = \{<x, 2x> | x \in A\}$

and $S = \{<x, 3x> | x \in A\}$

Compute (i) ROS, (ii) SOR

Solution : $A = \{1, 2, 3, ..., 29, 30\}$

$R = \{<x, 2x> | x \in A\}$
$= \{<1, 2>, <2, 4>, <3, 6>, <4, 8>, <5, 10>, <6, 12>,$
$<7, 14>, <8, 16>, <9, 18>, <10, 20>, <11, 22>,$
$<12, 24>, <13, 26>, <14, 28>, <15, 30>\}$

Also, $S = \{<x, 3x> | x \in A\}$
$= \{<1, 3>, <2, 6>, <3, 9>, <4, 12>, <5, 15>, <6, 18>,$
$<7, 21>, <8, 24>, <9, 27>, <10, 30>\}$

(i) To find ROS

$<1, 3> \in S, <3, 6> \in R$ $\therefore$ $<1, 6> \in ROS$

$<2, 6> \in S, <6, 12> \in R$ $\therefore$ $<2, 12> \in ROS$

$<3, 9> \in S, <9, 18> \in R$ $\therefore$ $<3, 18> \in ROS$

$<4, 12> \in S, <12, 24> \in R$ $\therefore$ $<4, 24> \in ROS$

$<5, 15> \in S, <15, 30> \in S$ $\therefore$ $<5, 30> \in ROS$

$\therefore$ $ROS = \{<1, 6>, <2, 12>, <3, 18>, <4, 24>, <5, 30>\}$

(ii) To find SOR

$<1, 2> \in R, <2, 6> \in S$ $\therefore$ $<1, 6> \in SOR$

$<2, 4> \in R, <4, 12> \in S$ $\therefore$ $<2, 12> \in SOR$

$<3, 6> \in R, <6, 18> \in S$ $\therefore$ $<3, 18> \in SOR$

$<4, 8> \in R, <8, 24> \in S$ $\therefore$ $<4, 24> \in SOR$

$<5, 10> \in R, <10, 30> \in S$ $\therefore$ $<5, 30> \in SOR$

$\therefore$ $SOR = \{<1, 6>, <2, 12>, <3, 18>, <4, 24>, <5, 30>\}$

Example 1.12 : Given the relation matrices M_R and M_S. Find M_{ROS} and M_{SOR}

$$M_R = \begin{bmatrix} 1 & 0 & 1 \\ 1 & 1 & 0 \\ 1 & 1 & 1 \end{bmatrix}, \quad M_S = \begin{bmatrix} 1 & 0 & 0 & 1 & 0 \\ 1 & 0 & 1 & 0 & 1 \\ 0 & 1 & 0 & 1 & 0 \end{bmatrix}$$

Solution : M_R is 3×3 matrix and M_S is 3×5 matrix. So we consider the set

$A = \{1, 2, 3, 4, 5\}$ on which the relations are defined

$$M_R = \begin{bmatrix} 1 & 0 & 1 & 0 & 0 \\ 1 & 1 & 0 & 0 & 0 \\ 1 & 1 & 1 & 0 & 0 \\ 0 & 0 & 0 & 0 & 0 \\ 0 & 0 & 0 & 0 & 0 \end{bmatrix} \quad M_S = \begin{bmatrix} 1 & 0 & 0 & 1 & 0 \\ 1 & 0 & 1 & 0 & 1 \\ 0 & 1 & 0 & 1 & 0 \\ 0 & 0 & 0 & 0 & 0 \\ 0 & 0 & 0 & 0 & 0 \end{bmatrix}$$

Now, $M_{ROS} = M_S \odot M_R = \begin{bmatrix} 1 & 0 & 0 & 1 & 0 \\ 1 & 0 & 1 & 0 & 1 \\ 0 & 1 & 0 & 1 & 0 \\ 0 & 0 & 0 & 0 & 0 \\ 0 & 0 & 0 & 0 & 0 \end{bmatrix} \odot \begin{bmatrix} 1 & 0 & 1 & 0 & 0 \\ 1 & 1 & 0 & 0 & 0 \\ 1 & 1 & 1 & 0 & 0 \\ 0 & 0 & 0 & 0 & 0 \\ 0 & 0 & 0 & 0 & 0 \end{bmatrix}$

$\therefore \quad M_{ROS} = \begin{bmatrix} 1 & 0 & 1 & 0 & 0 \\ 1 & 1 & 1 & 0 & 0 \\ 1 & 1 & 0 & 0 & 0 \\ 0 & 0 & 0 & 0 & 0 \\ 0 & 0 & 0 & 0 & 0 \end{bmatrix}$

$M_{SOR} = M_R \odot M_S = \begin{bmatrix} 1 & 0 & 1 & 0 & 0 \\ 1 & 1 & 0 & 0 & 0 \\ 1 & 1 & 1 & 0 & 0 \\ 0 & 0 & 0 & 0 & 0 \\ 0 & 0 & 0 & 0 & 0 \end{bmatrix} \odot \begin{bmatrix} 1 & 0 & 0 & 1 & 0 \\ 1 & 0 & 1 & 0 & 1 \\ 0 & 1 & 0 & 1 & 0 \\ 0 & 0 & 0 & 0 & 0 \\ 0 & 0 & 0 & 0 & 0 \end{bmatrix}$

$\therefore \quad M_{SOR} = \begin{bmatrix} 1 & 1 & 0 & 1 & 0 \\ 1 & 0 & 1 & 1 & 1 \\ 1 & 1 & 1 & 1 & 1 \\ 0 & 0 & 0 & 0 & 0 \\ 0 & 0 & 0 & 0 & 0 \end{bmatrix}$

Example 1.13 : Let A = {1, 2, 3, 4}. Let
R = {<1, 2>, <1, 3>, <1, 4>, <2, 3>, <3, 1>, <3, 3>, <4, 2>} and
S = {<1, 3>, <2, 2>, <3, 2>, <4, 2>}

Find (i) RO(SOS), (ii) IS ROS = SOR ? (iii) ROROR

Solution : $M_R = \begin{bmatrix} 0 & 1 & 1 & 1 \\ 0 & 0 & 1 & 0 \\ 1 & 0 & 1 & 0 \\ 0 & 1 & 0 & 0 \end{bmatrix}$, $M_S = \begin{bmatrix} 0 & 0 & 1 & 0 \\ 0 & 1 & 0 & 0 \\ 0 & 1 & 0 & 0 \\ 0 & 1 & 0 & 0 \end{bmatrix}$

(i) $M_{RO(SOS)} = M_{SOS} \odot M_R = (M_S \odot M_S) \odot M_R$

$= \begin{bmatrix} 0 & 0 & 1 & 0 \\ 0 & 1 & 0 & 0 \\ 0 & 1 & 0 & 0 \\ 0 & 1 & 0 & 0 \end{bmatrix} \begin{bmatrix} 0 & 0 & 1 & 0 \\ 0 & 1 & 0 & 0 \\ 0 & 1 & 0 & 0 \\ 0 & 1 & 0 & 0 \end{bmatrix} \begin{bmatrix} 0 & 1 & 1 & 1 \\ 0 & 0 & 1 & 0 \\ 1 & 0 & 1 & 0 \\ 0 & 1 & 0 & 0 \end{bmatrix}$

$= \begin{bmatrix} 0 & 1 & 0 & 0 \\ 0 & 1 & 0 & 0 \\ 0 & 1 & 0 & 0 \\ 0 & 1 & 0 & 0 \end{bmatrix} \begin{bmatrix} 0 & 1 & 1 & 1 \\ 0 & 0 & 1 & 0 \\ 1 & 0 & 1 & 0 \\ 0 & 1 & 0 & 0 \end{bmatrix} = \begin{bmatrix} 0 & 0 & 1 & 0 \\ 0 & 0 & 1 & 0 \\ 0 & 0 & 1 & 0 \\ 0 & 0 & 1 & 0 \end{bmatrix}$

∴ RO(SOS) = {<1, 3>, <2, 3>, <3, 3>, <4, 3>}

(ii) $M_{ROS} = M_S \odot M_R = \begin{bmatrix} 0 & 0 & 1 & 0 \\ 0 & 1 & 0 & 0 \\ 0 & 1 & 0 & 0 \\ 0 & 1 & 0 & 0 \end{bmatrix} \begin{bmatrix} 0 & 1 & 1 & 1 \\ 0 & 0 & 1 & 0 \\ 1 & 0 & 1 & 0 \\ 0 & 1 & 0 & 0 \end{bmatrix}$

∴ $M_{ROS} = \begin{bmatrix} 1 & 0 & 1 & 0 \\ 0 & 0 & 1 & 0 \\ 0 & 0 & 1 & 0 \\ 0 & 0 & 1 & 0 \end{bmatrix}$

∴ ROS = {<1, 1>, <1, 3>, <2, 3>, <3, 3>, <4, 3>}

$M_{SOR} = M_R \odot M_S = \begin{bmatrix} 0 & 1 & 1 & 1 \\ 0 & 0 & 1 & 0 \\ 1 & 0 & 1 & 0 \\ 0 & 1 & 0 & 0 \end{bmatrix} \begin{bmatrix} 0 & 0 & 1 & 0 \\ 0 & 1 & 0 & 0 \\ 0 & 1 & 0 & 0 \\ 0 & 1 & 0 & 0 \end{bmatrix}$

∴ $M_{SOR} = \begin{bmatrix} 0 & 1 & 0 & 0 \\ 0 & 1 & 0 & 0 \\ 0 & 1 & 1 & 0 \\ 0 & 1 & 0 & 0 \end{bmatrix}$

∴ SOR = {<1, 2>, <2, 2>, <3, 2>, <3, 3>, <4, 2>}
∴ ROS ≠ SOR

(iii) $M_{RoRoR} = M_R \odot M_R \odot M_R$

$$= \begin{bmatrix} 0 & 1 & 1 & 1 \\ 0 & 0 & 1 & 0 \\ 1 & 0 & 1 & 0 \\ 0 & 1 & 0 & 0 \end{bmatrix} \begin{bmatrix} 0 & 1 & 1 & 1 \\ 0 & 0 & 1 & 0 \\ 1 & 0 & 1 & 0 \\ 0 & 1 & 0 & 0 \end{bmatrix} \begin{bmatrix} 0 & 1 & 1 & 1 \\ 0 & 0 & 1 & 0 \\ 1 & 0 & 1 & 0 \\ 0 & 1 & 0 & 0 \end{bmatrix}$$

$$= \begin{bmatrix} 0 & 1 & 1 & 1 \\ 0 & 0 & 1 & 0 \\ 1 & 0 & 1 & 0 \\ 0 & 1 & 0 & 0 \end{bmatrix} \begin{bmatrix} 1 & 1 & 1 & 0 \\ 1 & 0 & 1 & 0 \\ 1 & 1 & 1 & 1 \\ 0 & 0 & 1 & 0 \end{bmatrix}$$

$$= \begin{bmatrix} 1 & 1 & 1 & 1 \\ 1 & 1 & 1 & 1 \\ 1 & 1 & 1 & 1 \\ 1 & 0 & 1 & 0 \end{bmatrix}$$

∴ RoR = {<1, 1>, <1, 2>, <1, 3>, <1, 4>, <2, 1>, <2, 2>, <2, 3>, <2, 4>, <3, 1>, <3, 2>, <3, 3>, <3, 4>, <4, 1>, <4, 3>}

Example 1.14 : Let R and S be the following relations on B = {a, b, c, d};

R = {(a, a), (a, c), (c, b), (c, d), (d, b)}

and S = {(b, a), (c, c), (c, d), (d, a)}

Find the following composite relations : (i) SOR   (ii) SOROS

Solution : The matrices of the relations R and S are

$$R = \begin{array}{c} \\ a \\ b \\ c \\ d \end{array} \begin{array}{cccc} a & b & c & d \\ \begin{bmatrix} 1 & 0 & 1 & 0 \\ 0 & 0 & 0 & 0 \\ 0 & 1 & 0 & 1 \\ 0 & 1 & 0 & 0 \end{bmatrix} \end{array} \quad S = \begin{array}{c} \\ a \\ b \\ c \\ d \end{array} \begin{array}{cccc} a & b & c & d \\ \begin{bmatrix} 0 & 0 & 0 & 0 \\ 1 & 0 & 0 & 0 \\ 0 & 0 & 1 & 1 \\ 1 & 0 & 0 & 0 \end{bmatrix} \end{array}$$

$$M_{SOR} = M_R \odot M_S = \begin{bmatrix} 1 & 0 & 1 & 0 \\ 0 & 0 & 0 & 0 \\ 0 & 1 & 0 & 1 \\ 0 & 1 & 0 & 0 \end{bmatrix} \begin{bmatrix} 0 & 0 & 0 & 0 \\ 1 & 0 & 0 & 0 \\ 0 & 0 & 1 & 1 \\ 1 & 0 & 0 & 0 \end{bmatrix}$$

$$\therefore \quad M_{SOR} = \begin{bmatrix} 0 & 0 & 1 & 1 \\ 0 & 0 & 0 & 0 \\ 1 & 0 & 0 & 0 \\ 1 & 0 & 0 & 0 \end{bmatrix}$$

$\therefore \quad SOR = \{(a, c), (a, d), (c, a), (d, a)\}$

(ii) $M_{SOROS} = M_{(SOR)OS} = M_S \odot M_{SOR}$

$$= \begin{bmatrix} 0 & 0 & 0 & 0 \\ 1 & 0 & 0 & 0 \\ 0 & 0 & 1 & 1 \\ 1 & 0 & 0 & 0 \end{bmatrix} \begin{bmatrix} 0 & 0 & 1 & 1 \\ 0 & 0 & 0 & 0 \\ 1 & 0 & 0 & 0 \\ 1 & 0 & 0 & 0 \end{bmatrix}$$

$$= \begin{bmatrix} 0 & 0 & 0 & 0 \\ 0 & 0 & 1 & 1 \\ 1 & 0 & 0 & 0 \\ 0 & 0 & 1 & 1 \end{bmatrix}$$

$\therefore \quad SOROS = \{(b, c), (b, d), (c, a), (d, c), (d, d)\}$

Example 1.15 : Given A = {1, 2, 3, 4, 5} and B = {1, 3, 5}. Let R be relation from A → B defined by "x is less than y". Write relation R, its matrix and draw its graph.

Solution : A = {1, 2, 3, 4, 5}, B = {1, 3, 5} $x \in A$ is related to $y \in B$ iff $x < y$

$\therefore \quad R = \{(1, 3), (1, 5), (2, 3), (2, 5), (3, 5), (4, 5)\}$

The matrix of R is $R = \begin{array}{c} \\ 1 \\ 2 \\ 3 \\ 4 \\ 5 \end{array} \begin{array}{ccc} 1 & 3 & 5 \\ \left[\begin{array}{ccc} 0 & 1 & 1 \\ 0 & 1 & 1 \\ 0 & 0 & 1 \\ 0 & 0 & 1 \\ 0 & 0 & 0 \end{array}\right] \end{array}$

Graphically R is represented as below.

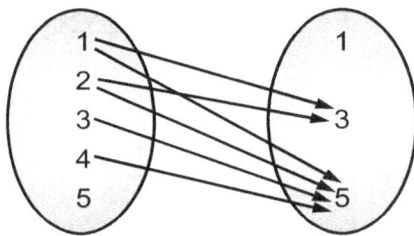

Fig. 1.9

Example 1.16 : Let R = {<1, 2>, <3, 4>, <2, 3>} and

S = {<4, 2>, <2, 5>, <3, 1>, <1, 3>}

Find SO(ROR) and (ROS)OR.

Solution : The relations and S are defined on the set A = {1, 2, 3, 4, 5}

$$M_R = \begin{bmatrix} 0 & 1 & 0 & 0 & 0 \\ 0 & 0 & 1 & 0 & 0 \\ 0 & 0 & 0 & 1 & 0 \\ 0 & 0 & 0 & 0 & 0 \\ 0 & 0 & 0 & 0 & 0 \end{bmatrix}, \quad M_S = \begin{bmatrix} 0 & 0 & 1 & 0 & 0 \\ 0 & 0 & 0 & 0 & 1 \\ 1 & 0 & 0 & 0 & 0 \\ 0 & 1 & 0 & 0 & 0 \\ 0 & 0 & 0 & 0 & 0 \end{bmatrix}$$

$$M_{ROR} = M_R \odot M_R = \begin{bmatrix} 0 & 1 & 0 & 0 & 0 \\ 0 & 0 & 1 & 0 & 0 \\ 0 & 0 & 0 & 1 & 0 \\ 0 & 0 & 0 & 0 & 0 \\ 0 & 0 & 0 & 0 & 0 \end{bmatrix} \begin{bmatrix} 0 & 1 & 0 & 0 & 0 \\ 0 & 0 & 1 & 0 & 0 \\ 0 & 0 & 0 & 1 & 0 \\ 0 & 0 & 0 & 0 & 0 \\ 0 & 0 & 0 & 0 & 0 \end{bmatrix}$$

$$= \begin{bmatrix} 0 & 0 & 1 & 0 & 0 \\ 0 & 0 & 0 & 1 & 0 \\ 0 & 0 & 0 & 0 & 0 \\ 0 & 0 & 0 & 0 & 0 \\ 0 & 0 & 0 & 0 & 0 \end{bmatrix}$$

$$M_{ROS} = M_S \odot M_R = \begin{bmatrix} 0 & 0 & 1 & 0 & 0 \\ 0 & 0 & 0 & 0 & 1 \\ 1 & 0 & 0 & 0 & 0 \\ 0 & 1 & 0 & 0 & 0 \\ 0 & 0 & 0 & 0 & 0 \end{bmatrix} \begin{bmatrix} 0 & 1 & 0 & 0 & 0 \\ 0 & 0 & 1 & 0 & 0 \\ 0 & 0 & 0 & 1 & 0 \\ 0 & 0 & 0 & 0 & 0 \\ 0 & 0 & 0 & 0 & 0 \end{bmatrix}$$

$$= \begin{bmatrix} 0 & 0 & 0 & 1 & 0 \\ 0 & 0 & 0 & 0 & 0 \\ 0 & 1 & 0 & 0 & 0 \\ 0 & 0 & 1 & 0 & 0 \\ 0 & 0 & 0 & 0 & 0 \end{bmatrix}$$

$$M_{SO(ROR)} = M_{ROR} \odot M_S = \begin{bmatrix} 0 & 0 & 1 & 0 & 0 \\ 0 & 0 & 0 & 1 & 0 \\ 0 & 0 & 0 & 0 & 0 \\ 0 & 0 & 0 & 0 & 0 \\ 0 & 0 & 0 & 0 & 0 \end{bmatrix} \begin{bmatrix} 0 & 0 & 1 & 0 & 0 \\ 0 & 0 & 0 & 0 & 1 \\ 1 & 0 & 0 & 0 & 0 \\ 0 & 1 & 0 & 0 & 0 \\ 0 & 0 & 0 & 0 & 0 \end{bmatrix}$$

$$= \begin{bmatrix} 1 & 0 & 0 & 0 & 0 \\ 0 & 1 & 0 & 0 & 0 \\ 0 & 0 & 0 & 0 & 0 \\ 0 & 0 & 0 & 0 & 0 \\ 0 & 0 & 0 & 0 & 0 \end{bmatrix}$$

∴   SO(ROR) = {<1, 1>, <2, 2>}

$M_{(ROS)OR} = M_R \odot M_{ROS}$

$$= \begin{bmatrix} 0 & 1 & 0 & 0 & 0 \\ 0 & 0 & 1 & 0 & 0 \\ 0 & 0 & 0 & 1 & 0 \\ 0 & 0 & 0 & 0 & 0 \\ 0 & 0 & 0 & 0 & 0 \end{bmatrix} \begin{bmatrix} 0 & 0 & 0 & 1 & 0 \\ 0 & 0 & 0 & 0 & 0 \\ 0 & 1 & 0 & 0 & 0 \\ 0 & 0 & 1 & 0 & 0 \\ 0 & 0 & 0 & 0 & 0 \end{bmatrix}$$

$$= \begin{bmatrix} 0 & 0 & 0 & 0 & 0 \\ 0 & 1 & 0 & 0 & 0 \\ 0 & 0 & 1 & 0 & 0 \\ 0 & 0 & 0 & 0 & 0 \\ 0 & 0 & 0 & 0 & 0 \end{bmatrix}$$

∴   (ROS)OR = {<2, 2>, <3, 3>}

EXERCISE (1.3)

1. Let R and S be two relations from set A = {1, 2, 3} to set B = {1, 2, 3, 4}.
   R = {(1, 3), (2, 4), (3, 2), (3, 3)}
   S = {(1, 1), (2, 1), (3, 1), (3, 4), (3, 2), (3, 3), (2, 3)}

   Compute (a) R ∪ S, (b) R ∩ S, (c) R ⊕ S (d) $\bar{R}$.

2. Let R and S be two relations defined on the set A = {1, 2, 3, 4, 5}.
   R = {(1, 1), (1, 3), (1, 4), (1, 5), (2, 2), (2, 3), (3, 1), (3, 4), (4, 1), (4, 3), (5, 2), (5, 3), (5, 4), (5, 5)}
   S = {(1, 1), (1, 2), (1, 5), (2, 4), (3, 1), (3, 2), (3, 5), (4, 2), (4, 4), (4, 5), (5, 1)}.

   Compute ROS and SOR.

3. Let A = {1, 2, 3, 4, 5} and R, S be two relations defined on A by
   R = {a, b); $a^2 \leq 2b$}
   S = {(a, c); $a^2 \leq 3c$}

   Compute ROS and SOR.

4. Let R and S be two relations defined on

A = {1, 2, 3, 4} as

R = {(1, 2), (1, 3), (2, 3), (2, 4), (3, 1)}

S = {(2, 1), (3, 2), (4, 2), (3, 1)}

By using matrices find the relations SOR and ROS and write them as ordered pairs.

5. Let R be the relation defined on A = {1, 2, 3, 4, 5} as below.

R = {(2, 2), (2, 3), (2, 4), (3, 4), (3, 5), (4, 2), (4, 5), (4, 1), (5, 3), (5, 1),

(1, 2), (1, 3), (1, 5)}

Find R^2 = ROR and R^3 = ROROR

6. Find the relation represented by the following digraph. Also write its matrix.

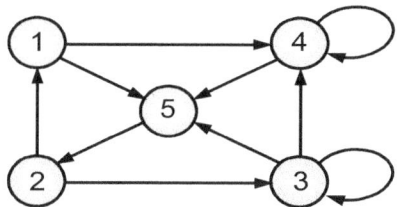

Fig. 1.10

7. Let A = {a, b, c, d, e} and R be the relation on A, whose matrix is

$$M_R = \begin{bmatrix} 1 & 1 & 0 & 0 & 0 \\ 0 & 0 & 1 & 1 & 0 \\ 0 & 0 & 0 & 1 & 1 \\ 0 & 1 & 1 & 0 & 0 \\ 1 & 0 & 0 & 0 & 0 \end{bmatrix}$$

Find R and draw its digraph.

8. A = {1, 2, 3, 4}. A relation R is defined on A as

R = {(1, 1), (1, 2), (1, 3), (1, 4), (2, 3), (3, 2), (4, 2), (4, 3), (4, 4)}

(a) Draw the graph of R and also write the matrix.

(b) Compute M_{R^2}, M_{R^3}, M_{R^4} and write your conclusion; where

$M_{R^2} = M_{RoR}$, M_{RoRoR}

(c) Compute M_{R^∞}.

ANSWERS (1.3)

1. (a) {(1, 3), (2, 4), (3, 2), (3, 3), (1, 1), (2, 1), (3, 1), (3, 4), (2, 3)}
   (b) {(3, 2), (3, 3)}
   (c) {(1, 3), (2, 4), (1, 1), (2, 1)}
   (d) {(1, 1), (1, 2), (1, 4), (2, 1), (2, 2), (2, 3), (3, 1), (3, 4)}

2. ROS = {(1, 1), (1, 3), (1, 4), (1, 5), (1, 2), (2, 1), (2, 3), (3, 1), (3, 3), (3, 4), (3, 5), (3, 2), (4, 2), (4, 3), (4, 1), (4, 4), (4, 5), (5, 1), (5, 3), (5, 4), (5, 5)}

   SOR = {(1, 1), (1, 2), (1, 5), (1, 4), (2, 4), (2, 1), (2, 2), (2, 5), (3, 1), (3, 2), (3, 5), (3, 4), (4, 1), (4, 2), (4, 5), (5, 4), (5, 1), (5, 2), (5, 5), (5, 4)}

3. ROS = SOR = {(1, 1), (1, 2), (1, 3), (1, 4), (1, 5)}

4. $M_{ROS} = \begin{bmatrix} 0 & 0 & 0 & 0 \\ 0 & 1 & 1 & 0 \\ 0 & 1 & 1 & 1 \\ 0 & 0 & 1 & 1 \end{bmatrix}$ ROS = {(2, 2), (2, 3), (3, 2), (3, 3), (3, 4), (4, 3), (4, 4)}

   $M_{SOR} = \begin{bmatrix} 1 & 1 & 0 & 0 \\ 1 & 1 & 0 & 0 \\ 0 & 0 & 0 & 0 \\ 0 & 0 & 0 & 0 \end{bmatrix}$ ∴ SOR = {(1, 1), (1, 2), (2, 1), (2, 2)}

5. $M_{R^2} = \begin{bmatrix} 1 & 1 & 1 & 1 & 1 \\ 1 & 1 & 1 & 1 & 1 \\ 1 & 1 & 1 & 0 & 1 \\ 1 & 1 & 1 & 1 & 1 \\ 0 & 1 & 1 & 1 & 1 \end{bmatrix}$

   R^2 = {(1, 1), (1, 2), (1, 3), (1, 4), (1, 5), (2, 1), (2, 2), (2, 3), (2, 4), (2, 5), (3, 1), (3, 2), (3, 3), (3, 5), (4, 1), (4, 2), (4, 3), (4, 4), (4, 5), (5, 2), (5, 3), (5, 4), (5, 5)}

   $M_{R^3} = \begin{bmatrix} 1 & 1 & 1 & 1 & 1 \\ 1 & 1 & 1 & 1 & 1 \\ 1 & 1 & 1 & 1 & 1 \\ 1 & 1 & 1 & 1 & 1 \\ 1 & 1 & 1 & 1 & 1 \end{bmatrix}$ $R^3 = A \times A$

6. R = {(1, 4), (1, 5), (2, 1), (2, 3), (3, 3), (3, 4), (3, 5), (4, 5), (4, 4), (5, 2)}

$$M_R = \begin{bmatrix} 0 & 0 & 0 & 1 & 1 \\ 1 & 0 & 1 & 0 & 0 \\ 0 & 0 & 1 & 1 & 1 \\ 0 & 0 & 0 & 1 & 1 \\ 0 & 1 & 0 & 0 & 0 \end{bmatrix}$$

7. R = {(a, a), (a, b), (b, c), (b, d), (c, d), (c, e), (d, b), (d, c), (e, a)}

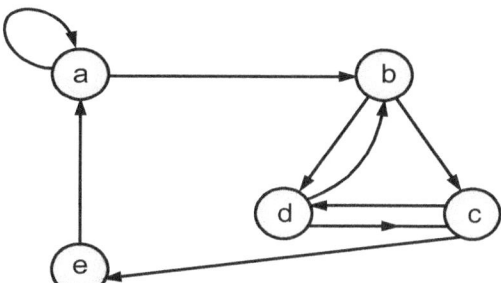

Fig. 1.11

8. (a) $$M_R = \begin{bmatrix} 1 & 1 & 1 & 1 \\ 0 & 0 & 1 & 0 \\ 0 & 1 & 0 & 0 \\ 0 & 1 & 1 & 1 \end{bmatrix}$$

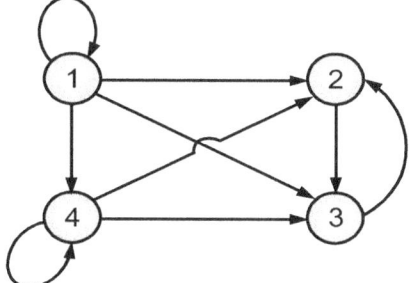

Fig. 1.12

(b) $$M_{R^2} = \begin{bmatrix} 1 & 1 & 1 & 1 \\ 0 & 1 & 0 & 0 \\ 0 & 0 & 1 & 0 \\ 0 & 1 & 1 & 1 \end{bmatrix} \quad M_{R^3} = \begin{bmatrix} 1 & 1 & 1 & 1 \\ 0 & 0 & 1 & 0 \\ 0 & 1 & 0 & 0 \\ 0 & 1 & 1 & 1 \end{bmatrix} \quad M_{R^4} = \begin{bmatrix} 1 & 1 & 1 & 1 \\ 0 & 1 & 0 & 0 \\ 0 & 0 & 1 & 0 \\ 0 & 1 & 1 & 1 \end{bmatrix}$$

Here $M_{R^2} = M_{R^4}$. The paths in the digraph of R, of length 4 and of length 2 are given by the same digraph.

(c) As $M_{R^4} = M_{R^2}$ we have

$$M_{R^\infty} = \begin{bmatrix} 1 & 1 & 1 & 1 \\ 0 & 0 & 1 & 0 \\ 0 & 1 & 0 & 0 \\ 0 & 1 & 1 & 1 \end{bmatrix} \vee \begin{bmatrix} 1 & 1 & 1 & 1 \\ 0 & 1 & 0 & 0 \\ 0 & 0 & 1 & 0 \\ 0 & 1 & 1 & 1 \end{bmatrix} \vee \begin{bmatrix} 1 & 1 & 1 & 1 \\ 0 & 0 & 1 & 0 \\ 0 & 1 & 0 & 0 \\ 0 & 1 & 1 & 1 \end{bmatrix}$$

$$= \begin{bmatrix} 1 & 1 & 1 & 1 \\ 0 & 1 & 1 & 0 \\ 0 & 1 & 1 & 0 \\ 0 & 1 & 1 & 1 \end{bmatrix}$$

1.4 TYPES OF RELATIONS

We always come across with the relations defined on the set A, instead of relations from set A to set B. We now discuss the properties satisfied (not satisfied) by the relations defined on set A.

Reflexivity : A relation R on the set A is called reflexive relation if every element of A is related to itself according to relation R i.e. aRa for every $a \in A$. Equivalently $(a, a) \in R$ for every $a \in A$.

If no element of A is related to itself according to relation R, then R is called irreflexive relation. Following are some examples of reflexive and irreflexive relations.

(a) The relation of equality in the set $\mathbb{R}$ of all real numbers is reflexive because every real number is equal to itself.

(b) The relation of divisibility in the set $\mathbb{N} = \{1, 2, 3, ...\}$ of positive integers is reflexive because every positive integer divides itself. We write this as $a | a$ for every $a \in \mathbb{N}$.

(c) Let n be any (but fixed) positive integer greater than 1. We define a relation R on the set $Z = \{0, \pm 1, \pm 2, \pm 3, ...\}$ of all integers as below.

For $a, b \in Z$ we have aRb iff n divides the difference $a - b$.

It is called 'congruence modulo n' relation. When aRb i.e. $n | (a - b)$ we denote this by $a \equiv b$ (mod. n) and read 'integer a is congruent to integer b modulo n'.

For example : 13 ≡ 5 (mod. 4) because 13 – 5 = 8 is divisible by 4. Also 9 ≡ – 21 (mod. 6), since 9 – (– 21) = 9 + 21 = 30 which is divisible by 6.

But 23 ≢ 6 (mod. 5) because 23 – 6 = 17 which is not divisible by 5.

If now a ∈ Z is any member of Z, then a – a = 0, which is clearly divisible by n. Hence a ≡ a (mod. n) for every a ∈ Z.

Therefore the congruence relation modulo n is reflexive relation.

(d) The relation R = {(a, b), (b, d), (c, c), (d, c), (d, d)} defined on the set A = {a, b, c, d} is not reflexive. The reason is that a ∈ A and (a, a) ∉ R. Also b ∈ A and (b, b) ∉ R.

(e) The relation R = {(1, 3), (2, 1), (4, 2), (2, 4)} on A = {1, 2, 3, 4} is irreflexive. For any a ∈ A, we see that (a, a) ∉ R.

(f) Consider the relation R = {(1, 1), (2, 4), (3, 2), (4, 1)} on

A = {1, 2, 3, 4}.

R is not reflexive because (2, 2) ∉ R, (3, 3) ∉ R, (4, 4) ∉ R. Also R is not irreflexive due to the presence of the pair (1, 1) ∈ R.

In the matrix M_R of reflexive relation R, on the set A; each entry on the main diagonal (top left to right bottom) must be 1; while in case of irreflexive relation, each entry on the main diagonal is 0.

When we look to the digraph of reflexive relation there is a loop at each vertex and in the digraph of irreflexive relation, there is no loop at any vertex.

Symmetric Relation

A relation R defined on the set A is called symmetric if, whenever (a, b) ∈ R, (b, a) ∈ R. i.e. if aRb ⇒ bRa.

From this it follows that if there exist two elements a and b ∈ A such that (a, b) ∈ R but (b, a) ∉ R, then the relation R fails to be symmetric.

A relation R on A is called asymmetric if whenever (a, b) ∈ R then (b, a) ∉ R. From this it follows that if there exist a, b ∈ A such that (a, b) ∈ R and (b, a) ∈ R, then R is not asymmetric.

A relation R on set A is called antisymmetric if whenever $(a, b) \in R$ and $(b, a) \in R$ then $a = b$. This is equivalent to say that if $a \neq b$ in A, then either $(a, b) \notin A$ or $(b, a) \notin A$.

(a) The relation of equality in the set $\mathbb{R}$ of all real numbers is symmetric because $a = b \Rightarrow b = a$.

(b) The relation of divisibility in the set $\mathbb{N}$ of positive integers is not symmetric because $5 | 20$ but $20 \nmid 5$. However, this relation is antisymmetric because if a and b are two positive integers with $a \neq b$ then either a does not divide b or b does not divide a.

(c) The congruence relation modulo n in the set Z of all integers is symmetric relation. This is because

$a \equiv b \pmod{n} \Rightarrow n | (a - b)$

$\Rightarrow a - b = nk;$ k is integer

$\Rightarrow b - a = n(-k);$ $-k$ is integer

$\Rightarrow b \equiv a \pmod{n}$

(d) Consider the relation 'less than' on the set Z of integers.

$aRb \Rightarrow a < b \Rightarrow b \not< a \Rightarrow bRa$. Therefore, it is not symmetric.

Further $a < b \Rightarrow b \not< a$. Therefore, it is asymmetric.

Also it is antisymmetric because, if $a \neq b$ then either $a \not< b$ or $b \not< a$.

(e) Consider the set A = {a, b, c, d} and relation R = {(a, b), (b, b), (c, d), (d, a)}.

R is not symmetric because $(a, b) \in R$ but $(b, a) \notin R$.

Also R is not asymmetric because $(b, b) \in R$. However R is antisymmetric because $a \neq b \Rightarrow (a, b) \notin R$ or $(b, a) \notin R$.

Now in a symmetric relation, we have $a_i R a_j \Leftrightarrow a_j R a_i$. This means in the matrix M_R of a symmetric relation; $a_{ij} = a_{ji}$. If $a_{ij} = 1$, then $a_{ji} = 1$ and if $a_{ij} = 0$ then $a_{ji} = 0$. Therefore the matrix of a symmetric relation is symmetric matrix.

In the matrix of asymmetric relation, we have the following result. If $m_{ij} = 1$, then $m_{ji} = 0$ and on the main diagonal $m_{ii} = 0$ for every i.

The matrix M_R of antisymmetric relation has the following property. If $i \neq j$, the neither $m_{ij} = 0$ or $m_{ji} = 0$.

Antisymmetric Relation :

A relation R defined on the set A is called antisymmetric, if 'for a, b ∈ A; whenever (a, b) ∈ R and (b, a) ∈ R then a = b'.

Equivalently if a ≠ b are two distinct elements of A then either (a, b) ∉ R or (b, a) ∉ R.

Consider the relation of divisibility in the set N of positive integers. We know that if two positive integers a and b divide each other then a = b. Hence the relation of divisibility in N is antisymmetric.

As another example, let A be any set and P(A) be the power set of A i.e. P(A) = Collection of all subsets of the set A. We define set inclusion relation ⊆ on P(A).

Thus, for S ∈ P(A), T ∈ P(A), S is related to T iff S ⊆ T.

Now of S ⊆ T and T ⊆ S, then clearly S = T.

Therefore, the set inclusion relation is antisymmetric.

Example 1.17 : Let $M_R = \begin{bmatrix} 0 & 1 & 1 & 0 \\ 1 & 1 & 0 & 0 \\ 1 & 0 & 1 & 1 \\ 0 & 0 & 1 & 1 \end{bmatrix}$

Examine the relation R for reflexivity and symmetry. Is R (i) irreflexive (ii) asymmetric (iii) antisymmetric ?

Solution : $M_R = \begin{bmatrix} 0 & 1 & 1 & 0 \\ 1 & 1 & 0 & 0 \\ 1 & 0 & 1 & 1 \\ 0 & 0 & 1 & 1 \end{bmatrix}$; A = {1, 2, 3, 4}

In M_R; $m_{11} = 0$ ∴ 1R̸1

∴ R is not reflexive.

The matrix M_R is a symmetric matrix because $m_{ij} = m_{ji}$ for i = 1, 2, 3, 4 and j = 1, 2, 3, 4.

∴ Relation R is symmetric.

R is not irreflexive because (2, 2) ∈ R.

In the matrix of asymmetric relation all diagonal elements must be 0. This condition is violated in M_R. Therefore relation R is not asymmetric.

Also the relation R is not antisymmetric, since 1 and 2 are distinct elements of A and (1, 2) ∈ R, (2, 1) ∈ R.

The digraph of a relation R possesses the following characteristics with respect to the above properties.

(i) In the reflexive relation R defined on set A, (a, a) ∈ R for every a ∈ A.

Therefore in the digraph of R, there is a loop at each vertex.

(ii) If R is irreflexive, then there cannot be a loop at any vertex.

(iii) The equirement of a symmetric relation viz. $(a_i, a_j) \in R \Rightarrow (a_j, a_i) \in R$ suggests that whenever there is an edge from vertex a_i to vertex a_j, there is also an edge from vertex a_j to vertex a_i.

Also it may or may not have a loop at some vertex.

(iv) In the digraph of asymmetric relation, again there is no loop at any vertex. Further whenever there is an edge from vertex a_i to vertex a_j; there is no edge from vertex a_j to vertex a_i.

(v) If R is antisymmetric relation then for $i \neq j$ there cannot be simultaneously edge from a_i to a_j and an edge from a_j to a_i. Further there is no any restriction about the loop at any vertex.

Example 1.18 : A digraph of a relation R is given below. Comment about R.

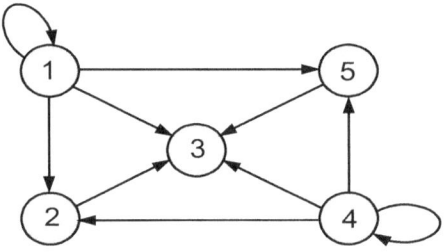

Fig. 1.13

Solution : In the given digraph, there is no loop at the vertex 2 and vertex 5.

∴ 2R̸2, 5R̸5

∴ Relation R is not reflexive.

The existence of loop at the vertex 1 and 4 suggests that 1R1, 4R4.

∴ Relation R is not irreflexive.

There are no antiparallel edges in the graph.

1R2 but 2R̸1

∴ Relation R is not symmetric.

Also 1R1, 4R4 suggests that R is not asymmetric.

The relation R is antisymmetric because from the diagraph, we see that for any two different vertices antiparallel edges are not there. The loop at vertex 1 and 4 is allowed.

Transitivity of a Relation

A relation R on the set A is called transitive if whenever aRb, and bRc then aRc; for a, b, c ∈ A.

Obviously then if there exist a, b, c ∈ A such that aRb and bRc but aR̸c then we can say R is not transitive.

(a) The relation of equality in the set $\mathbb{R}$ of real numbers is transitive since $a = b, b = c \Rightarrow a = c$.

(b) The relation of divisibility in the set $\mathbb{N}$ of all positive integers is transitive. Suppose $a|b$ and $b|c$.

Then we have $b = ak_1$, and $c = bk_2$ where k_1, k_2 are integers.

Then $c = bk_2 = (ak_1)k_2 = a(k_1k_2) = ak_3$ ∵ $k_3 = k_1k_2$ is integer

∴ $a|c$.

(c) Consider now the congruence relation modulo n in the set Z of all integers.

Let $a \equiv b \pmod{n}$ and $b \equiv c \pmod{n}$ where $a, b, c \in \mathbb{Z}$.

Then by the definition of congruence relation, we have

$n|(a - b)$ and $n|(b - c)$

∴ $a - b = nk_1$; k_1 is integer

and $b - c = nk_2$; k_2 is integer

Adding these two results,

$a - b + b - c = nk_1 + nk_2$

∴ $a - c = n(k_1 + k_2)$

∴   a − c = nk_3   ∵ $k_3 = k_1 + k_2$ is integer

∴   a ≡ c (mod. n)

Hence the relation is transitive.

(d) Consider the relation, R = {(1, 3), (2, 2), (2, 4), (3, 1), (4, 2)} defined on the set A = {1, 2, 3, 4}, we see that (1, 3) ∈ R, (3, 1) ∈ R but (1, 1) ∉ R.

Also (4, 2) ∈ R, (2, 4) ∈ R but (4, 4) ∉ R. Hence this relation fails to be transitive.

We note that a relation R on set A is transitive if and only if the following condition holds in M_R.

If m_{ij} = 1 and m_{jk} = 1 then m_{ik} = 1.

The 'if' part of this condition clearly suggests that in M_{R2} the i − kth entry is 1. So, the transitivity of relation R means that if M_{R2} has entry1 in any position, then M_R must have entry 1 in that position.

Hence, if $M_{R2} = M_R$, then the relation R is transitive. In other words, $M_{R2} = M_R$ is a sufficient condition for relation R to be transitive.

This condition however is not necessary condition for R to be transitive, i.e. a relation R can be transitive even if $M_{R2} \neq M_R$.

For example, consider the relation R = {(1, 2), (1, 3), (1, 4), (2, 3), (2, 4), (3, 4)} on the set A = {1, 2, 3, 4}.

In this relation (a, b) ∈ R, (b, c) ∈ R but (a, c) ∉ R such pairs are not there. Therefore R is transitive relation.

Now, $M_R = \begin{bmatrix} 0 & 1 & 1 & 1 \\ 0 & 0 & 1 & 1 \\ 0 & 0 & 0 & 1 \\ 0 & 0 & 0 & 0 \end{bmatrix}$

Then $M_{R2} = \begin{bmatrix} 0 & 1 & 1 & 1 \\ 0 & 0 & 1 & 1 \\ 0 & 0 & 0 & 1 \\ 0 & 0 & 0 & 0 \end{bmatrix} \odot \begin{bmatrix} 0 & 1 & 1 & 1 \\ 0 & 0 & 1 & 1 \\ 0 & 0 & 0 & 1 \\ 0 & 0 & 0 & 0 \end{bmatrix}$

$= \begin{bmatrix} 0 & 0 & 1 & 1 \\ 0 & 0 & 0 & 1 \\ 0 & 0 & 0 & 0 \\ 0 & 0 & 0 & 0 \end{bmatrix}$

Thus, $M_{R^2} \neq M_R$

A necessary and sufficient condition for a relation R defined on the set A to be transitive is that $R^n \subseteq R$, for all $n \geq 1$. We accept this result without proof.

EXERCISE (1.4)

1. Give example of a relation on the set A = {1, 2, 3} which is :
   (a) reflexive and symmetric but not transitive.
   (b) reflexive and transitive but not symmetric.
   (c) symmetric and transitive but not reflexive.

2. L is a set of straight lines in a plane. R is a relation of parallelism of lines and S is a relation of perpendicularity of lines.

   Determine whether or not R, S is (a) reflexive, (b) symmetric, (c) transitive.

3. A relation R on the set

   A = {a, b, c, d} is defined as R = {(a, a), (a, c), (c, a), (a, b), (c, c), (d, d)}.

   Determine whether or not R is reflexive, irreflexive, symmetric, asymmetric, antisymmetric, transitive.

4. The matrix M_R of a relation R on A = {1, 2, 3, 4} is

   $$M_R = \begin{bmatrix} 0 & 1 & 0 & 1 \\ 1 & 0 & 1 & 1 \\ 0 & 1 & 0 & 0 \\ 1 & 1 & 0 & 0 \end{bmatrix}$$

   Is R (a) symmetric, (b) transitive, (c) antisymmetric ?

5. A digraph of relation R is given below.

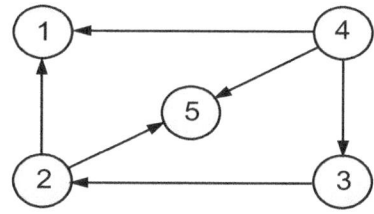

Fig. 1.14

Determine whether or not R is reflexive, symmetric, antisymmetric, transitive.

ANSWERS (1.4)

1. (a) R = {(1, 1), (2, 2), (3, 3), (1, 2), (2, 1), (2, 3), (3, 2)}
   (b) R = {(1, 1), (2, 2), (3, 3), (1, 2), (2, 3), (1, 3)}
   (c) R = {(1, 3), (3, 1), (1, 1), (3, 3)}
2. (a) R is reflexive, S is irreflexive.
   (b) R and S both are symmetric.
   (c) R is transitive but S is not transitive.
3. Not reflexive, not irrefleixve,
   Not symmetric, not asymmetric,
   Not antisymmetric, not transitive.
4. R is symmetric, not transitive, not antisymmetric.
5. Not reflexive, not symmetric, antisymmetric, not transitive.

1.5 CLOSURE PROPERTIES AND ITS EXAMPLES

Consider a relation R on the set A = {$a_1, a_2, ..., a_n$}. If for some or few values of i, $1 \leq i \leq n$ it happens that the pair (a_i, a_i) $\notin$ R, then the relation R fails to be reflexive. Now we extend the relation R by adding such missing pairs so that the new relation is reflexive. It is called reflexive closure of the relation.

Likewise if a pair (a_i, a_j) $\in$ R but (a_j, a_i) $\notin$ R, then R fails to be symmetric. If R is extended by adding such minimum pairs, then the resulting relation becomes symmetric.

For example let,

$$A = \{1, 2, 3, 4, 5\}$$

and $\quad R = \{(1, 2), (5, 4), (3, 3), (5, 5), (4, 5), (5, 1), (3, 2)\}$

This relation is not reflexive because (1, 1) $\notin$ R, (2, 2) $\notin$ R, (4, 4) $\notin$ R. We add these missing pairs to R and get the relation.

R_1 = {(1, 2), (5, 4), (3, 3), (5, 5), (4, 5), (5, 1), (3, 2), (1, 1), (2, 2), (4, 4)} which is reflexive closure of R.

Again (1, 2) $\in$ R but (2, 1) $\notin$ R

(5, 1) $\in$ R but (1, 5) $\notin$ R

(3, 2) $\in$ R but (2, 3) $\notin$ R

We add these missing pairs to the relation R and get,

$R_2 = \{(1, 2), (5, 4), (3, 3), (5, 5), (4, 5), (5, 1), (3, 2), (2, 1), (1, 5), (2, 3)\}$

which is symmetric closure of R.

It may be noted that it is not sometimes possible to find the reflexive closure or symmetric closure of a given relation R.

We now proceed to transitive closure of a relation. We recall that the transitivity needs whenever $(a_i, a_j) \in R$ and $(a_j, a_k) \in R$, then $(a_i, a_k) \in R$.

In the relation R discussed above, we note that $(4, 5) \in R$, $(5, 4) \in R$ but $(4, 4) \notin R$.

Again $(4, 5) \in R$, $(5, 1) \in R$ but $(4, 1) \notin R$.

$(5, 1) \in R$, $(1, 2) \in R$ but $(5, 2) \notin R$.

After adding the three missing terms to R, it is extended to

$R_3 = \{(1, 2), (5, 4), (3, 3), (5, 5), (4, 5), (5, 1), (3, 2), (4, 4), (4, 1), (5, 2)\}$.

R_3 is now a transitive relation. Here only three new terms are required to convert the relation R into a transitive one.

R_3 is transitive closure of R.

To find the transitive closure of a given relation, we use Warshall's algorithm.

In this algorithm, we start with the matrix W_0 of given relation R. We then go on improving this matrix step-by-step; $W_0 \to W_1 \to W_2 \to W_{k-1} \to W_k \to \ldots \to W_n$, where n denotes the number of elements in the set A on which the relation R is defined. For the improvement from W_{k-1} to W_k the following procedure is adopted. Suppose entries of W_{k-1} are denoted by s_{ij} and that of W_k be t_{ij}.

All the entries 1 in W_{k-1} will appear as 1 in W_k i.e. if $s_{ij} = 1$ then $t_{ij} = 1$.

In addition some entries 0 in W_{k-1} will be converted to 1 in W_k. For this we use the fact that if $s_{ik} = 1$ and $s_{kj} = 1$ then $t_{ij} = 1$; which is the requirement of transitivity. In this process the matrix W_n is the matrix of transitive closure of the relation R.

ILLUSTRATIVE EXAMPLES

Example 1.19 : Let A = {1, 2, 3} and R = {<1, 1>, <1, 2>, <1, 3>, <2, 3>, <3, 1>, <3, 2>}.

Find the transitive closure by using Warshall's algorithm.

Solution : A = {1, 2, 3}

R = {(1, 1), (1, 2), (1, 3), (2, 3), (3, 1), (3, 2)}.

The matrix of given relation is

$$W_0 = \begin{bmatrix} 1 & 1 & 1 \\ 0 & 0 & 1 \\ 1 & 1 & 0 \end{bmatrix}$$

Step 1 : To find W_1 ∴ k = 1

All entries 1 in W_0 appear as they are, in W_1.

In addition $s_{31} = 1$ and $s_{13} = 1$ ∴ $t_{33} = 1$

∴ $$W_1 = \begin{bmatrix} 1 & 1 & 1 \\ 0 & 0 & 1 \\ 1 & 1 & 1 \end{bmatrix}$$

Step 2 : To find W_2 ∴ k = 2

$s_{32} = 1$ and $s_{23} = 1$ implies $t_{33} = 1$

$s_{12} = 1$ and $s_{23} = 1$ implies $t_{13} = 1$

∴ $$W_2 = \begin{bmatrix} 1 & 1 & 1 \\ 0 & 0 & 1 \\ 1 & 1 & 1 \end{bmatrix}$$

Step 3 : To find W_3 ∴ k = 3

$s_{13} = 1$ and $s_{31} = 1$ implies $t_{11} = 1$

$s_{22} = 1$ and $s_{31} = 1$ implies $t_{21} = 1$

$s_{23} = 1$ and $s_{32} = 1$ implies $t_{22} = 1$

$s_{23} = 1$ and $s_{33} = 1$ implies $t_{23} = 1$

∴ $$W_3 = \begin{bmatrix} 1 & 1 & 1 \\ 1 & 1 & 1 \\ 1 & 1 & 1 \end{bmatrix}$$

∴ Transitive closure is

R* = {(1, 1), (1, 2), (1, 3), (2, 1), (2, 2), (2, 3), (3, 1), (3, 2), (3, 3)}

Example 1.20 : Use Warshall's algorithm, to find the transitive closure of the relation R = {(1, 2), (2, 3), (3, 4), (2, 1)} on A = {1, 2, 3, 4}.

Solution : A = {1, 2, 3, 4} and R = {(1, 2), (2, 3), (3, 4), (2, 1)}.

The matrix of the given relation is

$$W_0 = \begin{bmatrix} 0 & 1 & 0 & 0 \\ 1 & 0 & 1 & 0 \\ 0 & 0 & 0 & 1 \\ 0 & 0 & 0 & 0 \end{bmatrix}$$

Step 1 : To find W_1 ∴ k = 1

$s_{21} = 1$ and $s_{12} = 1$ ∴ $t_{22} = 1$

∴ $$W_1 = \begin{bmatrix} 0 & 1 & 0 & 0 \\ 1 & 1 & 1 & 0 \\ 0 & 0 & 0 & 1 \\ 0 & 0 & 0 & 0 \end{bmatrix}$$

Step 2 : To find W_2 ∴ k = 2

$s_{12} = 1$ and $s_{21} = 1$ ∴ $t_{11} = 1$

$s_{12} = 1$ and $s_{22} = 1$ ∴ $t_{12} = 1$

$s_{12} = 1$ and $s_{23} = 1$ ∴ $t_{13} = 1$

∴ $$W_2 = \begin{bmatrix} 1 & 1 & 1 & 0 \\ 1 & 1 & 1 & 0 \\ 0 & 0 & 0 & 1 \\ 0 & 0 & 0 & 0 \end{bmatrix}$$

Step 3 : To find W_3 ∴ k = 3

$s_{13} = 1$ and $s_{34} = 1$ ∴ $t_{14} = 1$

Also $s_{23} = 1$ and $s_{34} = 1$ ∴ $t_{24} = 1$

∴ $$W_3 = \begin{bmatrix} 1 & 1 & 1 & 1 \\ 1 & 1 & 1 & 1 \\ 0 & 0 & 0 & 1 \\ 0 & 0 & 0 & 0 \end{bmatrix}$$

Step 4 : To find W_4 ∴ k = 4

Since fourth row has all zeros, there is no further improvement in W_3

∴ $W_4 = W_3$

$$\therefore \quad W_4 = \begin{bmatrix} 1 & 1 & 1 & 1 \\ 1 & 1 & 1 & 1 \\ 0 & 0 & 0 & 1 \\ 0 & 0 & 0 & 0 \end{bmatrix}$$

∴ The transitive closure of a given relation is

R* = {(1, 1), (1, 2), (1, 3), (1, 4), (2, 1), (2, 2), (2, 3), (2, 4), (3, 4)}

Example 1.21 : Obtain the transitive closure of the following relational matrix using Warshall's algorithm.

$$M_R = \begin{bmatrix} 1 & 0 & 0 & 1 \\ 1 & 1 & 0 & 0 \\ 0 & 0 & 1 & 0 \\ 0 & 0 & 0 & 1 \end{bmatrix}$$

Solution : The matrix of the given relation is

$$W_0 = \begin{bmatrix} 1 & 0 & 0 & 1 \\ 1 & 1 & 0 & 0 \\ 0 & 0 & 1 & 0 \\ 0 & 0 & 0 & 1 \end{bmatrix}$$

Step 1 : To find W_1 ∴ k = 1

$s_{11} = 1$ and $s_{11} = 1$ ∴ $t_{11} = 1$

$s_{11} = 1$ and $s_{14} = 1$ ∴ $t_{14} = 1$

$s_{21} = 1$ and $s_{11} = 1$ ∴ $t_{21} = 1$

$s_{21} = 1$ and $s_{14} = 1$ ∴ $t_{24} = 1$

$$\therefore \quad W_1 = \begin{bmatrix} 1 & 0 & 0 & 1 \\ 1 & 1 & 0 & 1 \\ 0 & 0 & 1 & 0 \\ 0 & 0 & 0 & 1 \end{bmatrix}$$

Step 2 : To find W_2 ∴ k = 2

$s_{22} = 1$ and $s_{21} = 1$ ∴ $t_{21} = 1$

$s_{22} = 1$ and $s_{22} = 1$ ∴ $t_{22} = 1$

$$\therefore \quad W_2 = \begin{bmatrix} 1 & 0 & 0 & 1 \\ 1 & 1 & 0 & 1 \\ 0 & 0 & 1 & 0 \\ 0 & 0 & 0 & 1 \end{bmatrix}$$

Step 3 : To find W_3 $\therefore$ k = 3

$s_{33} = 1$ and $s_{33} = 1$ $\therefore$ $t_{33} = 1$

$$\therefore \quad W_3 = \begin{bmatrix} 1 & 0 & 0 & 1 \\ 1 & 1 & 0 & 1 \\ 0 & 0 & 1 & 0 \\ 0 & 0 & 0 & 1 \end{bmatrix}$$

Step 4 : To find W_4 $\therefore$ k = 4

$s_{14} = 1$ and $s_{44} = 1$ $\therefore$ $t_{14} = 1$

$s_{24} = 1$ and $s_{44} = 1$ $\therefore$ $t_{24} = 1$

$s_{44} = 1$ and $s_{44} = 1$ $\therefore$ $t_{44} = 1$

$$\therefore \quad W_4 = \begin{bmatrix} 1 & 0 & 0 & 1 \\ 1 & 1 & 0 & 1 \\ 0 & 0 & 1 & 0 \\ 0 & 0 & 0 & 1 \end{bmatrix}$$

Relation R = {(1, 1), (1, 4), (2, 1), (2, 2), (3, 3), (4, 4)}. Its transitive closure is

$$R^* = \{(1, 1), (1, 4), (2, 1), (2, 2), (2, 4), (3, 3), (4, 4)\}$$

Example 1.22 : Use Warshall's algorithm to find the transitive closure of the relation.

R = {(1, 2), (1, 3), (1, 4), (2, 3), (2, 4), (3, 4)} on A = {1, 2, 3, 4}.

Solution : The matrix of the relation is

$$W_0 = \begin{bmatrix} 0 & 1 & 1 & 1 \\ 0 & 0 & 1 & 1 \\ 0 & 0 & 0 & 1 \\ 0 & 0 & 0 & 0 \end{bmatrix}$$

Step 1 : To find W_1 $\therefore$ k = 1

In the first column, there are all zeros.

$$\therefore \quad W_1 = W_0 = \begin{bmatrix} 0 & 1 & 1 & 1 \\ 0 & 0 & 1 & 1 \\ 0 & 0 & 0 & 1 \\ 0 & 0 & 0 & 0 \end{bmatrix}$$

Step 2 : To find W_2 ∴ k = 2

$s_{12} = 1$ and $s_{23} = 1$ ∴ $t_{13} = 1$

$s_{12} = 1$ and $s_{24} = 1$ ∴ $t_{14} = 1$

∴ $W_2 = \begin{bmatrix} 0 & 1 & 1 & 1 \\ 0 & 0 & 1 & 1 \\ 0 & 0 & 0 & 1 \\ 0 & 0 & 0 & 0 \end{bmatrix}$

Step 3 : To find W_3 ∴ k = 3

$s_{13} = 1$ and $s_{34} = 1$ ∴ $t_{14} = 1$

$s_{23} = 1$ and $s_{34} = 1$ ∴ $t_{24} = 1$

∴ $W_3 = \begin{bmatrix} 0 & 1 & 1 & 1 \\ 0 & 0 & 1 & 1 \\ 0 & 0 & 0 & 1 \\ 0 & 0 & 0 & 0 \end{bmatrix}$

Step 4 : To find W_4 ∴ k = 4

Since fourth row contains all zeros, there is no further improvement in W_3.

∴ $W_4 = \begin{bmatrix} 0 & 1 & 1 & 1 \\ 0 & 0 & 1 & 1 \\ 0 & 0 & 0 & 1 \\ 0 & 0 & 0 & 0 \end{bmatrix}$

∴ Transitive closure of relation R is

R* = {(1, 2), (1, 3), (1, 4), (2, 3), (2, 4), (3, 4)}

Here R* = R

Example 1.23 : By using Warshall's algorithm find the transitive closure of the relation R = {(1, 1), (1, 4), (2, 2), (2, 3), (3, 2), (3, 3), (4, 1), (4, 4)} defined on the set

A = {1, 2, 3, 4}.

Solution : The matrix of the relation is

$W_0 = \begin{bmatrix} 1 & 0 & 0 & 1 \\ 0 & 1 & 1 & 0 \\ 0 & 1 & 1 & 0 \\ 1 & 0 & 0 & 1 \end{bmatrix}$

Step 1 : To find W_1 ∴ $k = 1$

$s_{11} = 1$ and $s_{11} = 1$ ∴ $t_{11} = 1$

$s_{11} = 1$ and $s_{14} = 1$ ∴ $t_{14} = 1$

$s_{41} = 1$ and $s_{11} = 1$ ∴ $t_{41} = 1$

$s_{41} = 1$ and $s_{14} = 1$ ∴ $t_{44} = 1$

∴ $W_1 = \begin{bmatrix} 1 & 0 & 0 & 1 \\ 0 & 1 & 1 & 0 \\ 0 & 1 & 1 & 0 \\ 1 & 0 & 0 & 1 \end{bmatrix}$

Step 2 : To find W_2 ∴ $k = 2$

$s_{22} = 1$ and $s_{22} = 1$ ∴ $t_{22} = 1$

$s_{22} = 1$ and $s_{23} = 1$ ∴ $t_{23} = 1$

$s_{32} = 1$ and $s_{22} = 1$ ∴ $t_{32} = 1$

$s_{32} = 1$ and $s_{23} = 1$ ∴ $t_{33} = 1$

∴ $W_2 = \begin{bmatrix} 1 & 0 & 0 & 1 \\ 0 & 1 & 1 & 0 \\ 0 & 1 & 1 & 0 \\ 1 & 0 & 0 & 1 \end{bmatrix}$

Step 3 : To find W_3 ∴ $k = 3$

$s_{23} = 1$ and $s_{32} = 1$ ∴ $t_{22} = 1$

$s_{23} = 1$ and $s_{33} = 1$ ∴ $t_{23} = 1$

$s_{33} = 1$ and $s_{32} = 1$ ∴ $t_{32} = 1$

$s_{33} = 1$ and $s_{33} = 1$ ∴ $t_{33} = 1$

∴ $W_3 = \begin{bmatrix} 1 & 0 & 0 & 1 \\ 0 & 1 & 1 & 0 \\ 0 & 1 & 1 & 0 \\ 1 & 0 & 0 & 1 \end{bmatrix}$

Step 4 : To find W_4 ∴ $k = 4$

$s_{14} = 1$ and $s_{41} = 1$ ∴ $t_{11} = 1$

$s_{14} = 1$ and $s_{44} = 1$ ∴ $t_{14} = 1$

$s_{44} = 1$ and $s_{41} = 1$ ∴ $t_{41} = 1$

$s_{44} = 1$ and $s_{44} = 1$ ∴ $t_{44} = 1$

∴ $W_4 = \begin{bmatrix} 1 & 0 & 0 & 1 \\ 0 & 1 & 1 & 0 \\ 0 & 1 & 1 & 0 \\ 1 & 0 & 0 & 1 \end{bmatrix}$

Transitive closure of R is

R* = R = {(1, 1), (1, 4), (2, 2), (2, 3), (3, 2), (3, 3), (4, 1), (4, 4)}

EXERCISE (1.5)

1. By using Warshall's algorithm find the transitive closure of the relation :

   (a) R = {(1, 2), (2, 3), (3, 4)} defined on A = {(1, 2, 3, 4}.

   (b) R = {(1, 3), (1, 1), (3, 1), (1, 2), (3, 3), (4, 4)} defined on

   A = {1, 2, 3, 4}

   (c) R = {(1, 1), (1, 2), (2, 2), (3, 3), (4, 2), (4, 4)} defined on

   A = {1, 2, 3, 4}

   (d) R = {(1, 3), (2, 1), (2, 3), (3, 1)} defined on A = {1, 2, 3}.

2. By using Warshall's algorithm find the transitive closure of the

   relation represented by the matrix $\begin{bmatrix} 0 & 0 & 0 & 1 \\ 0 & 0 & 0 & 0 \\ 0 & 1 & 0 & 0 \\ 0 & 0 & 1 & 0 \end{bmatrix}$

ANSWERS (1.5)

1. (a) R* = {(1, 2), (2, 3), (3, 4), (1, 3), (2, 4), (1, 4)}

   (b) R* = {(1, 3), (1, 1), (3, 1), (1, 2), (3, 3), (4, 4), (3, 2)}

   (c) R* = R

   (d) R* = {(1, 3), (2, 1), (2, 3), (3, 1), (1, 1), (3, 3)}

2. R* = {(1, 2), (1, 3), (1, 4), (3, 2), (4, 2), (4, 3)}

1.6 EQUIVALENCE RELATIONS AND PARTITIONS

A relation R on a set A is called an equivalence relation if it is reflexive, symmetric and transitive.

(a) Let A be the set of all people in Maharashtra state. Let R be the relation defined on A as follows. aRb if and only if a and b belong to the same district of Maharashtra state.

Clearly then for every a ∈ A, a and a belong to the same district i.e. aRa for every a ∈ A. Therefore R is a reflexive. Secondly, if a and b belong to the same district, then b and a belong to the same district. Thus aRb implies bRa. So the relation is symmetric.

Finally, if a and b belong to the same district and also b and c belong to the same district, then a and c belong to the same district. This means aRb and bRc implies aRc. Hence it is transitive relation.

The relation R satisfies all three properties required by an equivalence relation. Hence R is an equivalence relation.

(b) The relation of equality in the set of real numbers is reflexive symmetric and transitive. So the equality relation on $\mathbb{R}$ is an equivalence relation.

(c) The relation 'congruence modulo 3' defined on the set $\mathbb{Z}$ of all integers is an equivalence relation.

(d) Consider the relation of divisibility defined on the set $\mathbb{N}$ of positive integers. It is reflexive and transitive but not symmetric. Therefore it is not equivalence relation.

(e) Let A = {1, 2, 3, 4, 5}. Consider the relation R defined on A as a set of pairs.

R = {(1, 1), (2, 5), (1, 4), (3, 4), (1, 3), (3, 1), (3, 3), (4, 1), (4, 4), (4, 3), (5, 2), (5, 5), (2, 2)}

One can easily check that R is reflexive, symmetric and transitive, so it is an equivalence relation. Consider the equivalence relation in (e) above. We find the set of those elements of A which are related to 1 under this equivalence relation, and denote it by R(1).

R(1) = {x ∈ A; (1, x) ∈ R} = {1, 4, 3}

Similarly, we get

$R(2) = \{x \in A; (2, x) \in R\} = \{5, 2\}$

$R(3) = \{x \in A; (3, x) \in R\} = \{4, 1, 3\}$

$R(4) = \{x \in A; (4, x) \in R\} = \{1, 4, 3\}$

$R(5) = \{x \in A; (5, x) \in R\} = \{2, 5\}$

These sets are called equivalence classes; of respective elements. The equivalence class of an element a i.e. R(a) is also denote by [a].

In the above example, we have

$R(1) = [1] = \{1, 4, 3\}$ and $R(1) = R(3) = R(4)$.

Also, $R(2) = R(5)$.

Below, we prove some elementary results. We recall that a partition **P** = $\{A_1, A_2, ... A_k\}$ of a set A = $\{a_1, a_2, ..., a_n\}$ is a collection of non-empty and pairwise disjoint subsets of A, whose union is the set A.

The sets $A_1, A_2, ..., A_k$ in a partition are called blocks.

In the above example, P = $\{\{1, 4, 3\}, \{2, 5\}\}$ is a partition consisting of two blocks viz $\{1, 4, 3\}$ and $\{2, 5\}$.

We now prove that any partition of a given set defines an equivalence relation on that set.

Theorem : A partition **P** = $\{A_1, A_2, ..., A_k\}$ of the set A = $\{a_1, a_2, ..., a_n\}$ defines an equivalence relation on A.

Proof : Let **P** = $\{A_1, A_2, ..., A_k\}$ be the partition of the set

$A = \{a_1, a_2, ..., a_n\}$.

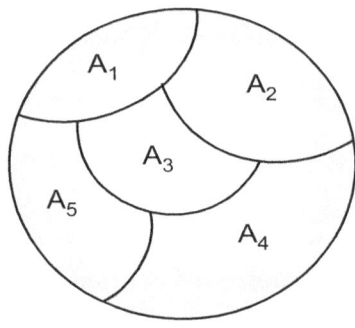

Fig. 1.15

We define a relation R on the set A as below.

$a_i R a_j$ if and only if a_i and a_j are in the same block of partition **P**.

Reflexivity : It is clear that for every i, a_i and a_i belong to the same block of **P**.

∴ $a_i R a_i$ for every i

∴ Relation R is reflexive.

Symmetry : Suppose $a_i R a_j$. Then a_i and a_j are in the same block of **P**. Therefore clearly it follows that a_j and a_i are in the same block of **P**. Therefore $a_j R a_i$.

Thus $a_i R a_j \Rightarrow a_j R a_i$.

∴ Relation R is symmetric.

Transitivity : Suppose $a_i R a_j$ and $a_j R a_k$.

Then a_i and a_j are in the same block of **P**.

Also a_j and a_k are in the same block of **P**.

Therefore, a_i and a_k must be in the same block of **P** in which a_j lies.

∴ $a_i R a_k$

Thus $a_i R a_j, a_j R a_k \Rightarrow a_i R a_k$

∴ Relation R is transitive.

The relation R being reflexive, symmetric and transitive, it is an equivalence relation on the set A, determined by the partition **P** of A.

We now proceed to the converse problem. Does every equivalence relation on the set A generates some partition of A ?

The answer to this question is YES. To prove it we need the following result.

Theorem : Let R be an equivalence relation on set A. If a and b are two elements of A, then aRb if and only if $R(a) = R(b)$.

Proof : R is an equivalence relation on set A. So R is reflexive, symmetric and transitive.

Let a, b be two elements in A.

First Part : Suppose $R(a) = R(b)$.

Now, $b \in R(b)$; by reflexivity

∴ $b \in R(a)$; ∵ $R(a) = R(b)$

∴ aRb.

Second Part : Suppose aRb.

Now to prove that $R(a) = R(b)$, we need to prove that

$R(a) \subseteq R(b)$ and $R(b) \subseteq R(a)$.

Let x be any member of $R(a)$. Then we have aRx.

Now aRb and aRx.

$\Rightarrow$ bRa and aRx; ∵ by symmetry of R

$\Rightarrow$ bRx; ∵ by transitivity of R

$\Rightarrow$ $x \in R(b)$

Thus $x \in R(a) \Rightarrow x \in R(b)$

Therefore $R(a) \subseteq R(b)$.

Again let y be any member of $R(b)$ i.e. $y \in R(b)$.

Then we have bRy.

Now aRb and bRy.

$\Rightarrow$ aRy ∵ by transitivity of R

$\Rightarrow$ $y \in R(a)$.

We have $y \in R(b) \Rightarrow y \in R(a)$

∴ $R(b) \subseteq R(a)$

Finally $R(a) \subseteq R(b)$ and $R(b) \subseteq R(a)$

Therefore $R(a) = R(b)$.

Now we are prepared to prove the following theorem.

Theorem : Let R be an equivalence relaion on the set A. Let **P** denote the collection of all disjoint equivalence classes $R(a)$; $a \in A$. Then **P** is a partition of A.

Proof : R is an equivalence relation on set A and **P** is a collection of all disjoint equivalence classes $R(a)$; $a \in A$.

To prove that **P** is a partition of A, we need to prove following two results.

(a) Every element of A is in some R(a).

But by reflexivity of R it is clear that a ∈ R(a).

(b) When R(a) ≠ R(b), then R(a) ∩ R(b) = φ.

To prove this result, we make use of contrapositive.

Assume that R(a) ∩ R(b) ≠ φ.

Then c ∈ R(a) ∩ R(b) for some c ∈ A.

∴ c ∈ R(a) and c ∈ R(b)

∴ aRc and bRc; by symmetry

∴ aRc and cRb; by symmetry

∴ aRb; by transitivity

∴ R(a) = R(b)

Thus, (b) part is proved.

Then **P** is a partition of A.

The collection of the sets in **P** above is also called the quotient set of A by R and it is denoted by A/R. Thus **P** = A/R.

ILLUSTRATIVE EXAMPLES

Example 1.24 : If {1, 3, 5}, {2, 4} is a partition of the set A = {1, 2, 3, 4, 5}, determine the corresponding equivalence relation.

Solution : A = {1, 2, 3, 4, 5} and **P** = {{1, 3, 5}, {2, 4}} is a partition of A.

The blocks in the partition **P** are {1, 3, 5} and {2, 4}.

Define a relation R on A as below. For a, b ∈ A; aRb if and only if a and b belong to the same block. Then we know that R is an equivalence relation.

∴ R = {<1, 1>, <1, 3>, <1, 5>, <3, 1>, <3, 3>, <3, 5>, <5, 1>,
<5, 3>, <5, 5>, <2, 2>, <2, 4>, <4, 2>, <4, 4>}

Example 1.25 : Let A = {1, 2, 3, 4, 5, 6, 7}. Define a relation R on A by aRb iff 3 divides (a − b). Show that R is an equivalence relation. Also, determine the partition generated by R.

Solution : A = {1, 2, 3, 4, 5, 6, 7}, aRb iff 3 divides (a − b).

∴ The relation R contains the following pairs

R = {(1, 1), (1, 4), (1, 7), (2, 2), (2, 5), (3, 3), (3, 6), (4, 1), (4, 4), (4, 7), (5, 2), (5, 5), (6, 3), (6, 6), (7, 1), (7, 4), (7, 7)}

We see that (a, a) ∈ R for every a ∈ A.

∴ Relation is reflexive.

If (a, b) ∈ R, then 3 divides.

∴ 3 divides b − a. Therefore bRa i.e. (b, a) ∈ R.

∴ Relation is symmetric.

If (a, b) ∈ R and (b, c) ∈ R, then 3 divides (a − b) and 3 divides (b − c).

∴ 3 divides [(a − b) + (b − c)] i.e. 3 divides a − c. Therefore aRc i.e. (a, c) ∈ R.

∴ Relation is transitive.

Hence R is an equivalence relation.

The equivalences of various elements are as below.

R(1) = R(4) = R(7) = {1, 4, 7}

R(2) = R(5) = {2, 5}

R(3) = R(6) = {3, 6}

∴ Partition generated by R is {{1, 4, 7}, {2, 5}, {3, 6}}.

Example 1.26 : Let A = {1, 2, 3, 4, 5, 6}.

Let R = {(a, b) | a ≡ b (mod. 2)}. Is R an equivalence relation ?

Solution : A = {1, 2, 3, 4, 5, 6} for a, b ∈ A; R = {(a, b) | a ≡ b (mod. 2)}.

Reflexivity : Let a be any element of A. Then clearly a − a = 0 is divisible by 2.

∴ a ≡ a (mod. 2) for every a ∈ A.

∴ Relation is reflexive.

Symmetry : Suppose a, b ∈ A such that a ≡ b (mod. 2)

Then by definition of congruence relation, 2 divides a − b.

Clearly then 2 divides b − a

∴ b ≡ a (mod. 2)

Thus $a \equiv b \pmod{2} \Rightarrow b \equiv a \pmod{2}$

∴ Relation is symmetric.

Transitivity : Suppose a, b, c ∈ A such that $a \equiv b \pmod{2}$ and $b \equiv c \pmod{2}$

Then 2 divides a − b and 2 divides b − c.

∴ 2 divides [(a − b) + (b − c)]

∴ 2 divides (a − c)

∴ $a \equiv c \pmod{2}$

∴ Relation is transitive. Hence R is an equivalence relation.

Example 1.27 : Let A = {1, 2, 3}. Determine whether the relations R and S whose matrices M_R and M_S are given below, are equivalence relations or not.

(i) $M_R = \begin{bmatrix} 1 & 0 & 0 \\ 0 & 1 & 1 \\ 0 & 1 & 1 \end{bmatrix}$, (ii) $M_S = \begin{bmatrix} 1 & 0 & 1 \\ 0 & 1 & 0 \\ 1 & 0 & 0 \end{bmatrix}$

Solution : (i) $M_R = \begin{bmatrix} 1 & 0 & 0 \\ 0 & 1 & 1 \\ 0 & 1 & 1 \end{bmatrix}$ Here all the diagonal elements are 1.

∴ 1R1, 2R2, 3R3

∴ R is reflexive.

The matrix M_R is symmetric $a_{ij} = a_{ji}$ for every i and j.

∴ Relation R is symmetric.

Now. $M_{R^2} = \begin{bmatrix} 1 & 0 & 0 \\ 0 & 1 & 1 \\ 0 & 1 & 1 \end{bmatrix} \odot \begin{bmatrix} 1 & 0 & 0 \\ 0 & 1 & 1 \\ 0 & 1 & 1 \end{bmatrix} = \begin{bmatrix} 1 & 0 & 0 \\ 0 & 1 & 1 \\ 0 & 1 & 1 \end{bmatrix}$

$M_{R^2} = M_R$ ∴ Relation R is transitive.

Therefore R is an equivalence relation.

(ii) $M_S = \begin{bmatrix} 1 & 0 & 1 \\ 0 & 1 & 0 \\ 1 & 0 & 0 \end{bmatrix}$ Here 3, 3 entry is 0. Therefore, relation S is not reflexive.

M_S is a symmetric matrix.

∴ Relation is a symmetric matrix.

Now 3, 1 entry is 1 and 1, 3 entry is 1.

∴ 3S1 and 1S3 but 3$\not{S}$3

∴ S is fails to be transitive.

∴ S is symmetric but not reflexive, not transitive.

∴ S is not an equivalence relation

Example 1.28 : A relation

R = {<1, 1>, <1, 2>, <1, 4>, <2, 1>, <2, 2>, <3, 2>, <3, 3>, <4, 4>} is defined over the set A = {1, 2, 3, 4}. Is R and equivalence relation ?

Solution : A = {1, 2, 3, 4}

R = {<1, 1>, <1, 2>, <1, 4>, <2, 1>, <2, 2>, <3, 2>, <3, 3>, <4, 4>}

We see that each element of A is related with itself according to relation R.

<1, 1> ∈ R, <2, 2> ∈ R, <3, 3> ∈ R, <4, 4> ∈ R.

Therefore R is reflexive.

Now <1, 4> ∈ R but <4, 1> ∉ R

Also <3, 2> ∈ R but <2, 3> ∉ R

Therefore relation R is not symmetric.

Again <2, 1> ∈ R and <1, 4> ∈ R but <2, 4> ∉ R

Also, <3, 2> ∈ R and <2, 1> ∈ R but <3, 1> ∉ R.

Therefore R is not transitive. Thus R is reflexive, not symmetric, not transitive.

Therefore R is not an equivalence relation.

Example 1.29 : If A = {a, e, i, o, u} and **P** = {{a, i}, {e, o}, {u}} is a partition of A, find the equivalence relation determined by **P**.

Solution : The set A = {a, e, i, o, u} and partition **P** = {{a, i}, {e, o}, {u}}.

We know that R is an equivalence relation determine by the partition **P** when each element of the same block is related to each element, including itself of that block.

∴ R = {(a, a), (a, i), (i, a), (i, i), (e, e), (e, o), (o, e), (o, o), (u, u)}

This is required equivalence relation.

Example 1.30 : Let X = {a, b, c, d, e} and C = {{a, b}, {c}, {d, e}}. Show that partition 'C' defines an equivalence relation on X.

Solution : X = {a, b, c, d, e} and C = {{a, b}, {c}, {d, e}} is a partition of X. The blocks in the partition C are {a, b}, {c} and {d, e}.

Consider the relation R on X such that two elements of X are related iff they belong to the same block. Then we have,

R = {(a, a), (a, b), (b, a), (b, b), (c, c), (d, d), (d, e), (e, d), (e, e)}

This relation R is an equivalence relation on set X, determined by partition C.

Example 1.31 : Let S = {1, 2, 3, 4} and A = S × S. Define a relation R on A = S × S as follows.

(a, b) R (c, d) if and only if a + b = c + d.

(a) Show that R is an equivalence relation.

(b) Compute A/R.

Solution : Two pairs (a, b) and (c, d) are R-related if and only if a + b = c + d.

(a) Reflexivity : Let (a, b) be any pair belonging to A = S × S.

We have a + b = a + b.

∴   (a, b) R (a, b)

∴   Relation R is reflexive.

Symmetry : Let (a, b) and (c, d) be two pairs in A such that (a, b) R (c, d).

Then a + b = c + d; by definition of R.

∴   c + d = a + b

∴   (c, d) R (a, b)

∴   Relation R is symmetric.

Transitivity : Let (a, b), (c, d), (e, f) be three pairs in A such that (a, b) R (c, d) and (c, d) R (e, f).

Then a + b = c + d and c + d = e + f; by definition of R

∴   a + b = e + f

∴ (a, b) R (e, f)

∴ Relation R is transitive. The relation R being reflexive, symmetric and transitive it is an equivalence relation on A = S × S.

(b) Now A = S × S consist of 4 × 4 = 16 pairs; (1, 1) (1, 2), ..., (4, 3), (4, 4).

Consider the first pair (1, 1), we have 1 + 1 = 2.

Then for any pair (a, b) ∈ A, we have a + b = 2 only when a = 1, and b = 1.

∴ Equivalence class of (1, 1) consists of (1, 1) itself.

$$R((1, 1)) = \{(1, 1)\}$$

Consider the next pair (1, 2) in A. We have 1 + 2 = 3, then for any pair (a, b) ∈ A,

a + b = 3 only when a = 1, b = 2 and a = 2, b = 1.

∴ Equivalence class of (1, 2) consists of two pairs.

$$R((1, 2)) = \{(1, 2), (2, 1)\} = R((2, 1))$$

After continuing in this way we get,

$$R((1, 3)) = \{(1, 3), (2, 2), (3, 1)\}$$
$$R((1, 4)) = \{(1, 4), (2, 3), (3, 2), (4, 1)\}$$
$$= R((2, 3)) = R((3, 2)) = R((4, 1))$$
$$R((2, 4)) = \{(2, 4), (4, 2), (3, 3)\}$$
$$= R((4, 2)) = R((3, 3))$$
$$R((3, 4)) = \{(3, 4), (4, 3)\} = R((4, 3))$$
$$R((4, 4)) = \{(4, 4)\}$$

∴ A/R = {A$_1$ = {(1, 1)}, A$_2$ = {(1, 2), (2, 1)}
A$_3$ = {(1, 3), (2, 2), (3, 1)}
A$_4$ = {(1, 4), (2, 3), (3, 2), (4, 1)}
A$_5$ = {(2, 4), (4, 2), (3, 3)} A$_6$ = {(3, 4), (4, 3)}
A$_7$ = {(4, 4)} }

Example 1.32 : Let R be a transitive and reflexive relation on A. Let T be a relation on A such that (a, b) is in T if and only if both (a, b) and (b, a) are in R. Show that T is an equivalence relation on A.

Solution : Given : R is transitive and reflexive.

Also given; (a, b) ∈ T if and only if (a, b) and (b, a) are in R.

Reflexivity of T : Let a be any element of A. Then by reflexivity of R, we have

$\quad$ (a, a) ∈ R and (a, a) ∈ R.

∴ (a, a) ∈ T; by definition of T.

∴ Relation T is reflexive.

Symmetry of T : Let a and b be two elements of A such that (a, b) ∈ T.

$\quad$ (a, b) ∈ T $\qquad$ ∴ (a, b) ∈ R and (b, a) ∈ R

$\qquad\qquad\qquad\quad$ ∴ (b, a) ∈ R and (a, b) ∈ R

$\qquad\qquad\qquad\quad$ ∴ (b, a) ∈ T $\quad$ by definition of T.

Thus, $\quad$ (a, b) ∈ T $\Rightarrow$ (b, a) ∈ T

∴ Relation T is symmetric.

Transitivity of T : Let a, b, c be elements of A such that (a, b) ∈ T and (b, c) ∈ T.

Then (a, b) ∈ R, (b, a) ∈ R, (b, c) ∈ R, (c, b) ∈ R by definition of T.

Now by transitivity of R, we have (a, b) ∈ R, (b, c) ∈ R $\Rightarrow$ (a, c) ∈ R.

Also (c, b) ∈ R, (b, a) ∈ R $\Rightarrow$ (c, a) ∈ R.

Finally, (a, c) ∈ R, (c, a) ∈ R $\Rightarrow$ (a, c) ∈ T; by definition of T.

Thus, (a, b) ∈ T, (b, c) ∈ T $\Rightarrow$ (a, c) ∈ T.

Hence the relation T is transitive.

We proved that relation T is reflexive, symmetric and transitive. Therefore it is an equivalence relation.

Example 1.33 : If R and S are equivalence relations on a set A, prove that R ∩ S is an equivalence relation on A.

Solution : Given that R and S are equivalence relations on set A.

∴ R and S both are reflexive, symmetric and transitive.

Now consider the relation R ∩ S.

Reflexivity : We have for any a ∈ A that (a, a) ∈ R and (a, a) ∈ S by reflexivity of R and S.

∴ (a, a) ∈ R ∩ S for every a ∈ A.

∴ R ∩ S is reflexive.

Symmetry : Suppose a R ∩ S b. Then (a,b) ∈ R ∩ S.

∴ (a, b) ∈ R and (a, b) ∈ S

∴ (b, a) ∈ R and (b, a) ∈ S; by symmetry of R and S

∴ (b, a) ∈ R ∩ S

∴ b R ∩ S a

Hence R ∩ S is symmetric.

Transitivity : Suppose a R ∩ S b and b R ∩ S c. Then (a, b) ∈ R ∩ S and (b, c) ∈ R ∩ S

∴ (a, b) ∈ R, (a, b) ∈ S, (b, c) ∈ R, (b, c) ∈ S.

Now (a, b) ∈ R, (b, c) ∈ R. ∴ (a, c) ∈ R by transitivity of R.

Also (a, b) ∈ S, (b, c) ∈ S ⇒ (a, c) ∈ S by transitivity of S.

Therefore (a, c) ∈ R ∩ S.

∴ a R ∩ S c

∴ Relation R ∩ S is transitive. Thus finally, R ∩ S being reflexive, symmetric and transitive, it is an equivalence relation.

EXERCISE (1.6)

1. By stating the required result, determine the equivalence relation on the set A, by the partition **P**.

    (a) A = {2, 4, 6, 8, 9, 10}

    P = {{2, 8, 9}, {6, 10}, {4}}

    (b) A = {p, q, r, s, t}

    P = {{p}, {q}, {r, s, t}}

    (c) A = {3, 4, 5, 6, 7, 8, 9}

    P = {{3, 7}, {4, 8}, {5, 9}, {6}}

2. A relation R is defined on the set A = {1, 3, 5, 6, 7, 9} as below. aRb if and only if a − b is divisible by 4. Determine the relation R. Show that it is an equivalence relation. Determine the partition of A generated by R. Draw the digraph of R.

3. Let A = {1, 2, 3, 4, 5, 6, 7} and R = {<x, y> | x − y is divisible by 3}, show that R is an equivalence relation. Draw the graph of R.

4. R and S are two relations on A = {1, 2, 3} whose matrices are given below.

$$M_R = \begin{bmatrix} 1 & 1 & 0 \\ 1 & 1 & 0 \\ 0 & 0 & 1 \end{bmatrix}, \quad M_S = \begin{bmatrix} 1 & 0 & 1 \\ 0 & 1 & 0 \\ 1 & 0 & 1 \end{bmatrix}$$

(a) Show that R and S both are equivalence relations.

(b) Write R ∩ S as a set of ordered pairs. Is R ∩ S an equivalence relation?

(c) Write R ∪ S as a set of ordered pairs. Is R ∪ S an equivalence relation?

5. A relation R is defined on the A = {1, 2, 3, 4} by the matrix

$$M_R = \begin{bmatrix} 1 & 0 & 0 & 0 \\ 0 & 1 & 1 & 1 \\ 0 & 1 & 1 & 1 \\ 0 & 1 & 1 & 1 \end{bmatrix}.$$ Show that R is an equivalence relation. Compute A/R.

6. Let S = {1, 2, 3, 4} and A = S × S. A relation R is defined on A = S × S as follows.

(a, b) R (c, d) if and only if ad = bc.

(a) Show that R is an equivalence relation.

(b) Compute A/R.

ANSWERS (1.6)

1. (a) R = {(2, 2), (2, 8), (2, 9), (8, 2), (8, 8), (8, 9), (9, 2), (9, 8), (9, 9), (6, 6), (6, 10), (10, 6), (10, 10), (4, 4)}

(b) R = {(p, p), (q, q), (r, r), (r, s), (r, t), (s, r), (s, s), (s, t), (t, r), (t, s), (t, t)}

(c) R = {(3, 3), (3, 7), (7, 3), (7, 7), (4, 4), (4, 8), (8, 4), (8, 8), (5, 5), (5, 9), (9, 5), (9, 9), (6, 6)}

2. R = {(1, 1), (1, 5), (1, 9), (3, 3), (3, 7), (5, 1), (5, 5), (5, 9), (6, 6), (7, 3), (7, 7), (9, 1), (9, 5), (9, 9)}

   P = {{1, 5, 9}, {3, 7}, {6}}

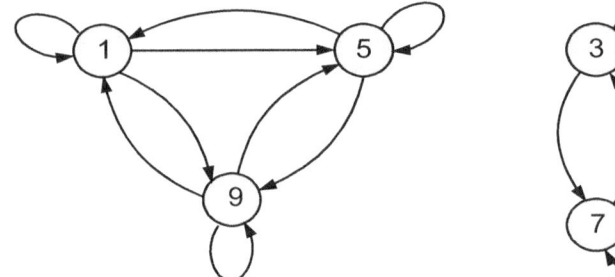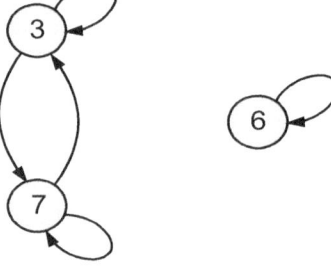

Fig. 1.16

3. R = {(1, 1), (1, 4), (1, 7), (4, 1), (4, 4), (4, 7), (7, 1), (7, 4), (7, 7), (2, 2), (2, 5), (5, 2), (5, 5), (3, 3), (3, 6), (6, 3), (6, 6)}

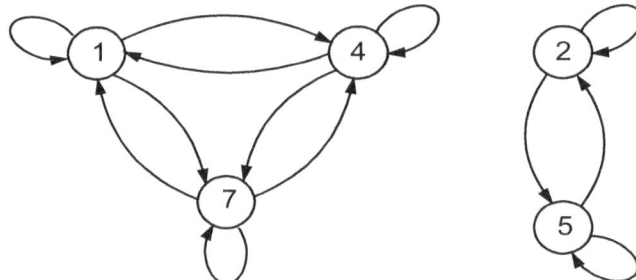

Fig. 1.17

4. (b) R ∩ S = {(1, 1), (2, 2), (3, 3)} It is an equivalence relation.

   (c) R ∪ S = {(1, 1), (2, 2), (3, 3), (1, 2), (2, 1), (1, 3), (3, 1)}

   It is not equivalence relation (3, 1) ∈ R ∪ S, (1, 2) ∈ R ∪ S but (3, 2) ∉ R ∪ S.

5.   A/R = {A_1 = {(1, 1)},

   A_2 = {(2, 2), (2, 3), (2, 4), (3, 2), (3, 3), (3, 4), (4, 2), (4, 3), (4, 4)}

6.   A/R = {A_1 = {(1, 1)},

   A_2 = {(1, 2), (2, 4)}

$A_3 = \{(1, 3)\}$

$A_4 = \{(1, 4)\}$

$A_5 = \{(2, 1), (4, 2)\}$

$A_6 = \{(2, 2), (3, 3), (4, 4)\}$

$A_7 = \{(2, 3)\}$

$A_8 = \{(3, 1)\}$

$A_9 = \{(3, 2)\}$

$A_{10} = \{(3, 4)\}$

$A_{11} = \{(4, 1)\}$

$A_{12} = \{(4, 3)\}\}$

1.7 PARTIAL ORDER RELATION

A relation R defined on the set A is called a partial order relation if R is reflexive i.e. aRa for every a ∈ A

Antisymmetric i.e. aRb and bRa $\Rightarrow$ a = b for a, b ∈ A.

Transitive i.e. aRb and bRc $\Rightarrow$ aRc for a, b, c ∈ A.

Illustration 1 : Consider the set $\mathbb{N}$ of all positive integers together with usual 'less than or equal to' relation ≤.

For every a ∈ $\mathbb{N}$, we have a ≤ a.

∴ ≤ relation is reflexive.

We know that a, b ∈ $\mathbb{N}$; a ≤ b and b ≤ a $\Rightarrow$ a = b.

∴ ≤ relation is antisymmetric.

Finally, for any three elements a, b, c ∈ $\mathbb{N}$; a ≤ b and b ≤ c $\Rightarrow$ a ≤ c.

∴ ≤ is transitive relation.

Hence ≤ is partial order relation on the set $\mathbb{N}$.

Illustration 2 : Consider the set S = {1, 2, 3, 4, 5, 6} and the relation of divisibility defined on S.

We have already seen that divisibility relation is a partial order relation.

A non-empty set P together with a partial order relation denoted by ≤ on it, is called a partially ordered set briefly written as **Poset** and denoted by (P, ≤).

Thus, in the above two illustrations ($\mathbb{N}$, ≤) and (S, |) are posets. Here the symbol '|' stands for divisibility.

Thus 4 divides 12 is written as 4|12; 3 divides 15 is denoted by 3|15 and 4 does not divide 25 is denoted by 4∤25.

At this stage, we note that the study of algebra of posets is the beginning of 'Boolean Algebra'.

Just like Venn diagrams used in set theory help us in better understanding of the algebra of sets; the posets are represented by diagrams known as Hasse diagrams. To draw Hasse diagram of a poset (P, ≤) we need a covering relation denoted by –< which is obtained from the partial order relation ≤.

Consider the partial order relation usual less than or equal to i.e. ≤; on the set P = {1, 2, 3, 4, 5}. We note that w.r.t. ≤ relation in P there is no x ∈ P such that 1 ≤ x ≤ 2. Also there is no y ∈ P such that 3 ≤ y ≤ 4.

It is described by saying that 1 is covered by 2 and likewise 3 is covered by 4. We denote this as 1 –< 2 and 3 –< 4.

Note that w.r.t. ≤ relation 3 ≤ 5 but 3 is not covered by 5. This is because there exists an element 4 ∈ P such that 3 ≤ 4 and 4 ≤ 5.

In the above example the covering relation is

$$-< \ = \ \{1 -< 2, \ 2 -< 3, \ 3 -< 4, \ 4 -< 5\}$$

Again consider the set, P = {1, 2, 3, 4, 5, 6} and the partial order relation of divisibility defined on P. Here 1 ∈ P is covered by 2 ∈ P, since there is no x ∈ P, such that 1|x and x|2. Therefore, 1 –< 2.

Also 1 –< 3 since there is no y ∈ P such that 1|y and y|3. ∴ 1 –< 3.

However, 1 ∈ P is not covered by 4 ∈ P. The reason is that w.r.t. divisibility there is 2 ∈ P, such that 1|2 and 2|4.

In this example the covering relation is

$$-< \ = \ \{1 -< 2, \ 1 -< 3, \ 1 -< 5, \ 2 -< 4, \ 2 -< 6, \ 3 -< 6\}$$

After preparing a covering relation, we draw Hasse diagram as below.

We denote the elements of the poset {P, ≤} by small circles.

If a $\prec$ b, then the circle corresponding to a is drawn at lower level and the circle corresponding to b is drawn at upper level and these two circles are joined by a straight line segment; either vertical or tilted. Note that there are no horizontal line segments in the Hasse diagram.

Consider the above example P = {1, 2, 3, 4, 5, 6} and the partial order relation of divisibility.

The covering relation is,

$\prec$ = {1 $\prec$ 2, 1 $\prec$ 3, 1 $\prec$ 5, 2 $\prec$ 4, 2 $\prec$ 6, 3 $\prec$ 6}

In this example, neither 2 divide 5 nor 5 divides 2. Such elements are said to be non-comparable (w.r.t. divisibility off course).

The Hasse diagram is as shown below.

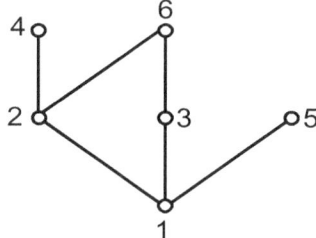

Fig. 1.18

In the first example, above P = {1, 2, 3, 4, 5} w.r.t. usual $\leq$ relation, we have

$\prec$ = {1 $\prec$ 2, 2 $\prec$ 3, 3 $\prec$ 4, 4 $\prec$ 5}

The Hasse diagram is

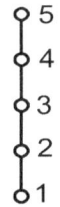

Fig. 1.19

It looks like a chain. It is called totally ordered set Toset or chain.

We note that Toset is a Poset but Poset need not be Toset.

Consider the set A = {a, b}.

The power set of set A is S = {ϕ, {a}, {b}, {a, b}}.

Then S is a poset w.r.t. partial order relation set inclusion relation $\subseteq$.

The covering relation is $-< = \{\phi -< \{a\}, \phi -< \{b\}, \{a\} -< \{a, b\}, b -< \{a, b\}\}$

The Hasse diagram is as below.

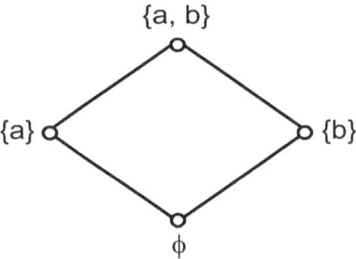

Fig. 1.20

This diagram looks like a diamond. It is called diamond poset.

In a poset $(P, \leq)$; an element $x \in P$ is called maximal element if there is no $y \in P$, such that $x \leq y$. Geometrically, in the Hasse diagram of P, the upward journey from x is not possible.

Likewise an element x is called minimal element in the poset $(P, \leq)$ if there is no $y \in P$, such that $y \leq x$.

Geometrically, in the Hasse diagram of P, the downward journey from x is not possible.

Further in the poset $(P, \leq)$ $x \in P$ is greatest element if $y \leq x$ for every $y \in P$ and x is the least element of P if $x \leq y$ for every $y \in P$.

In the Hasse diagram, the meaning of x is greatest element is that, we can start at any element of P, move in the upward direction and reach at x.

Also the meaning of x is least element of P is that, we can start at any element of P, move in the downward direction and reach at x.

It is clear that the greatest element of the poset is maximal element but maximal element may not be greatest.

Also the least element of the poset is minimal element but minimal element may not be least element.

In the poset represented by the diagram.

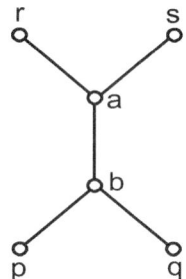

Fig. 1.21

r and s are maximal elements. p and q are minimal elements.

The greatest element does not exist because r and s are non-comparable. The least element does not exist because p and q are non-comparable.

We can easily prove that in poset the greatest element in poset the greatest element if it exists, it is unique.

For this if possible let x and y be two greatest elements in the poset (P, ≤).

Then by definition   x ≤ y   ∵ y is greatest

Also,   y ≤ x   ∵ x is greatest

Now by antisymmetry property of ≤, we have x = y. Proved.

Again suppose x and y are two least elements in P.

Then by definition,   x ≤ y   ∵ x is least

Also,   y ≤ x   ∵ y is least

∴   By antisymmetry again x = y. Proved.

EXERCISE (1.7)

1. Show that the relation of divisibility in the set of positive integers is a partial order relation.
2. Let P = {1, 2, 4, 5, 10, 20}. Write down the covering relation w.r.t. the relation of divisibility. Also draw Hasse diagram of P.
3. In the set $\mathbb{R}$ of all real numbers define the relation R by xRy iff x ≠ y.

    Is R a partial order relation ? Justify your answer.

4. Let A = {a, b} and P(A) the collection of all subsets of A. Show that the set inclusion relation defined on P(A) is partial order relation. Draw Hasse diagram.

5. Let A = {a, b, c} and P(A) the collection of all subsets of A. Show that P(A) forms a poset under set inclusion relation. Draw Hasse diagram of this poset.

ANSWERS (1.7)

2. $-< = \{1 -< 2, 1 -< 5, 2 -< 4, 2 -< 10, 4 -< 20, 5 -< 10, 10 -< 20\}$

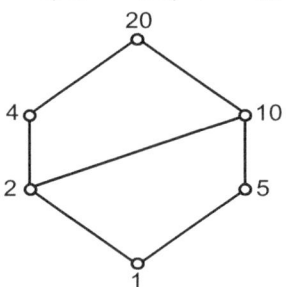

Fig. 122

3. R is not partial order relation.

4.
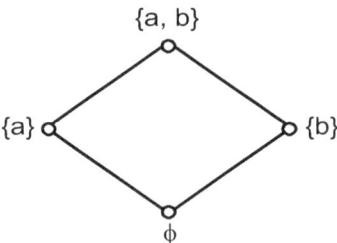

Fig. 1.23

5.
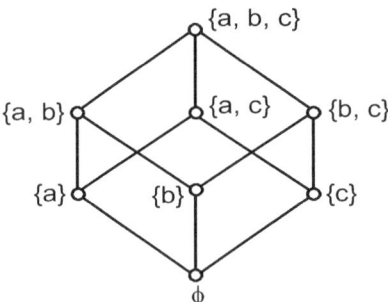

Fig. 1.24

1.8 CONGRUENCE RELATION

In this section, we continue the study of divisibility, but from a slightly different point of view. A congruence is nothing more than a statement about divisibility. However, it is more than just a convenient notation.

Congruence modulo n: Let a and b be any two integers and $n > 1$ be an integer. If $n \mid (a - b)$, we say that 'a is congruent to b modulo n' and write $a \equiv b \pmod{n}$. Clearly this defines a relation in the set of integers $\mathbb{Z}$, and is called *congruence relation modulo* n.

Thus $a \equiv b \pmod{n} \Rightarrow n \mid (a - b) \Rightarrow a - b = kn, k \in \mathbb{Z}$.

For instance, $5 \equiv 11 \pmod 6$, since $5 - 11 = -6$ is divisible by 6. Similarly, $-7 \equiv 10 \pmod{17}$, since $-7 - 10 = -17$ is divisible by 17.

Ex.: Show that congruence relation in $\mathbb{Z}$ is an equivalence relation:

(i) For any $a \in \mathbb{Z}$, we have $a - a = 0$ is divisible by n, hence $a \equiv a \pmod n$, for any $a \in \mathbb{Z}$.

∴ The relation is reflexive.

(ii) If $a \equiv b \pmod n$, then $n \mid (a - b)$, hence $n \mid (b - a)$, so $b \equiv a \pmod n$ and the relation is symmetric.

(iii) If $a \equiv b \pmod n$ and $b \equiv c \pmod n$, then $n \mid (a - b)$ and $n \mid (b - c)$. So that $n \mid [(a - b) + (b - c)]$, which implies $n \mid (a - c)$.

∴ $a \equiv c \pmod n$; and the relation is transitive.

Thus, the congruence relation modulo n is equivalence relation in $\mathbb{Z}$.

Simple properties of the congruence relation.

Theorem 7: Let a, b, c, d, x, y denote integers. Then

(a) If $a \equiv b \pmod n$, then

　(i) $ax \equiv bx \pmod n$.

　(ii) $(a + x) \equiv (b + x) \pmod n$.

(b) If $a \equiv b \pmod n$ and $c \equiv d \pmod n$, then

　(i) $(a + c) \equiv (b + d) \pmod n$

　(ii) $(ax + cy) \equiv (bx + dy) \pmod n$

　(iii) $ac \equiv bd \pmod n$

Proof: (a) As $a \equiv b \pmod{n}$, $n \mid (a - b)$, so $a - b = nk$, for $k \in Z$. ... (1)

(i) Now, $ax - bx = (a - b)x = nkx$, using (1)

$\Rightarrow ax - bx = n(kx)$

$\Rightarrow n \mid (ax - bx)$

$\Rightarrow ax \equiv bx \pmod{n}$

(ii) We have, $(a + x) - (b + x) = a - b = nk$ ... by (1)

$\Rightarrow (a + x) - (b + x) = nk$

$\Rightarrow n \mid [(a + x) - (b + x)]$

$\Rightarrow (a + x) \equiv (b + x) \pmod{n}$

(b) $a \equiv b \pmod{n} \Rightarrow n \mid (a - b)$, so $a - b = nk_1$ for some $k_1 \in Z$

$c \equiv d \pmod{n} \Rightarrow n \mid (c - d)$, so $c - d = nk_2$ for some $k_2 \in Z$ ... (2)

(i) Now $(a + c) - (b + d) = (a - b) + (c - d)$

$= nk_1 + nk_2$, ... using (2)

$= n(k_1 + k_2)$

which shows that $n \mid [(a + c) - (b + d)]$

i.e. $(a + c) \equiv (b + d) \pmod{n}$

(ii) We have,

$(ax + cy) - (bx + dy) = (ax - bx) + (cy - dy)$

$= (a - b)x + (c - d)y$

$= nk_1 x + nk_2 y$ ... using (2)

$= n[k_1 x + k_2 y]$

Hence $n \mid [(ax + cy) - (bx + dy)]$.

Proving that $(ax + cy) \equiv (bx + dy) \pmod{n}$

(iii) We have,

$ac - bd = ac - bc + bc - bd$

$= (a - b)c + b(c - d)$

$= nk_1 c + b(nk_2)$ ... using (2)

$= n(k_1 c + bk_2)$

So that $n \mid (ac - bd)$, hence
$$ac \equiv bd \pmod{n}.$$

Theorem 8: (a) If $a \equiv b \pmod{n}$ and $d \mid n$, $d > 0$, then
$$a \equiv b \pmod{d}$$

(b) If $ax \equiv bx \pmod{n}$ and $(x, n) = 1$, then

$a \equiv b \pmod{n}$. [cancellation law]

(c) If $(x, n) = d$ and $ax \equiv bx \pmod{n}$, then

$a \equiv b \pmod{w}$, where $n = dw$.

Proof: (a) Since $a \equiv b \pmod{n}$, we have $a - b = nk$, for some $k \in \mathbb{Z}$. Again, $d \mid n$, we have $n = dk_1$, for $k_1 \in \mathbb{Z}$. So that

$$a - b = nk = (dk_1) k, \quad \because n = dk_1$$

$\Rightarrow \qquad a - b = d(k_1 k)$

$\Rightarrow d \mid (a - b) \Rightarrow \quad a \equiv b \pmod{d}$

(b) If $ax \equiv bx \pmod{n}$, then $n \mid (ax - bx)$, i.e. $ax - bx = nk$, for $k \in \mathbb{Z}$.

$\Rightarrow (a - b) x = nk$, for $k \in \mathbb{Z}$

$\Rightarrow n \mid (a - b)x$

$\Rightarrow n \mid (a - b)$, since $(x, n) = 1$.

$\Rightarrow a \equiv b \pmod{n}$.

(c) Since $(x, n) = d$, let $x = dk_1$, and $n = dw$, for $k_1, w \in \mathbb{Z}$ ... (1)

and $\qquad (k_1, w) = 1$

Now, $\quad ax \equiv bx \pmod{n}$

$\Rightarrow n \mid (ax - bx)$

$\Rightarrow n \mid (a - b) x$

$\Rightarrow (a - b) x = nz$, for $z \in \mathbb{Z}$

$\Rightarrow (a - b) dk_1 = dwz,$ ... using (1)

$\Rightarrow (a - b) k_1 = wz,$ ($\because d \neq 0$, cancelling)

$\Rightarrow w \mid (a - b) k_1$

$\Rightarrow w \mid (a - b),$ ($\because (w, k_1) = 1$)

$\Rightarrow a \equiv b \pmod{w}$

Theorem 9: If $a \equiv b \pmod{n}$, then $(a, n) = (b, n)$.

Proof: We have $a - b = nk$, for some integer $k \in \mathbb{Z}$ ... (1)

Let $(a, n) = d$ and $(b, n) = g$. Then $d \mid a$ and $d \mid n$, we have $d \mid b$, from (1). So that $d \mid n$ and $d \mid b$ implies $d \mid g$. In similar manner, we can show $g \mid d$. Therefore $d = g$, since $d, g > 0$. Therefore $(a, n) = (b, n)$.

Theorem 10: Let a and b be any two integers and $n \in \mathbb{N}$. Then $a \equiv b \pmod{n}$ if and only if a and b leave the same remainder when divided by n.

Proof: Suppose $a \equiv b \pmod{n}$. Then we have to show that a and b leave the same remainder when divided by n.

Now $a \equiv b \pmod{n}$.

$\Rightarrow a - b = nk$, $k \in \mathbb{Z}$.

$\therefore \qquad a = b + nk$ ... (1)

Applying division algorithm to b and n, there exist q and r such that

$$b = nq + r, \qquad 0 \leq r < n \qquad ... (2)$$

i.e. r is the remainder when b is divided by n.

From (1) and (2), we have

$$a = (nq + r) + nk$$
$$= n(q + k) + r, \quad 0 \leq r < n$$

which shows that r is also the remainder when a is divided by n.

Conversely, suppose a and b leave the same remainder when divided by n. That is, by division algorithm, we have

$$a = nq + r \text{ and } b = nq' + r, 0 \leq r < n$$

$r, q, q' \in \mathbb{Z}$

Then, $\qquad a - b = (nq + r) - (nq' + r)$

$\qquad\qquad\qquad = n(q - q')$

$\qquad \Rightarrow \quad n \mid (a - b)$

$\qquad \Rightarrow \quad a \equiv b \pmod{n}$.

This completes the proof of the theorem.

We have seen that the relation "Congruence modulo n" is an equivalence relation in $\mathbb{Z}$. Hence we can define equivalence classes for the elements in $\mathbb{Z}$, which are called *congruent classes modulo* n or *residue classes modulo* n.

Residue classes modulo n: For $a \in \mathbb{Z}$, the set $\bar{a} = \{x \in \mathbb{Z} \mid x \equiv a \pmod{n}\}$ is called the *'congruent class of a modulo n'* or the 'residue class of a modulo n'.

Thus, the residue class of a is the set of all integers which are congruent to a modulo n.

Note: 1. For $a \in \mathbb{Z}$, we have

$$\bar{a} = \{x \in \mathbb{Z} \mid x \equiv a \pmod{n}\}$$
$$= \{x \in \mathbb{Z} \mid n \mid (x - a)\}$$
$$= \{x \in \mathbb{Z} \mid x - a = nz, z \in \mathbb{Z}\}$$

$$\bar{a} = \{x \in \mathbb{Z} \mid x = a + nz, z \in \mathbb{Z}\} \qquad \ldots (*)$$

If we apply division algorithm to a and n, we have unique q and r in $\mathbb{Z}$, such that

$$a = nq + r, \text{ where } 0 \leq r < n \qquad \ldots (**)$$

That is, r is the least positive remainder when 'a' is divided by n. Using (**) in (*), we get

$$\bar{a} = \{x \in \mathbb{Z} \mid x = r + nq + nz; q, z \in \mathbb{Z}\}$$
$$= \{x \in \mathbb{Z} \mid x = r + n(q + z); q, z \in \mathbb{Z}\}$$
$$= \{x \in \mathbb{Z} \mid x = r + nk; k \in \mathbb{Z}\}$$

This shows that, if $a \in \mathbb{Z}$ and r is the least positive integer obtained by dividing a by n; then

$$\bar{a} = \{\ldots, r - 2n, r - n, r, r + n, r + 2n, \ldots\} \qquad \ldots (*)'$$

2. In particular, let n = 5 and a = 2. Then by definition

$$\bar{2} = \{x \in \mathbb{Z} \mid x \equiv 2 \pmod{5}\}$$
$$= \{x \in \mathbb{Z} \mid x = 2 + nz, z \in \mathbb{Z}\}$$

so that $\bar{2} = \{\ldots, -8, -3, 2, 7, 12, \ldots\}$

Similarly, we can work-out

$$\bar{0} = \{..., -10, -5, 0, 5, 10, ...\}$$

$$\bar{7} = \{..., -8, -3, 2, 7, 12, ...\} \quad \text{(using note 1)}$$

Theorem 11: There are precisely n distinct residue classes modulo n.

Proof: Let $a \in \mathbb{Z}$ be an arbitrary integer. Applying division algorithm to a and n, we have unique q and r in $\mathbb{Z}$ such that

$$a = nq + r, \text{ where } 0 \le r < n$$

$\therefore \qquad a - r = nq \text{ or } n \mid (a - r)$

$\therefore \qquad a \equiv r \pmod{n}$

Therefore $a \in \bar{r}$.

But we know that $a \in \bar{r}$ iff $\bar{a} = \bar{r}$, the property of equivalence classes. Thus $\bar{a} = \bar{r}$. But $r = 0, 1, 2, ..., n-1$. This shows that every integer in $\mathbb{Z}$ belongs to one of the residue classes: $\bar{0}, \bar{1}, ..., \overline{n-1}$. That is, there are at most n residue classes modulo n.

We assert that $\bar{0}, \bar{1}, ..., \overline{n-1}$ are all distinct;

for if $\bar{i} = \bar{j}$, for $0 \le i, j < n$, then $i \equiv j \pmod{n}$

$\Rightarrow n \mid (i - j)$, which is impossible unless

$$i - j = 0, \text{ since } 0 \le i, j < n.$$

Hence $\qquad i - j = 0 \Rightarrow i = j$

Thus $\bar{0}, \bar{1}, ..., \overline{n-1}$ are all distinct, proving that there are precisely n distinct residue classes modulo n.

Notation: We denote by $\mathbb{Z}_n$, the set of all residue classes modulo n. That is,

$$\mathbb{Z}_n = \{\bar{0}, \bar{1}, \bar{2}, ..., \overline{n-1}\}$$

In particular, $\mathbb{Z}_5 = \{\bar{0}, \bar{1}, \bar{2}, \bar{3}, \bar{4}\}$ and $\mathbb{Z}_8 = \{\bar{0}, \bar{1}, \bar{2}, \bar{3}, \bar{4}, \bar{5}, \bar{6}, \bar{7}\}$

Definition: Let R denote a set. A mapping $\alpha: R \times R \to R$ is called a *binary operation* on R.

In other words, binary operation on a set combines two elements to form a new element in itself.

For instance, usual addition '+' and multiplication are binary operations on the set of real numbers. Another example can be given as follows: Let X be non-empty set; and P (X) denote the set of all subsets of X. Then *union* and *intersection* of any two members in P (X) is again a member of P (X), hence union and intersection are binary operations on P (X).

Definition: Let $\bar{i}, \bar{j} \in Z_n$. We define binary operations of *addition* and *multiplication* in Z_n as (i) $\bar{i} + \bar{j} = \overline{i+j}$ and (ii) $\bar{i} \cdot \bar{j} = \overline{i \cdot j}$

Note:
1. Addition and multiplication as defined above are well defined. That is, if we have $\bar{i} = \bar{i'}$ and $\bar{j} = \bar{j'}$ for $0 \leq i, i', j, j' < n$ the additions $\bar{i} + \bar{j}$ and $\bar{i'} + \bar{j'}$ i.e. $\overline{i+j}$ and $\overline{i'+j'}$ should be equal. This can be worked out by the properties of congruence relation.

   Since $\bar{i} = \bar{i'} \Rightarrow i \equiv i' \pmod{n}$

   and $\bar{j} = \bar{j'} \Rightarrow j \equiv j' \pmod{n}$

   Then we know $i + j \equiv i' + j' \pmod{n}$

   hence $\overline{i+j} = \overline{i'+j'}$

   Similarly, we can show that $\overline{i \cdot j} = \overline{i' \cdot j'}$

2. Sometimes addition and multiplication in Z_n are denoted by $+_n$ and $\times_n$ respectively, to distinguish these operations from our usual addition and multiplication.

   We illustrate these operations in Z_7. For $\bar{3}, \bar{4} \in Z_7$, we have $\bar{3} + \bar{4} = \overline{3+4} = \bar{7} = \bar{0}$ since in Z_7, $\bar{0} = \bar{7}$. And $\bar{3} \times \bar{4} = \overline{3 \times 4} = \overline{12} = \bar{5}$, since $\overline{12} = \bar{5}$ in Z_7.

Following are the composition tables for addition and multiplication in Z_7.

$Z_7 = \{\bar{0}, \bar{1}, \bar{2}, \bar{3}, \bar{4}, \bar{5}, \bar{6}\}$

$+_7$	$\bar{0}$	$\bar{1}$	$\bar{2}$	$\bar{3}$	$\bar{4}$	$\bar{5}$	$\bar{6}$
$\bar{0}$	$\bar{0}$	$\bar{1}$	$\bar{2}$	$\bar{3}$	$\bar{4}$	$\bar{5}$	$\bar{6}$
$\bar{1}$	$\bar{1}$	$\bar{2}$	$\bar{3}$	$\bar{4}$	$\bar{5}$	$\bar{6}$	$\bar{0}$
$\bar{2}$	$\bar{2}$	$\bar{3}$	$\bar{4}$	$\bar{5}$	$\bar{6}$	$\bar{0}$	$\bar{1}$
$\bar{3}$	$\bar{3}$	$\bar{4}$	$\bar{5}$	$\bar{6}$	$\bar{0}$	$\bar{1}$	$\bar{2}$
$\bar{4}$	$\bar{4}$	$\bar{5}$	$\bar{6}$	$\bar{0}$	$\bar{1}$	$\bar{2}$	$\bar{3}$
$\bar{5}$	$\bar{5}$	$\bar{6}$	$\bar{0}$	$\bar{1}$	$\bar{2}$	$\bar{3}$	$\bar{4}$
$\bar{6}$	$\bar{6}$	$\bar{0}$	$\bar{1}$	$\bar{2}$	$\bar{3}$	$\bar{4}$	$\bar{5}$

$\times_7$	$\bar{0}$	$\bar{1}$	$\bar{2}$	$\bar{3}$	$\bar{4}$	$\bar{5}$	$\bar{6}$
$\bar{0}$	$\bar{0}$	$\bar{0}$	$\bar{0}$	$\bar{0}$	$\bar{0}$	$\bar{0}$	$\bar{0}$
$\bar{1}$	$\bar{0}$	$\bar{1}$	$\bar{2}$	$\bar{3}$	$\bar{4}$	$\bar{5}$	$\bar{6}$
$\bar{2}$	$\bar{0}$	$\bar{2}$	$\bar{4}$	$\bar{6}$	$\bar{1}$	$\bar{3}$	$\bar{5}$
$\bar{3}$	$\bar{0}$	$\bar{3}$	$\bar{6}$	$\bar{2}$	$\bar{5}$	$\bar{1}$	$\bar{4}$
$\bar{4}$	$\bar{0}$	$\bar{4}$	$\bar{1}$	$\bar{5}$	$\bar{2}$	$\bar{6}$	$\bar{3}$
$\bar{5}$	$\bar{0}$	$\bar{5}$	$\bar{3}$	$\bar{1}$	$\bar{6}$	$\bar{4}$	$\bar{2}$
$\bar{6}$	$\bar{0}$	$\bar{6}$	$\bar{5}$	$\bar{4}$	$\bar{3}$	$\bar{2}$	$\bar{1}$

The following properties of addition and multiplication in Z_n, hold good, which can be proved by using the corresponding properties of + and · in Z. Let $\bar{i}, \bar{j}, \bar{k} \in Z_n$.

1. Addition in Z_n is commutative i.e. $\bar{i} + \bar{j} = \bar{j} + \bar{i}$

2. Addition in Z_n is associative, i.e. $(\bar{i} + \bar{j}) + \bar{k} = \bar{i} + (\bar{j} + \bar{k})$

3. $\bar{0}$ is an additive identity, i.e. neutral element in Z_n, w.r.t. addition.

    i.e. $\quad \bar{i} + \bar{0} = \bar{0} + \bar{i} = \bar{i}$

4. For $\bar{i} \in Z_n$, there is $\overline{n-i}$ in Z_n, such that

    $$\bar{i} + \overline{(n-i)} = \overline{1 + (n-i)} = \bar{n} = \bar{0}.$$

5. Multiplication in Z_n is commutative i.e. $\bar{i} \cdot \bar{j} = \bar{j} \cdot \bar{i}$

6. Multiplication in Z_n is associative i.e. $(\bar{i} \cdot \bar{j}) \cdot \bar{k} = \bar{i} \cdot (\bar{j} \cdot \bar{k})$.

7. $\bar{1} \in Z_n$ is identity (neutral) element w.r.t. multiplication in Z_n.

8. Multiplication distributes over addition in Z_n. That is,

    $$\bar{i} \cdot (\bar{j} + \bar{k}) = \bar{i} \cdot \bar{j} + \bar{i} \cdot \bar{k}.$$

Exercise: Students should establish the above eight properties as an exercise.

Note: In Z_n, for $\bar{i} \in Z_n$, it is not always possible to find $\bar{j} \in Z_n$ such that $\bar{i} \cdot \bar{j} = \bar{1}$. For instance $\bar{3} \in Z_7$, we have $\bar{5} \in Z_7$ such that $\bar{3} \cdot \bar{5} = \bar{1}$. Infact from the table, we see that to each $\bar{i} \neq \bar{0}$ in Z_7 there is $\bar{j} \in Z_7$ such that $\bar{i} \cdot \bar{j} = \bar{1}$ (List such pairs in Z_7). However, in Z_6, for $\bar{3}$ and $\bar{4}$, we cannot find such $\bar{j}$ in Z_6.

Theorem 12: For $\bar{i} \in Z_n$, there exists $\bar{j} \in Z_n$ with $\bar{i} \cdot \bar{j} = \bar{1}$ if and only if $(i, n) = 1$.

Proof: Suppose $\bar{i} \in Z_n$ and there is $\bar{j} \in Z_n$ such that $\bar{i} \cdot \bar{j} = \bar{1}$. We have to show that $(i, n) = 1$.

Now $\bar{i} \cdot \bar{j} = \bar{1} \Rightarrow \overline{i \cdot j} = \bar{1}$

$\Rightarrow i \cdot j \equiv 1 \pmod{n}$
$\Rightarrow n \mid (i.j - 1)$
$\Rightarrow i.j - 1 = nk$, for $k \in Z$
$\Rightarrow i.j - nk = 1$
$\Rightarrow i.j + n(-k) = 1$
$\Rightarrow (i, n) = 1$.

(See illustrated Example (2.1) followed by section 2.2)

Conversely suppose $(i, n) = 1$, then there exist integers p and q in Z such that

$1 = iq + np$

$\Rightarrow \bar{1} = \overline{iq + np}$

$\Rightarrow \bar{1} = \overline{i \cdot q} + \overline{n \cdot p}$, by definition of addition in Z_n.

$\Rightarrow \bar{1} = \bar{i} \cdot \bar{q} + \bar{n} \cdot \bar{p}$, by definition of multiplication in Z_n.

$\Rightarrow \bar{i} \cdot \bar{q} = \bar{1}$, since $\bar{n} = \bar{0}$, so $\bar{n} \cdot \bar{p} = \bar{0}$

This completes the proof of the theorem.

EXERCISE (1.8)

1. In $\mathbb{Z}_8$, list all the elements $\bar{i}$ such that there exists $\bar{j} \in \mathbb{Z}_8$ such that $\bar{i} \cdot \bar{j} = \bar{1}$.
2. Do the exercise (1) for $\mathbb{Z}_{12}$.
3. Prepare composition tables of addition and multiplication for (i) $\mathbb{Z}_6$ (ii) $\mathbb{Z}_{11}$.

ILLUSTRATIVE EXAMPLES

Example 1.34: *If p is prime and $a^2 \equiv b^2 \pmod{p}$, then show that either $p \mid (a + b)$ or $p \mid (a - b)$.*

Solution: Since $a^2 \equiv b^2 \pmod{p}$, $p \mid (a^2 - b^2)$.

i.e. $p \mid (a + b)(a - b)$

$\Rightarrow$ $p \mid (a + b)$ or $p \mid (a - b)$; by theorem (5), since p is prime.

Example 1.35: *List all integers x in the range $1 \leq x \leq 100$ that satisfy $x \equiv 7 \pmod{17}$.*

Solution: The integers x, which satisfy $x \equiv 7 \pmod{17}$ are nothing but $\bar{7}$, the members of $\bar{7}$, the residue class of 7 modulo 17 since 7 is the remainder when 7 is divided by 17, by (*)' of note of the residue class we have

$$\bar{7} = \{..., 7 - 2 \times 17, 7 - 17, 7, 7 + 17, 7 + 2 \times 17, ...\}$$
$$= \{..., -27, -10, 7, 24, 41, ...\}$$

We want the list in the range $1 \leq x \leq 100$, hence the required list is

$$\{7, 7 + 17, 7 + 2 \times 17, 7 + 3 \times 17, 7 + 4 \times 17, 7 + 5 \times 17\}$$

i.e. $\{7, 24, 41, 58, 75, 92\}$

Example 1.36: *Express each of the following elements of $\mathbb{Z}_3$ as $\bar{0}$, $\bar{1}$ and $\bar{2}$.*

$$(\bar{2})^3, \overline{100}, \overline{(-100)}^4, \overline{10} + \bar{1}.$$

Solution: $(\bar{2})^3 = \bar{2} \times \bar{2} \times \bar{2}$

$= \overline{2 \times 2 \times 2}$, by definition of multiplication in $\mathbb{Z}_3$

$= \overline{8}$

$= \overline{2}$ since $2 \equiv 8 \pmod 3$, $\overline{2} = \overline{8}$

$\overline{100}$, when 100 is divided by 3, the remainder (least positive) is 1, hence,

$$\overline{100} = \overline{1}.$$

$\overline{(-100)}^4$, when -100 is divided by 3, the least positive remainder is 2, since $-100 = 3 \times (-34) + 2$.

∴ $\overline{(-100)} = \overline{2}$, so $\left(\overline{-100}\right)^4 = (\overline{2})^4 = (\overline{2})^3 \times \overline{2} = \overline{2} \times \overline{2} = \overline{1}$.

$\overline{10} + \overline{1} = \overline{10+1} = \overline{11} = \overline{2}$; since $11 \equiv 2 \pmod 3$

Example 1.37: *Which elements of Z_6 satisfy $x^2 = x$?*

Solution: $Z_6 = \{\overline{0}, \overline{1}, \overline{2}, \overline{3}, \overline{4}, \overline{5}\}$

We have $(\overline{0})^2 = \overline{0}$, $(\overline{1})^2 = \overline{1} \times \overline{1} = \overline{1}$, $(\overline{2})^2 = \overline{2} \times \overline{2} = \overline{4}$

$(\overline{3})^2 = \overline{3} \times \overline{3} = \overline{3 \times 3} = \overline{9} = \overline{3}$, since $9 \equiv 3 \pmod 6$

$(\overline{4})^2 = \overline{4} \times \overline{4} = \overline{4 \times 4} = \overline{16} = \overline{4}$, since $16 \equiv 4 \pmod 6$

$(\overline{5})^2 = \overline{5} \times \overline{5} = \overline{25} = \overline{1}$, ∵ $25 \equiv 1 \pmod 6$

Thus, we see that

$(\overline{3})^2 = \overline{3}$ and $(\overline{4})^2 = \overline{4}$; so $\overline{3}$ and $\overline{4}$ satisfy the given condition.

Example 1.38: *Show that 19 is not divisor of $4n^2 + 4$ for any integer.*

Solution: If 19 is divisor of $4n^2 + 4$, we have

$4n^2 + 4 \equiv 0 \pmod{19}$

$\Rightarrow \qquad 4n^2 \equiv -4 \pmod{19}$

$\Rightarrow \qquad n^2 \equiv -1 \pmod{19}$, since $(4, 19) = 1$.

Since 19 is a prime of the form

$p \equiv 3 \pmod 4$ ($19 \equiv 3 \pmod 4$)

the congruence has no solution in integers
$$x^2 \equiv -1 \pmod{p}$$
Therefore there is no integer n, satisfying
$$n^2 \equiv -1 \pmod{19}. \text{ Hence } 19 \nmid (4n^2 + 4) \text{ for all } n.$$

Example 1.39: *If a is any integer, then prove that*
$$a^2 \equiv 0 \pmod{4}$$
$$a^2 \equiv 1 \pmod{4}$$
depending on whether a is even or odd respectively.

Solution: (i) To prove $a^2 \equiv 0 \pmod 4$, if a is even

a is even $\Rightarrow a = 2n, n \in \mathbb{Z}$
$\Rightarrow a^2 = 4n^2$
$\Rightarrow a^2 - 0 = 4n^2$
$\Rightarrow 4 \mid a^2 - 0$
$\Rightarrow a^2 \equiv 0 \pmod 4$

(ii) To prove $a^2 \equiv 1 \pmod 4$, if a is odd

a is odd $\Rightarrow a = 2n + 1, n \in \mathbb{Z}$
$\Rightarrow a^2 = 4n^2 + 4n + 1$
$\Rightarrow a^2 - 1 = 4(n^2 + n)$
$\Rightarrow a^2 - 1 = 4k, k = n^2 + n \in \mathbb{Z}$
$\Rightarrow 4 \mid a^2 - 1$
$\Rightarrow a^2 \equiv 1 \pmod 4$

Example 1.40: *Find all pairs $\bar{i}$ and $\bar{j}$ in Z_8 such that $\bar{i} \cdot \bar{j} = \bar{1}$.*

Solution : $Z_8 = \{\bar{0}, \bar{1}, \bar{2}, \bar{3}, \bar{4}, \bar{5}, \bar{6}, \bar{7}\}$

We know that for $\bar{i}$ in Z_n there is $\bar{j}$ in Z_n such that $\bar{i} \cdot \bar{j} = \bar{1}$ if and only if $(i, n) = 1$. Here $n = 8$, and $(1, 8) = 1, (3, 8) = 1, (5, 8) = 1, (7, 8) = 1$.

For $\bar{i}$, we have $\bar{1} \cdot \bar{1} = \bar{1}$, $\bar{3}$, we have $\bar{3} \cdot \bar{3} = \bar{9} = \bar{1}$ for $\bar{5}$, we have $\bar{5} \cdot \bar{5} = \overline{25} = \bar{1}$ and for $\bar{7}$, we have $\bar{7} \cdot \bar{7} = \overline{49} = \bar{1}$. Thus, $\bar{1}, \bar{3}, \bar{5}$ and $\bar{7}$ are paired with themselves.

Example 1.41: Z_{12}, Calculate: (i) $(\overline{2} \cdot \overline{9} + \overline{1})$, (ii) $-\overline{5} \cdot (\overline{4} + \overline{5})$.

Solution : (i) $(\overline{2} \cdot \overline{9} + \overline{1})^{-1} = (\overline{6} + \overline{1})^{-1} = (\overline{7})^{-1} = \overline{7}$

(ii) $-\overline{5} \cdot (\overline{4} + \overline{5}) = -\overline{5} \cdot \overline{9} = -\overline{9} = \overline{3}$

Example 1.42: *Show that 41 divides $2^{20} - 1$.*

Solution: Since $2^5 = 32$, we have

$$2^5 \equiv -9 \pmod{41}$$

$\therefore \quad 2^{20} = (2^5)^4 \equiv (-9)^4 \pmod{41}$

$\qquad \qquad \equiv 9^2 \times 9^2 \pmod{41}$

$\qquad \qquad \equiv 81 \times 81 \pmod{41}$

$\qquad \qquad \equiv (-1)(-1) \pmod{41} \qquad \because 81 \equiv - \pmod{41}$

$\qquad \qquad \equiv 1 \pmod{41}$

$\therefore \quad 2^{20} \equiv 1 \pmod{41}$

Hence 41 divides $2^{20} - 1$.

Example 1.43: *List all integers x with $-10 \le x \le 90$, which satisfy $x \equiv 7 \pmod{11}$.*

Solution: The integer x, which satisfies $x \equiv 7 \pmod{11}$ certainly belongs to the residue class of 7 modulo 11 and we know that the residue class of 7 modulo 11 is

$$\overline{7} = \{ \ldots -15, -4, 7, 18, 29, 40, 51, 62, 73, 84, 95, \ldots \}$$

Therefore, the integers x with $-10 \le x \le 90$ satisfying $x \equiv 7 \pmod{11}$ are

$$-4, 7, 18, 29, 40, 51, 62, 73, 84$$

IMPORTANT POINTS

- Well-ordering principle.
- Principles of mathematical induction 1 and 2.
- Properties of divisibility.
- Division algorithm.
- Greatest common divisor d of two integers a and b in the form d = ma + nb.
- Least common multiple of two integers a and b and the relation

$$[a, b] = \frac{|ab|}{(a, b)}.$$

- Relatively prime integers.
- Primes.
- Euclid's Lemma.
- Unique Factorization theorem or Fundamental theorem of arithmetic.
- Congruence relation modulo n and its properties.
- Addition and multiplication modulo n.

THEORY QUESTIONS

1. Prove that the product of any three consecutive integers is divisible by 6.
2. Show that, if (ac) | (bc), then a | b.
3. If a | b and c | d, then show that (ac) | (bd).
4. Show that any two consecutive integers are relatively prime.
5. Prove that no integers x, y exist satisfying x + y = 200 and (x, y) = 7.
6. Prove that if (b, c) = 1 and a | b, then (a, c) = 1.
7. If a and b are relatively prime and b | (ac), then show that b | c.
8. Show that the product of any two consecutive integers is divisible by 2.
9. Prove that an integer is divisible by 11 if and only if the difference between the sum of digits in odd places and the sum of the digits in the even places is divisible by 11.
10. If x and y are odd, prove that $x^2 + y^2$ cannot be a perfect square.
11. Prove that (a, a + 2) = 1 or 2 for every integer a.
12. If (a, b) = 1 and a | c, b | c, then show that ab | c.
13. Show that $\sqrt{3}$ is not rational number.
14. Write out addition, multiplication tables of (a) Z_3, (b) Z_6, (c) Z_8, (d) Z_{11}.
15. If m is any integer, then prove that $m^2 \equiv 0$ or 1 (mod 4), hence show that the equation $x^2 + y^2 = 4247$ has no solution in integers.

3. **Hint:** Product of any three consecutive integers is $(n-1) n (n+1) = n^3 - n$. By mathematical induction, show that $6 \mid (n^3 - n)$, for all $n \geq 0$.

NUMERICAL PROBLEMS

1. Find values of x and y which satisfy
   - (a) $243x + 198y = 9$;
   - (b) $71x - 50y = 1$;
   - (c) $43x + 64y = 1$;
   - (d) $93x - 81y = 3$.

2. Find the greatest common divisor d of the given two numbers a and b and find the integers x and y to satisfy $d = ax + by$, for each of the following:
   - (a) $a = 7469, b = 2464$;
   - (b) $a = 4001, b = 2689$;
   - (c) $a = 616, b = 427$;
   - (d) $a = 1357, b = 1166$.

3. Show that the integers 3927 and 377 are relatively prime and find integers x and y which satisfy $1 = 3927x + 377y$.

4. Show that g.c.d. 'd' of 2210 and 357 is 17 and find x and y such that $17 = 2210x + 357y$.

5. Find the least common multiple of 482 and 1687.

6. Find positive integers a and b satisfying the equations $(a, b) = 10$ and $[a, b] = 100$ simultaneously. Find all solutions.

7. If $(a, b) = p$, a prime, what are the possible values of (a^2, b), (a^3, b) and (a^2, b^3)?

8. Evaluate (ab, p^4) and $(a + b, p^4)$, given that $(a, p^2) = p$ and $(b, p^3) = p^2$, where p is prime.

9. Express in canonical form and hence find g.c.d. of 7007 and 2450.

10. List all the integers x in the range $1 \leq x < 80$, which satisfy $x \equiv 5 \pmod{8}$.

11. Find all the pairs $\bar{i}$ and $\bar{j}$, such that $\bar{i} \cdot \bar{j} = \bar{1}$ in (a) Z_3, (b) Z_6, (c) Z_8, (d) Z_{11}, (e) Z_5, (f) Z_{12}.

12. Express each of the following elements of Z_5 as $\bar{0}, \bar{1}, \bar{2}, \bar{3}, \bar{4}$.

   $-\bar{1}, -\bar{2}, (\overline{-3})^2, (\overline{-4})^3, \overline{(64)} \cdot \overline{(93)}, \overline{10001}$.

13. Which elements satisfy the equation $x^2 = x$? List all of them; where x belongs to (a) Z_6, (b) Z_8, (c) Z_7, (d) Z_{12}.

Answers

1. (a) x = 9, y = –11;   (b) x = 31, y = 44;
   (c) x = 3, y = – 2;   (d) x = 7, y = 8;
2. (a) d = 74, x = 1, y = – 3; (b) d = 1, x = – 1117, y = 1662;
   (c) d = 7, x = – 9, y = 13; (d) d = 1, x = 641, y = – 746.
3. x = – 12, y = 125.
4. x = – 5, y = 31.
5. **Hint:** Find g.c.d. d = (482, 1687), then
   l.c.m = (482 × 1687)/d ...... l.c.m. = 3374.
6. a = 10, b = 100 is a solution in positive integers. All solutions are given by a = ± 10, b = ± 100; a = ± 20, b = ± 50; a = ± 100, b = ± 10; a = ± 50, b = ± 20; with all arrangements of sign. There are 16 solutions in all.
8. p^2, p
9. 49.
10. 10.
11. (a) $\bar{2} \times \bar{2}$, (b) $\bar{5} \times \bar{5}$, (c) $\bar{3} \times \bar{3}, \bar{5} \times \bar{5}, \bar{7} \times \bar{7}$.

    (d) $\bar{2} \times \bar{6}, \bar{3} \times \bar{4}, \bar{5} \times \bar{9}, \bar{7} \times \bar{8}, \overline{10} \times \overline{10}$, (e) $\bar{2} \times \bar{3}, \bar{4} \times \bar{4}$.

    (f) $\bar{5} \times \bar{5}, \bar{7} \times \bar{7}, \bar{8} \times \bar{8}$. In each case $\bar{1} \times \bar{1}$ is always there.

12. $\bar{4}, \bar{3}, \bar{4}, \bar{1}, \bar{2}, \bar{1}$.

13. (a) $\bar{1}, \bar{3}, \bar{4}$, (b) No, (c) No, (d) $\bar{1}, \bar{4}, \bar{9}$.

MULTIPLE CHOICE QUESTIONS

1. If a, b, c are integers and a | (bc), then _____
   (a) a | b   (b) a | c
   (c) a divides both   (d) all of these may be true

2. If gcd (a, b) = d > 1, then _____
   (a) $gcd\left(\dfrac{a}{d}, \dfrac{b}{d}\right) = 1$
   (b) ax + by = 1, for x, y,∈, Z
   (c) $\dfrac{a}{d}$ and $\dfrac{b}{d}$ are not relatively prime
   (d) none of these
3. For any integer a, a(a + 1) is always _____
   (a) even integer   (b) odd integer
   (c) prime integer   (d) none of these
4. For any integer a, a(a + 1) (a + 2) is _____
   (a) even   (b) odd
   (c) square number   (d) none of these
5. How many prime numbers divide 30?
   (a) 10   (b) 40
   (c) 25   (d) 3
6. What is the remainder when the following sum is divided by 4?
   $1^5 + 2^5 + \ldots + 20^5$
   (a) 0   (b) 2
   (c) 3   (d) none of these
7. If a is odd integer then the remainder when $a^2 - 1$ divided by 8 is
   (a) 1   (b) 0
   (c) 3   (d) 5
8. $25^{97} \equiv ?$ (mod 97)
   (a) 1   (b) 25
   (c) 0   (d) none of these
9. The remainder when the sum 1! + 2! + 3! + ... + 1000 ! is divided by 12 is _____
   (a) 9   (b) 5
   (c) 0   (d) 11
10. If n > 4 is composite, then _____
    (a) n | (n − 1)!   (b) $n | (n^2 - 2)$
    (c) $n | (n^2 + 1)$ (d) none of these
11. If gcd(a, b) = 3 and lcm (a, b) = 30, if a = 6, then b = _____
    (a) 30   (b) 15
    (c) both 30 and 15   (d) none of these

Answers

1. (d)	2. (a)	3. (a)	4. (b)	5. (a)
6. (a)	7. (b)	8. (b)	9. (a)	10. (a)
11. (b)				

SAY TRUE OR FALSE WITH JUSTIFICATION

1. $a, b, \in Z$ then $ab = 1$, has four solutions.
2. If $a, b, x, y, \in Z$ and $ax + by = 1$, then a and x are relatively prime.
3. There are infinitely many primers.
4. A number is divisible by 4 iff the last digit of the number is divisible by 4.
5. If a is odd integer than $a^2 \equiv 1 \pmod 4$.
6. If $(a, b) = (a, c)$, then $[a, b] = [a, c]$.
7. If $(a, b) = (a, c)$, then $(a^2, b^2) = (a^2, c^2)$.
8. If p is a prime and $p \mid a$ and $p \mid (a^2 + b^2)$, then $p \mid b$.
9. If p is a prime and $p \mid a^7$, then $p \mid a$.
10. If $a^3 \mid c^3$, then $a \mid c$.
11. If $a^3 \mid c^2$, then $a \mid c$.
12. If $a^2 \mid c^3$, then $a \mid c$.
13. If p is a prime and $p \mid (a^2 + b^2)$ & $p \mid (b^2 + c^2)$ then $p \mid (a^2 - c^2)$.
14. If p is a prime and $p \mid (a^2 + b^2)$ & $p \mid (b^2 + c^2)$ then $p \mid (a^2 + c^2)$.
15. If $b \mid (a^2 + 1)$, then $b \mid (a^4 + 1)$.
16. If $b \mid (a^2 - 1)$, then $b \mid (a^4 - 1)$.

Answers

1. False	2. True	3. True	4. False	5. True
6. False, $a = 2, b = 6, c = 10$.	7. True	8. True	9. True	10. True
11. True	12. False, $a = 8, c = 4$.	13. True	14. False, $p = 5, a = 2, b = 1, c = 3$.	15. False, $a = 2, b = 5$
16. True				

CHAPTER 2

DIVISION ALGORITHM

2.1 INTRODUCTION

We know that the numbers ...... − 3, − 2, − 1, 0, 1, 2, 3, ... are called *integers* and *the set of all these numbers is* denoted by the symbol $\mathbb{Z}$. The numbers 0, 1, 2, 3, ... are called *non-negative integers* (or *whole numbers)*. The numbers 1, 2, 3, ... are called *positive integers* or *natural numbers* and the set of all these numbers is denoted by the symbol $\mathbb{N}$. The natural numbers form the primary subject matter of arithmetic, but it is often essential to regard them as a subclass of integers.

The 'Theory of Numbers', one of the major branches of Mathematics deals with only the set of natural numbers apart from the fact that its study involves not only real numbers but also the complex numbers. The set $\mathbb{N}$ of all natural numbers is a very basic tool for starting the study of mathematics. The set of integers is obtained by extending the set of natural numbers, since the simple equation like x + 6 = 1 cannot be solved in $\mathbb{N}$. In fact, the set of natural numbers is the foundation stone of the real number system. But, one may ask, from where the set of natural numbers came into existence. This question raises deep logical and philosophical problems, so we skip it to answer. However, we accept the existence of natural numbers and let us be contended with the words of the reknowned Mathematician Kronecker: 'God created the set of natural numbers and all the rest is the work of human being'.

We also assume that the operations of addition and multiplication in $\mathbb{N}$ satisfy the properties like commutativity, associativity etc. familiar to the students.

Further, we state only the following result, which will be frequently used in this chapter.

Law of trichotomy: For any m, n $\in \mathbb{N}$, either m = n or m < n or n < m.

Well-ordering property of $\mathbb{N}$: Every non-empty subset of $\mathbb{N}$ has a least member.

The above property can be stated as: If S is non-empty subset of $\mathbb{N}$, then there exists an integer m∈ S such that $m \leq k$, for all k∈ S.

The Italian mathematician G. Peano showed that the algebraic system $< \mathbb{N}, +, \times >$, the set $\mathbb{N}$ with usual addition and multiplication can be defined even more simply as an algebra. He used the **successor function** σ, we define it as:

Definition: A function $\sigma: \mathbb{N} \to \mathbb{N}$ which is defined by $\sigma(n) = n + 1$, for n∈ $\mathbb{N}$ is called **Peano's successor function.**

Note that the domain of σ is $\mathbb{N}$ and the range of σ is

$$R(\sigma) = \{2, 3, 4, ..., n, n + 1, ...\}.$$

The set of natural numbers $\mathbb{N}$ with the unary operation σ (as defined above) is characterised by a set of three simple conditions on σ. These conditions are the following **'Peano axioms'** for the successor function:

1. If $\sigma(m) = \sigma(n)$, then m = n (that is σ is injective on $\mathbb{N}$).
2. For no n∉ $\mathbb{N}$, $\sigma(n) = 1$ (that is 1 is not image of any integer in $\mathbb{N}$).
3. Let $S \subset \mathbb{N}$ satisfy (a) 1∈ S, (b) n∈ S implies that $\sigma(n)$∈ S. Then $S = \mathbb{N}$.

The third axiom (above) is called the **induction axiom.**

We now state two important principles which are the consequences of Peano's axioms and well-ordering principle.

First principle of induction:

If S is a subset of $\mathbb{N}$ satisfying

(i) 1∈ S and

(ii) If n∈ S then $n + 1 \in S$

Then $S = \mathbb{N}$; that S is the whole set of natural numbers $\mathbb{N}$.

Second principle of Induction:

Let S be a subset of $\mathbb{N}$ such that:

(i) 1∈ S and

(ii) If m∈ S for all positive integers $m < n$ implies n∈ S, then $S = \mathbb{N}$.

Note: The second principle of induction is also known as strong form of (i).

The above two principles are used to prove the statements which depend on n, the natural number. For example:

(i) If X is a set with n elements, the number of all subsets of X is 2^n. This statement is proved by using the first principle of induction.

(ii) **The fundamental theorem of arithmetic** is proved by using second principle of induction.

In mathematics at many places we need to use these two principles.

2.2 DIVISION ALGORITHM

Division Algorithm (D.A.): Let us observe the following:

$$51 = 8 \times 6 + 3, \quad 0 < 3 < 8 \quad \ldots (1)$$
$$51 = (-8)(-6) + 3, \quad 0 < 3 < |-8| = 8 \quad \ldots (2)$$
$$-51 = 8 \times (-7) + 5, \quad 0 < 5 < 8 \quad \ldots (3)$$
$$-51 = (-8)(7) + 5, \quad 0 < 5 < |-8| = 8 \quad \ldots (4)$$

From (1) we see that when we divide 51 by 8

i.e.
$$\begin{array}{r} 6 \\ 8\overline{)51} \\ \underline{-48} \\ 3 \end{array}$$

the quotient is 6 and the remainder is 3.

From (2) when 51 is divided by – 8.

i.e.
$$\begin{array}{r} -6 \\ -8\overline{)51} \\ \underline{-48} \\ 3 \end{array}$$

the quotient is – 6 and the remainder is 3.

In similar manner, we can interpret (3) and (4).

From these four examples, for any two integers a, b with a ≠ 0, can we have b = aq + r, where $0 \le r < |a|$? The answer is 'yes'. The following is the theorem related to the above illustration.

Theorem 1: (Division Algorithm): If a and b are any two integers with a ≠ 0 then there exist unique integers q and r such that

$$b = aq + r, \text{ where } 0 \le r < |a|$$

Proof: Case (i): If a > 0:

Let $S = \{b - ax \in \mathbb{Z} \mid b - ax \ge 0; x \in \mathbb{Z}\}$.

Since a > 0 implies a ≥ 1, we have,

$$|b| \cdot a \ge |b| \cdot 1 \qquad (\because |b| \ge 0)$$

∴ $\quad b + |b| \cdot a \ge |b| + b \ge 0$

⇒ $\quad b - (-|b|) \cdot a \ge 0$

⇒ $\quad b - (-|b|) \cdot a \in S$.

Hence S is a non-empty subset of $\mathbb{N} \cup \{0\}$.

∴ By 'Well Ordering Principle', S has a least element say r. Then r∈ S and r ≤ y, for all y∈ S. But r∈ S also implies that

$$r = b - aq, \text{ for some } q \in \mathbb{Z}$$

⇒ $\quad b = aq + r, \qquad 0 \le r \quad (\text{since } r \in S)$

Now, suppose r ≥ a, then r − a ≥ 0. But r − a = (b − aq) − a = b − (q + 1) a. Thus, r − a ≥ 0 and is of the form of the elements in S. Therefore r − a∈ S. By our assumption, r is the least element of S, since a > 0, r − a < r which is contradiction to the choice of r. Therefore r < a.

Thus, we have, q, r ∈ $\mathbb{Z}$ such that

$$b = aq + r, \qquad 0 \le r < |a| \qquad \ldots (1)$$

(Since a > 0, $|a| = a$)

Case (ii): If a < 0:

Then $|a| > 0$, so replacing 'a' by $|a|$ we can apply case (i) to b and $|a|$, therefore we have from (1) above,

$$b = |a| q' + r, \qquad 0 \le r < |a| \qquad \ldots (2)$$

for q', r ∈ $\mathbb{Z}$. Now $|a| = -a$, $\qquad (\because a < 0)$

So from (2), we get,

$$b = (-a)q' + r, \quad 0 \le r < |a|$$

$$\Rightarrow \quad b = a \cdot (-q') + r, \quad 0 \le r < |a|$$

$$\Rightarrow \quad b = aq + r, \ 0 \le r < |a|, \text{ put } (-q') = q.$$

Thus, in both the cases, we have, there exists $q, r \in \mathbb{Z}$ such that

$$b = aq + r, \quad 0 \le r < |a| \qquad \ldots (3)$$

This proves the existence of q and r and the required identity with given constraints.

Uniqueness of q and r:

Now, let us prove the uniqueness of q and r.

Suppose we have two pairs of integers q and r; q' and r' such that

$$b = aq + r, \quad \text{where} \quad 0 \le r < |a|$$

and $\quad b = aq' + r', \quad \text{where} \quad 0 \le r' < |a|$

On subtraction, we get,

$$0 = a(q - q') + (r - r'), \text{ with } 0 \le r, r' < |a| \qquad \ldots (4)$$

$$\Rightarrow \quad r - r' = a(q' - q), \text{ with } |r - r'| < |a|$$

$$\Rightarrow \quad a \mid (r - r'), \text{ with } |r - r'| < |a|.$$

But this is possible only if $r - r' = 0$, that is, $r = r'$. Using this fact in (4), we get $a(q' - q) = 0. \Rightarrow q' - q = 0; (\because a \ne 0)$

$$\Rightarrow q = q'$$

Hence, the uniqueness. This completes the proof of the theorem.

2.3 DIVISIBILITY

Hereafter we will mostly be working with the set $\mathbb{Z}$, of all integers, or we will sometimes restrict ourselves to the set $\mathbb{N}$ of all natural numbers. The difference of working in $\mathbb{Z}$ or in $\mathbb{N}$ can be seen from the following examples: We have $12 = 4.3$, that is, 12 is product of 4 and 3, where 4 and 3 belong to $\mathbb{N}$. However, we can also write $12 = (-4)(-3)$, and we see that -4 and -3 are in $\mathbb{Z}$ but not in $\mathbb{N}$. Similarly $m.n = 1$ iff $m = 1$ and n = 1 if we are working in ℕ, whereas mn = 1 iff m = 1 and n = 1 or m = – 1 and n = – 1, if we are working in ℤ. Thus, m.n = 12 and m.n = 1 have two solutions of each in ℤ, whereas each of these equations have only one solution in ℕ.

Now, we shall give abstract definitions and shall deal with abstract results, which are somewhat difficult to understand for the students. We will try to illustrate each definition or result by a particular numerical example.

We have 12 = 4·3, that is, the product of 4 and 3 equals to 12. This fact we describe in the following ways: '12 is multiple of 4' or '4 is factor of 12' or '4 divides 12' or '12 is divisible by 4'. In similar manner, for a and b given integers, if we can find an integer c such that
b = a.c, we say that 'a divides b'. So we have:

Divisibility: Let a and b be any two integers with a ≠ 0. Then we say that '*a divides b*' if there is an integer c such that b = a.c and we write this as a | b. Thus, a | b $\Rightarrow$ b = ac, c ∈ ℤ.

In case 'a does not divide b', we write this as a ∤ b.

Note:

1. If a | b we say that a is a *divisor* of b.
2. For any integer a ≠ 0, we have 0 = a.0, which shows by definition that a | 0. That is, 0 is divisible by any non-zero integer.
3. For any a ∈ ℤ, a ≠ 0, we have

    a = 1.a = a.1 = (– 1) . (– a) = (– a) · (– 1), so by definition, again 1, – 1, a, – a are the divisors of a. **That is, for given any non-zero integer a, it is always divisible by ± 1 and ± a.**

Remarks:

1. If a | b, then we say that a is a *proper divisor* of b; if a is not ± 1 or ± b.
2. Let a, b ∈ ℤ. If a | b, b ≠ 0 then $|a| \leq |b|$. For, since a | b, by definition, we have b = a.c for some c ∈ ℤ. As b ≠ 0, c ≠ 0, therefore $|b| = |ac| = |a| \cdot |c|$, which implies $|b| \geq |a|$, since

$c \neq 0$, $|c| \geq 1$. Note that if a is proper divisor of b, then $a \neq \pm b$, hence $|a| \neq |b|$, so that $|a| < |b|$.

3. Let a, b $\in$ Z and a.b = 1. Then by definition, 1 = a.b implies a | 1, hence by remark (2) above $|a| \leq |1| = 1$, that is $0 < |a| \leq 1$, since $a \neq 0$, hence $|a| = 1$. This shows $a = \pm 1$. Thus, a.b = 1 has solutions a = 1 and b = 1 or a = –1 and b = –1.

4. Let $a \neq 0$, $b \neq 0$ be in Z. If a | b and b | a, then $a = \pm b$. For, a | b implies b = ax for some x $\in$ Z and b | a implies a = by for some y $\in$ Z (by definition). Now a = by = (ax) y, since b = ax; so that a = a (xy). This implies xy = 1.

∴ By remark (3) above, x = 1 and y = 1 or x = –1 and y = –1. Therefore $a = \pm b$.

Note: Whenever we say a | b, we *always have a $\neq$ 0*.

Theorem 2: Let a, b, c, d be integers. Then

(i) If a | b, then a | (bx), for any x$\in$ Z.

(ii) If a | b and a | c, then a | (b + c), in fact a | (bx + cy) for any x, y$\in$ Z.

(iii) If a | b and b | c, then a | c.

(iv) If $m \neq 0$ is in Z and a | b, then am | bm.

(v) If a | b and c | d then ac | bd.

(vi) If (ab | bc), then a | c.

Proof:

(i) Since a | b, we have b = ac, for some c$\in$ Z. Multiplying both sides by any x$\in$ Z, we get bx = (ac) x = a. (cx); so that bx = a.c', where, c' = cx$\in$ Z, therefore a | (bx).

(ii) Since a | b, we have b = ak_1, $k_1 \in$ Z and a | c, we have c = ak_2, for $k_2 \in$ Z. Thus, b + c = $ak_1 + ak_2$ = a ($k_1 + k_2$) = ak, where, k = $k_1 + k_2 \in$ Z, so that b + c = a.k, k$\in$ Z. Therefore a | (b + c).

(**Note:** If a | b and a | c, then we can show that a | (b – c) also).

Now, since $a \mid b$ implies that $a \mid bx$ for any $x \in \mathbb{Z}$, and $a \mid c$ implies that $a \mid cy$ for any $y \in \mathbb{Z}$, (by using (1) above). Therefore $a \mid (bx + cy)$ (by earlier part of (2) itself); for any $x, y \in \mathbb{Z}$.

Note: The result (2) can be stated in generalised form as: If $a \mid b$, $a \mid c$, then $a \mid (bx \pm cy)$ for any $x, y \in \mathbb{Z}$.

(iii) Since $a \mid b$, we have $b = ax$, for some $x \in \mathbb{Z}$ and $b \mid c$ implies $c = by$, for some $y \in \mathbb{Z}$. Thus, we have $c = by = (ax) y$, ($\because b = ax$) $\therefore c = a(xy)$; that is $c = ax'$, $x' = xy \in \mathbb{Z}$. Therefore $a \mid c$.

Note: This result (3) shows that, the relation of divisibility in $\mathbb{Z}$ is transitive.

(iv) Note $m \neq 0$ implies that $am \neq 0$, since $a \neq 0$. Since $a \mid b$, we have $b = ax$, for some $x \in \mathbb{Z}$. Then multiplying both sides by m, we get $bm = (ax) m = (am) x$. Therefore $am \mid bm$.

(v) Since $a \mid b$, we have $b = ax$, for some $x \in \mathbb{Z}$. ... (1)

Also from $c \mid d$, we have $d = cy$, for some $y \in \mathbb{Z}$. ... (2)

Multiplying the corresponding sides of (1) and (2), we get $bd = (ax)(cy) = (ac)(xy)$; which implies $bd = (ac) k$, where, $k = xy \in \mathbb{Z}$. Therefore, $(ac) \mid (bd)$.

(vi) If $c = 0$, $a \mid c$, by note (2) of the definition of divisibility. Since $(ab) \mid (bc)$, we have $bc = (ab) x$, for some $x \in \mathbb{Z}$. Also $ab \neq 0$, implies $b \neq 0$. Therefore from $bc = b(ax)$, we get by cancelling b, $c = ax$, for $x \in \mathbb{Z}$, which shows $a \mid c$.

2.4 GREATEST COMMON DIVISOR (G.C.D.)

What are the divisors of 12 and 16? The positive divisors of 12 are: 1, 2, 3, 4, 6 and 12. The positive divisors of 16 are: 1, 2, 4, 8, 16. We see that 2 and 4 are divisors of both 12 and 16, we call 2 and 4 as *common divisors* (c.d.) of 12 and 16. The greatest of the common divisors 2 and 4 is 4, is called the greatest common divisor of 12 and 16. Thus, we have the following:

2.4.1 Common Divisor

Let a and b be any two integers not both zero. An integer d is said to be *common divisor* of a and b if $d \mid a$ and $d \mid b$.

Exercise: Find all common divisors of (1) 36 and 51 (2) 36 and 48 (3) 16 and 48.

Greatest common divisor: Let a and b be two non-zero integers. An integer d is said to be greatest common divisor (g.c.d.) of a and b if (i) d is common divisor of a and b, i.e. d | a and d | b and (ii) any common divisor of a and b divides d, i.e. if c | a and c | b, then c | d.

For instance, it is clear that 4 is the g.c.d. of 12 and 16.

Note:

1. If d is a g.c.d. of a and b, then so is − d. By g.c.d., hereafter we will always mean positive g.c.d. and it is denoted by (a, b). Thus, if d is g.c.d. of a and b, then d = (a, b).

2. The term Highest Common Factor (H.C.F.) is also used for g.c.d.

Observe that 4 = (12, 16) from the discussion in the beginning.

Exercise: Find all c.d.s and hence find g.c.d. in each case of the following: (1) 36 and 51 (2) 50 and 80 (3) 74 and 111.

Now, let us state and prove the theorem which establishes that g.c.d. for any two integers exists and is unique.

Theorem 3: Any two non-zero integers a and b have a unique (positive) g.c.d. d = (a, b) and it can be expressed in the form:

$$d = (a, b) = ma + nb, \text{ for some } m, n \in \mathbb{Z}.$$

Proof: Let $S = \{ax + by \mid x, y \in \mathbb{Z} \text{ and } ax + by > 0\}$

Since a and b are non-zero, $a^2 + b^2 > 0$ and $a^2 + b^2 = a.a + b.b > 0$. That is, $a^2 + b^2$ can be written in the form $ax + by$, where $x = a$ and $y = b$, and is greater than zero. Therefore, $a^2 + b^2 \in S$. Hence S is non-empty subset of N.

So by 'Well Ordering Principle', S has a least element, say d. That is $d \in S$ and $d \leq z$, for all $z \in S$. Also, $d \in S$ implies $d = ma + nb$, for some m, $n \in \mathbb{Z}$. ... (1)

Now, we prove that d is common divisor of a and b.

Applying division algorithm to a and d, there exists q and r in $\mathbb{Z}$, such that

$$a = dq + r, \quad \text{where } 0 \leq r < d \quad \ldots (2)$$

If $r \neq 0$, (2) gives

$$r = a - dq, \quad \text{with } 0 < r < d$$
$$= a - (ma + nb)q, \quad \text{[using (1)]}$$
$$= (1 - mq)a + (-nq)b, \quad 0 < r < d$$

Thus $r > 0$ and is of the form $ax + by$ with $x = (1 - mq)$ and $y = -nq$, hence $r \in S$. But this is contradiction to the choice of d, as $r < d$, hence $r = 0$.

So from (ii) we get $a = dq$, which shows, $d \mid a$. Similarly, we can show that $d \mid b$. Thus, d is common divisor of a and b.

Now, to show that d is g.c.d., we have to show that any c.d. of a and b also divides d. Let c be any c.d. of a and b, and let $a = ck_1$ and $b = ck_2$, for $k_1, k_2 \in \mathbb{Z}$. Using this in (1), we get,

$$d = m(ck_1) + n(ck_2)$$
$$\therefore \quad d = c(mk_1 + nk_2)$$

which shows that $c \mid d$.

Thus, d is g.c.d. of a and b.

It is remained to show the uniqueness of d.

Suppose d' is another g.c.d. of a and b. Since d' is g.c.d., it is c.d. of a and b. Therefore $d' \mid a$ and $d' \mid b$, hence $d' \mid d$, since d is g.c.d. Similarly d is g.c.d. of a and b, $d \mid a$, $d \mid b$, hence $d \mid d'$, as d' is g.c.d. of a and b. Thus, $d \mid d'$ and $d' \mid d$, hence $d' = \pm d$; but both d and d' are positive, so that $d' = d$.

This completes the proof of the theorem.

Note: The integers m and n in the expression $d = ma + nb$ are not unique for instance, we know $4 = (12, 16)$ and we have $4 = 12 \times (-1) + 16 \times 1$ with $m = -1$, and $n = 1$. But we can also have $4 = 12 \times (3) + 16 \times (-2)$, with $m = 3$ and $n = -2$.

In fact, $d = ma + nb$, we have

$$d = a(m - kb) + b(n + ka) \text{ for any}$$
$$k = 0, \pm 1, \pm 2, \ldots$$

which shows that there exist infinitely many pairs of m and n such that

$$d = ma + nb$$

Exercise: Find g.c.d. d and find also two pairs of m and n such that d = ma + nb, for each of the following: (1) a = 10, b = 18; (2) a = 31, b = 17; (3) a = 6, b = 24; (4) a = 50, b = 101.

2.5 PROPERTIES OF G.C.D. (Without Proof)

2.5.1 Theorem

Theorem 4 :

A positive integer d = g.c.d. (a, b) if and only if d has following two properties :

(i) d divides both a and b.

(ii) If c divides both a and b, then $c \mid d$.

2.5.2 Simple Properties of the Greatest Common Divisor (Without Proof)

1. g.c.d (a, b) = g.c.d. (b, a)

2. If x > 0, then g.c.d. (ax, bx) = x.g.c.d. (a, b)

3. If d = g.c.d. (a, b), then g.c.d. $\left(\dfrac{a}{d}, \dfrac{b}{d}\right) = 1$

4. For any integer x, g.c.d. (a, b) = g.c.d. (a, b + ax)

2.6 EUCLIDEAN ALGORITHM (E.A.) (Without Proof)

The process of finding g.c.d. of given two integers by applying D.A. successively, is known as *Euclidean Algorithm* (E.A.). We describe this process in the following.

Let a and b be two non-zero integers. Applying D.A. to a and b, there exist unique integers q_1 and r_1 such that

$$b = aq_1 + r_1, \quad \text{where } 0 \leq r_1 < |a| \qquad \ldots (1)$$

If $r_1 = 0$, then $a \mid b$ and $(a, b) = |a|$. If, $r_1 \neq 0$, i.e. $r_1 > 0$, then from (1) we see that c.d. of r_1 and a is also a divisor of b, and hence a c.d. of a and b. On the other hand, from (1), $r_1 = b - aq_1$, which shows that c.d. of a and b is also a divisor of r_1, hence c.d. of r_1 and a.

Thus, we have $(a, r_1) \mid (a, b)$ and $(a, b) \mid (a, r_1)$,

∴ $\qquad (a, b) = (a, r_1) \qquad \ldots (2)$

Applying D.A. to a and r_1, there exist unique integers q_2 and r_2 such that

$$a = r_1 q_2 + r_2 \text{ where } 0 \leq r_2 < r_1 \qquad \ldots (3)$$

If $r_2 = 0$, then $(a, r_1) = r_1$, hence from (2) we get $(a, b) = r_1$.

If $r_2 \neq 0$ i.e. $r_2 > 0$, then the similar arguments as applied to a, b, r, above we apply to a, r_1, r_2 we have

$$(r_1, r_2) = (a, r_1) = (a, b) \qquad \ldots (4)$$

Again, applying D.A. to r_1 and r_2 there exist unique integers q_3 and r_3 such that

$$r_1 = r_2 q_3 + r_3, \text{ where } 0 \leq r_3 < r_2 \qquad \ldots (5)$$

If $r_3 = 0$, $(r_1, r_2) = r_2 = (a, b)$, $\qquad \ldots$ (By (4))

If $r_3 > 0$, we continue as above. Obtain $q_4, r_4; q_5, r_5; \ldots$ etc.

We continue this process till we get the remainder zero.

As we observe $|a| > r_1, > r_2 > \ldots$, we will get a remainder zero after finite number of steps, say $r_{n+1} = 0$. So, we have

$$r_2 = r_3 q_4 + r_4, \text{ where } 0 \leq r_4 < r_3 \qquad \ldots (6)$$

$$\vdots$$

$$r_{n-2} = r_{n-1} q_n + r_n, \text{ where } 0 \leq r_n < r_{n-1} \qquad \ldots (7)$$

and $\qquad r_{n-1} = r_n q_{n+1} + 0$

As argued before, we have

$$r_n = (r_{n-1}, r_n) = (r_{n-2}, r_{n-1}) = \ldots = (r_1, r_2) = (b, r_1) = (a, b)$$

Thus, $\qquad r_n = (a, b)$, the g.c.d. of a and b.

Note: The above process (E.A.) not only describes how to find g.c.d. of given integers, but also provides the method of finding integers m and n such that $(a, b) = ma + nb$. We start with equation (7) above and express r_n in terms of r_{n-1} and r_{n-2}, then using previous equation, express r_{n-1} in terms of r_{n-2} and r_{n-3}, ... and so on, till we reach the equation (1), which gives r_n in the form $ma + nb$, for some m and n in $\mathbb{Z}$. Let us work out the following example to understand how E.A. helps to find. g.c.d. as well as to find the pair of integers m and n.

Find $(100, 15)$ and express it in the form $(100, 15) = 100 m + 15 n$, for $m, n \in \mathbb{Z}$. We have

$$100 = 15 \times 6 + 10 \quad \ldots (1)$$
$$15 = 10 \times 1 + 5 \quad \ldots (2)$$
$$10 = 5 \times 2 + 0$$
$$\therefore \quad (100, 15) = 5$$

Now from (2) we have

$$5 = 15 - 10 \times 1$$
$$5 = 15 - (100 - 15 \times 6) \times 1 \quad \text{Using (1) for 10.}$$
$$= 15 \times 7 + 100 \times (-1)$$

Thus, $\quad 5 = 15 \times 7 + 100 \times (-1)$,

where, $\quad m = 7$ and $n = -1$.

Exercise: 1. Find g.c.d. 'd' of 31 and 13, and obtain pair of integers m and n such that

$$d = 31m + 13n.$$

2. Do the same for $a = 24$ and $b = 114$.

From Euclidean Algorithm, we note that 'if d is the smallest positive integer of the form $ax + by$, then d is g.c.d. of a and b'.

2.7 RELATIVELY PRIME INTEGERS

Relatively Prime: Two integers a and b are said to be *relatively prime*, if

$$(a, b) = 1$$

The fact that $(a, b) = 1$ is sometimes expressed by saying that a and b are *coprime* or by saying that a is prime to b.

For instance, since $(13, 17) = 1$, 13 and 17 are relatively prime. Also, $(10, 21) = 1$, hence 10 and 21 are relatively prime.

Least Common Multiple: Let a and b be non-zero integers. Then the *least common multiple* (L.C.M.) of a and b is defined to be a positive integer d such that (i) $a \mid d$ and $b \mid d$ and (ii) if $a \mid c$ and $b \mid c$, then $d \mid c$. We write L.C.M. of a and b as $[a, b]$.

For instance, $[6, 10] = 30$, since $6 \mid 30$ and $10 \mid 30$. Also $[12, 50] = 300$.

Theorem 5: For any two non-zero integers a and b have unique L.C.M. [a, b] and $[a, b] = \dfrac{|ab|}{(a, b)}$.

Proof: Let $(a, b) = d$, then $a = dk_1$ and $b = dk_2$ where $(k_1, k_2) = 1$, by example (2). Let $g = |k_1 k_2| \, d$.

We shall show that g is L.C.M. of a and b. Clearly g is positive and observe that

$$g = |k_1||k_2| d = |k_1| \cdot |d| \cdot |k_2|, \quad \text{since } d > 0, |d| = d.$$
$$= (|k_1 d|) |k_2|$$

So $\quad g = |a| |k_2|$, since $\quad a = k_1 d$

$\quad g = \pm a |k_2|$, since $|a| = \pm a$.

$\therefore \; a \mid g$. Similarly we can show $b \mid g$. Let c be positive integer such that $a \mid c$ and $b \mid c$, and $c = ap$, $c = bq$, for $p, q \in Z$.

Now $(k_1, k_2) = 1$, implies that there exist integers m and n such that
$mk_1 + nk_2 = 1$

$\Rightarrow \quad c = mk_1 c + nk_2 c, \quad\quad\quad$ multiplying by c

$\quad\quad\quad = mk_1 bq + nk_2 ap, \quad\quad \because c = ap$ and $c = bq$.

$\quad\quad\quad = mk_1 k_2 dq + nk_2 k_1 dp, \quad \because b = k_2 d$ and $a = k_1 d$

$\quad c = (k_1 k_2 d) (mq + np)$

$\quad\quad\quad = \pm g (mq + np), \quad\quad\quad \because g = \pm k_1 k_2 d$

$\therefore \; g \mid c$.

Therefore, g is L.C.M. of a and b.

Again, we have, $\quad g = |k_1 k_2| \, d$

So $\quad gd = |k_1 k_2| \, d^2$

$\quad\quad\quad = |k_1 d| |k_2 d|, \quad \because d > 0$

$$= |a| \cdot |b|, \qquad \because a = k_1 d \text{ and } b = k_2 d$$

$$\therefore \quad g = \frac{|a||b|}{d} \quad \text{i.e. } [a, b] = \frac{|ab|}{(a, b)}.$$

Now, let us prove the uniqueness of g. If possible, suppose g' is another L.C.M. of a and b. Then g is L.C.M. and $a \mid g'$, $b \mid g'$, ($\because$ g' is L.C.M.).

$$\therefore \quad g \mid g'$$

Similarly, g' is L.C.M. and $a \mid g$, $b \mid g$,

$$\therefore \quad g' \mid g \qquad\qquad (\because \text{g is L.C.M.})$$

Therefore $g = \pm g'$, but g and g' are positive, hence $g' = g$.

ILLUSTRATIVE EXAMPLES

Example 2.1: Let a, b, x, y be non-zero integers and let $xa + yb = 1$. Then show that $(a, b) = (x, y) = (a, y) = (x, b) = 1$.

Solution: Suppose $d = (a, b)$ and let $a = dk_1$ and $b = dk_2$, for $k_1, k_2 \in Z$. Using this in $xa + yb = 1$, we get,

$$x(dk_1) + y(dk_2) = 1$$

$$\Rightarrow \quad d(xk_1 + yk_2) = 1$$

$$\Rightarrow \quad d \mid 1,$$

$$\Rightarrow \quad |d| = d \leq |1| = 1$$

i.e. $d \leq 1$, but $d > 0$ implies $d = 1$.

Thus $(a, b) = 1$. Similarly, we can show that $(x, y) = 1$ etc.

Example 2.2: Let a and b be non-zero integers and let $d = (a, b)$. If $a = dx$ and $b = dy$, show that $(x, y) = 1$.

Solution: Since $d = (a, b)$, we have

$$d = ma + nb, \text{ for some m, n in } Z.$$

$$= m(dx) + n(dy), \text{ since } a = dx \text{ and } b = dy$$

$$d = d(mx + ny)$$

$$\Rightarrow \quad mx + ny = 1, \text{ since } d \neq 0, \text{ by cancellation law.}$$

$$\Rightarrow \quad (x, y) = 1, \text{ by Example (2.1) above.}$$

Example 2.3: If $(a, m) = 1 = (b, m)$, then $(ab, m) = 1$.

(That is, if a and m are relatively prime and b and m are relatively prime, then ab and m are also relatively prime).

Solution: By theorem 3, there exist x_0, y_0, x_1, y_1 such that

$$ax_0 + my_0 = 1 \text{ and } bx_1 + my_1 = 1$$

Thus we write

$$(ax_0)(bx_1) = (1 - my_0)(1 - my_1)$$
$$= 1 - my_2,$$

where $y_2 = y_0 + y_1 - my_0 y_1$, so that we obtain $(ab)(x_0 x_1) + my_2 = 1$

By example (2.1), we get $(ab, m) = 1$.

Example 2.4: *For any integer x, show that $(a, b) = (a, b + ax)$.*

Solution: Let $(a, b) = d$ and $(a, b + ax) = g$.

Since $d = (a, b)$, $d \mid a$ and $d \mid b$, which implies that $d \mid a$ and $d \mid (b + ax)$, by definition d is c.d. of a and $b + ax$, hence $d \mid g$. ... (1)

On the other hand, since $g = (a, b + ax)$, so $g \mid a$ and $g \mid (b + ax)$.

$\Rightarrow a = gk_1$ and $(b + ax) = gk_2$, for $k_1, k_2 \in \mathbb{Z}$

$\Rightarrow a = gk_1$ and $b + gk_1 = gk_2$

$\Rightarrow a = gk_1$ and $b = g(k_2 - k_1)$

$\Rightarrow g \mid a$ and $g \mid b$ ... (2)

So g is c.d. of a and b, hence $g \mid d$, as d is g.c.d. of a and b. From (1) and (2), we get $g = d$, which proves the result.

Example 2.5 : *If a, b, c are integers such that $a \mid bc$ and $(a, b) = 1$, then show that $a \mid c$.*

Solution : Given that $a \mid bc$ and $(a, b) = 1$.

$(a, b) = 1$ so there exist integers m and n such that

$$ma + nb = 1$$

$\Rightarrow \quad mac + nbc = c$

$\Rightarrow \quad mac + nak = c \quad (\because a \mid bc)$

$\Rightarrow \quad a[mc + nk] = c$

$\Rightarrow \quad ax = c \quad (\because mc + nk = x \text{ is integer})$

$\Rightarrow \quad a \mid c \quad \text{proved.}$

Example 2.6: *Find g.c.d. 'd' of 3997 and 2947 and express it in the form d = 3997m + 2947n for some m, n∈Z.*

Solution: We have

$$3997 = 2947 \times 1 + 1050 \quad \ldots (6)$$
$$2947 = 1050 \times 2 + 847 \quad \ldots (5)$$
$$1050 = 847 \times 1 + 203 \quad \ldots (4)$$
$$847 = 203 \times 4 + 35 \quad \ldots (3)$$
$$203 = 35 \times 5 + 28 \quad \ldots (2)$$
$$35 = 28 \times 1 + 7 \quad \ldots (1)$$
$$28 = 7 \times 4 + 0$$

∴ (3997, 2947) = 7

Now from (1),
$$7 = 35 - 28 \times 1$$
$$= 35 - [203 - 35 \times 5] \times 1 \quad \text{by using (2)}$$
$$= 35 \times 6 - 203 \times 1$$
$$= [847 - 203 \times 4] \times 6 - 203 \times 1, \quad \text{by using (3)}$$
$$= 847 \times 6 - 203 \times 25$$
$$= 847 \times 6 - [1050 - 84 \times 1] \times 25, \quad \text{by using (4)}$$
$$= 847 \times 31 - 1050 \times 25$$
$$= [2947 - 1050 \times 2] \times 31 - 1050 \times 25, \quad \text{by using (5)}$$
$$= 2947 \times 31 - 1050 \times 87$$
$$= 2947 \times 31 - [3997 - 2947 \times 1] \times 87, \quad \text{by using (6)}$$

∴ $7 = 2947 \times 118 - 3997 \times 87$

∴ $7 = 3997 \times (-87) + 2947 \times 118$

Here $m = -87$ and $n = 118$

Example 2.7: *Show that 4999 and 1109 are relatively prime. Also find m and n such that 1 = 4999 m + 1109 n.*

Solution: We have,

$$4999 = 1109 \times 4 + 563 \quad \ldots (5)$$
$$1109 = 563 \times 1 + 546 \quad \ldots (4)$$

$$563 = 546 \times 1 + 17 \qquad \ldots (3)$$
$$546 = 17 \times 32 + 2 \qquad \ldots (2)$$
$$17 = 2 \times 8 + 1 \qquad \ldots (1)$$
$$2 = 1 \times 2 + 0$$

∴ (4999, 1109) = 1

That is 4999 and 1109 are relatively prime.

From (1), we have,

$$\begin{aligned}
1 &= 17 - 2 \times 8 & \text{by using (1)} \\
&= 17 - (546 - 17 \times 32) \times 8 & \text{by using (2)} \\
&= 17 \times 257 - 546 \times 8 \\
&= [563 - 546 \times 1] \times 257 - 546 \times 8 & \text{by using (3)} \\
&= 563 \times 257 - 546 \times 265 \\
&= 563 \times 257 - [1109 - 563 \times 1] \times 265 & \text{by using (4)} \\
&= 563 \times 522 - 1109 \times 265 \\
&= [4999 - 1109 \times 4] \times 522 - 1109 \times 265 & \text{by using (5)} \\
&= 4999 \times 522 - 1109 \times 2353
\end{aligned}$$

∴ $\quad 1 = 4999 \times 522 + 1109 \times (-2353)$

Here, $\quad m = 522$ and $n = -2353$

Example 2.8: *Find g.c.d. of 3587 and 1819 and express it in the form 3587 m + 1819 n. Find two distinct pairs of m and n.*

Solution: We have, by D.A.,

$$3587 = 1819 \times 1 + 1768 \qquad \ldots (4)$$
$$1819 = 1768 \times 1 + 51 \qquad \ldots (3)$$
$$1768 = 51 \times 34 + 34 \qquad \ldots (2)$$
$$51 = 34 \times 1 + 17 \qquad \ldots (1)$$
$$34 = 17 \times 2 + 0$$

∴ (3587, 1819) = 17

Now using (1), we have

$$17 = 51 - 34 \times 1$$

$$= 51 - [1768 - 51 \times 34] \times 1 \quad \text{by using (2)}$$
$$= 51 \times 35 - 1768 \times 1$$
$$= [1819 - 1768 \times 1] \times 35 - 1768 \times 1 \quad \text{by using (3)}$$
$$= 1819 \times 35 - 1768 \times 36$$
$$= 1819 \times 35 - [3587 - 1819 \times 1] \times 36 \quad \text{by using (4)}$$
$$= 1819 \times 71 - 3587 \times 36$$
$$= 3587 \times (-36) + 1819 \times 71$$

Here $\quad m = -36, n = 71$.

For another pair, we have a = 3587, b = 1819 and k = 1 in the formula

$$d = a(m - kb) + b(n + ka), \text{ we get}$$
$$17 = 3587 \times (-1855) + 1819 \times 3658$$

So $\quad m_1 = -1855 \text{ and } n_1 = 3658$

Example 2.9: *Prove that (i) If n is odd, $n^2 - 1$ is divisible by 8. (ii) If x and y are odd, then $x^2 + y^2$ is even but not divisible by 4.*

Solution: Any odd integer is of the form 2k − 1, k is any integer.

(i) ∴ If $\quad n = 2k - 1$, for $k \in Z$

$$n^2 - 1 = (2k - 1)^2 - 1$$
$$= 4k^2 - 4k + 1 - 1$$

∴ $\quad n^2 - 1 = 4k(k - 1)$

Now k and k − 1 are consecutive integers, hence k(k − 1) is divisible by 2.

i.e. $k(k - 1) = 2k_1$, where $k_1 \in Z$

Therefore $n^2 - 1 = 4 \times k(k - 1)$

$$= 4 \times 2k_1$$

i.e. $\quad n^2 - 1 = 8k_1$

$$\Rightarrow 8 \mid (n^2 - 1)$$

(ii) Since x and y are odd integers, let $x = 2k_1 - 1$ and $y = 2k_2 - 1$ for $k_1, k_2 \in \mathbb{Z}$. Then

$$x^2 + y^2 = (2k_1 - 1)^2 + (2k_2 - 1)^2$$
$$= 4k_1^2 - 4k_1 + 1 + 4k_2^2 - 4k_2 + 1$$
$$= 4k_1(k_1 - 1) + 4k_2(k_2 - 1) + 2$$

Clearly $x^2 + y^2$ is even integer. Further,

$$x^2 + y^2 = 4[k_1(k_1 - 1) + k_2(k_2 - 1)] + 2 \quad \ldots (*)$$

If suppose $x^2 + y^2$ is divisible by 4, and $x^2 + y^2 = 4k$, from (*), we get

$$2 = 4k - 4[k_1(k_1 - 1) + k_2(k_2 - 1)]$$

$\Rightarrow 4 \mid 2$, which is impossible.

Therefore $x^2 + y^2$ is even but not divisible by 4.

Example 2.10: *Prove that there are infinitely many pairs of x and y satisfying $x + y = 100$ and $(x, y) = 5$.*

Solution: As $(x, y) = 5$, $x = 5k_1$, and $y = 5k_2$, with $(k_1, k_2) = 1$. Now, using these in $x + y = 100$, we get

$$5k_1 + 5k_2 = 100$$
$$\Rightarrow k_1 + k_2 = 20$$
$$\therefore k_1 = 20 - k_2$$

Now, for any integer value of k_2, we have value of k_1 such that $k_1 + k_2 = 20$. This shows that there are infinitely many pairs of k_1 and k_2 satisfying $k_1 + k_2 = 20$. Hence, there are infinitely many corresponding pairs of x and y, where $x = 5k_1$ and $y = 5k_2$, which satisfy $(x, y) = 5$ and $x + y = 100$.

Example 2.11: *Show that $\dfrac{a(a^2 + 2)}{3}$ is an integer for all integers $a \geq 1$.* (Practical problem).

Solution: To show that $\dfrac{a(a^2 + 2)}{3}$ is an integer we need to show that $a(a^2 + 2)$ it is divisible by 3 for all integers $a \geq 1$.

First observe that if $a = 1$, $a(a^2 + 2) = 1(1 + 2) = 3$ is divisible by 3 and if $a = 2$, $a(a^2 + 2) = 2(2^2 + 2) = 2 \times 6$ again divisible by 3.

Now, to prove the result for all a ≥ 3, we apply division algorithm to a and 3, so we have

a = 3k + r, wher 0 ≤ r < 3.

First case, if r = 0, a = 3k, hence $a(a^2 + 2)$ is divisible by 3.

Next if r = 1, then

$$a(a^2 + 2) = (3k + 1)[(3k + 1)^2 + 2]$$
$$= (3k + 1)(9k^2 + 6k + 1 + 2)$$
$$= 3(3k + 1)(3k^2 + 2k + 1)$$

Hence $a(a^2 + 2)$ is divisible by 3.

Lastly, if r = 2 we have

$$a(a^2 + 2) = (3k + 2)[(3k + 2)^2 + 2]$$
$$= (3k + 2)(9k^2 + 12k + 4 + 2)$$

which shows that $a(a^2 + 2)$ is divisible by 3. Thus, $a(a^2 + 2)$ is divisible for all integers a ≥ 1.

2.8 PRIME AND COMPOSITE NUMBERS

Prime: A non-zero integer p (≠ ± 1) is called *Prime* if it has no divisors other than ± 1 and ± p.

For instance, ± 2, ± 3, ± 5, ± 7, ± 11 etc. are prime integers.

Note: 1. Thus, a prime integer is an integer which has no *proper* divisor.

2. Usually only positive primes are studied. If p and q are positive primes and if p | q, then p = q.

Composite: A non-zero integer 'a' is called composite if 'a' has a proper divisor. That is 'a' is called composite if we can write a = b.c, where 1 < |b| < |a| and 1 < |c| < |a| i.e. b is a proper divisor of a. For example, 4, 10, – 12 etc. are composite integers.

Exercise:

1. List all the primes between 1 and 100. How many primes are there?

2. List all the primes between 100 and 200. How many are they?

Theorem 6: (Euclid's Lemma): If p is prime and a, b are integers such that p | ab, then either p | a or p | b.

Proof: If p | a, then the theorem is obvious.

If p ∤ a, then $(p, a) = 1 \Rightarrow \exists\ x$ and $y \in \mathbb{Z}$ such that
$$1 = px + ay$$

Multiplying both sides by b, we get,
$$b = (px)b + (ay)b$$
$$\Rightarrow \quad b = p(xb) + (ab)y$$
$$\Rightarrow \quad b = p(xb) + (pk)y,$$

$\because$ p | ab, we have ab = pk, for some $k \in \mathbb{Z}$

$\Rightarrow \quad b = p(xb + ky)$

$\Rightarrow \quad p | b$

Thus, if p ∤ a, then p | b.

Hence p | ab $\Rightarrow$ either p | a or p | b.

We prove, in the following, the generalisation of the above theorem.

Corollary: If p is a prime and $p | (a_1 \cdot a_2 \cdots a_n)$, then $p | a_i$, for at least one i $(1 \leq i \leq n)$.

Proof: We prove the result by mathematical induction on n.

If n = 1, we have $p | a_1$, and the result is obvious.

If n = 2, we have proved it in theorem (above).

So suppose the result is true for n = k.

i.e. if $p | (a_1 \cdot a_2 \cdots a_k)$, then $p | a_i$, for at least one i $(1 \leq i \leq k)$.

Now, suppose $p | (a_1 \cdot a_2 \cdots a_k \cdot a_{k+1})$

$\Rightarrow p | (a_1 \cdot a_2 \cdots a_k)$ or $p | a_{k+1}$, by theorem. If $p | a_{k+1}$, then i = k + 1.

If $p | (a_1 \cdot a_2 \cdots a_k)$, then by induction hypothesis, $p | a_i$, for at least one i $(1 \leq i \leq k)$.

Thus, $p | a_i$ for at least one i $(1 \leq i \leq k + 1)$ and the result is true for n = k + 1

Hence by induction, the result is true for all n ≥ 1.

Among all integers, the integers ± 2, ± 3, ± 5, ± 7, ± 11, ... (all prime integers) are called prime integers, because all the composite integers are composed of primes. In fact what we are saying, nothing but the following theorem called 'Unique Factorisation Theorem' or is also called, 'The fundamental theorem of arithmetic'.

Theorem 7 (Unique Factorization Theorem): Every integer a > 1 can be expressed as a product of positive primes. This representation is unique apart from the order of the prime factors.

Proof: If a = 2, there is nothing to be proved as 2 itself is a prime factor.

So suppose a > 2. If 'a' is a prime then the integer itself stands as a 'product' with single factor. If a is not prime, then it is composite. Since 'a' is composite, it can be factorised as a = $n_1 n_2$, where $1 < n_1 < a$ and $1 < n_2 < a$. If n_1 is prime, let it stand; otherwise it will factor into, say, $n_1 = n_3, n_4$, where $1 < n_3 < n_1$ and $1 < n_4 < n_1$; similarly for n_2. This process of writing each composite number that arises as a product of factors must terminate because the factors are smaller than the composite number itself; and yet each factor is an integer greater than 1. Thus, we can write 'a' as a product of primes. This proves that 'a' can be expressed as a product of primes.

Now, let us establish uniqueness part.

Suppose a has two different factorings.

Let $a = p_1 \cdot p_2 \ldots p_k$ and also $a = q_1 \cdot q_2 \ldots q_r$ be two prime factorisations of a; p_i's and q_i's are all primes. So that we have

$$p_1 \cdot p_2 \ldots p_k = q_1 \ldots q_2 \ldots q_r \quad \ldots (1)$$

Therefore $p_1 | (q_1 \cdot q_2 \ldots q_r)$

$\Rightarrow p_1 | q_j$ for at least one j ($1 \le j \le r$), by using corollary of theorem 5, since p_1 is prime.

But q_j is also prime, hence $p_1 = q_j$.

Cancelling p_1 and q_j from corresponding sides of (1), we get,

$$p_2 \cdot p_3 \ldots p_k = q_1 \cdot q_2 \ldots q_{j-1} \cdot q_{j+1} \ldots q_r \quad \ldots (2)$$

Again $p_2 | (q_1 \cdot q_2 \ldots q_{j-1} \cdot q_{j+1} \ldots q_r)$, p_2 is prime it must divide at least one factor on right hand side, which is also prime, hence p_2 is equal to at least one member on right hand side of (2), so cancelling from both sides the like factors, we may obtain

$$p_3 \cdot p_4 \ldots p_k = q_1 \cdot q_2 \ldots q_{i-1} \cdot q_{i+1} \ldots q_{j-1} \cdot q_{j+1} \ldots q_r \qquad \ldots (3)$$

Continuing in this way every time we cancel one factor from both sides. Since the number of factors is finite, we will arrive at one stage, where factors on either side get exhausted or all factors on both sides get exhausted simultaneously, proving that $r = k$ and factorisation is unique. If possible only one side of (1) gets exhausted, then it means; whatever prime factors left on other side, their product will be equal to 1, which is impossible. Hence, both sides must exhaust simultaneously. This completes the proof of the theorem.

Corollary: Let $a (\neq \pm 1)$ be any non-zero integer. Then
$a = \pm p_1, p_2 \ldots p_k$, where p_i's are primes.

Proof: Clearly $|a| > 1$, so by previous theorem, we have

$|a| = p_1 \cdot p_2 \ldots p_k$, where p_i's are primes and the expression is unique. But we know

$$|a| = \pm a, \text{ hence}$$
$$\pm a = p_1 \cdot p_2 \ldots p_k$$
$$\Rightarrow a = \pm p_1 p_2 \ldots p_k$$

Note: 1. Let $a (\neq \pm 1)$ be any non-zero integer. The factorisation of 'a' as a product of primes, need not yield distinct primes, hence collecting together like primes, we may write 'a' as:

$$a = \pm p_1^{\alpha_1} \cdot p_2^{\alpha_2} \ldots p_r^{\alpha_r}, \qquad \ldots (*)$$

where, $p_1, p_2, \ldots, p_r$ are all distinct primes and $\alpha_i \geq 0$ are integers.

For instance, $100 = 2 \times 2 \times 5 \times 5$,
So $\qquad 100 = 2^2 \times 5^2 \times 3^0$
Also $\qquad 6750 = 2 \times 3 \times 3 \times 3 \times 5 \times 5 \times 5$
$\qquad\qquad\quad = 2 \times 3^3 \times 5^3 \times 7^0$

2. For any integer 'a', the expression (*) is called *"Canonical form"*.

Using the canonical forms of the given integers, it is easy to find g.c.d.

For example,

$$(100, 6750) = 2 \times 5^2 = 50$$

Exercise:

1. Express 1757051 in canonical form.
2. Find g.c.d. and *l*.c.m. by using canonical forms of 216 and 675.

ILLUSTRATIVE EXAMPLES

Example 2.12: (Euclid): *If the number of primes is infinite, then show that there is no end to the sequence of primes 2, 3, 5, 7, 11, 13, ...*

Solution: Suppose there are only finite number of primes $p_1, p_2, ..., p_k$. Then form the number

$$n = 1 + p_1 \cdot p_2 ... p_k \qquad ... (1)$$

If $p_1 \mid n$, $n = p_1 r$, for $r \in N$, so that from (1), we can write

$$1 = p_1 r - p_1 p_2 ... p_k = p_1 (r - p_2 \cdot p_3 ... p_k)$$

which shows that $p_1 \mid 1$, which is impossible, since p_1 is prime. Therefore $p_1 \nmid n$. Similarly $p_2, p_3, ..., p_k$ cannot divide n. Hence any prime divisor p of n is a prime distinct from $p_1, p_2, ..., p_k$. Since n is either a prime or has a prime factor p, this implies that there is a prime distinct from $p_1, p_2, ..., p_k$.

Adding this prime to our list, we can continue the above process, which will yield new prime every time and we can continue this indefinitely, hence there are infinitely many primes.

Let us prove one more interesting fact about distribution of primes.

Example 2.13: *Show that there are arbitrarily large gaps in the sequence of primes.*

OR

Given any integer k > 1, there exist k consecutive composite integers.

Solution: Let k > 1 be any integer. Consider the continuous sequence of consecutive integers: (k + 1) ! + 2, (k + 1) ! + 3, (k + 1) ! + 4, ... , (k + 1)! + k, (k + 1) ! + k + 1. Observe that each of these integers is composite (i.e. not prime). Since $(k + 1)!$ has a factor 2, $(k + 1)! + 2$ is divisible by 2. Similarly $(k + 1)!$ has factor 3, (if $3 < k + 1$), hence 3 divides $(k + 1)! + 3$, and so on. Thus, there are k continuous composite integers, hence there is a gap of at least k integers between the two primes p and q, where

$$p < (k + 1)! + 2 \text{ and } q > (k + 1)! + k + 1$$

Hence the result.

Example 2.14: *Prove that the product of two or more integers of the form $4n + 1$ is of the same form.*

Solution: It is sufficient to consider the product of just two integers. Let $k = 4n + 1$ and $k' = 4m + 1$. We have,

$$\begin{aligned} kk' &= (4n + 1)(4m + 1) \\ &= 16mn + 4n + 4m + 1 \\ &= 4(4mn + n + m) + 1 \\ &= 4n' + 1 \end{aligned}$$

which is of the desired form.

Example 2.15: *Show that there are infinitely many primes of the form $4n + 3$.*

Solution: Suppose on contrary there exist only finitely many primes of the form $4n + 3$. Let us call them $q_1, q_2, ..., q_s$. Consider the positive integer

$$N = 4q_1 q_2 ... q_s - 1 = 4(q_1 q_2 ... q_s - 1) + 3,$$

and let $N = r_1 r_2 ... r_k$ be its prime factorisation. Since N is an odd integer, we have $r_i \neq 2$ for all i, so that each r_i is of the form $4n + 1$ or $4n + 3$. By above result, the product of any number of primes of the form $4n + 1$ is again an integer of this type. For N to take the form $4n + 3$, as it clearly does, N must contain at least one prime factor r_i of the form $4n + 3$. But r_i can not be found among the list $q_1, q_2, ..., q_s$ for this would lead to the contradiction that $r_i \mid 1$. The only possible conclusion is that there are infinitely many primes of the form $4n + 3$.

Note: Any prime of the form $4n + 3$ is of the form $4n - 1$, since $4n + 3 = (4n + 4) - 1 = 4(n + 1) - 1 = 4n' - 1$. This fact and above example 2.15 together prove that there are infinitely many primes of the form $4n - 1$.

Example 2.16: *Show that there are infinitely many primes of the form $6n - 1$.*

Solution: Suppose there exist finitely many primes of the form $6n - 1$, say $q_1, q_2, ..., q_s$. We define a number N by

$$N = 6(q_1 q_2 ... q_s) - 1$$

Clearly N is of the form $6n - 1$. Let $p_1 \cdot p_2 ... p_k$ be prime factorisation of N; that is, $N = p_1 \cdot p_2 ... p_k$. As N is odd integer $p_i \neq 2$ or 3 for all i, so that each p_i is of the form $6n + 1$ or $6n - 1$. Observe that any prime number except 2 or 3 is of the form $6n + 1$ or $6n - 1$ and that the product of two primes of the form $6n + 1$ is again of the same form. N being integer of the form $6n - 1$, there must be at least one prime factor p_i of the form $6n - 1$. This p_i cannot be found among the list $q_1, q_2, ..., q_s$ for this would lead to the contradiction that $p_i \mid 1$. The only possible conclusion is that there are infinitely many primes of the form $6n - 1$.

Example 2.17: *If $(a, b) = 1$ and $a \mid bc$, then show that $a \mid c$.*

Solution: Since $(a, b) = 1$, we have

$1 = ma + nb$, for some $m, n \in Z$. Multiplying both sides by c, we get

$$c = (ma)c + (nb)c$$
$\Rightarrow \qquad c = a(mc) + n(bc)$
$\Rightarrow \qquad c = a(mc) + n(ak) \quad \because a \mid bc \Rightarrow bc = ak,\ \text{for some}\ k \in Z$
$\Rightarrow \qquad c = a[mc + nk]$
$\Rightarrow\ a \mid c.$

Example 2.18: *Show that $\sqrt{7}$ is not rational number.*

Solution: Suppose $\sqrt{7}$ is rational number. Let $\sqrt{7} = \dfrac{p}{q}$; $p, q \in Z$ and $(p, q) = 1$ so that $7 = \dfrac{p^2}{q^2}$

$$p^2 = 7q^2 \qquad \qquad ...(1)$$
$\Rightarrow \qquad 7 \mid p^2$
$\Rightarrow \qquad 7 \mid p$
$\Rightarrow \qquad \exists\ r \in Z\ \text{such that}$
$$p = 7r \qquad \qquad ...(A)$$

$\Rightarrow \qquad p^2 = 4qr^2 \qquad \ldots (2)$

(1) and (2) $\Rightarrow$

$\qquad 7q^2 = 4qr^2$

$\Rightarrow \qquad q^2 = 7r^2$

$\Rightarrow \qquad 7 \mid q^2 \Rightarrow 7 \mid q \Rightarrow q = 7r_1$ for some $r_1 \in \mathbb{Z}$ $\qquad \ldots$ (B)

(A) and (B) $\Rightarrow$

$\qquad (p, q) \geq 7$

which is contradiction to the fact that $(p, q) = 1$

Hence $\sqrt{7}$ cannot be rational number.

Example 2.19: *Express 540 and 126 as product of positive primes and hence find their g.c.d.*

Solution: We have,

$$540 = 2 \times 270$$
$$= 2 \times 2 \times 135$$
$$= 2 \times 2 \times 3 \times 45$$
$$= 2 \times 2 \times 3 \times 3 \times 15$$
$$= 2 \times 2 \times 3 \times 3 \times 3 \times 5 = 2^2 \cdot 3^3 \cdot 5^1$$

Similarly, $\quad 126 = 2 \times 63$
$$= 2 \times 3 \times 21$$
$$= 2 \times 3 \times 3 \times 7 = 2 \cdot 3^2 \cdot 7$$

$\therefore \quad (540, 126) = 2 \times 3^2$
$$= 18$$

Example 2.20: *(i) Prove that an integer is divisible by 3 if and only if the sum of its digits is divisible by 3. (ii) Prove that an integer is divisible by 9 if and only if the sum of its digits is divisible by 9.*

Solution: (i) Let $k = a_n \cdot a_{n-1} \ldots a_2 a_1$ be an integer with n – digits, $a_n \neq 0$, $0 \leq a_i \leq 9$, $i = 1$ to n. Then, we can write k as

$$k = a_n 10^{n-1} + a_{n-1} 10^{n-2} + \ldots + a_2 10 + a_1$$

(For instance, $3567 = 3 \times 10^3 + 5 \times 10^2 + 6 \times 10 + 7$)

Further, we have

$$k = (a_n 10^{n-1} - a_n) + (a_{n-1} 10^{n-2} - a_{n-1}) + \ldots$$
$$+ (a_2 10 - a_2) + a_1 - a_1 + (a_n + a_{n-1} + \ldots + a_2 + a_1)$$
$$k = a_n(10^{n-1} - 1) + a_{n-1}(10^{n-2} - 1) + \ldots$$
$$+ a_2(10-1) + (a_n + a_{n-1} + \ldots + a_2 + a_1) \quad \ldots (1)$$
$$\Rightarrow (a_n + a_{n-1} + \ldots + a_2 + a_1) = k - [a_n(10^{n-1} - 1)$$
$$+ a_{n-1}(10^{n-2} - 1) + \ldots + a_2(10-1)] \quad \ldots (2)$$

Observe that $10^{n-1} - 1$, $10^{n-2} - 1$, ..., $10 - 1 = 9$ are all multiples of 9, Therefore if $3 \mid k$, we see that R.H.S. of (2) is divisible by 3, hence the sum of the digits is divisible by 3. On the other hand, if the sum of the digits is divisible by 3, the R.H.S. of (1) is divisible by 3 and hence $3 \mid k$. Thus, k is divisible by 3 if and only if the sum of the digits is divisible by 3.

(ii) Similar arguments can be applied in case of 9.

Example 2.21: *Prove that $(a, a + k) \mid k$, for all integers a, k not both zero.*

Solution: Let $(a, a + k) = d$. Then $d \mid a$ and $d \mid (a + k)$.

$\Rightarrow \quad a = dz_1 \quad$ and $\quad a + k = dz_2$, for $z_1, z_2 \in \mathbb{Z}$.

$\Rightarrow \quad a = dz_1 \quad$ and $\quad k = dz_2 - a$

$\Rightarrow \quad a = dz_1 \quad$ and $\quad k = dz_2 - dz_1$

$$= d(z_2 - z_1)$$

which shows that $d \mid k$.

Thus, $d \mid k$ i.e. $(a, a + k) \mid k$.

Example 2.22: *Find all primes which divide 50!.*

Solution: Since $50! = 1 \times 2 \times 3 \times \ldots \times 49 \times 50$, the number of primes dividing 50! will be nothing but the number primes less than 50. 2, 3, 5, 7, 11, 13, 17, 19, 23, 29, 31, 37, 41, 43, 47 are primes less than 50, which are 15 in number.

IMPORTANT POINTS

- Well-ordering principle.
- Principles of mathematical induction 1 and 2.
- Properties of divisibility.
- Division algorithm.
- Greatest common divisor d of two integers a and b in the form d = ma + nb.
- Least common multiple of two integers a and b and the relation $[a, b] = \dfrac{|ab|}{(a, b)}$.
- Relatively prime integers.
- Primes.
- Euclid's Lemma.
- Unique Factorization theorem or Fundamental theorem of arithmetic.

THEORY QUESTIONS

1. Prove that the product of any three consecutive integers is divisible by 6.
2. Show that, if (ac) | (bc), then a | b.
3. If a | b and c | d, then show that (ac) | (bd).
4. Show that any two consecutive integers are relatively prime.
5. Prove that no integers x, y exist satisfying x + y = 200 and (x, y) = 7.
6. Prove that if (b, c) = 1 and a | b, then (a, c) = 1.
7. If a and b are relatively prime and b | (ac), then show that b | c.
8. Show that the product of any two consecutive integers is divisible by 2.
9. Prove that an integer is divisible by 11 if and only if the difference between the sum of digits in odd places and the sum of the digits in the even places is divisible by 11.
10. If x and y are odd, prove that $x^2 + y^2$ cannot be a perfect square.
11. Prove that (a, a + 2) = 1 or 2 for every integer a.
12. If (a, b) = 1 and a | c, b | c, then show that ab | c.
13. Show that $\sqrt{3}$ is not rational number.

Answer

3. **Hint:** Product of any three consecutive integers is
   $(n - 1) n (n + 1) = n^3 - n$. By mathematical induction, show that
   $6 \mid (n^3 - n)$, for all $n \geq 0$.

NUMERICAL PROBLEMS

1. Find values of x and y which satisfy
   (a) $243x + 198y = 9$;
   (b) $71x - 50y = 1$;
   (c) $43x + 64y = 1$;
   (d) $93x - 81y = 3$.

2. Find the greatest common divisor d of the given two numbers a and b and find the integers x and y to satisfy $d = ax + by$, for each of the following:
   (a) $a = 7469, b = 2464$; (b) $a = 4001, b = 2689$;
   (c) $a = 616, b = 427$; (d) $a = 1357, b = 1166$.

3. Show that the integers 3927 and 377 are relatively prime and find integers x and y which satisfy $1 = 3927x + 377y$.

4. Show that g.c.d. 'd' of 2210 and 357 is 17 and find x and y such that $17 = 2210x + 357y$.

5. Find the least common multiple of 482 and 1687.

6. Find positive integers a and b satisfying the equations $(a, b) = 10$ and $[a, b] = 100$ simultaneously. Find all solutions.

7. If $(a, b) = p$, a prime, what are the possible values of (a^2, b), (a^3, b) and (a^2, b^3)?

8. Evaluate (ab, p^4) and $(a + b, p^4)$, given that $(a, p^2) = p$ and $(b, p^3) = p^2$, where p is prime.

9. Express in canonical form and hence find g.c.d. of 7007 and 2450.

Answers

1. (a) $x = 9, y = -11$; (b) $x = 31, y = 44$; (c) $x = 3, y = -2$; (d) $x = 7, y = 8$;

2. (a) $d = 74, x = 1, y = -3$; (b) $d = 1, x = -1117, y = 1662$;
   (c) $d = 7, x = -9, y = 13$; (d) $d = 1, x = 641, y = -746$.

3. $x = -12, y = 125$.
4. $x = -5, y = 31$.
5. **Hint:** Find g.c.d. $d = (482, 1687)$, then
   $l.c.m = (482 \times 1687)/d$ ...... $l.c.m. = 3374$.
6. $a = 10, b = 100$ is a solution in positive integers. All solutions are given by $a = \pm 10$, $b = \pm 100$; $a = \pm 20$, $b = \pm 50$; $a = \pm 100$, $b = \pm 10$; $a = \pm 50$, $b = \pm 20$; with all arrangements of sign. There are 16 solutions in all.
8. p^2, p
9. 49.

MULTIPLE CHOICE QUESTIONS

1. If a, b, c are integers and a | (bc), then _____
   (a) a | b
   (b) a | c
   (c) a divides both
   (d) all of these may be true

2. If gcd (a, b) = d > 1, then _____
   (a) $\gcd\left(\dfrac{a}{d}, \dfrac{b}{d}\right) = 1$
   (b) ax + by = 1, for x, y, ∈ Z
   (c) $\dfrac{a}{d}$ and $\dfrac{b}{d}$ are not relatively prime
   (d) none of these

3. For any integer a, a(a + 1) is always _____
   (a) even integer
   (b) odd integer
   (c) prime integer
   (d) none of these

4. For any integer a, a(a + 1) (a + 2) is _____
   (a) even
   (b) odd
   (c) square number
   (d) none of these

5. How many prime numbers divide 30!
   (a) 10
   (b) 40
   (c) 25
   (d) 3

6. What is the remainder when the following sum is divided by 4?
   $1^5 + 2^5 + \ldots + 20^5$
   (a) 0
   (b) 2
   (c) 3
   (d) none of these

7. If a is odd integer then the remainder when $a^2 - 1$ divided by 8 is
   (a) 1
   (b) 0
   (c) 3
   (d) 5

8. $25^{97} \equiv ?$ (mod 97)
   (a) 1
   (b) 25
   (c) 0
   (d) none of these

9. The remainder when the sum $1! + 2! + 3! + \ldots + 1000!$ is divided by 12 is _____
   (a) 9
   (b) 5
   (c) 0
   (d) 11

10. If n > 4 is composite, then _____
    (a) $n \mid (n-1)!$
    (b) $n \mid (n^2 - 2)$
    (c) $n \mid (n^2 + 1)$
    (d) none of these

11. If gcd(a, b) = 3 and *l*cm (a, b) = 30, if a = 6, then b = _____
    (a) 30
    (b) 15
    (c) both 30 and 15
    (d) none of these

Answers

1. (d)   2. (a)   3. (a)   4. (b)   5. (a)
6. (a)   7. (b)   8. (b)   9. (a)   10. (a)
11. (b)

SAY TRUE OR FALSE WITH JUSTIFICATION

1. $a, b, \in \mathbb{Z}$ then $ab = 1$, has four solutions.
2. If $a, b, x, y, \in \mathbb{Z}$ and $ax + by = 1$, then a and x are relatively prime.
3. There are infinitely many primers.
4. A number is divisible by 4 iff the last digit of the number is divisible by 4.
5. If a is odd integer than $a^2 \equiv 1 \pmod 4$.
6. If $(a, b) = (a, c)$, then $[a, b] = [a, c]$.
7. If $(a, b) = (a, c)$, then $(a^2, b^2) = (a^2, c^2)$.
8. If p is a prime and $p \mid a$ and $p \mid (a^2 + b^2)$, then $p \mid b$.
9. If p is a prime and $p \mid a^7$, then $p \mid a$.
10. If $a^3 \mid c^3$, then $a \mid c$.
11. If $a^3 \mid c^2$, then $a \mid c$.
12. If $a^2 \mid c^3$, then $a \mid c$.
13. If p is a prime and $p \mid (a^2 + b^2)$ and $p \mid (b^2 + c^2)$ then $p \mid (a^2 - c^2)$.
14. If p is a prime and $p \mid (a^2 + b^2)$ and $p \mid (b^2 + c^2)$ then $p \mid (a^2 + c^2)$.
15. If $b \mid (a^2 + 1)$, then $b \mid (a^4 + 1)$.
16. If $b \mid (a^2 - 1)$, then $b \mid (a^4 - 1)$.

Answers

1. False	2. True	3. True	4. False	5. True
6. False,	7. True	8. True	9. True	10. True, $a = 2, b = 6, c = 10$.
11. True	12. False, $a = 8, c = 4$.	13. True	14. False, $p = 5, a = 2, b = 1, c = 3$.	15. False, $a = 2, b = 5$
16. True				

3
CHAPTER

MATHEMATICAL LOGIC

3.1 STATEMENTS (PROPOSITIONS)

In our everyday life we use different types of sentences for communication. Below are given some sentences :

(i) High! Hellow!

(ii) Please bring me cup of coffee.

(iii) What are you doing ?

(iv) Earth is round.

(v) 3 + 4 = 10

(vi) All students in MCA class are graduates.

(vii) The result of 5 multiplied by 2 is less than 100.

(viii) Sun rises in the west.

In the above list the sentences in (i), (ii), (iii) are exclamatory, order and question type sentences. They do not declare any result; whereas each of the sentences from (iv) – (viii) declare firmly something; which may be True (T) or False (F). They are called declarative sentences. The result declared in (iv), (vi) and (vii) is true but that in (v) and (viii) is false.

Let us consider the following declarative sentence.

'Their are four mistaks in this sentense'

Is it true or false ?

If we say it is true, then it is false since there are only three mistakes.

If we say it is false, then the result is true.

We shall avoid this type of declarative sentences.

3.1.1 Proposition

Definition : A declarative sentence which is either True (T) or False (F) but not both, is called a statement or proposition.

Thus the sentences (iv), (vi) and (vii) above are true statements and (v), (viii) are false statements. We denote the statements by small case letters p, q, r etc. If the statement p is true then we say that the truth value of p is T. If p is a false statement, then the truth value of p is F.

These results are denoted by writing $p \equiv T$ or $p \equiv F$ respectively.

Consider the following statements :

   p : Logic is easy.

   q : It is too hot today.

   r : 2x + 3 = 15.

The truth value of statement p changes from student to student. For a student X it may be that really it is easy but for another student Y it may seem to be rather difficult.

The truth value of q changes from place to place.

The statement r has truth value T only when x = 6 and for any other value of x it is false.

A statement whose truth value depends upon certain circumstances, is called a logical variable.

Thus p, q, r are logical variables.

A statement whose truth value never changes is called a logical constant.

   s : There are 26 letters in English alphabet.

   t : Integer 10 is not divisible by 2.

Here the statements s and t are logical constants and we have $s \equiv T$, $t \equiv F$.

3.1.2 Logical Connectives

We now proceed to the methods of forming new propositions (statements) from the given two or more propositions. While communicating with each other, we always come across with the words 'not', 'and', 'or', 'if – then', 'if and only if' etc. They are called 'Logical Connectives'.

A proposition which does not involve any logical connective is called a simple statement. The statements, we have seen in Article 1.1 are all simple statements.

A proposition which involves logical connective (s) is called a compound proposition or compound statement.

Thus,   p : 5 is odd and 9 is a perfect square

q : If traffic is jam, then buses are late.

r : Children like to watch 'chhota Bhim' or 3 is not prime.

are compound propositions.

While forming a compound proposition, we use different symbols for logical connectives. These symbols are called logical operators.

Definition : Let p be a proposition. Then the negation of p denoted by ¬p (or ~p or $\bar{p}$) is a proposition whose truth value is opposite to the truth value of p.

Thus suppose,

p : Signal mechanism has failed.

Then   ¬p : Signal mechanism has not failed.

We can also say.

¬p : It is not the case that signal mechanism has failed.

From the definition of ¬p, we have the following table called truth table for ¬p.

p	¬p
T	F
F	T

Definition : Let p and q be propositions. Then the conjunction of p and q, denoted by p ∧ q (read p and q) is the proposition whose truth value is T, when p and q both have value T and value F in all remaining cases.

We note that there are four possible combinations of the truth values of two propositions p and q. They are TT, TF, FT and FF.

As such the truth table for p ∧ q consists of 4 rows; as given below.

p	q	p ∧ q
T	T	T
T	F	F
F	T	F
F	F	F

Let p : 5 is prime

q : 4 is even

r : 7 is a perfect square.

Then we have p ≡ T, q ≡ T, r ≡ F. The compound position '5 is prime and 4 is even' has the truth value p ∧ q ≡ T ∧ T ≡ T (See table)

Also the proposition '5 is prime and 7 is a perfect square' has truth value

p ∧ r ≡ T ∧ F ≡ F (See table)

Sometimes the word 'still', 'but' can be used while writing the conjunction of two propositions. For example, let p : It is raining and q : we go for picnic.

Then p ∧ q : It is raining and we go for picnic.

can be written as

'It is raining, still we go for picnic' we can also write.

'It is raining but we go for picnic'.

Definition : Let p and q be propositions. Then the disjunction of p and q, denoted by p ∨ q (read p or q) is the proposition whose truth value is T when at least one of p and q has value T and value F when both p and q have value F.

The truth table for p ∨ q is as below.

p	q	p ∨ q
T	T	T
T	F	T
F	T	T
F	F	F

Consider the following propositions.

p : The word LOGIC contains 2 vowels

q : The word LOGIC contains 3 consonants

r : The world LOGIC contains 2 consonants

s : The word LOGIC contains 3 vowels.

We note that $p \equiv T, q \equiv T, r \equiv F, s \equiv F$.

The compound proposition.

'The word LOGIC contain 2 vowels or it contains 2 consonants'

$\equiv p \vee r \equiv T \vee F \equiv T$ (See table)

Also the proposition 'The word LOGIC contains 2 consonants or it contains 3 vowels' is $r \vee s \equiv F \vee F \equiv F$ (See table).

Again the proposition 'The word LOGIC contains 3 consonants or it contains 2 consonants

$\equiv q \vee r \equiv T \vee F \equiv T$ (See table)

Note : The word 'or' has two meanings viz. 'inclusive or' and 'exclusive or'.

In the above discussion, we have used 'or' in inclusive sense. It has value T when at least one of p and q has value T, and value F otherwise.

For exclusive 'or' we use the symbol $p \oplus q$. It has value T when exactly one of p and q has value T, and value F otherwise.

The examples of exclusive 'or' are :

(i) 5 is prime or 5 is not prime.

(ii) Today it is raining or not raining.

(iii) New baby is either male or female.

(iv) Today postman gave the letter or he did not.

The truth table for exclusive 'or' as given below.

p	q	$p \oplus q$
T	T	F
T	F	T
F	T	T
F	F	F

Conditional Statements :

Definition : Let p and q be propositions. Then the conditional statement denoted b $p \to q$ ($p \Rightarrow q$) is a proposition whose truth value F only when p is true and q is false. It has truth value T in all other cases.

We read p → q as 'p implies q' or 'if p then q'.

p is called anticident (hypothesis) and q is called consequent (conclusion).

The truth table for p → q is as shown below.

p	q	p → q
T	T	T
T	F	F
F	T	T
F	F	T

The following are equivalent meanings of p → q.

If p then q, q if p, p only if q, p is sufficient for q, q is necessary for p, whenever p, then q.

Consider two statements 'Today is holiday' and 'I go to movie'.

Then the conditional statement 'If today is holiday, then I go to movie' is symbolically written as below.

p : Today is holiday

q : I go to movie

∴ The symbolic form of the given statement is p → q.

From the given conditional statement p → q, we form three more conditional statements.

The converse of p → q is q → p.

The inverse of p → q is ¬p → ¬q.

Contrapositive of p → q is ¬q → ¬p.

In the above example, the

(i) converse is 'If I go to movie, then today is holiday'.

(ii) inverse is 'If today is not holiday, then I will not go to movie'.

(iii) contrapositive is 'If I do not go to movie, then today is not holiday'.

Let us now prepare a single truth value table which shows the truth values of above 4 implications; for all possible truth values of p and q.

Clearly the table consists of $2^2 = 4$ rows.

1	2	3	4	5	6	7	8
p	q	¬p	¬q	p → q	q → p	¬p → ¬q	¬q → ¬p
T	T	F	F	T	T	T	T
T	F	F	T	F	T	T	F
F	T	T	F	T	F	F	T
F	F	T	T	T	T	T	T
				Implication	Converse	Inverse	Contrapositive

Two compound propositions $P(p_1, p_2, \ldots, p_r)$ and $Q(p_1, p_2, \ldots, p_r)$ involving simple statements $p_1, p_2, \ldots, p_r$ are said to be logically equivalent if they have identical truth values in all possible combinations of the truth values of $p_1, p_2, \ldots, p_r$.

It is denoted by $P(p_1, p_2, \ldots, p_r) \equiv Q(p_1, p_2, \ldots, p_r)$.

From the above truth table, we observe the following results.

In column (5) and column (8), the two propositions p → q and ¬q → ¬p have identical truth values in all possible combinations of the truth values of p and q.

∴ p → q ≡ ¬q → ¬p

> The given implication and its contrapositive are logically equivalent.

Also from the column (6) and column (7) of the truth table, the compound propositions q → p and ¬p → ¬q have identical truth values in all possible combinations of the truth values of p and q.

∴ q → p ≡ ¬p → ¬q

> The converse and the inverse of given implication are logically equivalent.

Biconditional Statements :

Definition : Let p and q be two statements. Then the biconditional statement denoted by (p ⇔ q) is the proposition 'p if and only if q'. It has truth value T when p and q have identical truth values and value F when p and q have opposite truth values. It is also called double implication or bi-implication.

We read p ↔ q in the following ways. p implies and implied by q.

p is necessary and sufficient for q.

If p then q and conversely. The abbreviation p iff q is used for 'p if and only if q'.

Suppose p : I catch the train and q : I arrive at the station in time.

Then p ↔ q in words is

'I catch the train if and only if, I arrive at the station in time'.

As an another example, let p : x is odd, q : x^2 is odd.

Then p ↔ q is in words, 'x is odd iff x^2 is odd', i.e. 'The necessary and sufficient condition for x to be odd is that x^2 is odd'.

The truth table for biconditional statement is as below.

p	q	p ↔ q
T	T	T
T	F	F
F	T	F
F	F	T

Example 3.1 : By preparing a truth table show that p → q ≡ ~p ∨ q.

Solution :

(1)	(2)	(3)	(4)	(5)
p	q	~p	p → q	~p ∨ q
T	T	F	T	T
T	F	F	F	F
F	T	T	T	T
F	F	T	T	T

From column (4) and column (5) of the table the propositions p → q and ~p ∨ q have identical truth values in all possible combinations of the truth values of p and q.

∴ p → q ≡ (~p) ∨ q

Note : The above result p → q ≡ (~p) ∨ q is always useful in establishing the equivalence of two propositions by using the algebra of propositions.

3.1.3 Propositional Form

Compound Propositions

In the preceding article, we are acquainted with four logical connectives conjunction ($\wedge$), disjunction ($\vee$), implication ($\rightarrow$) and bi-implication ($\leftrightarrow$) together with negation ($\neg$).

Let now $P(p_1, p_2, \ldots, p_r)$ be a compound proposition involving r simple statements $p_1, p_2, \ldots, p_r$ and the logical connectives together with negation. As each simple statement p_i assumes 2 values i.e. T and F, there are $2 \times 2 \times \ldots \times 2 = 2^r$ possible combinations of the truth values of $p_1, p_2, \ldots, p_r$. Thus to prepare a truth table of $P(p_1, p_2, \ldots, p_r)$, we have to construct a table having 2^r rows.

Consider a compound proposition involving 3 simple statements p, q, r. The truth table for P(p, q, r) contains $2^3 = 8$ rows. While preparing a truth table we proceed as below.

The first three columns of the table are reserved for p, q, r as shown below.

p	q	r		...		P
T	T	T				
T	T	F				
T	F	T				
T	F	F				
F	T	T				
F	T	F				
F	F	T				
F	F	F				

Now the height of each column is 8.

In the column of p, we put first $4T^s$ and last $4F^s$. (See table).

Then in the column of q, we put first $2T^s$, next $2F^s$, next $2T^s$ and last $2F^s$ (See table).

In the column of r, we put T^s and F^s alternately. (See table).

After this, we fill-up the next columns successively as given in P(p, q, r).

3.1.4 Truth Table

There are five logical connectives.

(i) **Negation (not) :** It is denoted by ~.
If p is true then ~ p is false and vice versa.

(ii) **Conjunction (and) :** It is denoted as p ∧ q.
It is true only if both p and q are true.

(iii) **Disjunction (or) :** It is denoted by p ∨ q.
This is true if p is true or q is true or both are true.

(iv) **Conditional (implication) If .... then :** It is denoted as p → q.
This is false only if p is true and q is false.

(v) **Biconditional (double implication) equivalence .... if and only if .... :** It is denoted as p ↔ q.
This is true if both are true or both are false.

Remark : Negation is called a connective although it does not combine two or more statements.

The above terms can be represented in the truth table as follows.

p	q	~ p	p ∧ q	p ∨ q	p → q	p ↔ q
T	T	F	T	T	T	T
T	F	F	F	T	F	F
F	T	F	F	T	T	F
F	F	T	F	F	T	T

Example 3.2 : Construct a truth table for (q → ¬p) ∨ (¬p → ¬q).

Solution : P(p, q) ≡ (q → ¬p) ∨ (¬p → ¬q) involves 2 simple statements.

∴ Truth table consists of 2^2 = 4 rows. Also the expression for P(p, q) suggests that the table needs 7 columns; as shown below.

p	q	¬p	¬q	q → ¬p	¬p → ¬q	(q → ¬p) ∨ (¬p → ¬q)
T	T	F	F	F	T	T
T	F	F	T	T	T	T
F	T	T	T	F	F	T
F	F	T	T	T	T	T

Example 3.3 : Construct a truth table for $(\neg p \leftrightarrow \neg q) \leftrightarrow (q \leftrightarrow r)$

Solution : The given expression involves three simple statements. Therefore truth table consists of $2^3 = 8$ rows.

p	q	r	¬p	¬q	¬p ↔ ¬q	q ↔ r	(¬p ↔ ¬q) ↔ (q ↔ r)
T	T	T	F	F	T	T	T
T	T	F	F	F	T	F	F
T	F	T	F	T	F	F	T
T	F	F	F	T	F	T	F
F	T	T	T	F	F	T	F
F	T	F	T	F	F	F	T
F	F	T	T	T	T	F	F
F	F	F	T	T	T	T	T

By referring to the above examples, we see that the compound proposition $(q \to \neg p) \vee (\neg p \to \neg q)$ has truth value T in all possible combinations of the truth values of p and q. Such a compound proposition is called a tautology.

3.1.5 Tautology and Contradiction

Definition - Tautology : A compound proposition $P(p_1, p_2, ..., p_r)$ is called a tautology if P has truth value T in all possible combinations of the truth values of $p_1, p_2, ..., p_r$.

Definition - Contradiction : A compound proposition $P(p_1, p_2, ..., p_r)$ is called a contradiction of fallacy if P has truth value F in all possible combinations of the truth values of $p_1, p_2, ..., p_r$.

A proposition which is neither tautology nor contradiction is called a contingency.

Thus, $(\neg p \leftrightarrow \neg q) \leftrightarrow (q \leftrightarrow r)$ is a contingency.

From the definition of logical equivalence of two propositions $P(p_1, p_2, ..., p_r)$ and $Q(p_1, p_2, ..., p_r)$ and tautology it immediately follows that

[P ≡ Q] iff [(P ↔ Q) is a tautology].

The symbol ⇔ is used for logical equivalence.

Thus P ≡ Q and P ⇔ Q have the same meaning.

Example 3.4 : Show that $(\neg Q \wedge (P \to Q)) \to \neg P$ is a tautology.

Solution :

P	Q	¬P	¬Q	P → Q	¬Q ∧ (P → Q)	(¬Q ∧ (P → Q)) → ¬P
T	T	F	F	T	F	T
T	F	F	T	F	F	T
F	T	T	F	T	F	T
F	F	T	T	T	T	T

From the last column of the table, the proposition $(\neg Q \wedge (P \to Q)) \to \neg P$ has truth value T in all possible combinations of the truth values of P and Q. Hence it is a tautology.

3.1.6 Logical Equivalence

Logical Identities :

In the algebra of propositions there are some logical identities (logical equivalences). We can use them in establishing the equivalence of compound propositions. The following table gives the list of logical identities.

3.2 ALGEBRA OF PROPOSITIONS

Commutative laws	p ∨ q ≡ q ∨ p
	p ∧ q ≡ q ∧ p
Distributive laws	p ∨ (q ∧ r) ≡ (p ∨ q) ∧ (p ∨ r)
	p ∧ (q ∨ r) ≡ (p ∧ q) ∨ (p ∧ r)
Identity laws	p ∧ T ≡ p
	p ∨ F ≡ p
Negation laws	p ∧ ~p ≡ T
	p ∧ ~p ≡ F

Associative laws	$p \vee (q \vee r) \equiv (p \vee q) \vee r$
	$p \wedge (q \wedge r) \equiv (p \wedge q) \wedge r$
Domination laws	$p \vee T \equiv T$
	$p \wedge F \equiv F$
Double negation law	$\sim(\sim p) \equiv p$
De Morgan's laws	$\sim(p \vee q) \equiv \sim p \wedge \sim q$
	$\sim(p \wedge q) \equiv \sim p \vee \sim q$
Absorption laws	$p \wedge (p \vee q) \equiv p$
	$p \vee (p \wedge q) \equiv p$
Idempotency laws	$p \vee p \equiv p$
	$p \wedge p \equiv p$

We shall give the proof of some of these laws below. The proofs of the remaining are left as an exercise.

Proof of associative laws :

(1)	(2)	(3)	(4)	(5)	(6)	(7)
p	q	r	q ∨ r	p ∨ (q ∨ r)	p ∨ q	(p ∨ q) ∨ r
T	T	T	T	T	T	T
T	T	F	T	T	T	T
T	F	T	T	T	T	T
T	F	F	F	T	T	T
F	T	T	T	T	T	T
F	T	F	T	T	T	T
F	F	T	T	T	F	T
F	F	F	F	F	F	F

From column (5) and (7), we see that $p \vee (q \vee r)$ and $(p \vee q) \vee r$ have identical truth values in all the rows.

$$\therefore \quad p \vee (q \vee r) \equiv (p \vee q) \vee r$$

The other associative law i.e. $p \wedge (q \wedge r) \equiv (p \wedge q) \wedge r$ can be proved as above (Try yourself)

De Morgan's laws :

(1)	(2)	(3)	(4)	(5)	(6)	(7)	(8)	(9)	(10)
p	q	~p	~q	p ∨ q	~(p ∨ q)	~p ∧ ~q	p ∧ q	~(p ∧ q)	~p ∨ ~q
T	T	F	F	T	F	F	T	F	F
T	F	F	T	T	F	F	F	T	T
F	T	T	F	T	F	F	F	T	T
F	F	T	T	F	T	T	F	T	T

From column (6) and (7), we see that ~(p ∨ q) and ~p ∧ ~q have identical truth values in all the rows.

∴ ~(p ∨ q) ≡ ~p ∧ ~q

Also from column (9) and (10) the proposition ~(p ∧ q) and ~p ∨ ~q have identical truth values in all possible rows.

∴ ~(p ∧ q) ≡ ~p ∨ ~q

Absorption laws :

(1)	(2)	(3)	(4)	(5)	(6)
p	q	p ∧ q	p ∨ (p ∧ q)	p ∨ q	p ∧ (p ∨ q)
T	T	T	T	T	T
T	F	F	T	T	T
F	T	F	F	T	F
F	F	F	F	F	F

From column (1) and (4), we see that the proposition p ∨ (p ∧ q) and p have identical truth values in all the rows.

∴ p ∨ (p ∧ q) ≡ p

Also from column (1) and (6) the proposition p ∧ (p ∨ q) and p have identical truth values in all the rows.

∴ p ∧ (p ∨ q) ≡ p

With the help of truth table complete the proof of remaining laws given in the table.

The careful look to the table of logical identities immediately tells that all the identities (except that of double negation) occur in pairs. In each identity the second part (first part) can be obtained from the first part (second part) simply by interchanging all occurrences of (i) disjunction ($\vee$) and conjunction ($\wedge$) and (ii) T and F.

It is called 'principle of duality' in the algebra of propositions.

For example, consider first distributive law

$$p \vee (q \wedge r) \equiv (p \vee q) \wedge (p \vee r)$$

$\wedge$ by $\vee$ everywhere.

Then we get, $p \wedge (q \vee r) \equiv (p \wedge q) \vee (p \wedge r)$

which is second distributive law.

Again consider the first domination law i.e. $p \vee T \equiv T$.

Now we replace $\vee$ by $\wedge$ and also T by F.

Then, we get $p \wedge F \equiv F$; which is second domination law.

We have seen that logical equivalence of two propositions can be established with the help of a truth table.

If the two propositions whose logical equivalence is to be established, involve 2 or 3 simple statements, then we need to prepare a truth table of $2^2 = 4$ or $2^3 = 8$ rows.

It is manageable.

However, in case the number of simple statements involved is 4 or more it is quite unmanageable to prepare a truth table of $2^4 = 16$ rows or $2^5 = 32$ rows.

In such cases the equivalence can be established with the help of logical identities.

Let us prove that $A \rightarrow (B \vee C) \Leftrightarrow (A \wedge \sim B) \rightarrow C$.

We have,
$$\begin{aligned}
A \rightarrow (B \vee C) &\equiv (\sim A) \vee (B \vee C) &&\because p \rightarrow q \equiv \sim p \vee q \\
&\equiv ((\sim A) \vee B) \vee C &&\because \text{associative law} \\
&\equiv ((\sim A) \vee (\sim \sim B)) \vee C &&\because \text{double negation} \\
&\equiv [\sim (A \wedge \sim B)] \vee C &&\because \text{De Morgan's law} \\
&\equiv (A \wedge \sim B) \rightarrow C &&\because p \rightarrow q \equiv \sim p \vee q \quad \text{Proved.}
\end{aligned}$$

ILLUSTRATIVE EXAMPLES

Example 3.5 : Let   P : It rains

                     Q : The atmospheric humidity increases.

Write the following statements in symbolic form :

(i) Atmospheric humidity increases only if it rains.

(ii) Sufficient condition for it to rain is that atmospheric humidity increases.

(iii) Necessary condition for it to rain is that atmospheric humidity increases.

(iv) Whenever atmospheric humidity increases it rains.

Solution : (i) Atmospheric humidity increases only if it rains i.e. Q only if P.

Symbolically it is $Q \to P$.

(ii) Sufficient condition for it to rain is that atmospheric humidity increases i.e. sufficient condition for P is Q. i.e. Q is sufficient for P.

Symbolically $Q \to P$.

(iii) Necessary condition for it to rain is that atmospheric humidity increases i.e. necessary condition for P is Q i.e. Q is necessary for P.

Symbolically $P \to Q$.

(iv) Whenever atmospheric humidity increases it rains.

Symbolically $Q \to P$.

Example 3.6 : Construct truth table for the following :

(i) $P \vee \neg (P \wedge Q)$ (ii) $(P \vee Q) \vee \neg R$ (iii) $\neg (P \vee \neg Q)$.

Solution : (i)

P	Q	$P \wedge Q$	$\neg (P \wedge Q)$	$P \vee \neg (P \wedge Q)$
T	T	T	F	T
T	F	F	T	T
F	T	F	T	T
F	F	F	T	T

(ii)

P	Q	R	¬R	P ∨ Q	(P ∨ Q) ∨ ¬R
T	T	T	F	T	T
T	T	F	T	T	T
T	F	T	F	T	T
T	F	F	T	T	T
F	T	T	F	T	T
F	T	F	T	T	T
F	F	T	F	F	F
F	F	F	T	F	T

(iii)

P	Q	¬Q	P ∨ ¬Q	¬(P ∨ ¬Q)
T	T	F	T	F
T	F	T	T	F
F	T	F	F	T
F	F	T	T	F

Example 3.7 : Determine which is a tautology or fallacy

(i) $p \Rightarrow q \wedge q \Rightarrow p$ (ii) $(p \wedge q) \wedge (p \vee q)$

Solution : (i)

p	q	p ⇒ q	q ⇒ p	(p ⇒ q) ∧ (q ⇒ p)
T	T	T	T	T
T	F	F	T	F
F	T	T	F	F
F	F	T	T	T

From the truth values of $(p \Rightarrow q) \wedge (q \Rightarrow p)$ in the last column of the truth table, we conclude that the proposition $(p \Rightarrow q) \wedge (q \Rightarrow p)$ is neither a tautology nor fallacy.

(ii)

p	q	p ∧ q	p ∨ q	(p ∧ q) ∧ (p ∨ q)
T	T	T	T	T
T	F	F	T	F
F	T	F	T	F
F	F	F	F	F

From the truth values of (p ∧ q) ∧ (p ∨ q) in the last column of the table conclusion is that the proposition is neither a tautology nor a fallacy.

Example 3.8 : (a) Write the converse and contrapositive of the following statements :

(i) If it is raining the grass is wet.

(ii) Rain is necessary for it to be cloudy.

(b) Write the converse and inverse of the following statement. If I am not in good health, then I will go to clinic.

Solution : (a) (i) Given statement is

If it is raining the grass is wet.

Let p : It is raining.

q : Grass is wet.

Then symbolically the given statement is p → q.

Now ¬p : It is not raining

¬q : Grass is not wet.

Converse is q → p, i.e. If grass is wet then it is raining. Contrapositive is ¬q → ¬p.

i.e. If grass is not wet, then it is not raining.

(ii) Given statement is 'Rain is necessary for it to be cloudy'.

We know that p → q means q is necessary for p.

We take p : It is cloudy

q : It rains

∴ Symbolically given statement is p → q.

Now ¬p : It is not cloudy

¬q : It does not rain

Converse is q → p, i.e. 'If it rains, then it is cloudy'. Contrapositive is ¬q → ¬p.

i.e. 'If it does not rain, then it is not cloudy'.

(b) Given statement is 'If I am not in good health, then I will go to clinic'.

Let   p : I am not in good health.

q : I will go to clinic.

Then symbolically given statement is p → q.

Now ¬p : I am in good health.

¬q : I will not go to clinic.

Converse is q → p i.e. 'If I go to clinic, then I am not in good health'.

Inverse is ¬p → ¬q, i.e. 'If I am in good health, then I will not go to clinic.'

Example 3.9 : By using truth table examine whether or not the following statements are equivalent :

(i) $(P \to Q) \wedge (R \to Q) \Leftrightarrow (P \vee R) \to Q$

(ii) $P \to (Q \vee R) \rightleftharpoons (P \to Q) \vee (P \to R) \Leftrightarrow T$

Solution : (i)

(1)	(2)	(3)	(4)	(5)	(6)	(7)	(8)
P	Q	R	P → Q	R → Q	(P → Q) ∧ (R → Q)	P ∨ R	(P ∨ R) → Q
T	T	T	T	T	T	T	T
T	T	F	T	T	T	T	T
T	F	T	F	F	F	T	F
T	F	F	F	T	F	T	F
F	T	T	T	T	T	T	T
F	T	F	T	T	T	F	T
F	F	T	T	F	F	T	F
F	F	F	T	T	T	F	T

From column (6) and column (8) of the table the propositions $(P \rightarrow Q) \wedge (R \rightarrow Q)$ and $(P \vee R) \rightarrow Q$ have identical truth values in all possible combinations of the values of P, Q, R. Hence the propositions are equivalent.

(ii)

P	Q	R	Q ∨ R	P → (Q ∨ R) (A)	P → Q	P → R	(P → Q) ∨ (P → R) (B)	A ⇌ B
T	T	T	T	T	T	T	T	T
T	T	F	T	T	T	F	T	T
T	F	T	T	T	F	T	T	T
T	F	F	F	F	F	F	F	F
F	T	T	T	T	T	T	T	T
F	T	F	T	T	T	T	T	T
F	F	T	T	T	T	T	T	T
F	F	F	F	T	T	T	T	T

The last column of the table shows that

$$P \rightarrow (Q \vee R) \rightleftharpoons (P \rightarrow Q) \vee (P \rightarrow R) \text{ is not a tautology.}$$

Hence the propositions are not equivalent.

Example 3.10 : Show that the following statements are equivalent.

$$A \rightarrow (B \vee C) \Leftrightarrow (A \wedge \sim B) \rightarrow C$$

Solution :

(1)	(2)	(3)	(4)	(5)	(6)	(7)	(8)
A	B	C	B ∨ C	A → (B ∨ C)	~ B	A ∨ ~ B	(A ∧ ~ B) → C
T	T	T	T	T	F	F	T
T	T	F	T	T	F	F	T
T	F	T	T	T	T	T	T
T	F	F	F	F	T	T	F
F	T	T	T	T	F	F	T
F	T	F	T	T	F	F	T
F	F	T	T	T	T	F	T
F	F	F	F	T	T	F	T

From column (5) and column (8) of the table the two propositions $A \rightarrow (B \vee C)$ and $(A \wedge \sim B) \rightarrow C$ have identical truth values in all possible combinations of the truth values of A, B, C.

Hence $A \rightarrow (B \vee C) \Leftrightarrow (A \wedge \sim B) \rightarrow C$.

Example 3.11 : Two roads cross each other at the junction point where there are two restaurants diagonally opposite to each other. The owner of one restaurant displayed a board 'cheap food is not good'. The owner of the other restaurant displayed a board 'good food is not cheap'.

Are they saying the same thing ? Justify your answer.

Solution : Let p : Food is good
q : Food is cheap

Then $\neg p$: food is not good
and $\neg q$: food is not cheap.

Symbolically first board says $q \rightarrow \neg p$ and second board says $p \rightarrow \neg q$.

We know that the implication and its contrapositive are logically equivalent.

The contrapositive of $p \rightarrow \neg q$ is $\neg(\neg q) \rightarrow \neg p$ i.e. $q \rightarrow \neg p$

$\because$ double negation

$\therefore \quad p \rightarrow \neg q \equiv q \rightarrow \neg p$

The two boards are saying the same thing.

Example 3.12 : Establish the following equivalence by using :
(a) truth table   (b) logical identities

$$P \rightarrow (Q \vee R) \Leftrightarrow (P \rightarrow Q) \vee (P \rightarrow R)$$

Solution :

(1)	(2)	(3)	(4)	(5)	(6)	(7)	(8)
P	Q	R	$Q \vee R$	$P \rightarrow (Q \vee R)$	$P \rightarrow Q$	$P \rightarrow R$	$(P \rightarrow Q) \vee (P \rightarrow R)$
T	T	T	T	T	T	T	T
T	T	F	T	T	T	F	T
T	F	T	T	T	F	T	T
T	F	F	F	F	F	F	F
F	T	T	T	T	T	T	T
F	T	F	T	T	T	T	T
F	F	T	T	T	T	T	T
F	F	F	F	T	T	T	T

From column (5) and (8) of the table, the truth values of
$P \to (Q \vee R)$ and $(P \to Q) \vee (P \to R)$ are identical in all rows.

∴ $P \to (Q \vee R) \Leftrightarrow (P \to Q) \vee (P \to R)$

Use of Logical Identities :

$$\begin{aligned}
P \to (Q \vee R) &\equiv (\neg P) \vee (Q \vee R) && \because a \to b \equiv \neg a \vee b \\
&\equiv (\neg P \vee \neg P) \vee (Q \vee R) && \because \text{Idempotency law} \\
&\equiv \neg P \vee [\neg P \vee (Q \vee R)] && \because \text{Associative law} \\
&\equiv \neg P \vee [(\neg P \vee Q) \vee R] && \because \text{Associative law} \\
&\equiv \neg P \vee [(Q \vee \neg P) \vee R] && \because \text{Commutative law} \\
&\equiv \neg P \vee [Q \vee (\neg P \vee R)] && \because \text{Associative law} \\
&\equiv (\neg P \vee Q) \vee (\neg P \vee R) && \because \text{Associative law} \\
&\equiv (P \to Q) \vee (P \to R) && \because a \to b \equiv \neg a \vee b
\end{aligned}$$

Proved.

Example 3.13 : Establish the logical equivalence

$$[(\sim p \vee \sim q) \Rightarrow (p \wedge q \wedge r)] \Leftrightarrow (p \wedge q)$$

by using (a) truth table
  (b) logical identities.

Solution :

(1)	(2)	(3)	(4)	(5)	(6)	(7)	(8)	(9)
p	q	r	~p	~q	~p ∨ ~q	p ∧ q ∧ r	[(~p ∨ ~q) ⇒ p ∧ q ∧ r]	p ∧ q
T	T	T	F	F	F	T	T	T
T	T	F	F	F	F	F	T	T
T	F	T	F	T	T	F	F	F
T	F	F	F	T	T	F	F	F
F	T	T	T	F	T	F	F	F
F	T	F	T	F	T	F	F	F
F	F	T	T	T	T	F	F	F
F	F	F	T	T	T	F	F	F

From column (8) and (9) of the table, we see that the two propositions

$(\sim p \vee \sim q) \Rightarrow (p \wedge q \wedge r)$ and $p \wedge q$ have identical truth values in all the rows.

∴ $(\sim p \vee \sim q) \Rightarrow (p \wedge q \wedge r) \Leftrightarrow p \wedge q$.

Use of Logical Identities :

$(\sim p \vee \sim q) \Rightarrow (p \wedge q \wedge r) \equiv\ \sim (p \wedge q) \Rightarrow (p \wedge q \wedge r)$

∵ De Morgan's law

$\equiv [\sim \sim (p \wedge q)] \vee (p \wedge q \wedge r)$

∵ $a \rightarrow b \equiv \sim a \vee b$

$\equiv (p \wedge q) \vee ((p \wedge q) \wedge r)$ ∵ Double negation

$\equiv p \wedge q$ Proved. ∵ Absorption law

Example 3.14 : Show the following implications :

(i) $P \wedge Q \Rightarrow P \rightarrow Q$

(ii) $P \rightarrow (Q \rightarrow R) \Rightarrow (P \rightarrow Q) \rightarrow (P \rightarrow R)$

Solution : (i)

P	Q	P∧Q	P→Q	(P∧Q) → (P→Q)
T	T	T	T	T
T	F	F	F	T
F	T	F	T	T
F	F	F	T	T

In the last column the proposition $(P \wedge Q) \rightarrow (P \rightarrow Q)$ has truth value T in all possible cases.

∴ $(P \wedge Q) \rightarrow (P \rightarrow Q)$ is a tautology.

∴ $(P \wedge Q) \Rightarrow (P \rightarrow Q)$

(ii)

P	Q	R	Q → R	P → (Q → R) (A)	P → Q	P → R	(P → Q) → (P → R) (B)	A → B
T	T	T	T	T	T	T	T	T
T	T	F	F	F	T	F	F	T
T	F	T	T	T	F	T	T	T
T	F	F	T	T	F	F	T	T
F	T	T	T	T	T	T	T	T
F	T	F	F	T	T	T	T	T
F	F	T	T	T	T	T	T	T
F	F	F	T	T	T	T	T	T

In the last column the proposition

$[P \to (Q \to R)] \to [(P \to Q) \to (P \to R)]$ has truth value T in all possible cases.

∴ $[P \to (Q \to R)] \to [(P \to Q) \to (P \to R)]$ is a tautology.

∴ $[P \to (Q \to R)] \Rightarrow [(P \to Q) \to (P \to R)]$.

Example 3.15 : Show that the following formula is contradiction or not :

(i) $(P \wedge \neg Q) \wedge (P \to Q)$

(ii) $P \leftrightarrow (\neg Q \wedge R)$

Solution : (i) We prepare a truth table.

P	Q	¬Q	P ∧ ¬Q	P → Q	(P ∧ ¬Q) ∧ (P → Q)
T	T	F	F	T	F
T	F	T	T	F	F
F	T	F	F	T	F
F	F	T	F	T	F

In the last column of the truth table the truth value is F in all the possible cases of the truth values of P and Q. Therefore it is a contradiction. Alternatively,

$(P \wedge \neg Q) \wedge (P \to Q) \equiv (\neg Q \wedge P) \wedge (P \to Q)$ ∵ Commutative law

$\equiv \neg Q \wedge [P \wedge (P \to Q)]$ ∵ Associative law

$\equiv \neg Q \wedge Q$ ∵ P, P → Q ∴ Q

$\equiv F$

(ii) We prepare a truth table.

P	Q	R	¬Q	¬Q ∧ R	P ↔ (¬Q ∧ R)
T	T	T	F	F	F
T	T	F	F	F	F
T	F	T	T	T	T
T	F	F	T	F	F
F	T	T	F	F	F
F	T	F	F	F	F
F	F	T	T	T	F
F	F	F	T	F	F

In the third row of the table the truth value of given proposition is T. Therefore it is not a contradiction.

Example 3.16 Show that ¬P is valid from ¬(P ∧ ¬Q), (¬Q ∨ R), ¬R.

Solution : Given : ¬(P ∧ ¬Q), (¬Q ∨ R), ¬R.

∴ ¬P ∨ Q, ¬Q ∨ R, ¬R   ∵ By DeMorgan's law

∴ P → Q, Q → R, ¬R

∴ ¬R, ¬R → ¬Q, ¬Q → ¬P

Now ¬R, ¬R → ¬Q ∴ ¬Q   ∵ Law of syllogism

Further ¬Q, ¬Q → ¬P ∴ ¬P   ∵ law of syllogism

Proved.

Example 3.17 : Show that $\neg(p \vee (\neg p \wedge q))$ and $\neg p \wedge \neg q$ are logically equivalent by developing a series of logical equivalences.

Solution :

$$\begin{aligned}
\neg(p \vee (\neg p \wedge q)) &\equiv \neg((p \vee \neg p) \wedge (p \vee q)) &\because \text{By distributive law} \\
&\equiv \neg(T \wedge (p \vee q)) &\because p \vee \neg p \equiv T \\
&\equiv \neg(p \vee q) &\because T \wedge a = a \\
&\equiv \neg p \wedge \neg q &\because \text{By DeMorgan's law}
\end{aligned}$$

Proved.

EXERCISE (3.1)

1. Let p : Logic is difficult

    q : All houses have balcony

    r : Dogs bark

    Write each of the following in symbolic form :

    (a) Either dogs bark or both logic is difficult and all houses have balcony.

    (b) If dogs do not bark, then all houses have balcony.

    (c) Logic is difficult and if some houses do not have balcony then dogs will not bark.

2. Write the following in symbolic form :

    (a) He helps you (H) only if you are rich (R).

    (b) It is necessary to be more than 18 years old (M) to get a driving licence (L).

    (c) It is sufficient to have an average I.Q. (Q) and well guided hard work (W) to score more than 90% (S).

3. If p, q are true statements and r, s are false statements, then find the truth value of :

    (a) $p \vee (q \wedge r)$

    (b) $(p \wedge \sim r) \wedge (\sim q \vee s)$

    (c) $(p \rightarrow q) \vee (r \leftrightarrow s)$.

4. Write negation of the following :
   (a) Either economy is improving or dollar is being devalued.
   (b) If the domestic production of oil increases, then we shall not import crude oil.
   (c) The leader must have both, charisma and diplomacy.

5. Prepare a truth table and write your conclusion :
   (a) $(\sim p \vee q) \rightarrow p \wedge (q \vee \sim q)$
   (b) $\neg (P \leftrightarrow Q) \leftrightarrow [P \wedge (\neg Q)] \vee [Q \wedge (\neg P)]$
   (c) Write dual of $P \wedge (\neg P \vee Q) \equiv P \wedge Q$

6. Identify the pairs of statements having the same meaning : Justify your answer :
   (a) If party has majority, then the government will survive.
   (b) If party has no majority, then government will collapse.
   (c) If government survives, then party has majority.
   (d) If government collapses, then party has no majority.

7. Identify the pairs of statements having the same meaning :
   (a) If thieves are caught, then police department is admired.
   (b) If thieves are not caught, then police department is not admired.
   (c) If police department is admired, then thieves are caught.
   (d) If police department is not admired, then thieves are not caught.

8. Construct a truth table for the following :
   (a) $\neg (p \leftrightarrow (Q \rightarrow (R \vee P)))$
   (b) $\neg (P \wedge \neg Q)$
   (c) $P \vee \neg (Q \wedge R)$
   (d) $(P \wedge \neg Q) \vee R$
   (e) $((P \vee Q) \wedge R) \rightarrow (P \vee R)$

9. By using truth table verify that the following implication is a tautology.
   $$[(P \vee Q) \wedge (P \rightarrow R) \wedge (Q \rightarrow R)] \rightarrow R.$$

10. Prepare a truth table and verify that the following implication is a tautology :
    (a) $(P \wedge (P \rightarrow Q)) \rightarrow Q$
    (b) $((P \rightarrow Q) \wedge (Q \rightarrow R)) \rightarrow (P \rightarrow R)$

11. Check the equivalence of the following statements :
    (a) $(P \leftrightarrow q) \equiv ((p \rightarrow q) \wedge (q \rightarrow p))$
    (b) $(p \rightarrow q) \equiv (\sim q) \rightarrow (\sim p)$

12. By using truth table examine whether or not
    (a) $A \rightarrow (B \vee C) \Leftrightarrow (A \wedge \neg B) \rightarrow C$
    (b) $(A \rightarrow C) \wedge (B \rightarrow C) \Leftrightarrow (A \vee B) \rightarrow C$

13. Establish the following equivalence by using :
    (a) truth table.
    (b) laws of logic
    $(P \rightarrow C) \wedge (Q \rightarrow C) \Leftrightarrow (P \vee Q) \rightarrow C$

14. Write the converse and inverse of the following statement.
    'If it is cold weather, then I wear sweater'.

15. Write the converse and inverse of the statement 'If I am not in good health, then I will go to clinic'.

16. Write the converse, inverse and contrapositive of each of the following statements :
    (a) If I run fast, then I can win the race.
    (b) $(\sim p) \Rightarrow q$.

17. (a) If $p \rightarrow q$ is false, find the truth value of $(\sim p \vee \sim q) \rightarrow q$.
    (b) If $p \rightarrow q$ is true, find the truth value of $\sim p \vee (p \leftrightarrow q)$.

18. Write the converse and contrapositive of the following statement.
    'If the flood destroys my house or the fire destroys my house, then my insurance company will pay me'.

19. By preparing truth table, complete the proof of all logical identities.

20. Determine whether or not :
    (a) $P \Leftrightarrow (Q \leftrightarrow (P \rightarrow Q))$
    (b) $((A \rightarrow B) \rightarrow C) \Leftrightarrow (A \rightarrow (B \rightarrow C))$

ANSWERS (3.1)

1. (a) $r \vee (p \wedge q)$ (b) $(\sim r) \rightarrow q$ (c) $p \wedge [\sim q \rightarrow \sim r]$
2. (a) $H \rightarrow R$ (b) $L \rightarrow M$ (c) $Q \wedge W \rightarrow S$
3. (a) T   (b) F   (c) T
4. (a) Economy is not improving and dollar is not being devalued.
   (b) The domestic production of oil increases, still we import crude oil.
   (c) Either the leader has no charisma or he has no diplomacy.
5. (a)

p	q	~p	~q	~p ∨ q	q ∨ ~q	p ∧ (q ∨ ~q)	(~p ∨ q) → p ∧ (q ∨ ~q)
T	T	F	F	T	T	T	T
T	F	F	T	F	T	T	T
F	T	T	F	T	T	F	F
F	F	T	T	T	T	F	F

   (b) Last column is TTFT

   (c) $P \vee (\neg P \wedge Q) \equiv P \vee Q$

6. (a) and (d) are contrapositives of each other. $\therefore a \equiv d$
   (b) and (c) are contrapositives of each other. $\therefore b \equiv c$
7. $a \equiv d$, $b \equiv c$
14. **Converse :** If I wear sweater, then it is cold weather.
    Inverse : If it is not cold weather, then I will not wear sweater.
15. **Converse :** If I go to clinic, then I am not in good health.
    Inverse : If I am in good health, then I win not go to clinic.
16. (a) **Converse :** If I win the race, then I run fast.
    Inverse : If I do not run fast, then I cannot with the race.
    Contrapositive : If I cannot win the race, then I don't run fast.
    (b) **Converse :** $q \Rightarrow \sim p$
    Inverse : $p \Rightarrow \sim q$
    Contrapositive : $\sim q \Rightarrow p$

17. (a) F   (b) T

18. **Converse :** If my insurance company pays me then the flood destroys my house or the fire destroys my house.

    Contrapositive : If my insurance company does not pay me, then the flood does not destroy my house and the fire does not destroy my house.

20. (a) No   (b) No

3.3 ARGUMENT AND VALIDITY

In this section, we begin our discussion with the following examples :

Consider the following sequences of propositions.

(i) If I were a movie star, then I would be famous.

But; I am not a movie star. Therefore, I am not famous.

(ii) If it is a Lux soap then it is a good soap.

It is a Lux soap. Hence, it is a good soap.

(iii) If my brother stands first in the class, I give him a T-shirt.

Either he stood first or I was out of station. I did not give him a T-shirt.

Therefore, I was out of station.

In each of the above examples there is a sequence of propositions; which are divided into two parts. In the first part there are some hypothetical propositions. They are called 'hypothesis' or 'premises'.

In the second part there is a proposition called 'conclusion'. It is some inference drawn from the premises.

The premises together with conclusion is called an 'argument'.

In the first example, above there are two premises viz.

'If I were a movie star, then I would be famous' and 'I am not a movie star'.

The conclusion is 'I am not famous' we write this argument as below.

If I were a movie star, then I would be famous.

I am not a movie star.
───────────────────────
∴   I am not famous.

We write the above argument symbolically as below.

Let   p : I were a movie star

         q : I would be famous

Then   ~p : I am not a movie star

         ~q : I am not famous.

Hence the argument is;

   p → q

   ~p
   ─────────
   ∴ ~q

The same is also written as,

   p → q, ¬p ⊢ ¬q

The symbol ⊢ is used for 'yields'.

In the second example,

Let p : It is a Lux soap

     q : It is a good soap

Then symbolically the argument is

   p → q

   p
   ─────────
   ∴ q

or p → q, p ⊢ q

Also in the third example,

Let   p : My brother stands first

       q : I give him a T-shirt

       r : I was out of station

Then ¬q : I did not give him a T-shirt. Therefore argument is

   p → q

   p ∨ r   or p → q, p ∨ r, ¬q ⊢ r

   ¬q
   ─────────
   ∴ r

Let now $P_1, P_2, \ldots, P_n \vdash C$ be an argument where each premise P_i; $1 \leq i \leq n$ and the conclusion C are functions of simple statements p, q, ..., r etc.

In an argument $P_1, P_2, \ldots, P_n \vdash C$ each premise P_i can have truth value either T or F.

Also the conclusion C can have value either T or F.

Definition : The argument $P_1, P_2, \ldots, P_n \vdash C$ is called **valid** argument if 'whenever all the premises are true then conclusion is also true'. Otherwise, it is called **invalid** argument.

It follows from the definition that 'if $P_1 \wedge P_2 \wedge \ldots \wedge P_n$ is true, then C is true' is the condition for argument to be valid.

Equivalently if the condition "$(P_1 \wedge P_2 \wedge \ldots \wedge P_n) \to C$ is a tautology" then the argument "$P_1, P_2, \ldots, P_n \vdash C$" is valid argument.

Illustration : Consider the argument $P \vee Q, \neg P \therefore Q$.

We prepare a truth table as below.

(1)	(2)	(3)	(4)
P	Q	P ∨ Q	¬P
T	T	T	F
T	F	T	F
F	T	T	T
F	F	F	T

From this table, we see that in the third row both the premises P ∨ Q and ¬P are true and the conclusion Q is also true.

Therefore, given argument is valid.

3.4 RULES OF INFERENCE

Consider the proposition $((P \vee Q) \wedge \neg P) \to Q$.

We can easily verify that this implication is a tautology.

P	Q	¬P	P ∨ Q	(P ∨ Q) ∧ ¬P	((P ∨ Q) ∧ ¬P) → Q
T	T	F	T	F	T
T	F	F	T	F	T
F	T	T	T	T	T
F	F	T	F	F	T

Such tautological propositions are called as 'Theorems' or 'Rules of Inference' in propositional calculus. We can use the rules of inference to establish the validity of argument (without preparing a truth table).

Below is the list of some rules of inference which are useful for our purpose of validity of arguments. The readers are supposed to verify these rules by truth table.

Inference Rules :

Sr. No.	Rule	Name of Rule
1.	$P \vee \neg P$	Excluded middle
2.	$P \leftrightarrow \neg \neg P$	Double negation
3.	$(P \wedge Q) \rightarrow P$	Separation
4.	$P \rightarrow (P \vee Q)$	Joining
5.	$(P \wedge (P \rightarrow Q)) \rightarrow Q$	Modus ponens or law of detachment
6.	$(P \rightarrow Q) \leftrightarrow (\neg Q \rightarrow \neg P)$	Contrapositive
7.	$((\neg P \rightarrow Q) \wedge (\neg P \rightarrow \neg Q)) \rightarrow P$	Proof by contradiction
8.	$((P \vee Q) \wedge \neg Q) \rightarrow P$	Disjunctive syllogism
9.	$(P \vee Q) \leftrightarrow (\neg P \rightarrow Q)$	Switcheroo
10.	$((P \rightarrow Q) \wedge (Q \rightarrow R)) \rightarrow (P \rightarrow R)$	Deduction
11.	$(((P \rightarrow Q) \wedge (R \rightarrow S)) \wedge (P \vee R)) \rightarrow (Q \vee S)$	Constructive dilemma
12.	$\neg (P \vee Q) \leftrightarrow (\neg P \wedge \neg Q)$	De Morgan's law
13.	$\neg (P \wedge Q) \leftrightarrow (\neg P \vee \neg Q)$	De Morgan's law
14.	$(P \rightarrow R) \vee (Q \rightarrow R) \equiv (P \wedge Q) \rightarrow R$	
15.	$(P \rightarrow R) \wedge (Q \rightarrow R) \equiv (P \vee Q) \rightarrow R$	
16.	$(P \rightarrow Q) \equiv \neg P \vee Q$	

Illustration : Test the validity of the following argument :

If it rains, then I wear a raincoat.

If it shines, then I do not need a sweater.

Either it rains or it shines.

Moreover, I do need a sweater.

Therefore, I wear a raincoat.

Solution : Let P : It rains
Q : It shines
R : I wear a raincoat
S : I need a sweater

Then given argument in symbolic form is

$$P \to R$$
$$Q \to \neg S$$
$$P \vee Q$$
$$S$$
$$\therefore R$$

$\therefore$ $Q \to \neg S$	$\therefore$ $S \to \neg Q$	$\because$ Contrapositive
$S, S \to \neg Q$	$\therefore$ $\neg Q$	$\because$ Detachment
$P \vee Q$ $\therefore$ $Q \vee P$	$\therefore$ $\neg Q \to P$	$\because$ $a \to b \equiv \sim a \vee b$
$\neg Q, \neg Q \to P,$	$\therefore$ P	$\because$ Detachment
$P, P \to R$	$\therefore$ R	$\because$ Detachment

Hence, the argument is valid.

3.5 METHODS OF PROOF

In the above illustration in which the argument involved two simple statements P and Q, we need to prepare a truth table involving $2^2 = 4$ rows and test the validity.

If the argument under consideration involves more than two atomic statements it is required to prepare reasonably a large table containing $2^3 = 8$ or $2^4 = 16$ rows etc.

Consider the following argument $P \to \neg Q, \neg R \vee Q, R \vdash \neg P$

3.5.1 Direct Method of Proof

We have the following truth table.

(1)	(2)	(3)	(4)	(5)	(6)	(7)	(8)
P	Q	R	¬P	¬Q	¬R	P → ¬Q	¬R ∨ Q
T	T	T	F	F	F	F	T
T	T	F	F	F	T	F	T
T	F	T	F	T	F	T	F
T	F	F	F	T	T	T	T
F	T	T	T	F	F	T	T
F	T	F	T	F	T	T	T
F	F	T	T	T	F	T	F
F	F	F	T	T	T	T	T

The premises P → ¬Q, ¬R ∨ Q and R are as shown in column (7) and column (8) and column (3) respectively. The conclusion ¬P is given by column (4).

Now in the 5th row of the table all three premises are true and conclusion is true. Therefore, given argument is valid.

3.5.2 Indirect Method of Proof

We can establish the validity of an argument in the above illustration, by a truth table containing 4 rows only (instead of 8 rows). For this we make use of contrapositive of given implication. We know that an implicative statement is logically equivalent to its contrapositive i.e. $(P \to Q) \equiv (\neg Q \to \neg P)$.

Now argument is valid means 'whenever all premises are true then conclusion is true'.

This is equivalent to its contrapositive which states as below.

The argument is valid means 'whenever conclusion is false, then at least one premise is false'.

By noting the above fact, we prepare a truth table in which the conclusion is false always.

In this table if we observe that in each row at least one premise is false, then we conclude that argument is valid.

Also if we observe that in some row all the premises are true, then argument is invalid.

In the above illustration, we assume that the conclusion ¬P is false i.e. P is true always. Then Q and R are free to assume any value. There are exactly 4 combinations of the values of Q and R. Thus, we prepare a table with 4 rows only.

P	Q	R	¬P	¬Q	¬R	P → ¬Q	¬R ∨ Q
T	T	T	F	F	F	F	T
T	T	F	F	F	T	F	T
T	F	T	F	T	F	T	F
T	F	F	F	T	T	T	T

This table shows that whenever conclusion ⌈P is false, at least one of the three premises viz. P → ¬ Q, ¬ R ∨ Q and R is false.

Hence, the argument is valid.

ILLUSTRATIVE EXAMPLES

Example 3.18 : By preparing truth table test the validity of the following argument :

(i) p ∨ q, ~q   ∴ p

(ii) (~p ∧ q) ∧ (q → p), p   ∴ p → ~q

(iii) I become famous or I will be a poet. I will not be a poet.

As a result, I will become famous.

(iv) Sudhir is either clever or lucky. Sudhir is not lucky.

If Sudhir is lucky, then he will win the lottery.

Therefore, Sudhir is clever.

Solution : (i)

p	q	~q	p ∨ q
T	T	F	T
T	F	T	T
F	T	F	T
F	F	T	F

In the second row of the table both the premises ~q and p ∨ q are true and the conclusion p is also true.

∴ Argument is valid.

(ii)

(1)	(2)	(3)	(4)	(5)	(6)	(7)	(8)
p	q	~p	~q	~p ∧ q	q → p	(~p ∧ q) ∧ (q → p)	p → ~q
T	T	F	F	F	T	F	F
T	F	F	T	F	T	F	T
F	T	T	F	T	F	F	T
F	F	T	T	F	T	F	T

Column (1) and column (7) show the two premises and column (8) shows the conclusion.

Both the premises are true, does not appear in any row.

Equivalently, when the conclusion is false (see first row) then at least one premise is false.

Therefore, argument is valid.

(iii) Let p : I become famous

q : I become poet

Then argument is, p ∨ q, ~q ∴ p

The truth table is as below.

p	q	~q	p ∨ q
T	T	F	T
T	F	T	T
F	T	F	T
F	F	T	F

In the second row of the table both the premises ~q and p ∨ q are true and the conclusion p is also true.

∴ Argument is valid.

(iv) Let p : Sudhir is clever
q : Sudhir is lucky
r : Sudhir wins lottery

The argument is, $p \vee q$, $\sim q$, $q \to r$ $\therefore p$

We prepare a table with $2^3 = 8$ rows.

p	q	r	~q	p ∨ q	q → r
T	T	T	F	T	T
T	T	F	F	T	F
T	F	T	T	T	T
T	F	F	T	T	T
F	T	T	F	T	T
F	T	F	F	T	F
F	F	T	T	F	T
F	F	F	T	F	T

(The last three columns above are the Premises.)

In the third row of the table all three premises are true and conclusion is also true.

∴ Argument is valid.

Example 3.19 : By preparing a truth table determine whether the following argument is valid or not.

$$((A \to B) \wedge (C \to D)), (\neg B \vee \neg D) \quad \therefore (\neg A \vee \neg C)$$

Solution : The given argument involves 4 statements A, B, C and D. So we have to prepare a truth table having $2^4 = 16$ rows. However this number 16 can be reduced to 4 rows only, as below.

Assume that the conclusion $\neg A \vee \neg C$ is false. Then $\neg(A \wedge C)$ is false.

∵ De Morgan's law

∴ $A \wedge C$ is true.

This happens only when both A and C have truth value T.

Also then B and D are free to assume any value.

∴ Truth table is as below.

A	B	C	D	¬B	¬D	A → B	C → D	(A → B) ∧ (C → D)	¬B ∨ ¬D
T	T	T	T	F	F	T	T	T	F
T	T	T	F	F	T	T	F	F	T
T	F	T	T	T	F	F	T	F	T
T	F	T	F	T	T	F	F	F	T

In this table in each row at least one premise is false.

∴ Argument is valid.

Example 3.20 : Show that the conclusion C is valid under the premises for the following without constructing truth table

$P_1 : \sim (A \land \sim B)$, $P_2 : \sim B \lor D$, $P_3 : \sim D$ ∴ $C : \sim A$

Solution : Given argument is, $\sim (A \land \sim B)$, $\sim B \lor D$, $\sim D$ ∴ $\sim A$

Now $\sim (A \land \sim B) \equiv \sim A \lor \sim \sim B \equiv \sim A \lor B$; De Morgan's law

$\sim B \lor D \equiv B \to D$

$\equiv \sim D \to \sim B$ ∵ Contrapositive

Then $\sim D$, $\sim D \to \sim B$

∴ $\sim B$ ∵ Law of detachment

Also, $\sim A \lor B \equiv A \to B$

$\equiv \sim B \to \sim A$ ∵ Contrapositive

$\sim B$, $\sim B \to \sim A$

∴ $\sim A$ ∵ Law of detachment

Hence, the argument is valid.

Note : This is direct method of establishing the validity.

Example 3.21 : Without constructing truth table, determine whether the conclusion C follows logically from the premises H_1, H_2, H_3 where

$H_1 : \neg P \lor Q$, $H_2 : \neg(Q \land \neg R)$, $H_3 : \neg R$, $C : \neg P$

Solution : $H_1 : \neg P \lor Q$

$\neg P \lor Q \equiv P \to Q$

$H_2 : \neg(Q \wedge \neg R)$

$\qquad \neg(Q \wedge \neg R) \equiv \neg Q \vee \neg \neg R \equiv \neg Q \vee R \equiv Q \rightarrow R$

Then $P \rightarrow Q, Q \rightarrow R \quad \therefore P \rightarrow R \qquad \because$ Deduction

Then $\qquad P \rightarrow R, \neg R$

$\therefore \qquad \neg R \rightarrow \neg P, \neg R$

$\therefore \qquad \neg R, \neg R \rightarrow \neg P$

$\therefore \qquad \neg P \qquad\qquad\qquad\qquad\qquad$ Law of detachment

Therefore argument is valid.

Example 3.22 : Without using truth table show that the conclusion C is valid from the premises H_1, H_2, H_3 where $H_1 : P \vee Q$, $H_2 : P \rightarrow R$, $H_3 : Q \rightarrow R$ and $C : R$

Solution : $(P \rightarrow R) \wedge (Q \rightarrow R) \equiv (P \vee Q) \rightarrow R$

Now, $(P \vee Q), ((P \vee Q) \rightarrow R)$

$\therefore \quad R \qquad\qquad\qquad$ by law of detachment

Therefore, argument is valid.

Example 3.23 : Establish the validity of the following arguments :

(i) $(A \rightarrow (B \rightarrow C)), B \quad \therefore A \rightarrow C$

(ii) $(R \rightarrow P), ((P \wedge Q) \vee R), (R \rightarrow Q) \quad \therefore P \wedge Q$

Solution : (i) Premises : $(A \rightarrow (B \rightarrow C)), B$

$B, B \rightarrow C \quad \therefore C \qquad\qquad\qquad\qquad \because$ Detachment

Then $\qquad A \rightarrow (B \rightarrow C) \equiv A \rightarrow C$; which is the conclusion.

Therefore, argument is valid.

(ii) Premises : $(R \rightarrow P), ((P \wedge Q) \vee R), (R \rightarrow Q)$

Now, $\qquad\qquad R \rightarrow P \equiv \neg P \rightarrow \neg R$

$\qquad\qquad\qquad R \rightarrow Q \equiv \neg Q \rightarrow \neg R$

$\therefore \qquad (R \rightarrow P) \wedge (R \rightarrow Q) \equiv (\neg P \rightarrow \neg R) \wedge (\neg Q \rightarrow \neg R)$

$\qquad\qquad\qquad\qquad\qquad \equiv (\neg P \vee \neg Q) \rightarrow \neg R$

$\qquad\qquad\qquad\qquad\qquad \equiv (\neg (P \wedge Q)) \rightarrow \neg R \qquad \because$ De Morgan's law

$\qquad\qquad\qquad\qquad\qquad \equiv (P \wedge Q) \vee (\neg R) \qquad\qquad\qquad \ldots (1)$

Also, $(P \wedge Q) \vee R$; given ... (2)

From equation (1) and (2), we get

$((P \wedge Q) \vee \neg R) \wedge ((P \wedge Q) \wedge R) \equiv (P \wedge Q) \vee (\neg R \wedge R)$ ∵ Distributive law
$\equiv (P \wedge Q) \vee F$
$\equiv P \wedge Q$ which is the conclusion.

Therefore, argument is valid.

Example 3.24 : Show the validity of the conclusion $\neg A \vee \neg D$ from the premises

$A \to (B \to C)$ and $D \to (B \wedge \neg C)$.

Solution : Assume that the conclusion $\neg A \vee \neg D$ is false.

∴ $\neg (A \wedge D)$ is false

∴ $A \wedge D$ is true

∴ $A \equiv T$ and $D \equiv T$

Now first premise is

$A \to (B \to C) \equiv \neg A \vee (B \to C) \equiv F \vee (B \to C)$
$\equiv B \to C \equiv \neg B \vee C$ ... (1)

Second premise is

$D \to (B \wedge \neg C) \equiv \neg D \vee (B \wedge \neg C) \equiv F \vee (B \wedge \neg C)$
$\equiv B \wedge \neg C = \neg (\neg B \vee C)$ ... (2)

From equation (1) and (2) at least one of them must be false.

Thus, when conclusion is false, at least one premise is false.

Therefore argument is valid.

Example 3.25 : Determine the validity of the argument.

If I study, then I will pass.

If I do not go to movie, then I will study.

I failed.

Therefore, I went to a movie.

Solution : Let   P : I study
Q : I pass
R : I go to movie

In symbolic form the argument is, $P \to Q, \neg R \to P, \neg Q \quad \therefore R$

Now, $\quad P \to Q \equiv \neg Q \to \neg P$

$\quad\quad\quad \neg Q, \neg Q \to \neg P \quad \therefore \neg P \quad\quad\quad \because$ By law of detachment

$\quad\quad\quad \neg P, \neg R \to P$

$\therefore \quad\quad \neg P, \neg P \to R \quad\quad\quad\quad\quad\quad\quad \because$ Contrapositive

$\therefore \quad\quad R \quad\quad\quad\quad\quad\quad\quad\quad\quad\quad\quad\quad \because$ By law of detachment

Therefore, argument is valid.

Example 3.26 : Test the validity of the following argument :

If I study, the I will not fail in Mathematics.

If I do not play basket ball, then I will study.

But I failed in Mathematics.

Therefore, I must have played basket ball.

Solution : Let $\quad\quad$ P : I study

$\quad\quad\quad\quad\quad\quad\quad$ Q : I failed in Mathematics

$\quad\quad\quad\quad\quad\quad\quad$ R : I played basket ball

In symbolic form the argument is;

$\quad\quad\quad P \to \neg Q, \neg R \to P, Q \quad \therefore R$

Now $\quad P \to \neg Q \equiv Q \to \neg P \quad\quad\quad\quad\quad \because$ Contrapositive

$\quad\quad\quad Q, Q \to \neg P \quad \therefore \neg P \quad\quad\quad\quad\quad$ By law of detachment

$\quad\quad\quad \neg P, \neg R \to P$

$\therefore \quad\quad \neg P, \neg P \to R \quad\quad\quad\quad\quad\quad\quad \because$ Contrapositive

$\therefore \quad\quad R \quad\quad\quad\quad\quad\quad\quad\quad\quad\quad\quad\quad \because$ Law of detachment

$\therefore \quad$ Argument is valid.

Example 3.27 : Test the validity of the following argument :

If my plumbing plans do not meet the construction code, then I cannot build my house.

If I hire a licensed contractor, then my plumbing plans will meet the construction code.

I hire a licensed contractor. Therefore, I can build my house.

Solution : Let P : My plumbing plans meet the construction code

Q : I can build my house

R : I hire a licenced contractor.

Symbolically the argument is, $\neg P \to \neg Q$, $R \to P$, R $\therefore$ Q

We make use of contrapositive. Suppose the conclusion Q is false.

The variables P and R are free. The truth table is as below.

P	Q	R	$\neg P$	$\neg Q$	$\neg P \to \neg Q$	$R \to P$
T	F	T	F	T	T	T
T	F	F	F	T	T	T
F	F	T	T	T	T	F
F	F	F	T	T	T	T

The first row of truth table suggests that all three premises $\neg P \to \neg Q$, $R \to P$ and R are true but the conclusion Q is false.

Therefore, argument is invalid.

Example 3.28 : Test the validity of the following argument :

If I like Mathematics, then I will study.

Either I don't study or I pass Mathematics.

If I don't graduate, then I don't pass Mathematics.

Therefore, If I graduated, then I studied.

Solution : Let   P : I like Mathematics

Q : I study

R : I pass Mathematics

S : I become graduate

Then symbolically argument is, $P \to Q$, $\neg Q \vee R$, $\neg S \to \neg R$ $\therefore S \to Q$

We use the method of contrapositive. So suppose the conclusion $S \to Q$ is false. This happens when S is true and Q is false.

The variables P and R are free.

$\therefore$ Truth table consists of 4 rows.

P	Q	R	S	¬Q	¬R	¬S	P → Q	¬Q ∨ R	¬S → ¬R
T	F	T	T	T	F	F	F	T	T
T	F	F	T	T	T	F	F	T	T
F	F	T	T	T	F	F	T	T	T
F	F	F	T	T	T	F	T	T	T

In the 3rd and 4th row all premises are true and conclusion is false.

∴ Argument is invalid.

Example 3.29 : Test the validity of the following argument :

If there was a game, then swimming was impossible.

If they started on right time, then swimming was possible.

They started on right time.

Therefore, there was no game.

Solution : Let P : There was a game

Q : Swimming was possible

R : They started on right time.

In symbolic form the argument is, P → ¬Q, R → Q, R ∴ ¬P.

We shall prove in two ways that the argument is valid.

Use of Truth Table :

Assume that the conclusion ¬P is false. This means P is true. The variables Q and R are free. The truth table is as below.

P	Q	R	¬Q	P → ¬Q	R → Q
T	T	T	F	F	T
T	T	F	F	F	T
T	F	T	T	T	F
T	F	F	T	T	T

We see that when ¬P is false i.e. P is true then in each row at least one of three premises i.e. P → ¬Q, R → Q, R is false.

∴ Argument is valid.

Use of rules of inference :

R, R → Q   ∴ Q   By law of detachment

Q, P → ¬Q

∴   Q, Q → ¬P   ∵ Contrapositive

∴   ¬P   ∵ Law of detachment

Therefore, argument is valid.

Example 3.30 : Test the validity of the following argument :

If Lucy has bought a fur coat, then either she has robbed a bank or her rich uncle has died.

Her rich uncle has not died.

Therefore, if Lucy has not robbed a bank, she has not bought a fur coat.

Solution : Let   P : Lucy bought a fur coat
                      Q : Lucy robbed a bank
                      R : Her rich uncle died

Then symbolically the argument is, P → Q ∨ R, ¬R   ∴ ¬Q → ¬P

We use the method of contrapositive. So we assume that the conclusion ¬Q → ¬P is false.

This happens when ¬Q is true and ¬P is false i.e. when Q is false and P is true.

The variable R is free.

∴   Truth table consists of two rows only.

P	Q	R	Q ∨ R	P → (Q ∨ R)	¬S
T	F	T	T	T	F
T	F	F	F	F	T

In this table in each row at least one of the premise is false.

Therefore, argument is valid.

Example 3.31 : Examine the validity of the following argument :

If there is life on mars, then the experts are wrong and the government is lying.

If the government is lying, then the experts are right or there is no life on mars.

The government is lying.

Therefore, there is life on mars.

Solution : Let P : There is life on mars

Q : Experts are right

R : Government is lying

Then the given argument is symbolically, $P \to \neg Q \wedge R$, $R \to Q \vee \neg P$, R ∴ P

We use the method of contrapositive. Assume that the conclusion P is false.

Then the truth table is as below.

P	Q	R	¬P	¬Q	¬Q ∧ R	Q ∨ ¬P	R → Q ∨ ¬P	P → ¬Q ∧ R
F	T	T	T	F	F	T	T	T
F	T	F	T	F	F	T	T	T
F	F	T	T	T	T	T	T	T
F	F	F	T	T	F	T	T	T

From column (3), (8), (9) of the three premises R, $R \to Q \vee \neg P$ and $P \to \neg Q \wedge R$ we see that in the first and third row all the premises are true and the conclusion is false.

Therefore, argument is invalid.

Example 3.32 : Show that the following set of premises are inconsistent.

$$A \to (B \to C), D \to (B \wedge \neg C), \text{ and } A \wedge D$$

Solution : $A \to (B \to C) \equiv A \to (\neg B \vee C)$

$D \to (B \wedge \neg C) \equiv \neg (B \wedge \neg C) \to \neg D$

$\equiv \neg B \vee \neg \neg C \to \neg D$

$\equiv \neg B \vee C \to \neg D$

Now, $A \to (\neg B \vee C), (\neg B \vee C) \to \neg D$

∴ $A \to \neg D \equiv \neg A \vee \neg D$

$\equiv \neg (A \wedge D)$

This is inconsistent with $A \wedge D$.

Example 3.33 : Show that the following premises are inconsistent.

If Jack misses many classes through illness, then he fails in the examination.

If Jack fails in the examination then he is uneducated.

If Jack reads a lot of books, then he is educated.

Jack misses many classes through illness and reads a lot of books.

Solution : Let
- P : Jack misses many classes through illness
- Q : Jack fails in the examination
- R : Jack is uneducated
- S : Jack reads lot of books

Then symbolically given premises are $P \to Q$, $Q \to R$, $S \to \neg R$, $P \wedge S$.

Now $P \to Q$, $Q \to R$ $\therefore P \to R$ (Deduction)

and $S \to \neg R \equiv R \to \neg S$ $\because$ Contrapositive

Then $P \to R$, $R \to \neg S$

$\therefore \quad P \to \neg S$ $\because$ Deduction

$$P \to \neg S \equiv \neg P \vee \neg S$$
$$\equiv \neg (P \wedge S) \quad \text{De Morgan's law}$$

$P \wedge S$ and $\neg (P \wedge S)$ have opposite truth values.

Therefore, the given premises are inconsistent.

EXERCISE (3.2)

1. Prove by using (i) direct method and (ii) indirect method that the following argument is valid :

    $P \to \neg Q$, $Q \vee R$, P $\quad \therefore R$

2. Test the validity of the following argument :

    $R \to C$, $S \to \neg W$, $R \vee S$, $W \vdash C$

3. Test the validity of the following argument by using indirect method :

    $p \vee q$, $p \to r$, $\sim r \vdash q$

4. Give indirect proof of validity of the following argument :

    $P \vee \neg Q$, $\neg Q \to R$, $P \to S$, $\neg R$ $\quad \therefore S$

5. Test the validity of :
   (i) $\sim p \wedge q,\ r \to p,\ \sim r \to s,\ s \to t \vdash t$
   (ii) $r \to c,\ s \to \sim w,\ r \vee s,\ w \vdash c$
6. Test the validity of the following arguments :
   (i) $p \vee \sim q,\ r \to \sim q,\ q \vdash r$
   (ii) $R \to P,\ G \to M,\ P \vee M \to S,\ \neg S \vdash \neg (R \vee G)$
   (iii) $P \vee Q,\ Q \to R,\ P \to M,\ \neg M\ \ \therefore R \wedge (P \vee Q)$
7. Show that the conclusion C follows from the premises H_1 and H_2.
   $H_1 : B \wedge C,\ H_2 : (B \rightleftharpoons C) \to (H \vee G),\ C : G \vee H$
8. Use statement calculus to derive the following argument :
   $P,\ P \to (Q \to (R \wedge S)) \vdash (Q \to S)$
9. Test the validity of the following argument by using method of indirect proof :

   If my brother stands first in the class, then I give him T-shirt.

   Either he stood first or I was out of station.

   I did not give him T-shirt.

   Therefore conclusion is that I was out of station.
10. Test the validity of the following argument :
    (i) Team A will win the cricket match if and only if they are playing against team B.

    I team A does not win then team C will take away the trophy.

    Team C does not get the trophy.

    Hence, team A does not play against team B.

    (ii) Wages will increase only if there is inflation.

    If there is inflation, then the cost of living will increase. Wages will increase.

    Therefore, the cost of living will increase.

    (iii) Either Hari attends the lecture or he watches the movie.

    If Hari attends the lecture, then he will have a cup of coffee.

    Hari will go to hotel, if he watches the movie.

    Therefore, either Hari will have a cup of coffee or he will go to hotel.

(iv) If I clear my backlogs then I shall be allowed to go to the next class.

If I am not allowed to go to the next class then I will have to leave my studies.

However, I cleared my backlogs. Hence, I won't have to leave my studies.

(v) If I work, I cannot study.

Either I work or I pass in C.A.

I passed in C.A.

Therefore, I studied.

(vi) If Teena marries Rahul, she will be in Pune.

If Teena marries Ganesh, she will be in Mumbai.

If she is either in Pune or in Mumbai, she will definitely be settled in life.

But Teena is not settled in life.

Therefore, she did not marry Rahul or Ganesh.

(vii) The project will complete iff Prasanna does the field work fast. Either Prasanna does the field work fast or he reads a book. Prasanna does not read a book. Hence the project will be incomplete.

11. Show that the following statements are inconsistent :

If Mugdha does not take a course in Discrete Mathematics, then she will not graduate. If Mugdha does not graduate then she is not qualified for the job appointment. If Mugdha reads this book then she is qualified for the job appointment. Mugdha does not take a course in Discrete Mathematics however she reads this book.

ANSWERS (3.2)

2. Valid
3. Valid
5. (i) Valid   (ii) Valid
6. (i) Invalid   (ii) Valid   (iii) Invalid
9. Valid
10. (i) Invalid   (ii) Valid   (iii) Valid   (iv) Invalid   (v) Invalid   (vi) Valid
    (vii) Invalid

3.6 PREDICATES AND QUANTIFIERS

Consider the open sentence '$x + 4 = 10$'. We denote it by

$P(x) : x + 4 = 10$.

We cannot determine the truth value of $P(x)$ unless we assign some particular value to x.

Thus, when $x = 1$, $P(1) : 1 + 4 = 10$ has truth value F and when $x = 6$, the truth value of $P(6)$ is T.

In the above example $P(x) : x + 4 = 10$, x is called a variable and the property P : 'plus 4 equals to 10' is called predicate.

The predicate becomes a proposition after assigning some particular value to the variable, and P is a function of x.

It can be such that there are 2 or more variables appearing in the propositions.

For example, if $Q(x, y) : x + 3y = 10$ then $Q(1, 3) = 1 + 3 \times 3 = 1 + 9 = 10$.

∴ $Q(1, 3)$ has truth value T but, $Q(3, 1) = 3 + 3 \times 1 = 3 + 3 = 6 \neq 10$

∴ $Q(3, 1)$ has value F

Also if $R(x, y, z) : x^2 + y^2 = z^2$ then $R(3, 4, 5) \equiv 3^2 + 4^2 = 5^2$ i.e. $9 + 16 = 25$ i.e. $25 = 25$.

∴ $R(3, 4, 5)$ has value T but $R(1, 2, 3) : 1^2 + 2^2 = 3^2$ i.e. $1 + 4 = 9$ i.e. $5 = 9$ which is not true.

∴ $R(1, 2, 3)$ has value F.

A proposition involving n variables $x_1, x_2, ..., x_n$ is called 'n place' predicate.

In the above examples,

$P(x)$ is 1 place predicate, $Q(x, y)$ is 2 place predicate and $R(x, y, z)$ is 3 place predicate.

Quantifiers :

In order to determine the truth value of $P(x)$; for a specified value of x; the variable x is allowed to assume the values from some set. This set is called the 'universe of discourse' or 'domain of discourse'.

For example, consider $P(x) : 2x < 5$ and the universe of discourse is the set

$$S = \{1, 2, 3, 4, 5\}$$

As x varies in S, we observe that

$P(1) : (2)(1) < 5$ i.e. $2 < 5$ is T

$P(2) : (2)(2) < 5$ i.e. $4 < 5$ is T

But $P(3) : (2)(3) < 5$ i.e. $6 < 5$ is F

Similarly, $P(4)$ and $P(5)$ have value F.

Again let $Q(x, y) : x + y$ is odd, and the universe of discourse is $S = \{1, 2, 3, 4, 5\}$.

Then x and y can assume the values from S.

We have $Q(2, 3) : 2 + 3$ is odd i.e. 5 is odd.

It is true statement.

But $Q(1, 3) : 1 + 3$ is odd i.e. 4 is odd.

It is false statement.

In the first example above, there is at least one value of x in the set S; which satisfies the required property $2x < 5$. In fact in our example, there are 2 values of x viz. 1 and 2.

In verbal language we write this situation as below.

'There exists at least one $x \in S$ such that $2x < 5$ holds'.

We write this symbolically as below.

We use the symbol $\exists$ for 'there exists'.

Then symbolically above statement can be written as '$\exists x\, P(x)$'.

This symbol $\exists$ is called 'existential quantifier'.

Illustration : Suppose the universe of discourse is the set $S = \{1, 2, 3\}$ and for $x \in S$; $P(x) : 2x + 1$ is a perfect square.

Then $P(1) : (2)(1) + 1 = 3$ is a perfect square which is not true.

∴ $P(1)$ is false.

In the same manner $P(2)$ and $P(3)$ are false statements.

In this example there is no $x \in S$ for which the property $P(x)$ holds. Therefore the quantification $\exists x\, P(x)$ has the truth value F.

Now with the same universal set S = {1, 2, 3}

Let Q(x) : 2x + 3 is a perfect square.

Then Q(1) is false since (2) (1) + 3 = 2 + 3 = 5 which is not a perfect square.

Also Q(2) is false since (2) (2) + 3 = 4 + 3 = 7 which is not a perfect square.

However, when x = 3, we have Q(3) : (2) (3) + 3 = 6 + 3 = 9; which is a perfect square.

Therefore Q(3) is true.

Thus, there exists at least one x in the universe of discourse S such that Q(x) holds.

∴ The quantification $\exists x\ Q(x)$ has truth value T.

Note : From the algebra of propositions, we know that if $p_1, p_2, \ldots, p_n$ are n statements, then their disjunction $p_1 \vee p_2 \vee \ldots \vee p_n$ has true value T iff at least one p_i has truth value T.

It then immediately follows that,

If the universe of discourse is the finite set $S = \{x_1, x_2, \ldots, x_n\}$, then the existential quantification $\exists x\ P(x)$ has truth value T iff at least one of $P(x_1)$, $P(x_2), \ldots, P(x_n)$ has truth value T.

Next we introduce another quantifier called universal quantifier. We consider the following example from our everyday life.

Suppose the universe of discourse is the set S of 2 staired houses; in a certain area of the city. Now for x ∈ S [i.e. x is a 2-staired house].

Let P(x) : x has electric bulb operated by two switches.

We know that in a 2 staired house always there is a bulb in the staircase which is operated by two switches, one switch located at the ground floor and the other switch located at the first floor.

In this case, we see that the property holds for all members of the set S.

Symbolically, we write this as $\forall x\ P(x)$ [or (x) P(x)] and read as 'for every x, P(x)'.

The symbol $\forall$ is called universal quantifier.

Illustration : Suppose the universe of discourse is the set S = {1, 2, 3}.

Let $P(x) : x^3 < 30$ and $Q(x) : x^3 < 25$.

Firstly, consider the truth value of P(x).

For x = 1, $P(1) : 1^3 < 30$ i.e. 1 < 30. It is true.

For x = 2, $P(2) : 2^3 < 30$ i.e. 8 < 30, it is true.

Finally for x = 3, $P(3) : 3^3 < 30$ i.e. 27 < 30, it is true.

Thus, P(x) is true for all x ∈ S.

Symbolically, we have $\forall x\ P(x)$ has the truth value T.

Now, consider the truth value of Q(x).

    For x = 1, $Q(1) : 1^3 < 25$ i.e. 1 < 25; it is true.

    For x = 2, $Q(2) : 2^3 < 25$ i.e. 8 < 25; it is true.

    For x = 3, $Q(3) : 3^3 < 25$ i.e. 27 < 25; it is false.

We see that the property Q(x) does not hold for all x ∈ S.

For some values of x ∈ S; Q(x) is true but not for all values of x ∈ S.

Symbolically, we write $\forall (x)\ Q(x)$ has truth value F.

Example 3.34 : What is the truth value of $\exists x\ (x^2 \leq x)$ if the domain consists of all real numbers ? What is the truth value of this statement if the domain consists of all integers ? Justify.

Solution : Consider $\exists x\ (x^2 \leq x)$ and x is a real number. We note that for any real number from 0 to 1, $x^2 \leq x$.

For example,   x = 0, $x^2 = 0$ ∴ $x^2 = x$

                       $x = \frac{1}{2}, x^2 = \frac{1}{4}$ ∴ $x^2 < x$

                       x = 1, $x^2 = 1$ ∴ $x^2 = x$

Given statement is true. Again $\exists x\ (x^2 \leq x)$ and x is integer

                       x = 0, $x^2 = 0$ ∴ $x^2 = x$

                       x = 1, $x^2 = 1$ ∴ $x^2 = x$

Given statement is true.

Note : From the algebra of propositions, we note that if $p_1, p_2, \ldots, p_n$ are n statements, then their conjunction $p_1 \wedge p_2 \wedge \ldots \wedge p_n$ has truth value T iff each p_i has truth value T.

It then follows that if the universe of discourse is the set $S = \{x_1, x_2, \ldots, x_n\}$ then the universal quantification $\forall x\, P(x)$ has truth value T iff each of $P(x_1), P(x_2), \ldots, P(x_n)$ has truth value T.

Example 3.35 : Suppose that the universe of discourse of the propositional function P(x) is the set $S = \{-2, -1, 0, 1, 2\}$ write each of the following propositions using disjunction, conjunction and negation.

(a) $\exists x\, P(x)$ (b) $\forall x\, P(x)$ (c) $\exists x\, \neg P(x)$ (d) $\forall x\, \neg P(x)$

Solution : We know that if the universe of discourse is the set $S = \{x_1, x_2, \ldots, x_n\}$ then

$$\exists x\, P(x) \equiv P(x_1) \vee P(x_2) \vee \ldots \vee P(x_n)$$

and

$$\forall x\, P(x) \equiv P(x_1) \wedge P(x_2) \wedge \ldots \wedge P(x_n)$$

(a) $\exists x\, P(x) \equiv P(-2) \vee P(-1) \vee P(0) \vee P(1) \vee P(2)$

(b) $\forall x\, P(x) \equiv P(-2) \wedge P(-1) \wedge P(0) \wedge P(1) \wedge P(2)$

(c) $\exists x\, \neg P(x) \equiv \neg P(-2) \vee \neg P(-1) \vee \neg P(0) \vee \neg P(1) \vee \neg P(2)$

(d) $\forall x\, \neg P(x) \equiv \neg P(-2) \wedge \neg P(-1) \wedge \neg P(0) \wedge \neg P(1) \wedge \neg P(2)$

Restricted Domain :

In some instances, we need to restrict the domain to some elements in it, by avoiding the remaining ones.

Consider the following situation. The universe of discourse is the set of all those students who have passed XII science examination. Some of these students may not have offered Mathematics as one of their subjects. Such students are not eligible to apply for engineering degree course admission. So we restrict our domain to those students who have offered Mathematics as one of their subjects at the XII science examination.

Let now P(x) : x applied for admission for engineering degree course.

We write this situation symbolically as below.

$\forall x$, (x offered Mathematics) P(x).

Here the condition 'x offered Mathematics' appears immediately to the right of quantifier.

The meaning of this symbolic statement is that all those students who have offered Mathematics can apply for admission to engineering degree course.

Equivalently 'if x has offered Mathematics then he can apply for admission'.

Thus, the restriction of a universal quantification is universal quantification of a conditional statement.

$$\boxed{\forall x \text{ (condition) } (P(x)) \equiv \forall x \text{ (condition} \rightarrow P(x))}$$

In the above problem, we note that there is at least one student who has offered Mathematics and applied for the admission. Symbolically this is written as :

∃x, (x offered Mathematics) (x applied for admission)

Thus, the restriction of existential quantification is equivalent to existential quantification of the conjunction of the condition and P(x).

$$\boxed{\exists x \text{ (condition) } (P(x)) \equiv \exists x \text{ (condition} \wedge P(x))}$$

Example 3.36 : Explain the meaning of the following; assuming that the universe of discourse is the set of real numbers.

(a) $\forall x < 0 \ (x^2 > 0)$

(b) $\forall x \neq 0 \ (x^3 \neq 0)$

(c) $\exists x > 0 \ (x^2 = 3)$

Solution : We know that,

$\forall x$ (condition) $P(x) \equiv \forall x$ (condition $\rightarrow P(x)$)

and $\exists x$ (condition) $P(x) \equiv \exists x$ (condition $\wedge P(x)$)

(a) $\quad \forall x < 0 \ (x^2 > 0) \equiv \forall x \ (x < 0) \ (x^2 > 0)$

$\equiv \forall x \ [(x < 0) \rightarrow x^2 > 0]$

In words 'the square of any negative number is positive'.

(b) $\quad \forall x \neq 0 \ (x^3 \neq 0) \equiv \forall x \ (x \neq 0) \ (x^3 \neq 0)$

$\equiv \forall x \ [(x \neq 0) \rightarrow (x^3 \neq 0)]$

In words 'the cube of non-zero real number is non-zero'.

(c) $\quad \exists x > 0\ (x^2 = 3) \equiv \exists x\ (x > 0)\ (x^2 = 3)$
$\quad\quad\quad\quad\quad\quad\quad \equiv \exists x\ [(x > 0) \wedge (x^2 = 3)]$

In words 'there is a positive real number whose square is 3'.

Note : We know that in the algebra of real numbers while evaluating the given arithmetic expression, we perform the arithmetic operations in a particular order 'BEDMAS'. It is called hierarchy of operations.

B : bracket evaluation, E : exponentiation, D : division, M : multiplication,

A : addition, S : subtraction.

For example, $(2 + 3 \times 4) - 4^3 + 12 \div 4 = (2 + 12) - 64 + 3 = 14 - 64 + 3 = 17 - 64 = -47$

In the algebra of propositions while evaluating logical expression the top priority goes to quantifiers $\forall$ and $\exists$.

Thus, $\forall x\ P(x) \wedge Q(x)$ means $(\forall x\ P(x)) \wedge Q(x)$.

It is different from $\forall x\ (P(x) \wedge Q(x))$.

Similarly, $\exists x\ P(x) \vee Q(x)$ means $(\exists x\ P(x)) \vee Q(x)$; and it is different from $\exists x\ (P(x) \vee Q(x))$.

Binding Variables :

In the logical expression, when a quantifier is used on the variable x, we say that this occurrence of the variable is bound. On the other hand the occurrence of a variable which is not bound by a quantifier nor it is assigned some particular value is described by saying that the variable is free.

In order to be able for us to determine the truth value of a propositional function it is quite necessary that all the variables appearing in it must be bound or they are assigned some particular value. This is achieved with the help of universal quantifiers, existential quantifiers and the value assignments.

In the logical expression that part to which a quantifier is applied is called 'scope' of that quantifier.

In the statement $\exists x\ (x + y = 5)$ the variable x is bound by the existential quantifier $\exists x$. The variable y is not bound by any quantifier nor that y is assigned any particular value. So y is free variable.

Also in $\forall x\, (P(x) \lor Q(x)) \land \exists x\, R(x)$ the scope of $\forall x$ is $P(x) \lor Q(x)$ and the scope of $\exists x$ is $R(x)$.

Let now P and Q be two statements involving quantifiers and predicates. We say that P is logically equivalent to Q and write $P \equiv Q$ if and only if they have the same truth value irrespective of the predicates substituted in them and irrespective of the universe of discourse.

We show that $\forall x\, (P(x) \land Q(x)) \equiv \forall x\, P(x) \land \forall x\, Q(x)$.

In words 'the universal quantifier distributes over the conjunction.

Let $P(x)$ and $Q(x)$ be two given statements. Without any loss, we can assume that the universe of discourse is the same for both $P(x)$ and $Q(x)$.

We establish the equivalence by considering two parts.

In the first part, we assume that $\forall x\, (P(x) \land Q(x))$ has truth value T and show that

$\forall x\, P(x) \land \forall x\, Q(x)$ has truth value T.

In the second part, we assume that $\forall x\, P(x) \land \forall x\, Q(x)$ has truth value T and prove that $\forall x\, (P(x) \land Q(x))$ has truth value T.

First Part : $\forall x\, (P(x) \land Q(x))$ has truth value T (assumption).

Then if a is any element in the universe of discourse, we have $P(a) \land Q(a)$ is true.

∴ $P(a)$ is true and $Q(a)$ is true.

Now $P(a)$ is true and $Q(a)$ is true, this holds for every a in the universe of discourse.

∴ $\forall x\, P(x)$ is true and

$\forall(x)\, Q(x)$ is true.

∴ $\forall x\, P(x) \land \forall x\, Q(x)$ is true.

Second Part : Assume that $\forall x\, P(x) \land \forall x\, Q(x)$ is true.

Then, $\forall x\, P(x)$ is true and

$\forall x\, Q(x)$ is true.

∴   If a is any element in the universe of discourse, then $P(a)$ is true and $Q(a)$ is true.

∴   for all a, $P(a) \land Q(a)$ is true.

∴ $\forall x\, (P(x) \land Q(x))$ is true.

This completes the proof and we have

$$\forall x(P(x) \land Q(x)) \equiv (\forall x\, P(x)) \land (\forall x\, Q(x))$$

Note : The generalization to more than two propositions is possible i.e.

$$\forall x\, (P_1(x) \wedge P_2(x) \wedge \ldots \wedge P_n(x)) \equiv (\forall x\, P_1(x)) \wedge \ldots \wedge (\forall x\, P_n(x))$$

Note : The universal quantifier does not distribute over disjunction. For this, suppose the universe of discourse is the set S = {3, 5, 16, 19, 25}.

Let $\qquad$ P(x) : x is odd

and $\qquad$ Q(x) : x is a perfect square

Then P(x) ∨ Q(x) is the statement 'x is odd or perfect square'.

We have $\forall x\, (P(x) \vee Q(x))$ is true since each member of S is odd or a perfect square.

But $\forall x\, P(x)$ is false because 16 ∈ S is not odd.

Also $\forall x\, Q(x)$ is false because 5 ∈ S and 5 is not a perfect square.

∴ $(\forall x\, P(x)) \vee (\forall x\, Q(x))$ has truth value F ∨ F ≡ F.

Therefore $\forall x\, (P(x) \vee Q(x))$ and $\forall x\, P(x) \vee \forall x\, Q(x)$ are not logically equivalent.

Negation of Quantified Expression :

Consider the statement :

'All students in the class passed in the Discrete Mathematics course'.

Symbolically it is $\forall x\, P(x)$.

Clearly we cannot say that the negation of the above statement is 'all students in the class failed in Discrete Mathematics course'.

We note that if at least one student in the class failed in Discrete Mathematics course then we cannot say all students in the class passed.

Thus 'all students passed' and 'at least one student failed' have opposite truth values.

Now 'at least one student failed' is symbolically $\exists x\, \neg P(x)$.

∴ $\qquad \neg \forall x\, P(x) \equiv \exists x\, \neg P(x)$.

Consider now the universe of discourse S = {1, 2, 3, 4, 5}.

Let P(x) : x is a perfect square.

The statement $\exists x\, P(x)$ has truth value T since at least one member i.e. 4 ∈ S is a perfect square.

The corresponding statement whose truth value is F will be as below.

No element of S is a perfect square i.e. every element in S is a non-square quantity. Symbolically it is $\forall x \neg P(x)$.

Thus, $\neg \exists x\, P(x) \equiv \forall x \neg P(x)$

Illustration :

(a) Let P(x) be the statement.

P(x) : For every positive integer x, $x^2 + 41x + 41$ is a prime number.

Symbolically it can be written as $\forall x\, P(x)$.

Now, negation of the above statement is

$\neg \forall x\, P(x) \equiv \exists x \neg P(x)$

In words 'there is at least one positive integer x for which $x^2 + 41x + 41$ is not a prime number.

(b) Let Q(x) be the statement.

Q(x) : There is some integer x for which $4x = 20$.

Symbolically it can be written as $\exists x\, Q(x)$.

Now negation of the above statement is

$\neg \exists x\, Q(x) \equiv \forall x \neg Q(x)$

For every integer x, $4x \neq 20$.

ILLUSTRATIVE EXAMPLES

Example 3.37 : Let P(x), Q(x), R(x) be the statements 'x is a clear explanation', 'x is satisfactory' and 'x is an acuse'.

Suppose that the universe of discourse for x is the set of all English texts. Express each of the following statements using quantifiers :

(a) All clear explanations are satisfactory.

(b) Some excuses are not clear explanations.

Solution : (a) $\forall x\, (P(x) \to Q(x))$

(b) $\exists x\, (R(x) \to \neg Q(x))$

Example 3.38 : If the universe of discourse is the set {a, b, c}, eliminate the quantifiers in the following formulae :

(a) $(x)(P(x) \to Q(x))$

(b) $(x) R(x) \lor (\exists x) S(x)$

Solution : (a) Given statement $(x)(P(x) \to Q(x))$ is $\forall x (P(x) \to Q(x))$

$\equiv (P(a) \to Q(a)) \land (P(b) \to Q(b)) \land (P(c) \to Q(c))$

(b) Given statement $(x) R(x) \lor (\exists x) S(x)$ is $\forall x R(x) \lor (\exists x) S(x)$

$\equiv [R(a) \land R(b) \land R(c)] \lor [S(a) \lor S(b) \lor S(c)]$

Example 3.39 : Indicate the variables that are free and bound and scope of the quantifiers.

(a) $(P(x) \land (\exists x) Q(x)) \lor ((\forall x) P(x) \to Q(x))$

(b) $(\forall x) R(x) \land (\forall x) S(x)$

Solution : (a) The variable x is bound by the quantifiers $\exists x$ and $\forall x$.

Scope of $\exists x$ is $Q(x)$.

Scope of $\forall x$ is $P(x)$.

(b) Given statement is $\forall x R(x) \land (\forall x) S(x)$ which is equivalent to $\forall x (R(x) \land S(x))$.

The variable x is bound by the quantifier $\forall x$.

The scope of $\forall x$ is $R(x) \land S(x)$.

Example 3.40 : Let $P(x, y)$ denote '$x + y = 0$'.

Find the truth values of quantifications $\exists y \forall x P(x, y)$ and $\forall x \exists y P(x, y)$; the universe of discourse being the set of all real numbers.

Solution : The quantification $\exists y \forall x P(x, y)$ says that there exists a value of y such that for any real value of x, $x + y = 0$ holds.

For a given value of y there is only one value of x viz. $x = -y$ satisfying $x + y = 0$.

Therefore, the value of the quantification $\exists y \forall x P(x, y)$ is F.

Next, consider $\forall x \exists y P(x, y)$. This quantification says that for every real value of x, we can find y such that $x + y = 0$.

We note that if x is any real number then $y = -x$ satisfies $x + y = 0$.

Therefore the value of the quantification $\forall x \exists y P(x, y)$ is T.

Example 3.41 : Write each of the following propositions using quantifiers and predicates.

(a) A man qualifies for the marathon if his best previous time is less than 3 hours and a woman qualifies for the marathon if her best previous time is less than 3.5 hours.

(b) x is father of mother of y.

Solution : (a) We write $M(x)$: x is a male person. Then $\neg M(x)$: x is a female person.

Let $T(x, y)$: A person x has best previous time less than y hours.

Let $Q(x)$: Person x is qualified for the marathon.

Then symbolic form of the given proposition is

$$\forall x\,(((M(x) \wedge T(x, 3)) \vee (\neg M(x) \wedge T(x, 3.5))) \to Q(x))$$

(b) Consider $P(x)$: x is person

$F(x, y)$: x is father of y.

$M(x, y)$: x is mother of y.

Then the given proposition 'x is father of mother of y' is in symbolic form

$$\exists x\, \exists y\, \exists z\; F(x, z) \wedge M(z, y)$$

Example 3.42 : Write the negation of the following statements :

(a) All roses in the garden are either pink or white.

(b) For some real numbers x and y, $x^2 - y^4$ is negative.

Solution : (a) Let $\quad P(x)\;:\;$ Rose is pink

$\qquad\qquad\qquad Q(x)\;:\;$ Rose is white

Then given statement in symbolic form is $\forall x\, (P(x) \vee Q(x))$.

Its negation is

$$\neg\, \forall x\, (P(x) \vee Q(x)) \equiv \exists x\, \neg\, (P(x) \vee Q(x))$$
$$\equiv \exists x\, ((\neg P(x)) \wedge \neg Q(x))$$

i.e. there is at least one rose in the garden, which is neither pink nor white.

(b) In symbolic form the given statement is $\exists x \, \exists y \, (x^2 - y^4 < 0)$.

Its negation is

$$\neg \exists x \, \exists y \, (x^2 - y^4 < 0) \equiv \forall x \, \neg \exists y \, (x^2 - y^4 < 0)$$
$$\equiv \forall x \, \forall y \, \neg (x^2 - y^4 < 0)$$
$$\equiv \forall x \, \forall y \, (x^2 - y^4 \geq 0)$$

In words, for any two real numbers x and y, $x^2 - y^4 \geq 0$.

Example 3.43 : Write the negation of :

(a) $\exists x \, (P(x) \wedge \neg Q(x))$

(b) $\exists x \, P(x) \wedge \neg Q(x)$

(c) $\forall x \, (P(x) \wedge Q(x))$

(d) $\forall x \, (P(x) \to Q(x))$

Solution : (a) Given statement is $\exists x \, (P(x) \wedge \neg Q(x))$

$$\neg \exists x \, (P(x) \wedge \neg Q(x)) \equiv \forall x \, \neg (P(x) \wedge \neg Q(x))$$
$$\equiv \forall x \, (\neg P(x) \vee \neg \neg Q(x)) \quad \because \text{De Morgan's law}$$
$$\equiv \forall x \, (\neg P(x) \vee Q(x)) \quad \because \text{Double negation}$$

(b) Given statement is $\exists x \, P(x) \wedge \neg Q(x)$

$$\neg [\exists x \, P(x) \wedge \neg Q(x)] \equiv \neg \exists x \, P(x) \vee \neg \neg Q(x) \quad \because \text{De Morgan's law}$$
$$\equiv \forall x \, (\neg P(x)) \vee Q(x)$$

(c) Given statement is $\forall x \, (P(x) \wedge Q(x))$

$$\neg \forall x \, (P(x) \wedge Q(x)) \equiv \exists x \, \neg (P(x) \wedge Q(x))$$
$$\equiv \exists x \, (\neg P(x) \vee \neg Q(x))$$

(d) Given statement is $\forall x \, (P(x) \to Q(x))$

$$\neg \forall x \, (P(x) \to Q(x)) \equiv \neg \forall x \, (\neg P(x) \vee Q(x)) \quad \because p \to q \equiv \sim p \vee q$$
$$\equiv \exists x \, \neg (\neg P(x) \vee Q(x))$$
$$\equiv \exists x \, (\neg \neg P(x) \wedge \neg Q(x))$$
$$\equiv \exists x \, (P(x) \wedge \neg Q(x)) \quad \because \text{Double negation}$$

Example 3.44 : Express the negation of the following propositions using quantifiers. Then write the negation in verbal language :

(a) There is some one in this class who does not have a good attitude.

(b) No one can keep a secret.

Solution : (a) Let the universe of discourse be the set of all students in a class and P(x) : x has a good attitude.

Then symbolically given statement is $\exists x\, (\neg P(x))$.

Its negation is

$$\neg \exists x\, (\neg P(x)) \equiv \forall x\, \neg (\neg P(x))$$
$$\equiv \forall x\, P(x) \because \text{By double negation}$$

In words 'All students in the class have a good attitude'.

(b) Let the universe of discourse be the set of all people and P(x) : x keeps a secret.

Then the given proposition in symbolic form is $\forall x\, (\neg P(x))$

Its negation is

$$\neg \forall x\, (\neg P(x)) \equiv \exists x\, \neg (\neg P(x))$$
$$\equiv \exists x\, P(x) \because \text{By double negation}$$

In words 'there is at least one person who keeps the secret'.

This can also be described by saying that 'some persons keep secret'.

Example 3.45 : Prove that, $\exists x\, (P(x) \vee Q(x)) \equiv (\exists x\, P(x)) \vee (\exists x\, Q(x))$ i.e. the existential quantifier distributes over disjunction.

Give example to show that $\exists x\, (P(x) \wedge Q(x))$ and $\exists x\, P(x) \wedge \exists x\, Q(x)$ are not logically equivalent.

Solution : Let P(x) and Q(x) have the same universe of discourse. We establish the equivalence

$$\exists x\, (P(x) \vee Q(x)) \equiv (\exists x\, P(x)) \vee (\exists x\, Q(x))$$

By proving that whenever left side expression has value F, right side expression has value F. Further whenever right side expression has value F, then left side expression has value F.

First Part : Suppose $\exists x\, (P(x) \vee Q(x))$ has value F. Then for some a in the universe of discourse, we have $P(a) \vee Q(a)$ has value F.

∴   P(a) has value F and Q(a) has value F.

∴ $\exists x\, P(x)$ has value F and $\exists x\, Q(x)$ has value F.

∴ $\exists x\, P(x) \vee \exists x\, Q(x)$ has value F.

Second Part : Assume that $\exists x\, P(x) \vee \exists x\, Q(x)$ has value F.

Then $\exists x\, P(x)$ has value F and $\exists x\, Q(x)$ has value F.

∴ $P(a)$ is F and $Q(a)$ is F for some a in the universe of discourse.

∴ $P(a) \vee Q(a)$ is F.

∴ $P(x) \vee Q(x)$ is F for some x.

∴ $\exists x\, (P(x) \vee Q(x))$ is F.

The proof is complete and we have

$$\exists x\, (P(x) \vee Q(x)) \equiv \exists x\, P(x) \vee \exists x\, Q(x)$$

Now consider the following example $S = \{1, 2, 3, \ldots, 10\}$ is the universe of discourse.

Let $P(x)$: x is divisible by 3

and $Q(x)$: x is divisible by 4.

The elements $3, 6, 9 \in S$ are divisible by 3.

∴ $\exists P(x)$ is true.

Also $4, 8 \in S$ are divisible by 4.

∴ $\exists x\, Q(x)$ is true.

Hence $(\exists x\, P(x)) \wedge (\exists x\, Q(x))$ is $T \wedge T \equiv T$.

Next we note that there is no element $x \in S$ which is divisible by 3 and 4 both.

∴ $\exists x\, (P(x) \wedge Q(x))$ has value F.

Thus, $\exists x\, (P(x) \wedge Q(x))$ and $\exists x\, P(x) \wedge \exists x\, Q(x)$ do not possess identical truth values.

∴   These two propositions are not logically equivalent.

Example 3.46 : Let $P(x)$, $Q(x)$, $R(x)$ be the statements 'x is a professor', x is ignorant' and 'x is vain' respectively. Express the following statements using quantifiers :

(a) No professors are ignorant.

(b) All ignorant people are vain.

Solution : The universe of discourse is $S = \{$all people$\}$. The given problem is that of restricted domain.

(a) Given statement is 'No professors are ignorant'. This means if a person x is a professor then he/she is not ignorant.

Here 'x is a professor' is a condition and this condition implies 'x is not ignorant', we know that

$$\forall x \text{ (condition)} \land (x) \equiv \forall x \text{ (condition} \to A(x))$$

∴ $\forall x$ (x is a professor → x is not ignorant)

$$\equiv \forall x \text{ (x is a professor) (x is not ignorant)}$$
$$\equiv \forall x \, (P(x)) \, (\neg Q(x))$$

(b) Given statement is 'all ignorant people are vain'.

This means 'if a person is ignorant then he/she is vain'.

Here 'a person is ignorant' is the condition and this condition implies 'a person is vain'.

We know that,

$$\forall x \text{ (condition) } (A(x)) \equiv \forall x \text{ (condition} \to A(x))$$

∴ $\forall x$ (x is ignorant → x is vain) $\equiv \forall x$ (x is ignorant) (x is vain)

$$\equiv \forall x \, (Q(x)) \, (R(x))$$

EXERCISE (3.3)

1. In the universe of discourse **Z** of all integers, let P(x) : x is even, Q(x) : x is a prime number and R(x, y) : x + y is even.

   (a) Write the following as a sentence in English.

   (i) $\exists x \, \neg Q(x)$

   (ii) $\forall x \, P(x)$

   (iii) $\forall x \, \exists y \, R(x, y)$

   (iv) $\exists x \, \forall y \, R(x, y)$

   (b) Write each of the following by using quantifiers :

   (i) Every integer is an odd integer.

   (ii) The sum of any two integers is an even number.

   (iii) There are no even primes.

   (iv) Every integer is even or prime.

   (c) Find the values of P(2), P(3), Q(2), Q(6) and R(3, 4).

2. In the set of all integers, determine the truth value of
   (a) $\exists x\ (x^3 < 4)$
   (b) $\forall x\ (x^2 > 0)$
   (c) $\forall x\ (x > 4x)$
   (d) $\forall x\ (x^2 \geq x)$
   (e) $\exists x\ (x < -x)$

3. Let $P(x)$: x is a baby
   $Q(x)$: x is logical
   $R(x)$: x is able to manage crocodile
   $S(x)$: x is dispised.

   The universe of discourse consists of all people. Express the following using quantifiers.
   (a) Babies are illogical.
   (b) Nobody is dispised who can manage crocodile.
   (c) Illogical persons are dispised.
   (d) Babies cannot manage crocodile.

4. The universe of discourse is the set $U = \{1, 2, 3, 4, 5\}$
   Write truth set of the following predicates :
   (a) $\exists x\ ((x^2 - 3x + 2) = 0)$
   (b) $\forall x\ x^2 \geq 9$
   (c) $\forall x\ ((x^2 - 6x + 8 = 0) \wedge (x^2 - 5x + 4 = 0))$

5. Write the truth value of :
   (a) $\forall x\ P(x)$ and (b) $\exists x\ \neg P(x)$
   where $P(x)$: $x^2 < 25$ and the universe of discourse is the set of non-negative integers not greater than 5.

6. Let $D = \{1, 2, 3, 4\}$ be the domain of discourse. Eliminate the quantifier from each of the following :
   (a) $\forall x\ P(x)$
   (b) $\exists x\ P(x)$
   (c) $\neg \exists x\ P(x)$
   (d) $\exists x\ \neg P(x)$

7. If the universe of discourse is $\{a, b, c\}$, eliminate the quantifiers in the following :
   (a) $\forall x\ (P(x) \rightarrow Q(x))$
   (b) $\exists x\ R(x) \wedge (x)\ S(x)$

8. Over the set of integers, let

$$A(x, y) : x + y \text{ is even}$$
$$B(x) : x \text{ is a prime number}$$
$$C(x, y) : x + y \text{ is odd.}$$

Write the following into simple English sentences :

(a) $\forall x \exists y\, A(x, y)$ (b) $\forall x \exists y\, C(x, y)$

(c) $\forall x\, (\forall y\, C(x, y))$

9. Rewrite the following propositions using the symbols $\exists$ and $\forall$.

   (a) All elephants have trunks.

   (b) Every clever student is successful.

   (c) Some people know all the answers.

   (d) Only judges admire judges.

   (e) All good students study hard.

   (f) There is a triangle whose sum of angles is not equal to 180°.

10. Prove that $\neg\, \forall x\, (P(x) \rightarrow Q(x))$ is logically equivalent to $\exists x\, (P(x) \wedge \neg Q(x))$.

11. Prove that the following are tautologies :

    (a) $\exists x\, (P(x) \wedge Q(x)) \Rightarrow \exists x\, P(x) \wedge \exists x\, Q(x)$

    (b) $\forall x\, (P(x) \vee Q(x)) \Rightarrow [\forall x\, P(x)] \vee [\forall x\, Q(x)]$

12. Let $Q(x, y, z) : x + y = z$. What are the truth values of :

    (a) $\forall x\, \forall y\, \exists z\, Q(x, y, z)$?   (b) $\exists z\, \forall x\, \forall y\, Q(x, y, z)$?

    Assume that $x = 1, y = 2, z = 3$.

13. Let $Q(x, y)$: x has sent e-mail message to y; and the domain D = all students in the class. Express the following in words :

    (a) $\exists x\, \exists y\, Q(x, y)$ (b) $\exists x\, \forall y\, Q(x, y)$

    (c) $\forall x\, \exists y\, Q(x, y)$ (d) $\exists y\, \forall x\, Q(x, y)$

    (e) $\forall y\, \exists x\, Q(x, y)$ (f) $\forall x\, \forall y\, Q(x, y)$

14. Write the following sentences in predicate formula :

    (i) All that glitters is not gold.

    (ii) Some birds cannot fly.

15. Translate the following sentence in symbolic form. "Some lawyers who are politicians are not congressmen".

16. Using quantifiers symbolize the following; if the universe of discourse is the set of real numbers.

    (i) For any real value of x, x^2 is atmost equal to 10.

    (ii) There is some x such that $x^2 + 3x - 2 = 0$

    (iii) For any value of x, there is some value of y such that $x \cdot y = 1$.

    (iv) There is a value of x and y such that $x^2 + y^2$ is negative.

17. Let Q(x, y) be the statement "$x^2 = y - 3$". What are the truth values of the propositions Q(1, 2), Q(3, 0) and Q(2, 7).

ANSWERS (3.3)

1. (a) (i) There is some integer x, which is not prime.

    (ii) Every integer is even integer.

    (iii) For any value of x, we can find a value of y such that x + y is even.

    (iv) There is some integer x such that for every integer y, x + y is even integer.

   (b) (i) $\forall x \neg P(x)$

    (ii) $\forall x \forall y\, R(x, y)$

    (iii) $\neg (P(x) \wedge Q(x))$ or $\neg P(x) \vee \neg Q(x)$

    (iv) $\forall x\, (P(x) \vee Q(x))$

   (c) P(2) : 2 is even; T

    P(3) is F, Q(2) is T, Q(6) is F, R (3, 4) is F.

2. (a) T (b) F (c) F (d) T (e) T

3. (a) $\forall x\, (P(x) \rightarrow \neg Q(x))$

   (b) $\forall x \neg (R(x) \wedge S(x))$

   (c) $\forall x\, ((\neg Q(x)) \rightarrow S(x))$ or $\forall x\, (Q(x) \vee S(x))$

   (d) $\forall x\, (P(x) \rightarrow \neg R(x))$

4. (a) {1, 2} (b) {3, 4, 5} (c) {4}

5. (a) T (b) F

6. (a) $P(1) \wedge P(2) \wedge P(3) \wedge P(4)$

   (b) $P(1) \vee P(2) \vee P(3) \vee P(4)$

   (c) $(\neg P(1)) \wedge (\neg P(2)) \wedge (\neg P(3)) \wedge (\neg P(4))$

   (d) $(\neg P(1)) \vee (\neg P(2)) \vee (\neg P(3)) \vee (\neg P(4))$

7. (a) $[P(a) \rightarrow Q(a)] \wedge [P(b) \rightarrow Q(b)] \wedge [P(c) - Q(c)] [P(c) \rightarrow Q(c)]$

   i.e. $[\neg P(a) \vee Q(a)] \wedge [\neg P(b) \vee Q(b)] \wedge [\neg P(c) \vee Q(c)]$

   (b) $[R(a) \vee R(b) \vee R(c)] \wedge [S(a) \wedge S(b) \wedge S(c)]$

8. (a) If x is any given integer, we can find integer y such that the sum of x and y is even integer.

   (b) If x is any given integer, we can find integer y such that they add upto odd integer.

   (c) For all integers x and y their sum is odd integer.

9. (a) U = Set of all animals.

       P(x) : animal x is elephant

       Q(x) : animal x has trunk

   ∴ $\forall x (P(x) \rightarrow Q(x))$

   (b) U = Set of all students

       P(x) : student x is clever

       Q(x) : student x is successful

   ∴ $\forall x (P(x) \rightarrow Q(x))$

   (c) U = Set of all people

       P(x) : person x knows all answers

   ∴ $\exists x P(x)$

   (d) U = Set of all people

       P(x) : person x is a judge

       A(x, y) : x admires y.

   ∴ $\forall x \forall y [P(x) \wedge P(y)) \rightarrow A(x, y)] \wedge [(\neg P(x) \wedge P(y)) \rightarrow \neg A(x, y)]$

   (e) U = Set of all students

       P(x) : x is a good student

       Q(x) : x studies hard

   ∴ $\forall x (P(x) \rightarrow Q(x))$

(f) U = Set of all triangles

   P(x) : In a triangle x the sum of angles is 180°

   ∴ ∃x (¬ P(x))

12. (a) T   (b) F

13. (a) There are two students x and y in a class such that x has sent e-mail message to y.

   (b) There is a student x in the class, who has sent e-mail message to every student of the class.

   (c) Every student in the class has sent e-mail message to at least one student in the class.

   (d) There is some student in the class who received e-mail message from every student of the class.

   (e) Every student in the class received e-mail message from at least one student of the class.

   (f) All students in the class sent e-mail message to each other.

14. (i) P(x) : x glitters

   Q(x) : x is gold

   ∃x (P(x) ∧ ¬Q (x))

   (ii) S = {all birds}

   P(x) : x files

   ∃x (¬P(x))

15. Domain S = {all people}

   P(x) : x is a lawyer

   Q(x) : x is a politician

   R(x) : x is a congressman

   ∃x (P(x) ∧ Q(x) ∧ ¬R(x))

16. (i) $\forall x\ (x^2 \leq 10)$,   (ii) $\exists x\ (x^2 + 3x - 2 = 0)$,   (iii) $\forall x\ \exists y\ (xy = 1)$,

   (iv) $\exists x\ \exists y\ (x^2 + y^2 < 0)$

17. F, F, T

4
CHAPTER

GRAPH THEORY

4.1 INTRODUCTION

A graph consists of two types of objects viz. vertices and edges such that each edge is associated with unordered pair of vertices. Consider the situation which describes the road map of a city joining some important places like garden (g), hospital (h), bus station (b), railway station (r), swimming tank (s), temple (t) and telephone booth (p). By taking into consideration their locations, we can represent this situation diagrammatically as shown below.

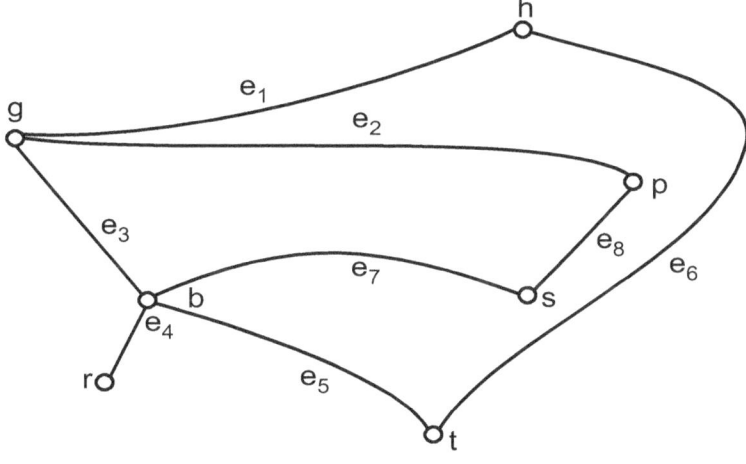

Fig. 4.1

This diagram represents a graph with 7 vertices g, b, r, t, s, p, h and 8 edges $e_1, e_2, e_3, e_4, e_5, e_6, e_7, e_8$.

Some other examples of graphs are :

(i) Communication lines joining military stations of a country.

(ii) A river together with its tributories and subtributories.

(iii) Ranking of workers in an office according to their ranks.

(4.1)

(iv) A plot of land with the walls to prevent the water from flowing.

(v) Railway route map of the country.

(vi) Nerves in the human body.

Definition : A graph $G = G(V, E)$ consists of two sets : A non-empty set V called vertex set whose elements are called vertices (or nodes) and a set E called edge set whose elements are called edges, such that each edge $e \in E$ is associated with an unordered pair (v_1, v_2) of vertices $v_1, v_2 \in V$.

If both the sets V and E are finite then the graph is called a finite graph. If both the sets V and E or either of them is infinite set then the graph is called an infinite graph. For our purpose, the word graph would mean a finite graph.

In the above definition whether the edge e_i is associated with vertex pair (v_j, v_k) or (v_k, v_j) is immaterial. This means we are not yet assigning the directions to the edges. Such graphs in which the edges are not assigned the directions are called undirected graphs.

Fig. 4.1 shows the diagrammatic representation of a graph. In the diagrammatic representation of a graph, the vertices are denoted by small circles and the edges are denoted either by straight lines or curved lines. Another way of representing a graph is to list the edges as vertex pairs. Thus, a graph shown in Fig. 4.1 can be represented as {(g, h), (g, p), (g, b), (h, t), (p, s), (s, b), (b, t), (b, r)}.

If the edge set E of a graph G is empty then G is called a null graph. The null graphs N_1, N_2, N_3, N_4 of 1, 2, 3, 4 vertices respectively are shown below.

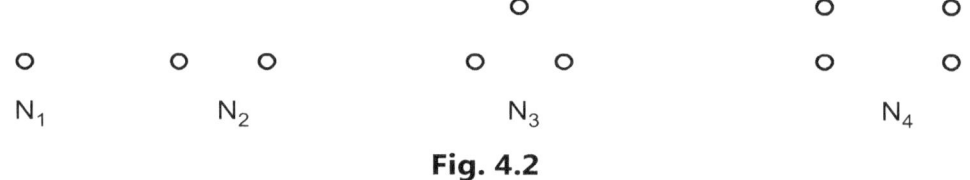

Fig. 4.2

In the graph G (V, E), if the edge e_i is associated with the vertex pair (v_j, v_k) then v_j, v_k are end vertices of e_i and equivalently we say that edge e_i is incident on v_j and v_k. Also, in this case, the vertices v_j and v_k are said to be adjacent vertices. The two edges e_i and e_j are called adjacent if they have a vertex in common. In the graph of Fig. 4.1, the vertices h and t are adjacent vertices but h and p are not adjacent because there is no edge joining h and p. Also the edges e_2 and e_8 are adjacent edges as they have a vertex p in common.

In the graph G (V, E) if two edges have the same end vertices then they are called parallel edges. If an edge e_i of a graph G has its two end vertices coincident then e_i is said to form a loop at that vertex. A graph without loops and without parallel edges is called a simple graph (or linear graph). A graph with parallel edges but having no loop is called a multigraph. A graph having parallel edges and loops is called a pseudograph.

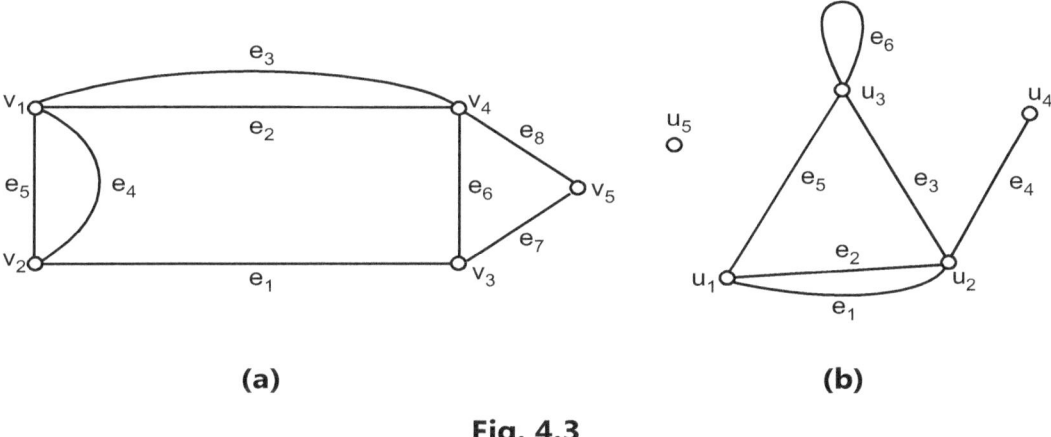

(a)   (b)

Fig. 4.3

Fig. 4.3 (a) shows a multigraph having e_2 and e_3 as parallel edges and also e_4 and e_5 as parallel edges.

Fig. 4.3 (b) shows a pseudograph. Here e_1 and e_2 are parallel edges and the edge e_6 forms a loop at the vertex u_3.

4.1.1 Degree of a Vertex

Let v be a vertex in a graph G(V, E). The number of edges incident on v is called the degree of v and is denoted by d (v).

We note that every edge of the graph G contributes two degrees, one at each end vertex. Also the loop at the vertex v contributes two degrees at v. The total degree of the graph G is the sum of the degrees of all the vertices. Hence, we have the following result.

4.1.2 Hand Shaking Lemma

Theorem 1 : The total degree of a graph G is equal to twice the number of edges in G.

This result is known as Hand Shaking Lemma; the name follows from the fact that at a party if n hand shakes occur then because each hand shake involves two hands, the total number of hands involved in hand shakes is 2n.

A vertex of degree 1 in a graph is called a pendant vertex and the corresponding edge is called a pendant edge. A vertex of degree 0 is called *isolated vertex*.

In Fig. 4.3 (a) we have $d(v_1) = 4$, $d(v_2) = 3$, $d(v_3) = 3$, $d(v_4) = 4$, $d(v_5) = 2$. The total degree is $4 + 3 + 3 + 4 + 2 = 16$. Also there are 8 edges and $2 \times 8 = 16$. This verifies Hand Shaking Lemma.

In Fig. 4.3 (b), $d(u_1) = 3$, $d(u_2) = 4$, $d(u_3) = 4$, $d(u_4) = 1$, $d(u_5) = 0$. Here u_4 is a pendant vertex and e_4 is a pendant edge. The vertex u_5 is isolated vertex. We note that the edge e_6 which forms a loop at u_3 contributes 2 degrees at u_3.

As a corollary to Hand Shaking Lemma i.e. theorem 1, we have the following result.

4.1.3 Theorem: An Undirected Graph has Even Number of Vertices of Odd Degree

Theorem 2 : In a graph G (V, E) the number of vertices of odd degree is even.

Proof : Let G (V, E) be a graph with p vertices and q edges. Then by Hand Shaking Lemma, the total degree of G is 2q.

i.e.
$$\sum_{i=1}^{p} d(v_i) = 2q$$

We separate the sum on left hand side into two parts viz. in the first part we consider vertices of even degree and in the second part the vertices of odd degree.

$$\therefore \sum_{\text{even degree vertices}} d(v_i) + \sum_{\text{odd degree vertices}} d(v_j) = 2q$$

The first sum on left side is even. Also the right side 2q is even. Therefore, the second sum on left side must be even.

i.e. $\sum_{\text{odd degree vertices}} d(v_j)$ is even number.

Hence, the number of odd degree vertices must be even.

4.2 TYPES OF GRAPHS

4.2.1 Complete Graph

(i) Weighted graph : A weighted graph is a graph in which every edge is assigned to it some positive number called weight of that edge. If we interpret the vertices of the graph as cities and the edges as the roads joining the cities, then the weight $w(e_i)$ of edge e_i joining the cities v_j and v_k may be actual length of the road or it may be the cost of constructing that road or it may be the bus fare for travelling from v_j to v_k.

The total weight of the graph G is the sum of the weights of all edges of G.

(ii) Complete graph : A simple graph with n vertices such that there exists an edge between every pair of vertices is called a complete graph and it is denoted by K_n.

The graphs K_1, K_2, K_3, K_4, K_5 are shown below.

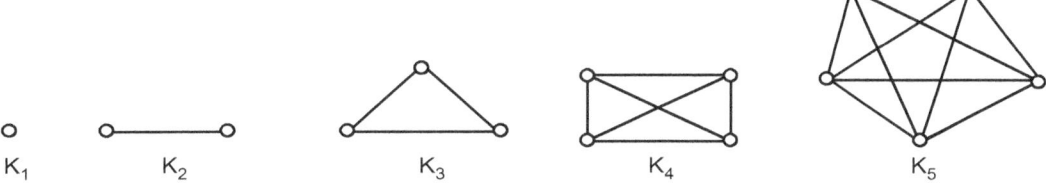

Fig. 4.4

We note that in a complete graph K_n, each vertex is joined to remaining $n-1$ vertices by an edge. Hence, the degree of each vertex is $n-1$. The total degree is $n(n-1)$. Therefore, the number of edges in K_n is $\frac{n(n-1)}{2}$.

4.2.2 Regular Graph

Let K be a positive integer. A simple graph G in which every vertex is of degree K is called k-regular graph. A graph G is called regular if it is K-regular for some positive integer K. A graph G shown below is 2-regular.

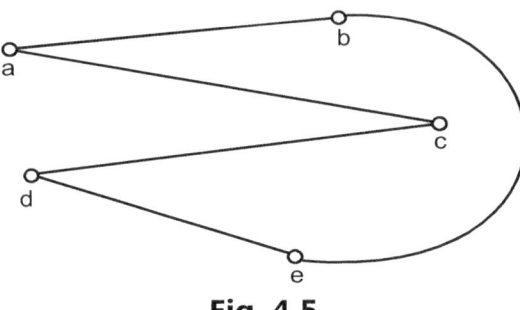

Fig. 4.5

A complete graph K_n is $n - 1$ regular. We see that a complete graph is regular but regular graph need not be complete.

4.2.3 Bipartite Graph

Let G(V, E) be a simple graph. If the vertex set V of G can be partitioned into two non-empty disjoint subsets V_1 and V_2 ($V_1 \cup V_2 = V$, $V_1 \cap V_2 = \phi$) in such a way that every edge of G has its one end vertex in V_1 and the other end vertex in V_2; then G is called a bipartite graph and the collection $\{V_1, V_2\}$ is called a bipartition.

4.2.4 Complete Bipartite Graph

A bipartite graph in which there exists an edge between every vertex in V_1 and every vertex in V_2 is called a *complete bipartite graph*. A complete bipartite graph with bipartition V_1, V_2 having m vertices in V_1 and n vertices in V_2 is denoted by $K_{m, n}$. Following figures illustrate this.

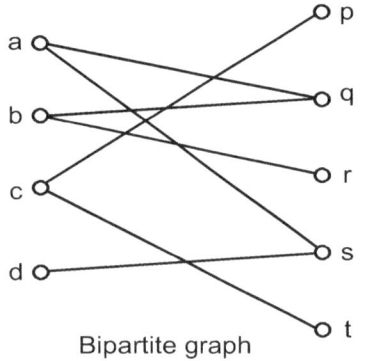

Bipartite graph

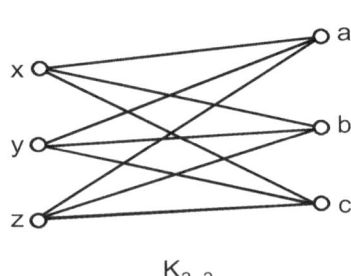

$K_{3, 3}$

Fig. 4.6

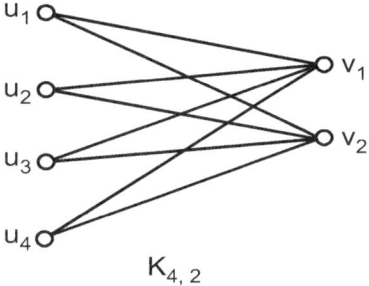

Fig. 4.7

In $K_{m,n}$ every vertex in

$V_1 = \{u_1, u_2, ..., u_m\}$ is joined to every vertex in $V_2 = \{v_1, v_2, ..., v_n\}$. Therefore $K_{m,n}$ has mn edges.

The graph $K_{1,n}$ is called a star.

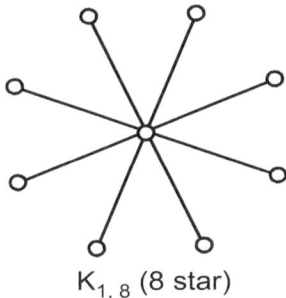

$K_{1,8}$ (8 star)

Fig. 4.8

From the star graph, we get a wheel graph.

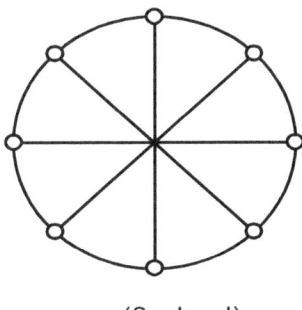

w_8 (8 wheel)

Fig. 4.9

Consider the graph shown below.

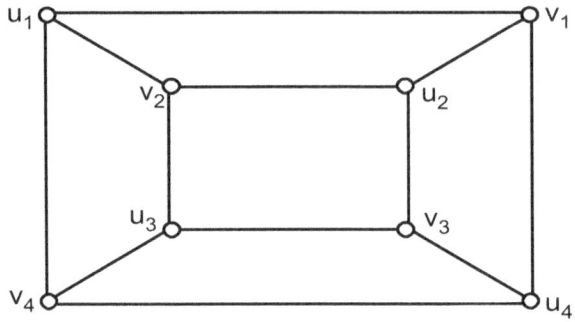

Fig. 4.10

In this graph, we observe that every edge is such that it joins u type vertex to v type vertex.

Therefore, $V_1 = \{u_1, u_2, u_3, u_4\}$ and $V_2 = \{v_1, v_2, v_3, v_4\}$ is a bipartition of the vertex set. We can redraw the above graph as below.

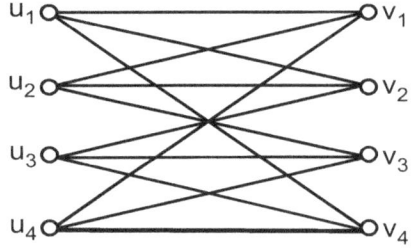

Fig. 4.11

It is a bipartite graph.

4.2.5 Operations on Graphs: Introduction

Definition : Let G (V, E) be a graph. A graph H (V', E') is called a subgraph of the graph G if $V' \subseteq V$ and $E' \subseteq E$.

Consider the graphs G, G', G" given below.

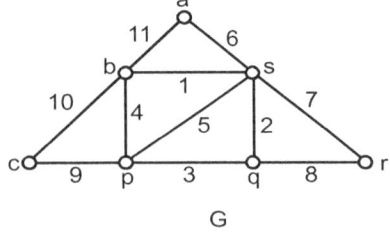 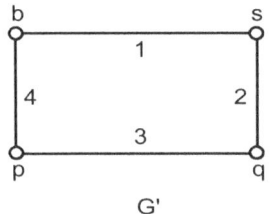 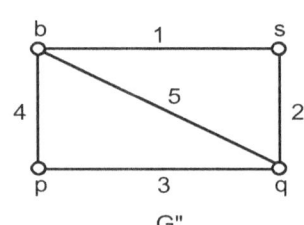

Fig. 4.12

We see that G' is a subgraph of both G and G" but G" is not a subgraph of G because the edge joining the vertices b and q is in G" but not in G.

Clearly every graph is its own subgraph; called improper or trivial subgraph. A subgraph H (V', E') of a graph G (V, E) is a proper subgraph if $V \neq V'$ or $E \neq E'$.

Vertex Deletion : Let G (V, E) be a graph and $v \in V$. A subgraph of G obtained by deleting the vertex v and by deleting those edges of G which are incident on v is called a vertex deleted subgraph of G. It is denoted by G – v.

Thus, G – v is a subgraph of G whose vertex set is V – {v} and whose edge set consists of those edges of G which are not incident on v.

The idea of deletion of a vertex can be extended as follows. Let G (V, E) be a graph and $H = \{v_1, v_2, ..., v_r\} \subset V$. Then the subgraph G – H has the vertex set V – H and the edge set of G – H consists of those edges of G which are not incident on any one of $v_1, v_2, ..., v_r$.

Edge Deletion : Let G (V, E) be a graph and $e \in E$. A subgraph of G obtained by deleting the edge e (but not any one of its end vertices) is called edge deleted subgraph of G. It is denoted by G – e.

The vertex set of G – e is V and edge set is E – {e}.

As in the case of vertex deletion, the idea of edge deletion is also extended. If G (V, E) be a graph and $F = \{e_1, e_2, ..., e_r\} \subset E$ then the subgraph G – F of G has vertex set V and the edge set E – F.

We illustrate the above by an example. Consider the graph given below.

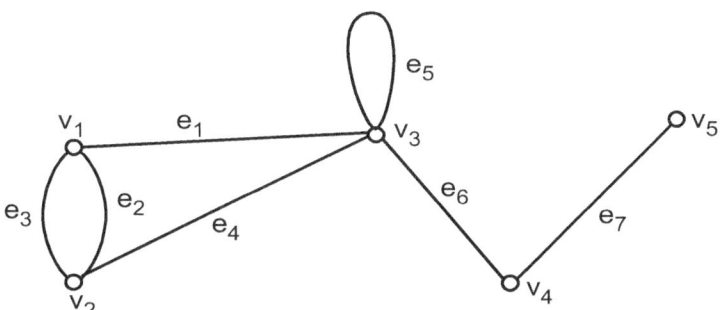

Fig. 4.13

Then (i) $G - v_2$ is   (ii) If $H = \{v_1, v_3, ..., v_5\}$ then $G - H$ is (See Fig. 4.15)

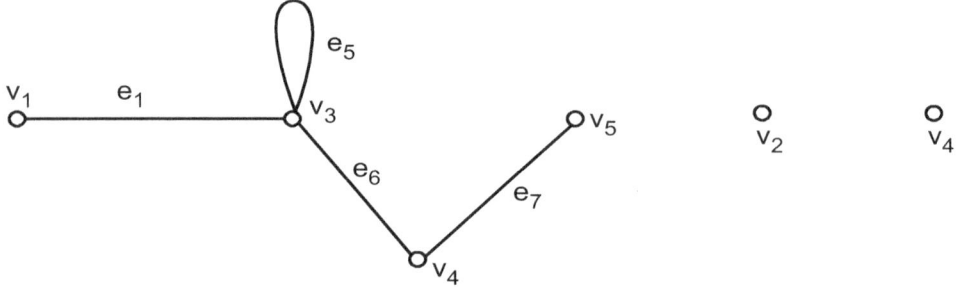

Fig. 4.14   Fig. 4.15

(iii) $G - e_3$ is

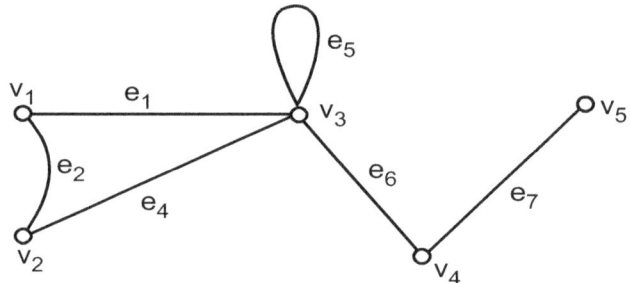

Fig. 4.16

(iv) If $F = \{e_1, e_2, e_5\}$ then $G - F$ is

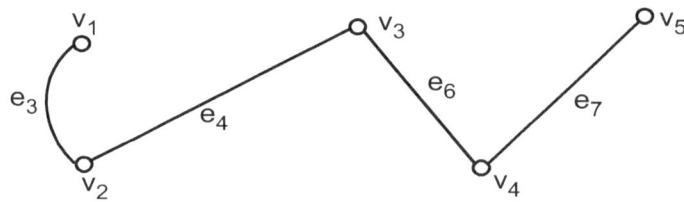

Fig. 4.17

Spanning Subgraph : A subgraph $H(V', E')$ of a graph $G(V, E)$ is called a spanning subgraph of G if $V = V'$. From the graph G, (i) if all the loops are removed and (ii) from every set of parallel edges all edges are removed except one then the resulting subgraph is a spanning subgraph without loops and without parallel edges. It is called a simple spanning subgraph of G or underlying graph of G.

Consider the following graph.

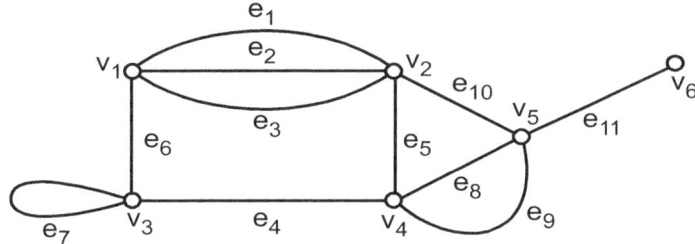

Fig. 4.18

One underlying graph of G is

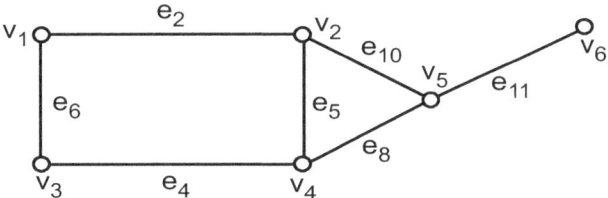

Fig. 4.19

Note that the above graph G has in all 6 underlying graphs. We have mentioned one here. The students are asked to draw remaining 5 underlying graphs of G.

Edge Disjoint Subgraphs : The two subgraphs G_1 and G_2 of a graph G are called edge disjoint if they have no edge in common. If G_1 and G_2 have no vertex in common then they are called vertex disjoint. Obviously, if G_1 and G_2 have no vertex in common then they cannot have any edge in common. Thus, two vertex disjoint subgraphs of a given graph are automatically edge disjoint. For this reason, the vertex disjoint subgraphs are called disjoint subgraphs.

Let G be a graph.

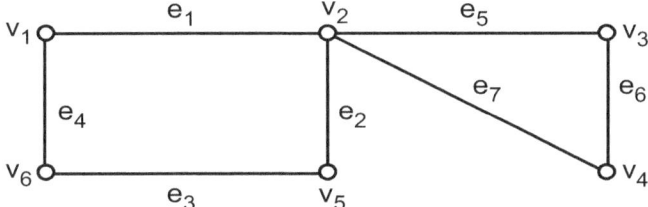

Fig. 4.20

Consider the following subgraphs of G (See Fig. 4.21).

G_1 and G_2 are edge disjoint subgraphs but not vertex disjoint because v_2 is a common vertex.

G_1 and G_3 are vertex disjoint and hence disjoint subgraphs.

G_2 and G_3 are neither edge disjoint nor vertex disjoint.

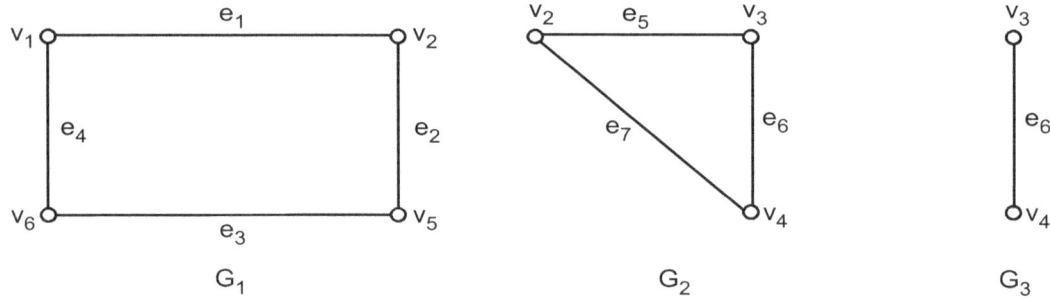

Fig. 4.21

In order to obtain the vertex deleted subgraph of the graph G, we remove from G those vertices in which we are not interested and the appropriate set of some edges. Similarly, edge deleted subgraph is obtained by removing a particular set of edges (but not any vertex). Consider the situation opposite to this. The subgraphs of G containing (i) the desired set of vertices and appropriate edges or (ii) desired set of edges and appropriate vertices are called *induced subgraphs*.

Definition : Let G (V, E) be a graph and H = $\{v_1, v_2, \ldots v_r\} \subset V$. A subgraph of G, whose vertex set is H and edge set consists of those edges in G whose both the end vertices are in H; is called a vertex induced subgraph.

It is denoted by < H >.

Definition : Let G (V, E) be a graph and F = $\{e_1, e_2 \ldots e_r\} \subset E$. A subgraph of G, whose edge set is E and vertex set consists of those vertices in G which are end vertices of edges in F; is called edge induced subgraph.

It is denoted by < F >.

Consider the graph G below.

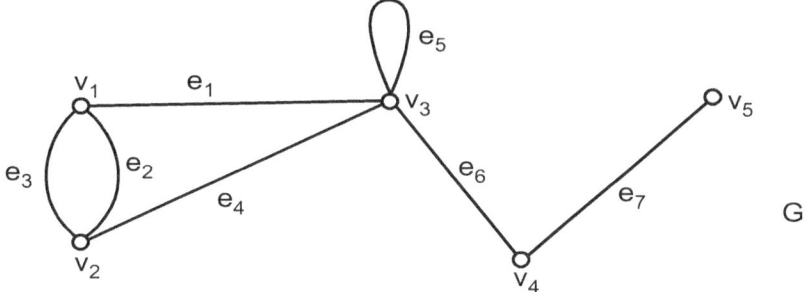

Fig. 4.22

If $H = \{v_1, v_3, v_4\}$ then the subgraph induced by H is

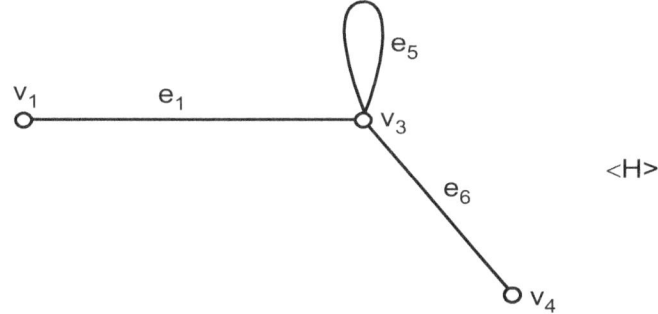

Fig. 4.23

Also if $F = \{e_1, e_4, e_6\}$ then the subgraph induced by F is

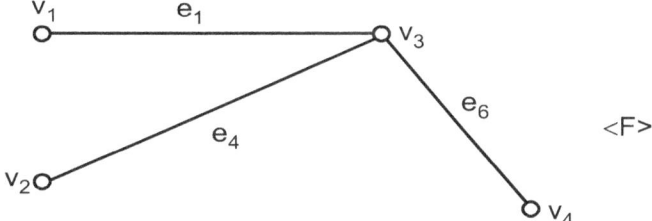

Fig. 4.24

Complement of a Graph

Definition : Let G (V, E) be a graph. Then the complement $\overline{G}$ of G is a graph whose vertex set is V itself and the edge set consists precisely of the edges (v_i, v_j) such that there is no edge in G joining v_i and v_j.

This means (v_i, v_j) is an edge in $\overline{G}$ iff it is not edge in G. We know that in the complete graph K_n on n vertices there exists an edge between every pair of distinct vertices. Therefore, in the complement $\overline{K}_n$, any vertex v_i is not joined to any other vertex v_j i.e. $\overline{K}_n$ consists of n vertices alone, without any edge. Thus, the complement of K_n is a null graph on n vertices and conversely the complement of a null graph is a complete graph. It immediately follows that if G is a graph then $\overline{\overline{G}} = G$ i.e. the complement of the complement of G is G itself. A graph on 5 vertices and its complement are shown below.

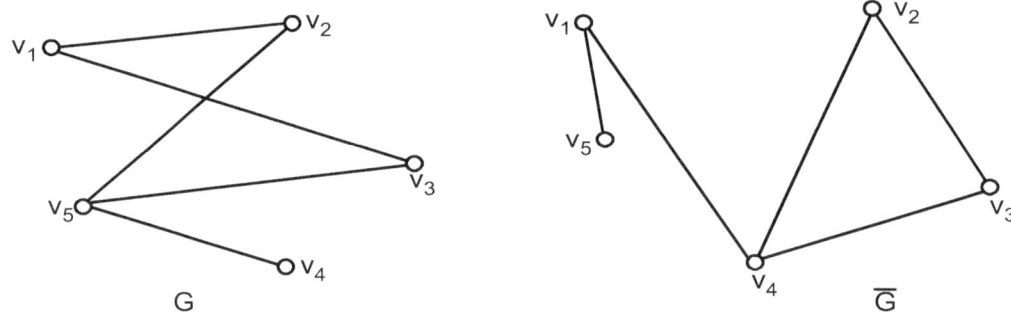

Fig. 4.25

Definition : A graph G is called self complementary if it is isomorphic with its own complement i.e. $G \cong \overline{G}$.

In the example preceding this definition, the two graphs G and $\overline{G}$ are not isomorphic because in the graph G a vertex of degree 3 is adjacent to a vertex of degree 1 and in $\overline{G}$ a vertex of degree 3 is not adjacent to a vertex of degree 1. Hence G is not self complementary. If however we consider the following graph on 5 vertices (See Fig. 4.26) then its complement is (See Fig. 4.27) and these two graphs are isomorphic (verify).

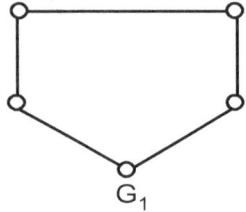 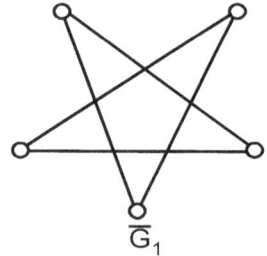

Fig. 4.26   **Fig. 4.27**

Therefore, G_1 is a self complementary graph.

The complement of a graph G is obtained by deleting the edges of G from the complete graph K_n.

∴ Number of edges in G + Number of edges in $\bar{G}$ = Number of edges in K_n.

∴ Number of edges in G + Number of edges in $\bar{G}$ = $\dfrac{n(n-1)}{2}$.

Now, we prove the following result.

Theorem 1 : The number of vertices in a self-complementary graph is of the type 4K or 4K + 1; where K is a integer.

Proof : Let G be a simple graph on n vertices and G be self-complementary.

We know that,

Number of edges in G + Number of edges in $\bar{G}$ = $\dfrac{n(n-1)}{2}$.

But G is given to be self-complementary.

∴ Number of edges in G = Number of edges in $\bar{G}$ (∵ $G \cong \bar{G}$)

∴ Number of edges in G = $\dfrac{n(n-1)}{4}$

Now, the number $\dfrac{n(n-1)}{4}$ is integer and one of n and n – 1 is odd.

Therefore, 4 must divide n or n – 1 i.e. 4 | n or 4 | n – l.

∴   n = 4 K or n – 1 = 4 K

∴   n = 4 K or n = 4 K + 1.   Hence proved.

Union and Intersection of Graphs

We can obtain new graphs from the given collection of two or more graphs. We discuss these operations one by one below.

Union of Two Graphs : Let $G_1(V_1, E_1)$ and $G_2(V_2, E_2)$ be two graphs. Then their union $G = G_1 \cup G_2$ is a graph $G(V, E)$ in which vertex set is $V = V_1 \cup V_2$ and edge set is $E = E_1 \cup E_2$.

Intersection of Two Graphs : Let $G_1(V_1, E_1)$ and $G_2(V_2, E_2)$ be two given graphs. Then their intersection $G = G_1 \cap G_2$ is a graph $G(V, E)$ in which vertex set is $V = V_1 \cap V_2$ and edge set is $E = E_1 \cap E_2$.

Ring Sum of Two Graphs : Let $G_1(V_1, E_1)$ and $G_2(V_2, E_2)$ be two given graphs. Then their ring sum $G = G_1 \oplus G_2$ is a graph in which vertex set is $V = V_1 \cup V_2$ and edge set E consists of those edges which are in E_1 or E_2 but not in both.

The extension of these operations to more than two sets is obvious.

The two graphs G_1 and G_2 and their union, intersection, ring sum are shown below.

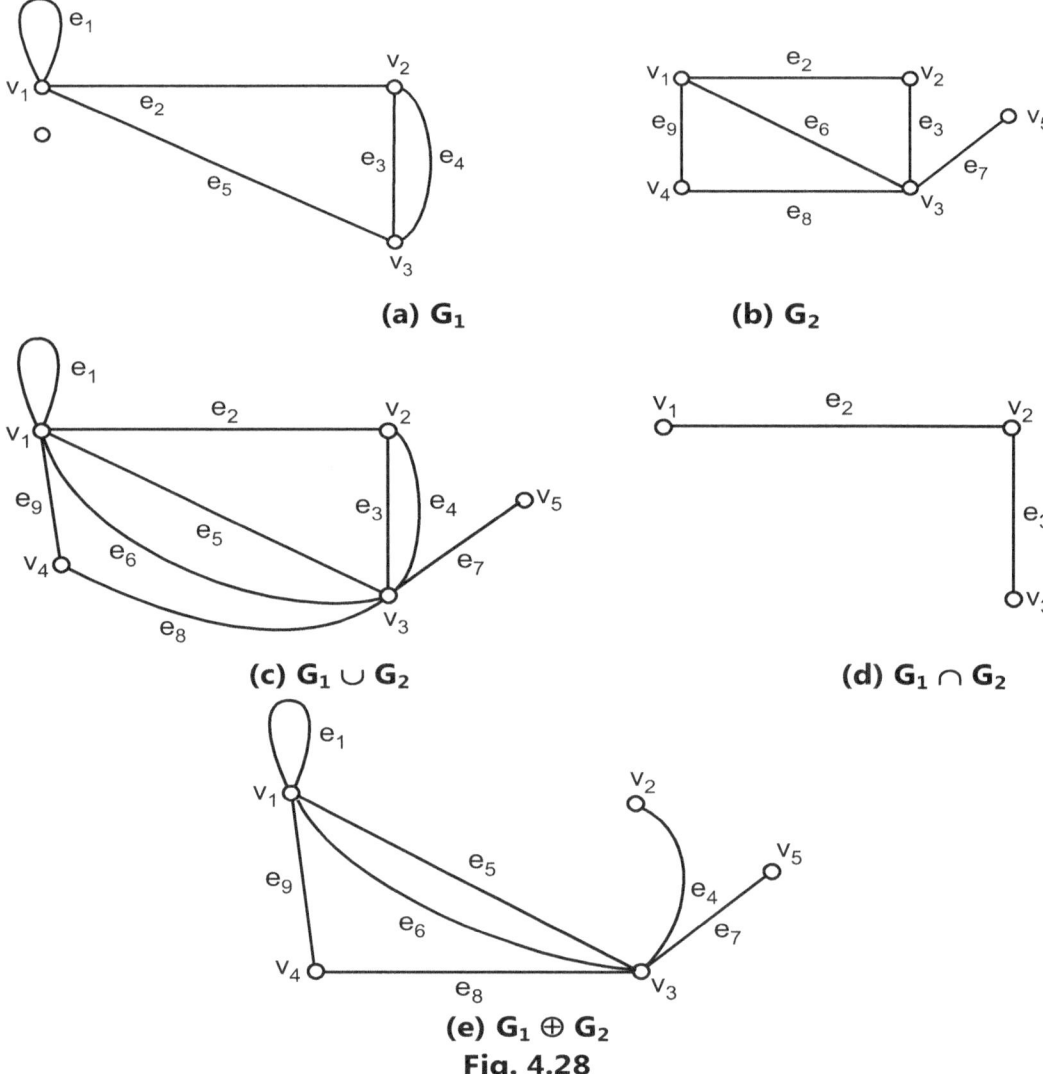

Fig. 4.28

From the definitions of the operations of union and intersection in set theory, it follows that $G_1 \cup G_2 = G_2 \cup G_1$, $G_1 \cap G_2 = G_2 \cap G_1$ and $G_1 \oplus G_2 = G_2 \oplus G_1$.

Also for any graph G, we have $G \cup G = G$ and $G \cap G = G$.

However, $G \oplus G$ consists of all the vertices of G without any edge. Thus, the ring sum of any graph with itself is a null graph.

Product of Two Graphs : Let $G_1(V_1, E_1)$ and $G_2(V_2, E_2)$ be two simple graphs. Then their product $G = G_1 \times G_2$ is a graph in which vertex set is the Cartesian product $V_1 \times V_2$ and the edge set consists of the edges such that two vertices (x, y) and (z, t) in $V_1 \times V_2$ are joined if x = z and y, t are adjacent or y = t and x, z are adjacent. We illustrate this by considering the two graphs G_1 and G_2 below.

(a) G_1 (b) G_2

Fig. 4.29

The Cartesian product $V_1 \times V_2$ has 9 pairs (a, p), (a, q), (a, r), (b, p), (b, q), (b, r), (c, p), (c, q), (c, r).

We plot these 9 vertices in 3 rows.

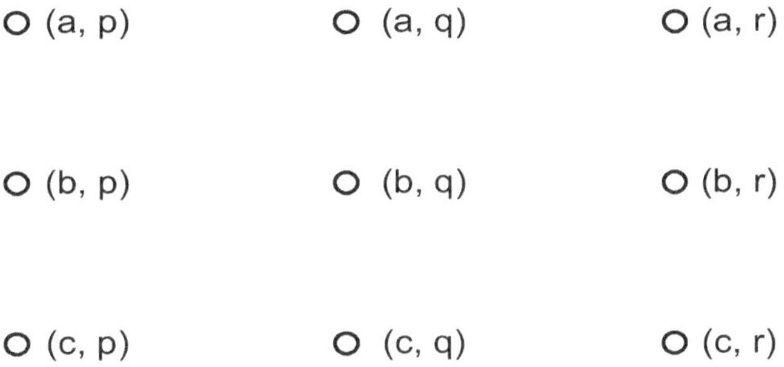

      O (a, p)   O (a, q)   O (a, r)

      O (b, p)   O (b, q)   O (b, r)

      O (c, p)   O (c, q)   O (c, r)

Fig. 4.30

Now keeping 'a' fixed, we make a copy of the graph G_2 as below.

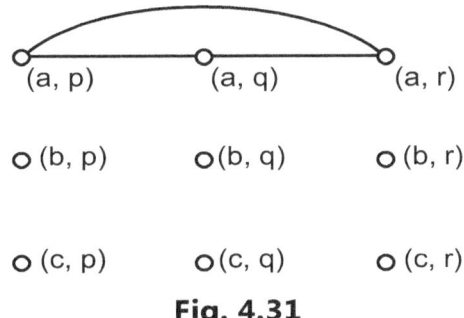

Fig. 4.31

Similarly by keeping b and c fixed, we make two more copies of G_2.

Also by keeping p, q, r fixed, we make three copies of G_1.

The resulting graph is $G_1 \times G_2$.

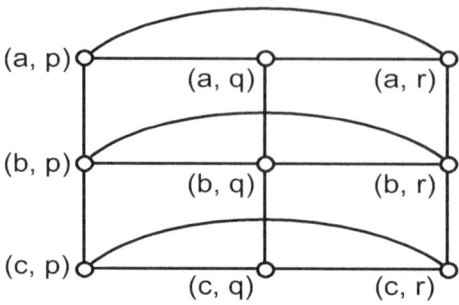

Fig. 4.32

We observe that if G_1 has p_1 vertices, q_1 edges and G_2 has p_2 vertices, q_2 edges then $G_1 \times G_2$ has $p_1 p_2$ vertices and $p_1 q_2 + p_2 q_1$ edges.

Fusion of Vertices : The fusion (merging) of two vertices v_1 and v_2 of a graph G means these two vertices are replaced by a single vertex (at v_1 or v_2) in such a manner that all the edges in G which were incident on v_1 and v_2 are now made incident on that single vertex. Thus, the fusion of two vertices reduces the number of vertices by 1 but it does not alter the number of edges.

In a like manner, three or more vertices of a graph can be fused together. This is illustrated below.

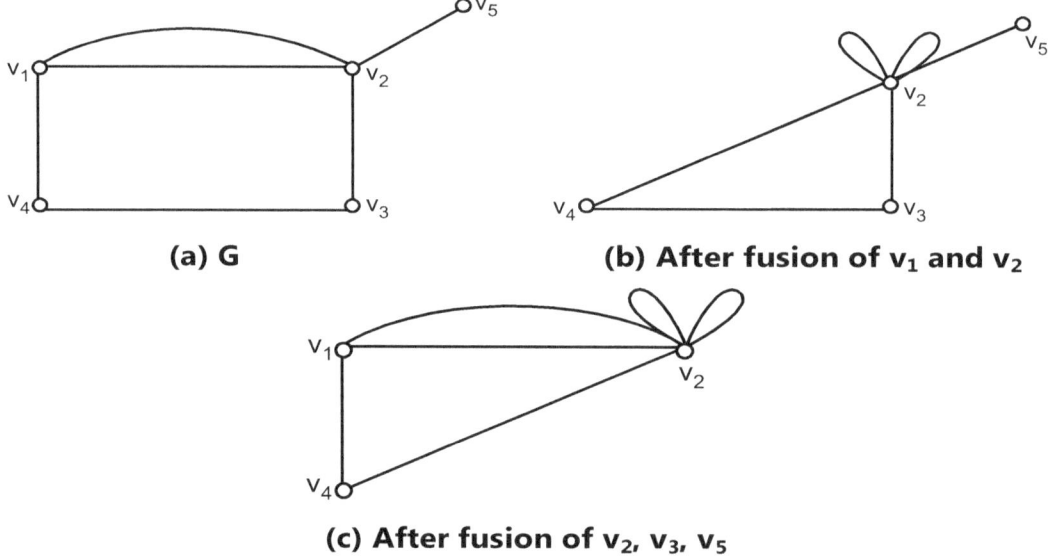

Fig. 4.33

Decomposition : We say that a graph G is decomposed into two edge disjoint subgraphs G_1 and G_2 if $G_1 \cup G_2 = G$ and $G_1 \cap G_2$ is a null graph. In the decomposition of G into G_1 and G_2, the two subgraphs G_1 and G_2 have no any edge in common but they may have possibly some vertices in common.

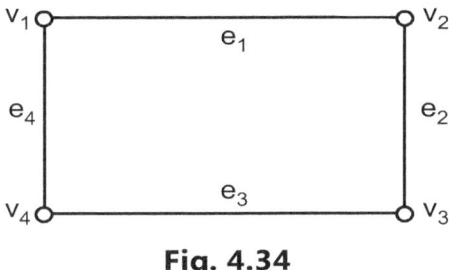

Fig. 4.34

If we have a graph then there are following seven pairs of subgraphs G_1 and G_2 yielding a decomposition of G into two subgraphs.

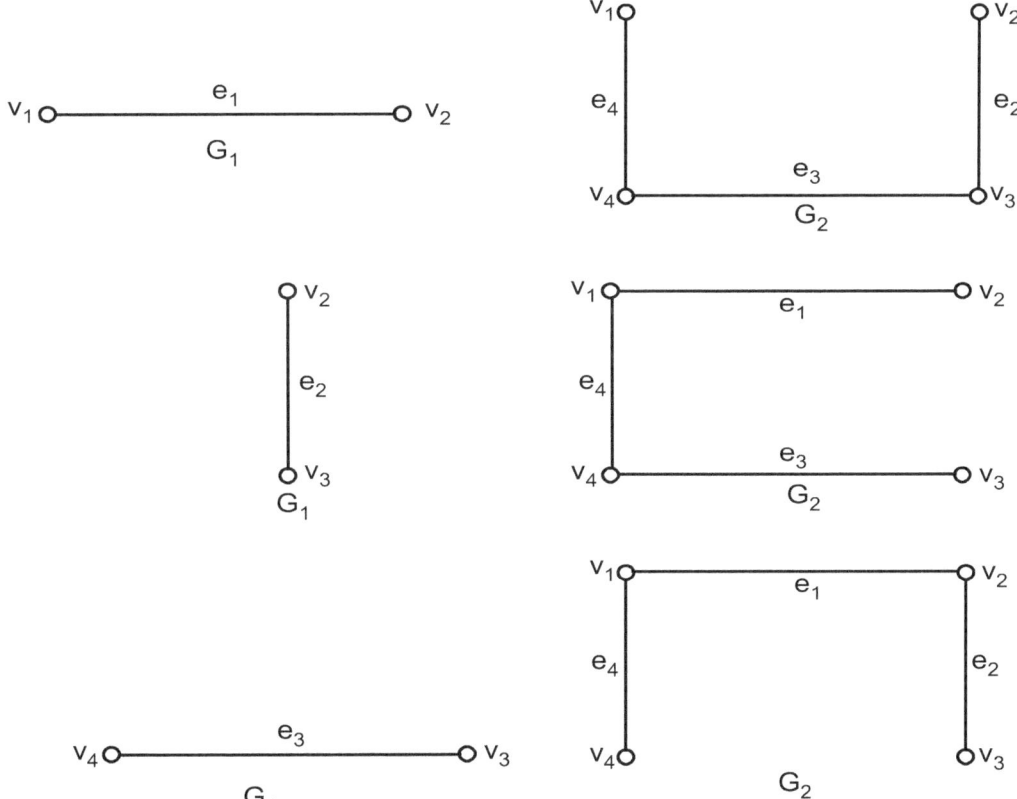

Fig. 4.35 (a)

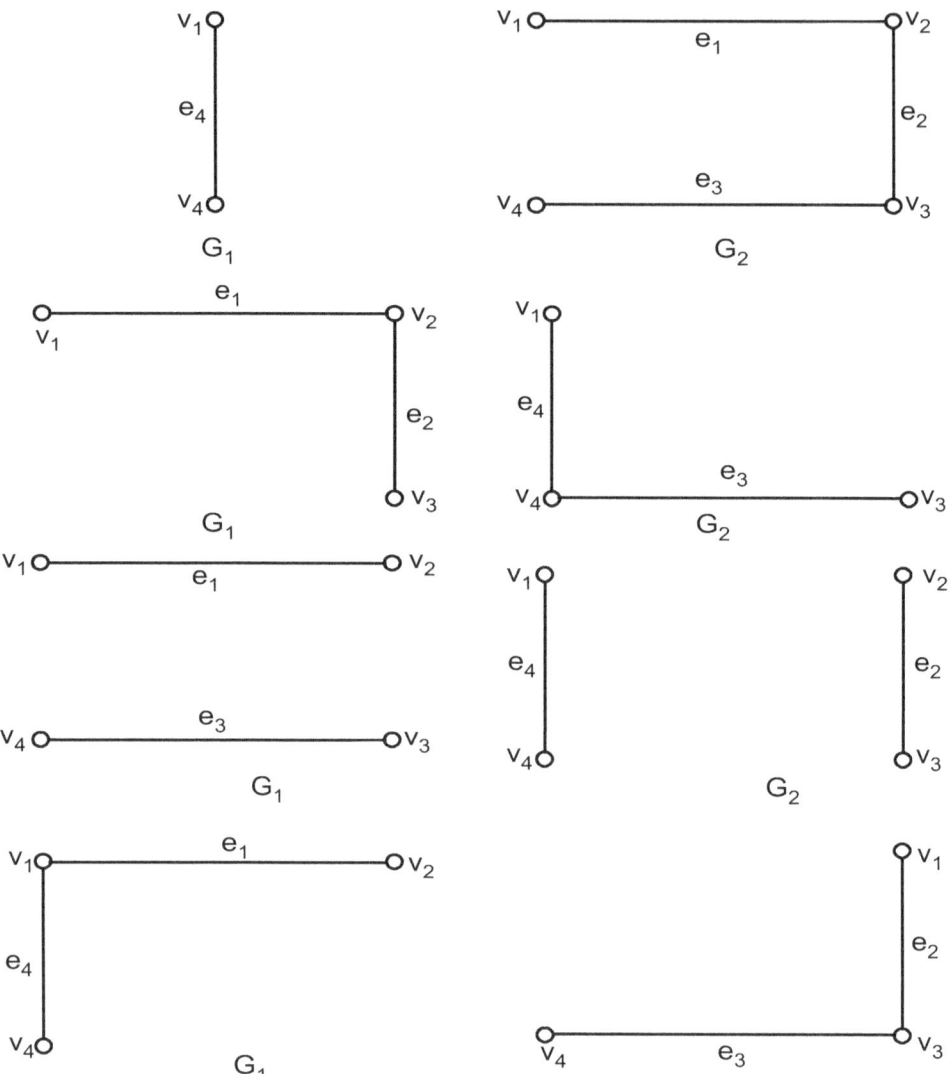

Fig. 4.35 (b)

There is no any more pair of subgraphs yielding the decomposition of G into two subgraphs. In the exercise we ask the students to show that if a graph G contains m edges $e_1, e_2, ..., e_m$ then it can be decomposed in $2^{m-1} - 1$ different ways into the pairs of subgraphs G_1 and G_2.

ILLUSTRATIVE EXAMPLES

Example 4.1 : *Let G be a simple graph on n vertices and $\bar{G}$ its complement.*

(a) *Prove that, for each vertex v in G, $d_G(v) + d_{\bar{G}}(v) = n - 1$, where $d_G(v)$ denotes the degree of v in G.*

(b) *Suppose that G contains exactly one vertex of even degree. Find the number of odd degree vertices in $\bar{G}$.*

(c) *Verify the results in (a) and (b) for wheel W_4.*

Solution : (a) G is a simple graph on n vertices. Suppose the n vertices of G are $v, x_1, x_2, ..., x_r, y_1, y_2, ..., y_{n-r-1}$.

We suppose that in the graph G, the vertex v is joined to r vertices $x_1, x_2, ..., x_r$ by the edges. Therefore, $d_G(v) = r$.

Now by definition of $\bar{G}$, the vertex v is joined to the vertices $y_1, y_2, ..., y_{n-r-1}$ in the graph $\bar{G}$.

Therefore, $\quad d_{\bar{G}}(v) = n - r - 1$

∴ $\quad d_G(v) + d_{\bar{G}}(v) = r + n - r - 1$

∴ $\quad d_G(v) + d_{\bar{G}}(v) = n - 1$.

(b) Let G be a simple graph on n vertices having exactly one vertex of even degree. So the remaining n − 1 vertices are of odd degree. They must be even in number. i.e. n − 1 is even number.

Now from part (a) above, we have for any vertex v of G,

$\quad d_G(v) + d_{\bar{G}}(v) = n - 1$; (even number)

If v is even degree vertex in G then $d_G(v)$ is even and n − 1 is even. Therefore, $d_{\bar{G}}(v)$ is also even. i.e. v is even degree vertex in $\bar{G}$ also.

Also let w be odd degree vertex in G. Then $d_G(w)$ is odd number and n − 1 is even number.

Therefore, $d_{\bar{G}}(w)$ must be odd number. i.e. w is odd degree vertex in $\bar{G}$ also.

Thus, odd degree vertices in $\overline{G}$ are precisely the odd degree vertices in G. They are n − 1 in number.

(c) The wheel W_4 is a graph as shown below.

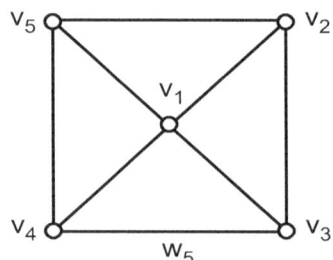

Fig. 4.36

Its complement is

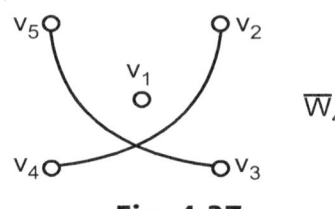

Fig. 4.37

We have, $d_{W_4}(v_1) + d_{\overline{W}_4}(v_1) = 4 + 0 = 4$

$d_{W_4}(v_2) + d_{\overline{W}_4}(v_2) = 3 + 1 = 4$

$d_{W_4}(v_3) + d_{\overline{W}_4}(v_3) = 3 + 1 = 4$

$d_{W_4}(v_4) + d_{\overline{W}_4}(v_4) = 3 + 1 = 4$

$d_{W_4}(v_5) + d_{\overline{W}_4}(v_5) = 3 + 1 = 4$

This verifies the part (a).

Now for verification of part (b), we see that there is exactly one vertex of even degree in W_4 viz. v_1 and the remaining 4 vertices are of odd degree viz. v_2, v_3, v_4, v_5. Also in $\overline{W}_4$, the vertices v_2, v_3, v_4, v_5 are odd degree vertices and they are 4 in number. This verifies the part (b).

Example 4.2 : *Consider the given graph G.*

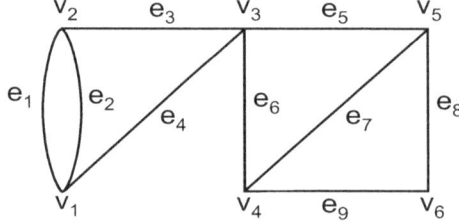

Fig. 4.38

(a) *Find induced subgraph G < V > where V = $\{v_1, v_2, v_5, v_6\}$.*

(b) *Find G − A where A = $\{e_1, e_2, e_8, e_9\}$.*

Solution : (a) Induced subgraph G < V > where V = {v_1, v_2, v_5, v_6}.

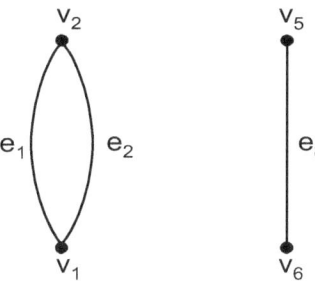

Fig. 4.39 (a)

(b) G – A where A = {e_1, e_2, e_8, e_9}.

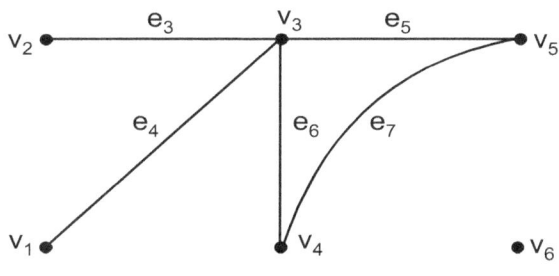

Fig. 4.39 (b)

Example 4.3 : *For the given graphs G_1 and G_2, find (1) $G_1 \cap G_2$, (2) $G_1 \oplus G_2$.*

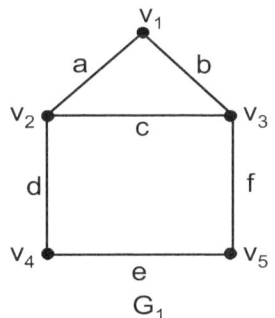
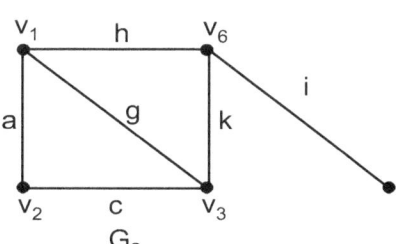

Fig. 4.40

Solution :

V_1 = {v_1, v_2, v_3, v_4, v_5} V_2 = {v_1, v_2, v_3, v_5, v_6}

E_1 = {a, b, c, d, e, f} E_2 = {a, c, g, h, i, k}

$V_1 \cap V_2$ = {v_1, v_2, v_3, v_5} $V_1 \cup V_2$ = {$v_1, v_2, v_3, v_4, v_5, v_6$}

$E_1 \cap E_2$ = {a, c} $E_1 \cup E_2$ = {a, b, c, d, e, f, g, h, i, k}

(1) $G_1 \cap G_2$

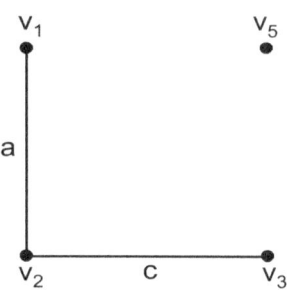

Fig. 4.41

(2) $G_1 \oplus G_2$

$$E_1 \oplus E_2 = (E_1 \cup E_2) - (E_1 \cap E_2)$$
$$= \{b, d, e, f, g, h, i, k\}$$
$$V_1 \oplus V_2 = V_1 \cup V_2$$
$$= \{v_1, v_2, v_3, v_4, v_5, v_6\}$$

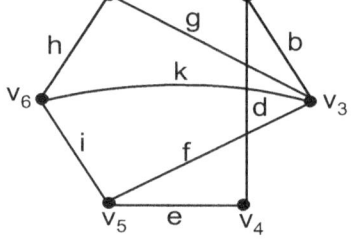

Fig. 4.42

Example 4.4 : *Draw the complement of the given graph G.*

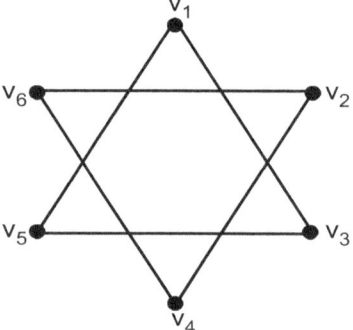

Fig. 4.43

Solution : Complement of G is given below (Fig. 4.44).

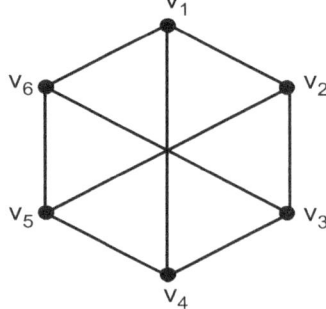

Fig. 4.44

Example 4.5 : *Draw the complement of graph.*

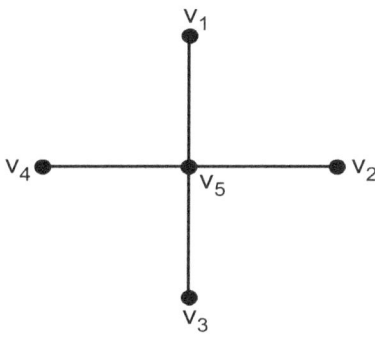

Fig. 4.45

Solution : *Fig. 4.46 shows compliment of G*

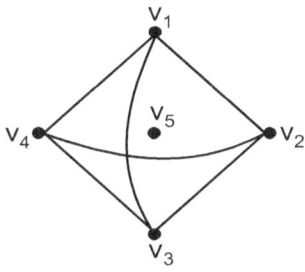

Fig. 4.46

Example 4.6 : *Find $G_1 \cup G_2$.*

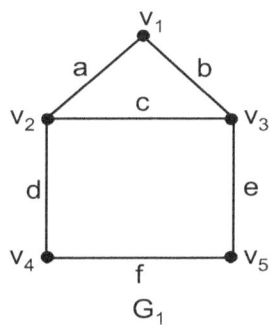
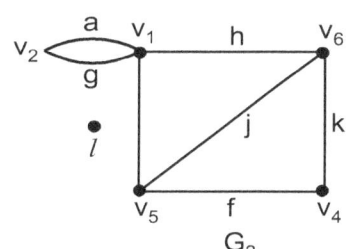

Fig. 4.47

Solution : $V_1 = \{v_1, v_2, v_3, v_4, v_5\}$

$E_1 = \{a, b, c, d, e, f\}$

$V_2 = \{v_1, v_2, v_3, v_4, v_5, v_6\}$

$$E_2 = \{a, f, g, h, i, j, k\}$$
$$V_1 \cup V_2 = \{v_1, v_2, v_3, v_4, v_5, v_6\}$$
$$E_1 \cup E_2 = \{a, b, c, d, e, f, g, h, i, j, k\}$$

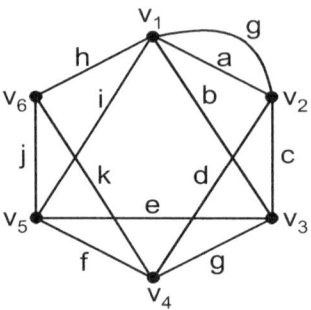

Fig. 4.48

Example 4.7 : *Is graph is complete graph ? If so, draw it complement.*

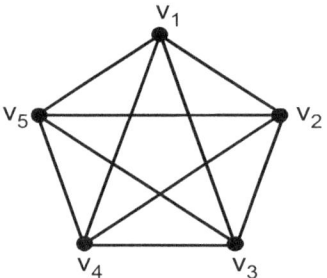

Fig. 4.49

Solution : The complement of given graph is null, becuase given graph G is complete i.e. each pair of vertices are adjacent to each other.

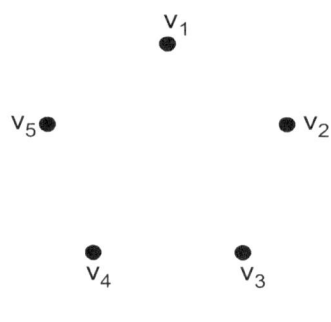

Fig. 4.50

EXERCISE 4.1

1. Find all subgraphs of the graph given below, having at least one vertex.

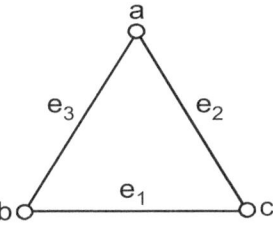

Fig. 4.51

2. The two graphs G_1 and G_2 are given below. Find $G_1 \cup G_2$, $G_1 \cap G_2$, $G_1 \oplus G_2$.

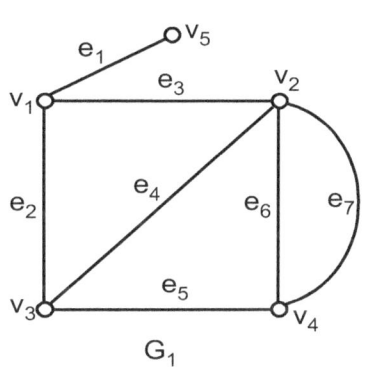 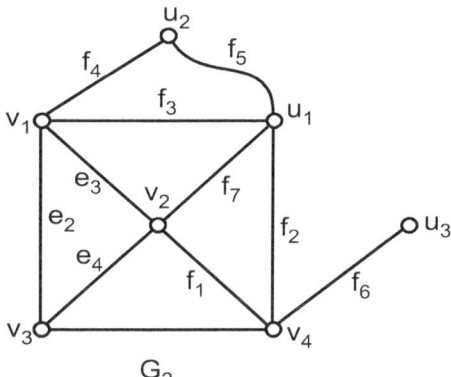

Fig. 4.52

3. For the graphs G_1, G_2, G_3 given below, find $G_2 \oplus (G_1 \cap G_3)$.

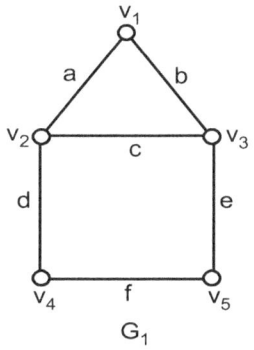 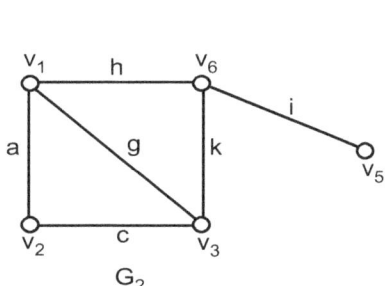 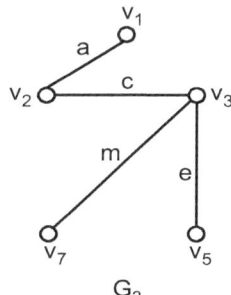

Fig. 4.53

4. For the graph G given below, find

   (a) underlying graph of G
   (b) $G - V_3$
   (c) $G - e_3$
   (d) $G - U$; $U = \{V_1, V_2\}$
   (e) $G - F$; $F = \{e_1, e_2, e_5, e_{11}\}$
   (f) $< H >$; $H = \{V_2, V_3, V_5\}$
   (g) $< F >$; $F = \{e_1, e_3, e_5, e_7, v_9\}$

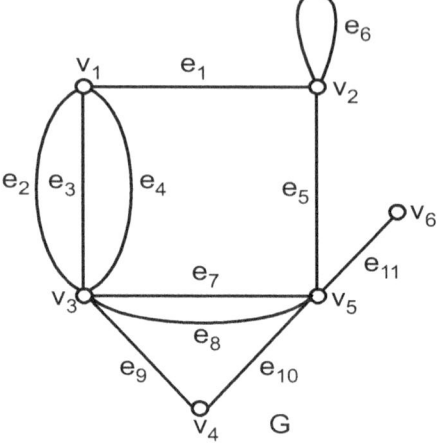

Fig. 4.54

5. A simple graph G has m edges. Prove that there are $2^{m-1} - 1$ pairs of subgraphs of G which yield the decomposition of G.

6. If G is a graph as shown below, draw the graph after the fusion of u and v.

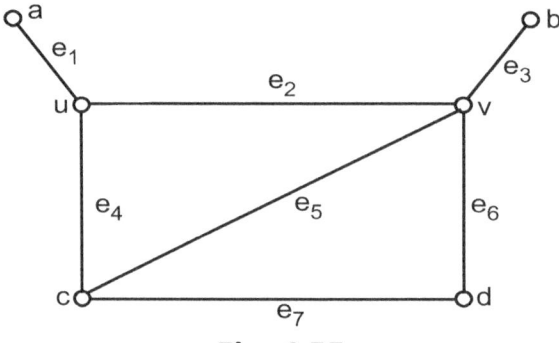

Fig. 4.55

7. If G_1 and G_2 are two regular graphs then $G_1 \oplus G_2$ is regular. State whether it is true or false. Justify.

8. List all self-complementary graphs on 4 vertices.

9. Find the product $G_1 \times G_2$ for each of the following pairs of graphs.

   (a)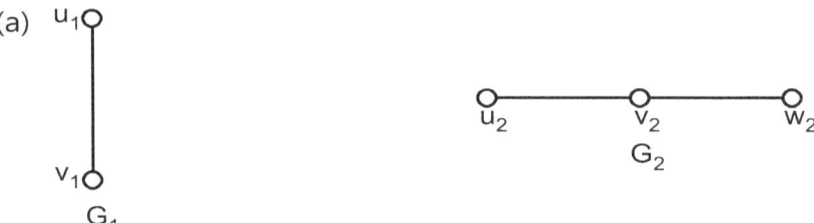

Fig. 4.56 (a)

(b)

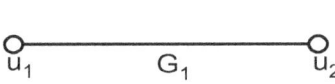
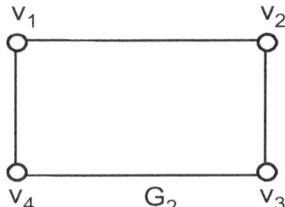

Fig. 4.56 (b)

(c)

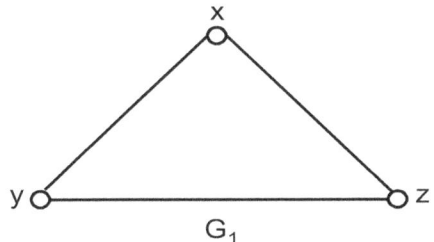
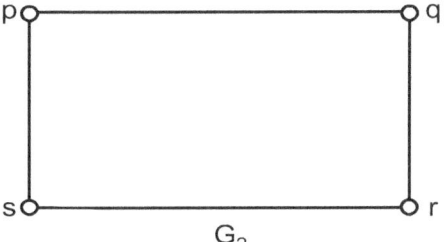

Fig. 4.56 (c)

ANSWERS 4.1

1. **Hint :** There are 17 such subgraphs.
2.
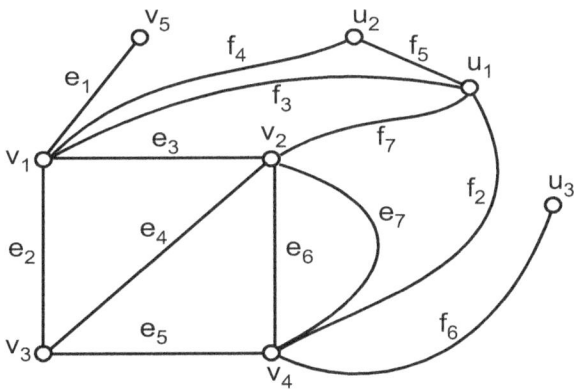

Fig. 4.57 : $G_1 \cup G_2$

For the graph $G_1 \cap G_2$, we have,

$$V_1 \cap V_2 = \{v_1, v_2, v_3, v_4\} \text{ and}$$
$$E_1 \cap E_2 = \{e_2, e_3, e_4, e_5\}$$

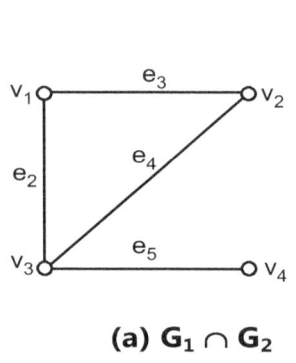

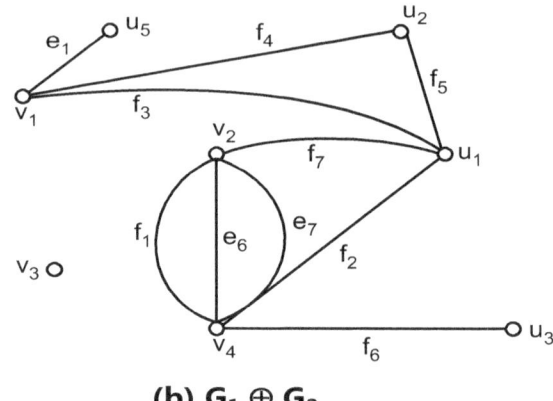

(a) $G_1 \cap G_2$ (b) $G_1 \oplus G_2$

Fig. 4.58

3.

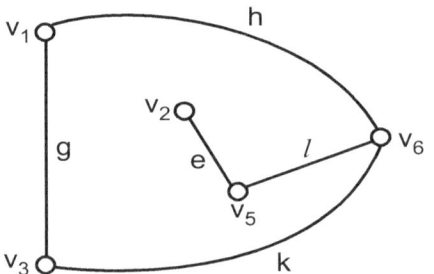

Fig. 4.59 : $G_2 \oplus (G_1 \cap G_3)$

4. (a)　　　　　　　　　　　　(b)

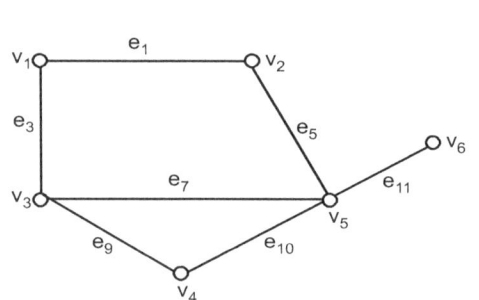
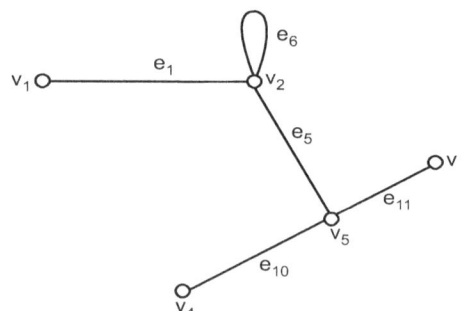

Fig. 4.60 (a) : Underlying graph of G　　**Fig. 4.60 (b) : G – v_3**

(c)

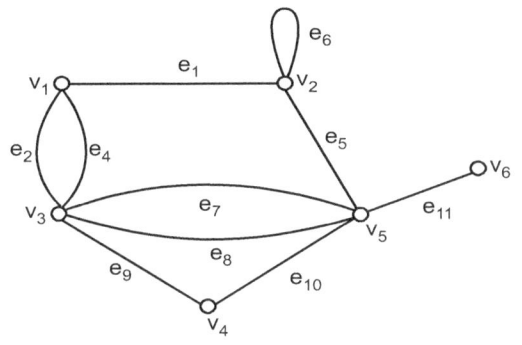

Fig. 4.60 (c) : G – e₃

(d)

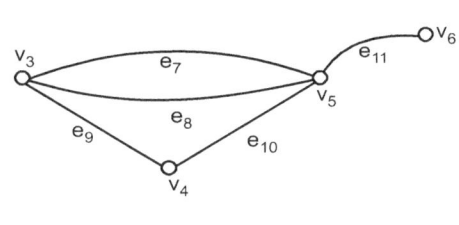

Fig. 4.60 (d) : G – U

(e)

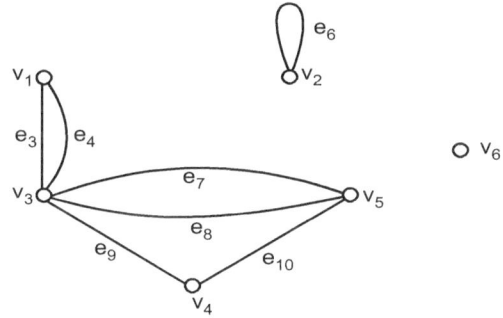

Fig. 4.60 (e) : G – F

(f)

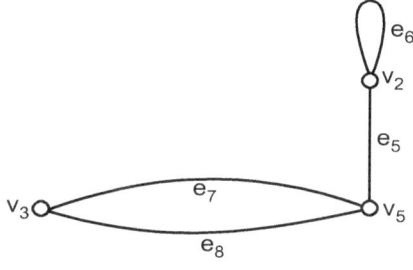

Fig. 4.60 (f) : < H >

(g)

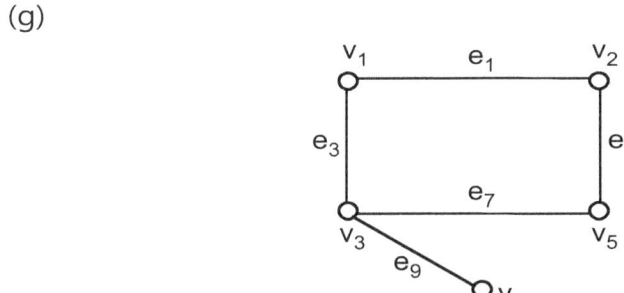

Fig. 4.60 (g) : < F >

6.

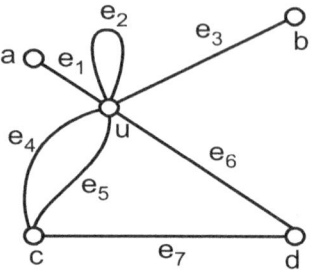

Fig. 4.61

7. False.

8. One such graph is

Fig. 4.62

10.

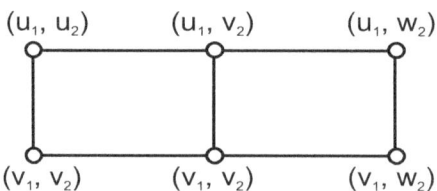

Fig. 4.63 (a) : $G_1 \times G_2$

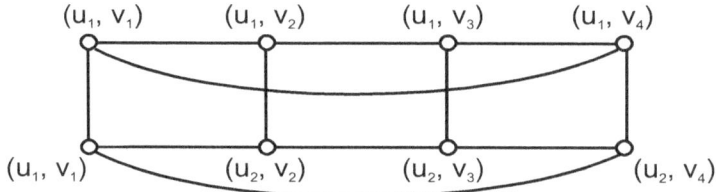

Fig. 4.63 (b) : $G_1 \times G_2$

(c)

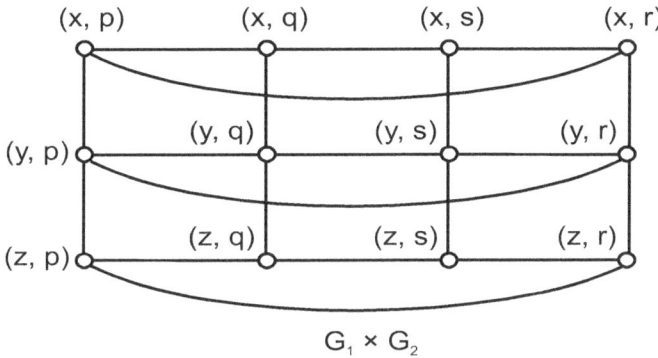

$G_1 \times G_2$

Fig. 4.63 (c) : $G_1 \times G_2$

4.3 MATRIX REPRESENTATION OF A GRAPH

4.3.1 Adjacency Matrix

We have seen that a graph is represented in two different ways :

(i) by listing the edges as vertex pairs and (ii) by a diagram.

There is another way of representing a graph i.e. by using matrices and this representation is used by a computer. We study two types of matrix representations of a graph; one by adjacency matrix and the other by incidence matrix of a graph.

Adjacency Matrix : Let G be a graph with n vertices $v_1, v_2, ..., v_n$. Then the adjacency matrix A(G) of G is $n \times n$ matrix in which the $(i-j)^{th}$ element a_{ij} is the number of edges in G joining the vertex pair (v_i, v_j).

Consider the graph G with 5 vertices shown below.

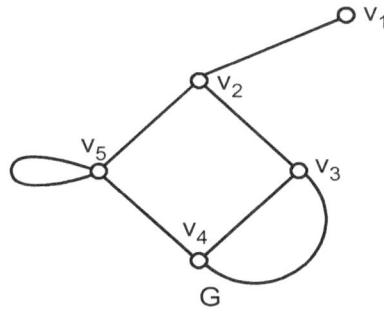

Fig. 4.64

The adjacency matrix corresponding to this graph is

$$\begin{array}{c} \\ v_1 \\ v_2 \\ v_3 \\ v_4 \\ v_5 \end{array} \begin{array}{c} \begin{array}{ccccc} v_1 & v_2 & v_3 & v_4 & v_5 \end{array} \\ \begin{bmatrix} 0 & 1 & 0 & 0 & 0 \\ 1 & 0 & 1 & 0 & 1 \\ 0 & 1 & 0 & 2 & 0 \\ 0 & 0 & 2 & 0 & 1 \\ 0 & 1 & 0 & 1 & 1 \end{bmatrix} \end{array}$$

We have the following observations about the adjacency matrix of a graph :

(i) As the number of edges joining v_i, v_j is the same as v_j, v_i, we have $a_{ij} = a_{ji}$.

Therefore, the adjacency matrix of a graph is a symmetric matrix.

(ii) The diagonal entries on the main diagonal (top left to bottom right) are 0 except when there is a loop. If there are loops at the vertex v_i then a_{ii} = number of loops at v_i.

(iii) If there is no loop at the vertex v_i then the sum of all the entries in the column of v_i gives the degree of v_i.

(iv) If there are no parallel edges and loops in G then all the entries of A(G) will be 0 or 1.

(v) If two graphs G_1 and G_2 are isomorphic then we can obtain $A(G_1)$ from $A(G_2)$ by permuting rows of $A(G_1)$ into themselves and that for columns in the same w and converse is also true.

Now we consider the converse problem i.e. given a n × n symmetric matrix whose elements are non-negative integers then to draw a graph associated with this matrix. This is done simply by joining the vertices v_i, v_j by the number of edges equal to a_{ij}.

4.3.2 Incidence Matrix

Let G be a graph with n vertices $v_1, v_2, ..., v_n$ and q edges $e_1, e_2, ..., e_q$. Then the incidence matrix $M = [m_{ij}]$ is n × q matrix in which the entry m_{ij} represents the number of times the vertex v_i is incident on the edge e_j.

i.e. $m_{ij} = \begin{cases} 0 & \text{if } v_i \text{ is not end vertex of } e_j \\ 1 & \text{if } v_i \text{ is end vertex of } e_j \text{ (not loop)} \\ 2 & \text{if } v_i \text{ is end vertex of } e_j \text{ (loop)} \end{cases}$

We also denote incidence matrix of graph G by I(G).

For example, consider the following graph.

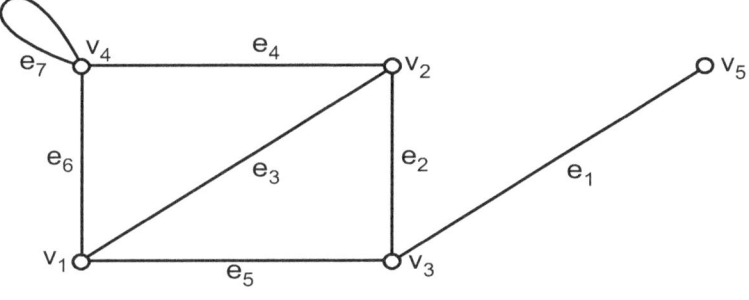

Fig. 4.65

This graph has 5 vertices and 7 edges. Therefore. incidence matrix is 5×7 matrix.

$$\begin{array}{c c} & \begin{array}{ccccccc} e_1 & e_2 & e_3 & e_4 & e_5 & e_6 & e_7 \end{array} \\ \begin{array}{c} v_1 \\ v_2 \\ v_3 \\ v_4 \\ v_5 \end{array} & \left[\begin{array}{ccccccc} 0 & 0 & 1 & 0 & 1 & 1 & 0 \\ 0 & 1 & 1 & 1 & 0 & 0 & 0 \\ 1 & 1 & 0 & 0 & 1 & 0 & 0 \\ 0 & 0 & 0 & 1 & 0 & 1 & 2 \\ 1 & 0 & 0 & 0 & 0 & 0 & 0 \end{array} \right] \end{array}$$

We observe that the sum of the entries in the row of v_i gives the degree of v_i. Also the sum of the entries in each column is 2; its being the contribution of 2 degrees by any edge.

If two graphs are isomorphic then we can obtain $I(G_2)$ from $I(G_1)$ by permuting rows of $I(G_1)$ into themselves and permuting columns into themselves in the same way. Also converse is true.

ILLUSTRATIVE EXAMPLES

Example 4.8 : *Let G be a graph with p vertices, r of which have degree k and the others have degree k + 1. Prove that $r = (k + 1) p - 2q$, where, q is the number of edges in G.*

Solution : A graph G has p vertices and q edges.

By hand shaking lemma, the total degree is 2q. ... (1)

Also out of p vertices, r of them have degree k and remaining p − r vertices have degree k + 1.

∴ Total degree = rk + (p − r) (k + 1)   ... (2)

From equations (1) and (2), we have,

rk + (p − r) (k + 1) = 2q

∴ − r + p (k + 1) = 2q

∴ r = p (k + 1) − 2q

Example 4.9 : *A graph G has n vertices and n − 1 edges. Prove that G has either a vertex of degree 1 or an isolated vertex.*

Solution : A graph G has n vertices and n − 1 edges.

By hand shaking lemma, the total degree is 2 (n − 1) = 2n − 2.

Assume that G does not have a vertex of degree 1 and no isolated vertex.

Then degree of each of n vertices is greater than or equal to 2. Therefore, total degree ≥ 2n. This contradicts to the fact that the total degree is 2n − 2.

Hence our assumption is wrong.

∴ G must have a vertex of degree 1 or an isolated vertex.

Example 4.10 : *How many edges are there in a graph with 10 vertices each of degree 6 ?*

Solution : Graph G has 10 vertices each of degree 6.

Therefore, total degree is 10 × 6 = 66. We know that each edge in a graph contributes 2 degrees. Therefore, the number of edges = $\frac{60}{2}$ = 30.

Example 4.11 : *The five military stations of a country are to be connected by express highway roads. The cost in ₹ crores of constructing a road between two stations is given in the following table. The infinity cost implies that a road cannot be constructed between two stations due to the geographical conditions.*

	a	b	c	d	e
a	–	4	5	∞	∞
b	4	–	∞	7	∞
c	5	∞	–	6	∞
d	∞	7	6	–	2
e	∞	∞	∞	2	–

(a) Represent the situation by a graph.
(b) Find the degree of each vertex.
(c) Find the total weight of the graph.

Solution : (a)

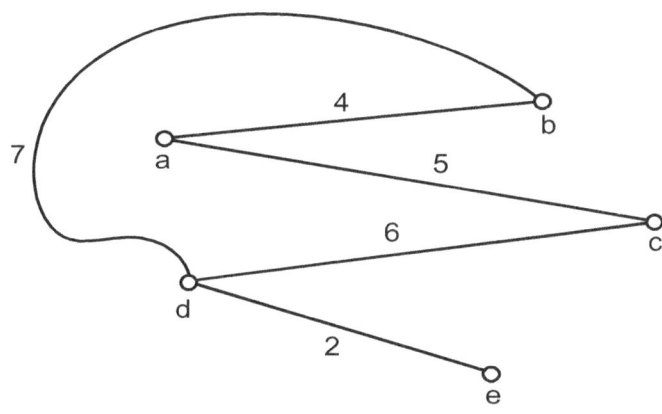

Fig. 4.66

(b) $d(a) = 2$, $d(b) = 2$, $d(c) = 2$, $d(d) = 3$, $d(e) = 1$.

(c) Total weight of the graph is $4 + 5 + 7 + 6 + 2 = 24$ crores ₹.

Example 4.12 : *Draw a multigraph corresponding to the adjacency matrix.*

$$\begin{array}{c} \quad\quad v_1\ v_2\ v_3\ v_4 \\ \begin{matrix} v_1 \\ v_2 \\ v_3 \\ v_4 \end{matrix} \begin{bmatrix} 1 & 1 & 1 & 2 \\ 1 & 0 & 0 & 0 \\ 1 & 0 & 0 & 2 \\ 2 & 0 & 2 & 2 \end{bmatrix} \end{array}$$

Solution : The given matrix is 4×4 symmetric matrix. Hence, the associated graph G has 4 vertices. We see that $a_{11} = 1$ which implies that there is a loop at the vertex v_1. Also there are 2 loops at v_4. Further, $a_{14} = 2$ means there are 2 edges joining v_1 and v_4.

Similarly for other entries of the matrix.

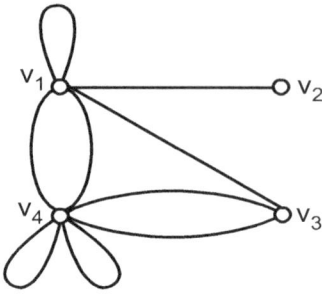

Fig. 4.67

Example 4.13 : *Draw the graph represented by the incidence matrix*

$$\begin{array}{c} \\ v_1 \\ v_2 \\ v_3 \\ v_4 \\ v_5 \end{array} \begin{array}{c} \begin{array}{cccccc} e_1 & e_2 & e_3 & e_4 & e_5 & e_6 \end{array} \\ \begin{bmatrix} 0 & 1 & 0 & 0 & 1 & 1 \\ 0 & 1 & 2 & 0 & 1 & 0 \\ 0 & 0 & 0 & 0 & 0 & 1 \\ 1 & 0 & 0 & 1 & 0 & 0 \\ 1 & 0 & 0 & 1 & 0 & 0 \end{bmatrix} \end{array}$$

Solution : The given matrix M is 5 × 6 matrix. Therefore, associated graph has 5 vertices and 6 edges. We see that edge e_1 has v_4 and v_5 as its end vertices. Similarly, e_2 has v_1 and v_2 as its end vertices. The edge e_3 forms a loop at v_2. The graph is as shown below.

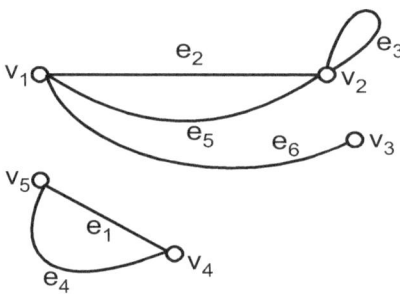

Fig. 4.68

We note that the identical columns in the incidence matrix correspond to parallel edges of the associated graph.

Example 4.14 : *Draw the following graphs :*

(i) Non-complete bipartite graph.

(ii) Complete graph which is complete bipartite.

(iii) Regular graph but not complete.

(iv) $^3R_6$ i.e. 3 regular graph with 6 vertices.

(v) Wheel graph with outside 5 vertices.

(vi) Star of outside 5 vertices.

Solution :

(i) Non-complete bipartite graph.

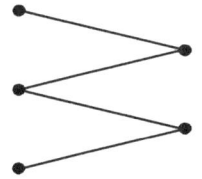

Fig. 4.69

(ii) Complete graph which is complete bipartite.

Fig. 4.70

(iii) Regular graph but not complete.

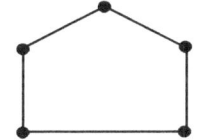

Fig. 4.71

(iv) $^3R_6$ i.e. 3 regular graph with 6 vertices.

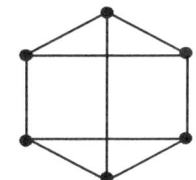

Fig. 4.72

(v) Wheel graph with outside 5 vertices.

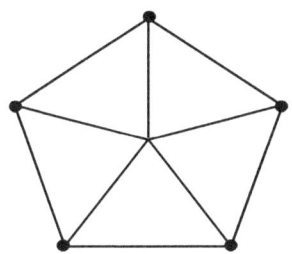

Fig. 4.73

(vi) Star of outside 5 vertices.

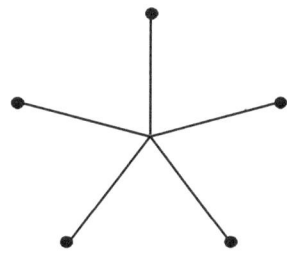

Fig. 4.74

Example 4.15 : *Find adjacency matrix of following graph.*

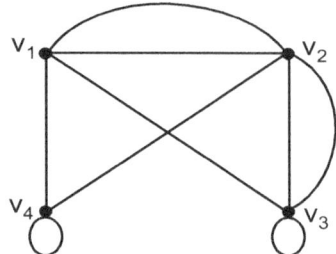

Fig. 4.75

Solution : Graph G has 4 vertices. Adjacent matrix of it is given below :

	v_1	v_2	v_3	v_4
v_1	0	2	1	1
v_2	2	0	2	1
v_3	1	2	1	0
v_4	1	1	0	1

Example 4.16 : *Write incidence and adjacency matrix of the following graph :*

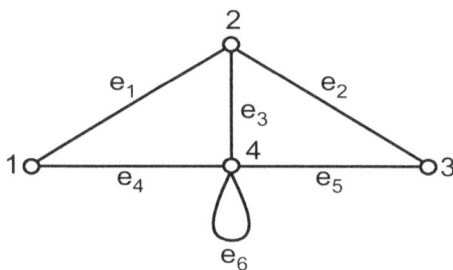

Fig. 4.76

Solution : Give graph G has 4 vertices and 6 edges. Incidence matrix $I(G) = [m_{ij}]$.

$i = 1, 2, 3, 4, \quad j = 1, 2, 3, 4, 5, 6$ is 4×6 matrix.

$$M(G) = \begin{matrix} 1 \\ 2 \\ 3 \\ 4 \end{matrix} \begin{bmatrix} 1 & 0 & 0 & 1 & 0 & 0 \\ 1 & 1 & 1 & 0 & 0 & 0 \\ 0 & 1 & 0 & 0 & 1 & 0 \\ 0 & 0 & 1 & 1 & 1 & 2 \end{bmatrix}$$

Graph G has 4 vertices. The adjacency matrix A(G) is 4 × 4 matrix.

$$A(G) = \begin{array}{c} \\ 1 \\ 2 \\ 3 \\ 4 \end{array} \begin{array}{c} \begin{array}{cccc} 1 & 2 & 3 & 4 \end{array} \\ \left[\begin{array}{cccc} 0 & 1 & 0 & 1 \\ 1 & 0 & 1 & 1 \\ 0 & 1 & 0 & 1 \\ 1 & 1 & 1 & 1 \end{array} \right] \end{array}$$

Example 4.17 : *Draw the graph represented by the adjacency matrix.*

$$\begin{array}{c} \\ p \\ q \\ r \\ s \end{array} \begin{array}{c} \begin{array}{cccc} p & q & r & s \end{array} \\ \left[\begin{array}{cccc} 0 & 1 & 2 & 0 \\ 1 & 2 & 1 & 1 \\ 2 & 1 & 0 & 0 \\ 0 & 1 & 0 & 0 \end{array} \right] \end{array}$$

Solution : Adjacency matrix has four rows and four columns. Therefore, the graph of given adjacency matrix is given in Fig. 4.77 below.

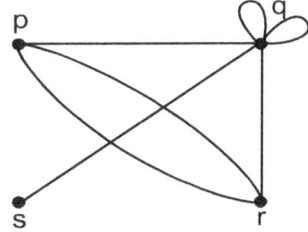

Fig. 4.77

Example 4.18 : *Consider a circle centered (1, 1) and having radius 3 units. Is it a graph? Justify.*

Solution : Circle with centre (1, 1) and radius 3 is not graph because circumference of circle is not forms an edge.

Example 4.19 : *State Handshaking lemma and justify with proper example.*

Solution : **Statement of Handshaking lemma :** The sum of the degrees of all the vertices is equal to twice the number of edges in graph.

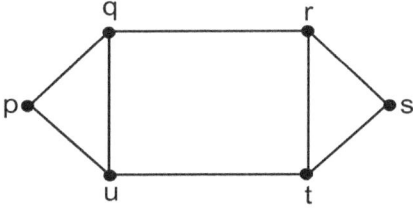

Fig. 4.78

$$d(p) = 2$$
$$d(q) = 3$$
$$d(r) = 3$$
$$d(s) = 2$$
$$d(t) = 3$$
$$d(u) = 3$$
$$\Rightarrow \sum_{V \in G} d(v) = 2 + 3 + 3 + 2 + 3 + 3 = 16$$

number of edges of graph are 8.

∴ $\sum_{V \in G} d(v) = 2.8 = 2 \times$ number of edges in G.

∴ Handshaking lemma is verified.

Example 4.20 : *For the following graphs G_1 and G_2, find $G_1 \times G_2$.*

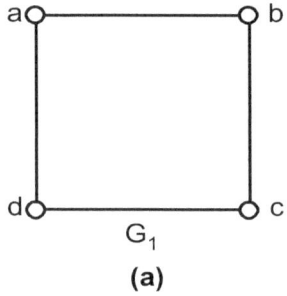
G_1
(a)

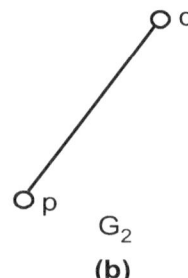
G_2
(b)

Fig. 4.79

Solution : The vertex set of $G_1 \times G_2$ is (a, p), (a, q), (b, p), (b, q), (e, p), (e, q), (d, p), (d, q).

```
(a, p) O————————O (a, q)
(b, p) O————————O (b, q)
(c, p) O————————O (c, q)
(d, p) O————————O (d, q)
```

Fig. 4.80

By keeping 'a' fixed, we make a copy of G_2. Similarly, by keeping 'b', 'c', 'd' fixed, we make copy of G_2.

Also by keeping 'p' fixed and 'q' fixed, we make a copy of G_1. The resulting graph $G_1 \times G_2$ is as below.

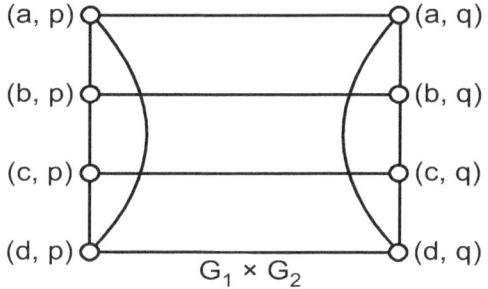

Fig. 4.81

Example 4.21 : *How many edges in a graph with 10 vertices with each of degree 6 ?*

Solution : Given that G(V, E) is a graph with $|V| = 10$ and $d(v) = 6 \ \forall \ v \in V$.

∴ By handshaking lemma,

$$\sum_{V \in G} d(v) = 2|E|$$

∴ $$\sum_{V \in G} 6 = 2|E| \qquad (\because d(v) = 6 \ \forall \ v \in V)$$

∴ $$6 \times |V| = |E|$$

∴ $$\boxed{30 = |E|}$$

Example 4.22 : *Find the smallest integer n such that k_n has atleast 600 edges.*

Solution : Given that k_n has atleast 600 edges

∴ $$|E| \geq 600$$

But by handshaking lemma, for k_n, we have

$$|E| = \frac{n(n-1)}{2}$$

∴ We have, $\frac{n(n-1)}{2} \geq 600$

$$n(n-1) \geq 1200$$

i.e. we have $35 \times 34 = 1190 < 1200$ and $36 \times 35 = 1260 > 1200$

∴ $$\boxed{n = 36}$$

Example 4.23 : *Let G is k regular graph and k is odd integer. Prove that number of edges in G is multiple of k.*

Solution : Given that G(V, E) is a graph with $d(v) = k \ \forall v \in V$ and k is odd.

By handshaking lemma,

$$\sum_{v \in V} d(v) = 2|E|$$

$$\therefore \sum_{v \in V} k = 2|E| \qquad (\because d(v) = k \ \forall v \in V)$$

$$\therefore k \times |V| = 2|E|$$

$(\because 2|E|$ is even and K is odd $\Rightarrow |V|$ is even)

$$\therefore k \times \left(\frac{|V|}{2}\right) = |E|$$

$\therefore$ Hence proof.

Example 4.24 : *Let G be a simple graph with atleast two vertices. Show that G contains atleast two vertices of same degree.*

Solution : Given that G(V, E) be a graph with $|V| \geq 2$.

Let $|V| = n$

we observe that,

G has vertex of degree n iff G does not have an isolated vertex. ... (1)

Let A_i = set of vertices in G having degree i, we have atmost n – 1 such non-empty sets.

Namely $A_0, A_1, A_2 \ldots A_n$ (from equation (1) A_0 or A_n is empty)

If we want to put vertices in V into sets A_i's, by pigeon-hole principle atleast two A_i's contain more than 2 vertices say u, v.

Hence we get, $d(v) = d(u)$

Example 4.25 : *Which complete bipartite graphs are complete graphs ?*

Solution : K_1 and K_2 are only complete bipartite graphs which are complete graphs.

[$\because$ If G is complete bipartite graph with partition $V = X \cup Y$ then $|X| \not> $ and $|Y| \not> 1$ otherwise G will not be complete graph]

Example 4.26 : *Write all possible adjacency matrices and incidence matrices for following graphs*

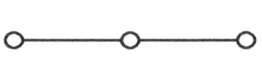 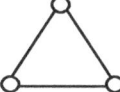

Fig. 4.82 (a)

Solution : Consider the graph

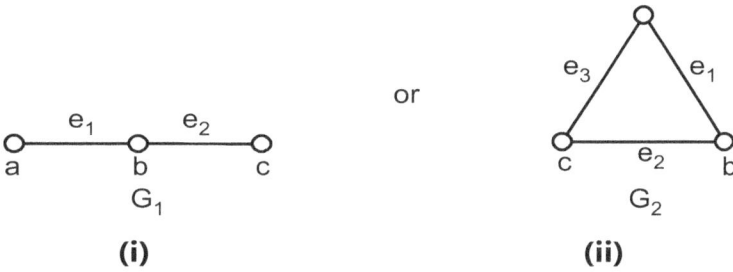

Fig. 4.82 (b)

∴ Adjacency matrices are

$$A(G_1) = \begin{array}{c} \\ a \\ b \\ c \end{array} \begin{array}{ccc} a & b & c \\ \begin{bmatrix} 0 & 1 & 0 \\ 1 & 0 & 1 \\ 0 & 1 & 0 \end{bmatrix} \end{array}, \quad A(G_2) = \begin{array}{c} \\ a \\ b \\ c \end{array} \begin{array}{ccc} a & b & c \\ \begin{bmatrix} 0 & 1 & 1 \\ 1 & 0 & 1 \\ 1 & 1 & 0 \end{bmatrix} \end{array}$$

Permuting rows into themselves and columns into themselves in similar way as that of rows, we get another adjacency matrices. Now incidence matrices are

$$I(G_1) = \begin{array}{c} \\ a \\ b \\ c \end{array} \begin{array}{cc} e_1 & e_2 \\ \begin{bmatrix} 1 & 0 \\ 1 & 1 \\ 0 & 1 \end{bmatrix} \end{array} \quad I(G_2) = \begin{array}{c} \\ a \\ b \\ c \end{array} \begin{array}{ccc} e_1 & e_2 & e_3 \\ \begin{bmatrix} 1 & 0 & 1 \\ 1 & 1 & 0 \\ 0 & 1 & 1 \end{bmatrix} \end{array}$$

Permuting the headings of rows into themselves and column into themselves and changing entries accordingly, we get another incidence matrices.

Example 4.27 : *Draw the graphs of the following adjacency matrix.*

$$\begin{bmatrix} 0 & 1 & 0 & 0 \\ 1 & 0 & 2 & 2 \\ 0 & 2 & 1 & 2 \\ 0 & 2 & 2 & 1 \end{bmatrix}$$

Solution : Let G be a graph with A(G) as shown above.

$$\therefore \quad A(G) = \begin{array}{c} \\ a \\ b \\ c \\ d \end{array} \begin{array}{cccc} a & b & c & d \\ \begin{bmatrix} 0 & 1 & 0 & 0 \\ 1 & 0 & 2 & 2 \\ 0 & 2 & 1 & 2 \\ 0 & 2 & 2 & 1 \end{bmatrix} \end{array} \quad \text{where a, b, c, d are vertices of G}$$

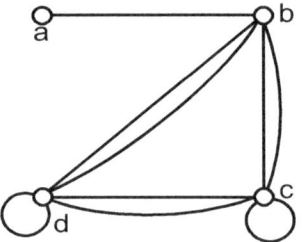

Fig. 4.83

Example 4.28 : *Let G be a bipartite graph, show that we can list the vertices of G so that corresponding adjacency matrix of G has the form*

$$A(G) = \begin{bmatrix} O & C \\ D & O \end{bmatrix}$$

Solution : Let vertex set V of G has partition

{X, Y} i.e. $X \cup Y = V \quad X \cap Y = \phi$

and no two vertices of X are adjacent and no two vertices of Y are adjacent.

Let $\quad\quad\quad\quad X = \{x_1, x_2 \ldots x_m\}$
$\quad\quad\quad\quad\quad\quad Y = \{y_1, y_2 \ldots y_l\}$

Write A(G) with row headings $x_1, x_2 \ldots x_m, y_1 \ldots y_l$ and column headings $x_1, x_2, \ldots, x_m, y_1 \ldots y_l$.

We get, $\quad\quad A(G) = \begin{bmatrix} O & C \\ D & O \end{bmatrix}$

Example 4.29 : *Consider the graph G*

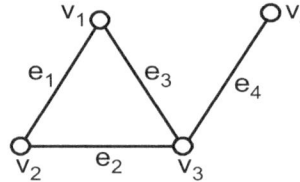

Fig. 4.84

Find A(G) and I(G).

Solution :

$$A(G) = \begin{array}{c} \\ v_1 \\ v_2 \\ v_3 \\ v_4 \end{array} \begin{array}{c} v_1\ v_2\ v_3\ v_4 \\ \left[\begin{array}{cccc} 0 & 1 & 1 & 0 \\ 1 & 0 & 1 & 0 \\ 0 & 1 & 1 & 1 \\ 0 & 0 & 1 & 0 \end{array}\right] \end{array} \quad I(G) = \begin{array}{c} \\ v_1 \\ v_2 \\ v_3 \\ v_4 \end{array} \begin{array}{c} e_1\ e_2\ e_3\ e_4 \\ \left[\begin{array}{cccc} 1 & 0 & 1 & 0 \\ 1 & 1 & 0 & 0 \\ 0 & 1 & 1 & 1 \\ 0 & 0 & 0 & 1 \end{array}\right] \end{array}$$

Example 4.30 : *Prove that it is impossible to have a group of 9 people at a party such that each one knows exactly five of the others in the group.*

Solution : Let us represent persons at party by set of vertices (p_1, p_2, p_3, p_4, p_5, p_6, p_7, p_8, p_9} we join p_i to p_j by an edge, if p_i knows p_j (obviously p_j knows p_i)

∴ Each p_i has degree 5.

∴ Sum of degrees = $5 \times 9 = 45$

But by handshaking lemma sum of degrees = $2 \times |E|$

where, $|E|$ = Number of edges

∴ $\qquad 45 = 2 \times |E|$

∴ 45 is even, which is absurd.

∴ Hence it is impossible to have a group of 9 people at a party such that each one knows exactly five of others in the group.

EXERCISE 4.2

1. Find the adjacency matrix and incidence matrix of the graph.

   (a)   (b)

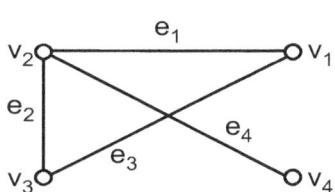
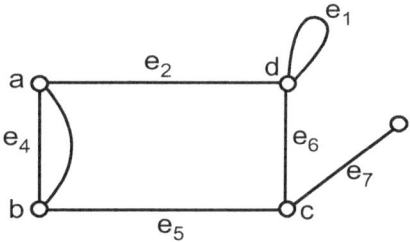

       Fig. 4.85 (a)   **Fig. 4.85 (b)**

(c) (d)

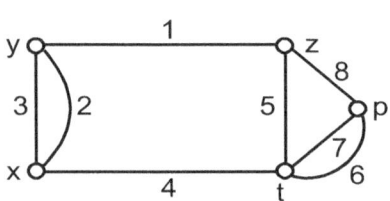 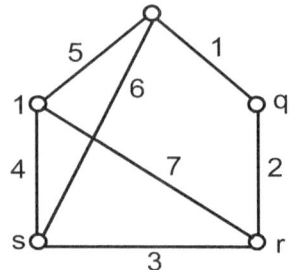

Fig. 4.85 (c)   **Fig. 4.85 (d)**

2. The adjacency matrix of the graph is given below. Draw the graph.

(a) $\begin{bmatrix} 1 & 1 & 2 & 0 \\ 1 & 2 & 1 & 3 \\ 2 & 1 & 0 & 1 \\ 0 & 3 & 1 & 0 \end{bmatrix}$
(b) $\begin{bmatrix} 1 & 3 & 0 & 0 \\ 3 & 0 & 2 & 1 \\ 0 & 2 & 1 & 2 \\ 0 & 1 & 2 & 0 \end{bmatrix}$

(c) $\begin{bmatrix} 0 & 2 & 0 & 1 \\ 2 & 1 & 1 & 1 \\ 0 & 1 & 0 & 1 \\ 1 & 1 & 1 & 0 \end{bmatrix}$
(d) $\begin{bmatrix} 1 & 1 & 1 & 2 \\ 1 & 0 & 0 & 0 \\ 1 & 0 & 0 & 2 \\ 2 & 0 & 2 & 2 \end{bmatrix}$

3. Draw a graph G with vertex set {1, 2, 3, 4, 5, 6, 7} and exactly one edge between the members of each of the following pairs of vertices: (1, 2), (1, 3) (2, 4), (2, 5), (3, 6), (3, 7). Is G simple ?

4. Determine the number of edges in a graph with 6 vertices, 2 of degree 4 and 4 of degree 2.

   Draw two such graphs one simple and the other not simple.

5. Verify hand shaking lemma for the graph shown in Fig. 4.86.

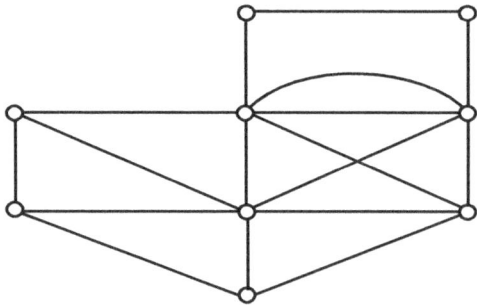

Fig. 4.86

6. Prove that it is impossible to have a group of nine people at a party such that each one knows exactly five of the others in the group.

7. Let G be a simple graph with at least two vertices. Show that G contains at least two vertices of the same degree.

8. Draw the graphs $K_{2,4}$ and $K_{3,2}$.

9. Find the smallest integer n such that K_n has at least 600 edges.

10. G is a K-regular graph where K is odd number. Prove that the number of edges in G is a multiple of K.

ANSWERS 4.2

1. (a)

$$A(G) = \begin{array}{c} \\ v_1 \\ v_2 \\ v_3 \\ v_4 \end{array} \begin{array}{cccc} v_1 & v_2 & v_3 & v_4 \\ \left[\begin{array}{cccc} 0 & 1 & 1 & 0 \\ 1 & 0 & 1 & 1 \\ 1 & 1 & 0 & 0 \\ 0 & 1 & 0 & 0 \end{array}\right] \end{array}$$

$$M(G) = \begin{array}{c} \\ v_1 \\ v_2 \\ v_3 \\ v_4 \end{array} \begin{array}{cccc} e_1 & e_2 & e_3 & e_4 \\ \left[\begin{array}{cccc} 1 & 0 & 1 & 0 \\ 1 & 1 & 0 & 1 \\ 0 & 1 & 1 & 0 \\ 0 & 0 & 0 & 1 \end{array}\right] \end{array}$$

(b)

$$A(G) = \begin{array}{c} \\ a \\ b \\ c \\ d \\ e \end{array} \begin{array}{ccccc} a & b & c & d & e \\ \left[\begin{array}{ccccc} 0 & 2 & 0 & 1 & 0 \\ 2 & 0 & 1 & 0 & 0 \\ 0 & 1 & 0 & 1 & 1 \\ 1 & 0 & 1 & 1 & 0 \\ 0 & 0 & 1 & 0 & 0 \end{array}\right] \end{array}$$

$$M(G) = \begin{array}{c} \\ a \\ b \\ c \\ d \\ e \end{array} \begin{array}{c} e_1 \quad e_2 \quad e_3 \quad e_4 \quad e_5 \quad e_6 \quad e_7 \\ \left[\begin{array}{ccccccc} 0 & 1 & 1 & 1 & 0 & 0 & 0 \\ 0 & 0 & 1 & 1 & 1 & 0 & 0 \\ 0 & 0 & 0 & 0 & 1 & 1 & 1 \\ 2 & 1 & 0 & 0 & 0 & 1 & 0 \\ 0 & 0 & 0 & 0 & 0 & 0 & 1 \end{array} \right] \end{array}$$

(c) $$A(G) = \begin{array}{c} \\ x \\ y \\ z \\ t \\ p \end{array} \begin{array}{c} x \quad y \quad z \quad t \quad p \\ \left[\begin{array}{ccccc} 0 & 2 & 0 & 1 & 0 \\ 2 & 0 & 1 & 0 & 0 \\ 0 & 1 & 0 & 1 & 1 \\ 1 & 0 & 1 & 0 & 2 \\ 0 & 0 & 1 & 2 & 0 \end{array} \right] \end{array}$$

$$M(G) = \begin{array}{c} \\ x \\ y \\ z \\ t \\ p \end{array} \begin{array}{c} 1 \quad 2 \quad 3 \quad 4 \quad 5 \quad 6 \quad 7 \quad 8 \\ \left[\begin{array}{cccccccc} 0 & 1 & 1 & 1 & 0 & 0 & 0 & 0 \\ 1 & 1 & 1 & 0 & 0 & 0 & 0 & 0 \\ 1 & 0 & 0 & 0 & 1 & 0 & 0 & 1 \\ 0 & 0 & 0 & 1 & 1 & 1 & 1 & 0 \\ 0 & 0 & 0 & 0 & 0 & 1 & & \end{array} \right] \end{array}$$

(d) $$A(G) = \begin{array}{c} \\ p \\ q \\ r \\ s \\ t \end{array} \begin{array}{c} p \quad q \quad r \quad s \quad t \\ \left[\begin{array}{ccccc} 0 & 1 & 0 & 1 & 1 \\ 1 & 0 & 1 & 0 & 0 \\ 0 & 1 & 0 & 1 & 1 \\ 1 & 0 & 1 & 0 & 1 \\ 1 & 0 & 1 & 1 & 0 \end{array} \right] \end{array}$$

$$M(G) = \begin{array}{c} \\ p \\ q \\ r \\ s \\ t \end{array} \begin{array}{c} 1 \quad 2 \quad 3 \quad 4 \quad 5 \quad 6 \quad 7 \\ \left[\begin{array}{ccccccc} 1 & 0 & 0 & 0 & 1 & 1 & 0 \\ 1 & 1 & 0 & 0 & 0 & 0 & 0 \\ 0 & 1 & 1 & 0 & 0 & 0 & 1 \\ 0 & 0 & 1 & 1 & 0 & 1 & 0 \\ 0 & 0 & 0 & 1 & 1 & 0 & 1 \end{array} \right] \end{array}$$

2. (a)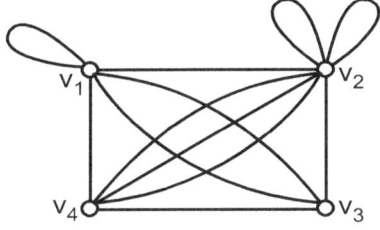

Fig. 4.87 (a)

(b)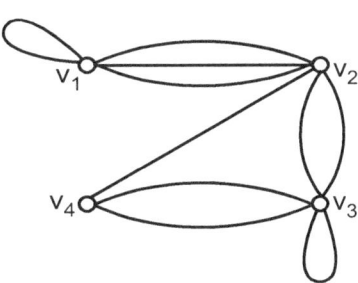

Fig. 4.87 (b)

(c)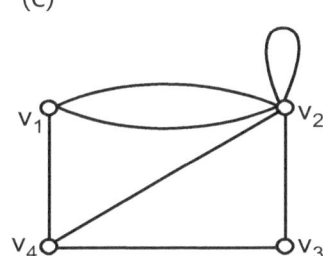

Fig. 4.87 (c)

(d)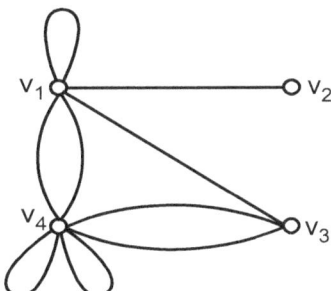

Fig. 4.87 (d)

3.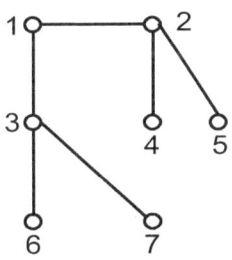

Fig. 4.88

Yes this graph is simple.

4. 8

8.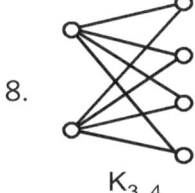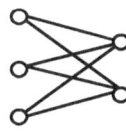

$K_{3,4}$ $K_{3,2}$

4.4 CONNECTIVITY

Introduction

We are now acquainted with the adjacency and incidence relationships in a graph. These relationships lead us to various concepts like path, cycle etc. which in turn enable us to give the definition of a connected graph. First we define those concepts.

Walk : Let G be a graph. A finite alternating sequence $\{v_1 \; e_1, v_2 \; e_2 \ldots v_i \; e_i \; v_{i+1} \ldots v_n\}$ of vertices and edges of G, beginning and ending with a vertex such that every edge involved in it is incident on a vertex which precedes and succeeds it, is called a walk in G.

This definition clearly allows the repetition of a vertex/edge in a walk.

Consider the graph given below.

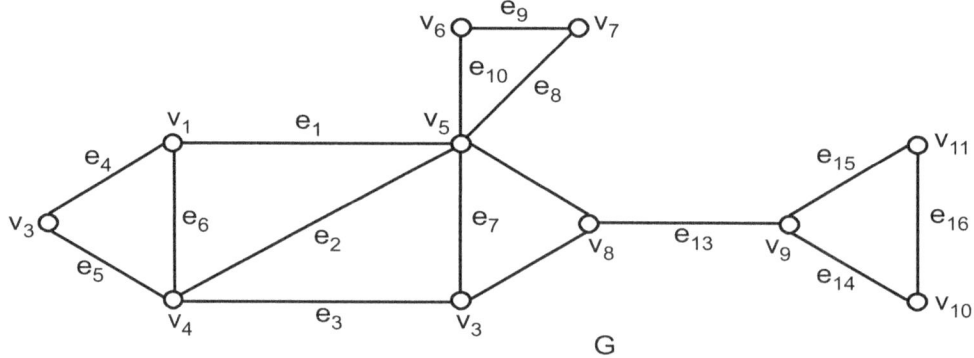

Fig. 4.90

The following are some walks in G :

W_1 : $v_4 \; e_2 \; v_2 \; e_{10} \; v_6 \; e_9 \; v_7 \; e_8 \; v_2 \; e_{11} \; v_8 \; e_{13} \; v_9 \; e_{13} \; v_8 \; e_{12} \; v_5$

W_2 : $v_4 \; e_2 \; v_2 \; e_{10} \; v_6 \; e_9 \; v_7 \; e_8 \; v_2 \; e_7 \; v_5$

W_3 : $v_1 \; e_1 \; v_2 \; e_{10} \; v_6 \; e_9 \; v_7 \; e_8 \; v_2 \; e_2 \; v_4 \; e_6 \; v_1$

W_4 : $v_3 \; e_5 \; v_4 \; e_3 \; v_5 \; e_{12} \; v_8$

W_5 : $v_4 \; e_2 \; v_2 \; e_{11} \; v_8 \; e_{12} \; v_5 \; e_3 \; v_4$

These walks differ from one another in a slight manner. For example, in the walk W_1, there is a repetition of v_2 and v_5, also the edge e_{13} is repeated. But in W_2, a vertex v_2 is repeated without repetition of any edge.

Trail : A walk in which there is no repetition of any edge is called a trail.

Thus, the walk W_2 is a trail. In any walk the vertices with which it begins and ends are called end vertices of that walk; in particular the beginning vertex is called initial vertex and the ending vertex is called terminal vertex. Any other vertex in the walk is called an intermediate vertex.

A walk is called open or closed according as its end vertices are distinct or coincident. We see that W_3 and W_5 are closed walks and the remaining 3 are open walks.

Tour : A closed trail is called a tour. Accordingly, the walk W_3 above is a tour.

Path : A walk in which any vertex is non-repeated (hence there cannot be repetition of any edge) is called a path.

Cycle : A closed path is called a cycle (or circuit). Thus, W_4 is a path and W_5 is a cycle.

The number of edges in a path (cycle) is called length of that path (cycle).

The path W_4 above is of length 3 because there are 3 edges in it and the cycle W_5 is of length 4. A single vertex is a path of length 0. A single vertex together with a loop is a cycle of length 1 and a single edge together with its two distinct vertices is a path of length 1.

If now a and b are two vertices of a graph G then there exist in general various paths of different lengths from the vertex a to the vertex b. (Note that we are assuming the existence of at least one such path.) In the graph G above, for example,

$$p_1 : v_1 \, e_1 \, v_2 \, e_{11} \, v_8$$
$$p_2 : v_1 \, e_1 \, v_2 \, e_7 \, v_5 \, e_{12} \, v_8$$
$$p_3 : v_1 \, e_6 \, v_4 \, e_2 \, v_2 \, e_7 \, v_5 \, e_{12} \, v_8$$

are paths joining v_1 to v_8 of lengths 2, 3, 4 respectively. If P is the path of minimum length joining the vertices a and b then it is called the shortest path from a to b. The length of the shortest path joining the vertices a and b of a graph G is called the distance between a and b and it is denoted by d(a, b). In the graph G mentioned above, we see that $v_4\ e_2\ v_2\ e_{11}\ v_8$ and $v_4\ e_3\ v_5\ e_{12}\ v_8$ are two different shortest paths; having path length 2. Therefore, $d(v_4, v_8) = 2$.

This shows that the shortest path joining the two given vertices is not unique but its length is unique.

Theorem 1 : In a graph G there exists a path from the vertex u to the vertex v if and only if there exists a walk from u to v.

Proof : First Part : We know that every path is a walk. Therefore, if there is a path from u to v then it can be considered as a walk from u to v.

Second Part : Suppose now that there is a walk W from u to v and W : $u\ e_1\ v_1\ e_2\ v_2\ ...\ v$.

If in W each vertex has frequency 1 i.e. appears only once then W is itself a path from u to v.

If not then some vertices in W are repeated. Let v_i be the first vertex which is repeated in W. Therefore, walk W is of the form

$$W\ :\ u\ e_1\ v_1\ ...\ e_{i-1}\ v_{i-1}\ e_i\ v_i\ e_{i+1}\ v_{i+1}\ ...\ e_j\ v_i\ ...\ v$$

From W now we delete the portion $e_{i+1}\ v_{i+1}\ ...\ e_j$.

Then W reduces to W' : $u\ e_1\ v_1\ ...\ e_i\ v_i\ ...\ v$. If there is no repetition of any vertex in W' then W' is a path from u to v. Otherwise suppose the vertex v_j is the first vertex in W' which is repeated. As before we delete the portion $e_{j+1}\ v_{j+1}\ ...\ e_k$ from W' and get W''. We continue this process of deletion until we get W* where there is no repetition of any vertex. Then W* is the required path from u to v.

Edge Sequence :

Definition : Let G(V, E) be a graph connected or disconnected and u, v be two vertices of G. An edge sequence of length n from the vertex u to the vertex v is the set S of n edges which are arranged so that

$$S\ =\ \{(u, x_1), (x_1, x_2), (x_2, x_3), ..., (x_{n-1}, v)\}.$$

In the edge sequence, the repetition of vertices and edges is permitted. The edges in the edge sequence are so arranged that every edge in it from the second edge starts with a vertex in which the preceding edge ends.

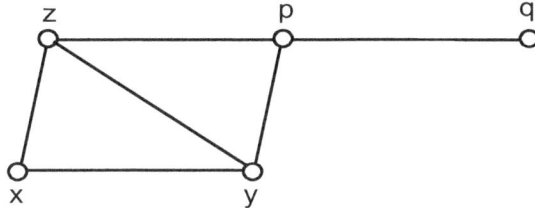

Fig. 4.91

In the above graph, consider the vertices z and q.

$$S_1 = \{(z, p), (p, q)\}$$
$$S_2 = \{(z, y), (y, p), (p, q)\}$$
$$S_3 = \{(z, x), (x, y), (y, p), (p, q)\}$$
$$S_4 = \{(z, x), (x, y), (y, z), (z, p), (p, q)\}$$

are the edge sequences of lengths 2, 3, 4, 5 respectively from the vertex z to the vertex q.

A single edge can be considered as an edge sequence of length 2 from one of its end vertex to itself. In the above graph, the set S = {(x, y), (y, x)} is an edge sequence of length 2 from x to x itself.

Suppose that G is a simple graph whose adjacency matrix is A = A(G). Then the i-jth element in the matrix A^n gives the number of edge sequences of length n from the vertex v_i to the vertex v_j. This result can be proved by induction on n.

In the above example, the adjacency matrix of G is

$$A = \begin{array}{c} \\ x \\ y \\ z \\ p \\ q \end{array} \begin{array}{c} \begin{array}{ccccc} x & y & z & p & q \end{array} \\ \left[\begin{array}{ccccc} 0 & 1 & 1 & 0 & 0 \\ 1 & 0 & 1 & 1 & 0 \\ 1 & 1 & 0 & 1 & 0 \\ 0 & 1 & 1 & 0 & 1 \\ 0 & 0 & 0 & 1 & 0 \end{array} \right] \end{array}$$

$$A^2 = \begin{bmatrix} 0 & 1 & 1 & 0 & 0 \\ 1 & 0 & 1 & 1 & 0 \\ 1 & 1 & 0 & 1 & 0 \\ 0 & 1 & 1 & 0 & 1 \\ 0 & 0 & 0 & 1 & 0 \end{bmatrix} \begin{bmatrix} 0 & 1 & 1 & 0 & 0 \\ 1 & 0 & 1 & 1 & 0 \\ 1 & 1 & 0 & 1 & 0 \\ 0 & 1 & 1 & 0 & 1 \\ 0 & 0 & 0 & 1 & 0 \end{bmatrix}$$

$$A^2 = \begin{array}{c} \\ x \\ y \\ z \\ p \\ q \end{array} \begin{array}{c} \begin{array}{ccccc} x & y & z & p & q \end{array} \\ \begin{bmatrix} 2 & 1 & 1 & 2 & 0 \\ 1 & 3 & 2 & 1 & 1 \\ 1 & 2 & 3 & 1 & 1 \\ 2 & 1 & 1 & 3 & 0 \\ 0 & 1 & 1 & 0 & 1 \end{bmatrix} \end{array}$$

Consider the row of p and column of x in the matrix A^2. The corresponding entry is 2; and in the graph G, there are exactly two edge sequences of length 2 from p to x. They are

$$S_1 = \{(p, z), (z, x)\}$$
$$\text{and } S_2 = \{(p, y), (y, x)\}$$

Again there are exactly 3 edge sequences of length 2 from z to z viz. $\{(z, p), (p, z)\}$, $\{(z, y), (y, z)\}$ and $\{(z, x), (x, z)\}$.

Further computations give us

$$A^3 = \begin{array}{c} \\ x \\ y \\ z \\ p \\ q \end{array} \begin{array}{c} \begin{array}{ccccc} x & y & z & p & q \end{array} \\ \begin{bmatrix} 2 & 5 & 5 & 2 & 2 \\ 5 & 4 & 5 & 6 & 1 \\ 5 & 5 & 4 & 6 & 1 \\ 2 & 6 & 6 & 2 & 3 \\ 2 & 1 & 1 & 3 & 0 \end{bmatrix} \end{array}$$

We see that from the vertex x to the vertex p, there are two edge sequences of length 3 viz. $\{(x, y), (y, z), (z, p)\}$ and $\{(x, z), (z, y), (y, p)\}$.

Also the entry in the row of x and column of p in A^3 is 2.

Connected Graph

In a graph G, we say that vertex a is connected to the vertex b if there exists a path (at least one) from a to b. If a is connected to b then just by reversing the path from a to b, we get a path from b to a. Thus, if a is connected to b then b is also connected to a and we say that the pair of vertices a and b is connected.

Definition : A graph G in which every pair of vertices is connected, is called a connected graph.

If G is not connected then it is said to be disconnected. In a disconnected graph, there is at least one pair of vertices which is not connected.

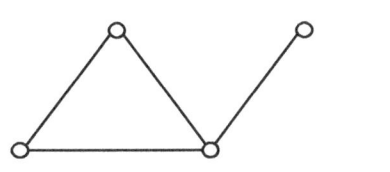
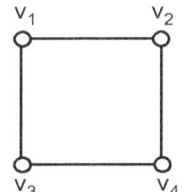

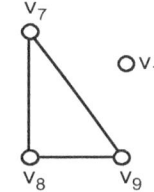

Connected graph G_1   **Disconnected graph G_2**

Fig. 4.92

A graph G_1 is connected graph with 4 vertices and 4 edges. In the graph G_2, there is no path from v_4 to v_6 or from v_6 to v_{10}. Therefore, G_2 is disconnected graph with 10 vertices and 8 edges. In addition to the two numbers (i) the number of vertices and (ii) the number of edges, there is one more number associated with any graph G.

In the above Fig. 4.93, we see that the graph A is a connected subgraph of G_2 such that it is not properly contained in any other proper subgraph of G_2.

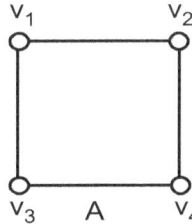

Fig. 4.93

A connected subgraph of a disconnected graph G, which is not properly contained in any proper subgraph of G is called a 'component' of G.

There are four components of the disconnected graph G_2 above. They are A, B, C, D.

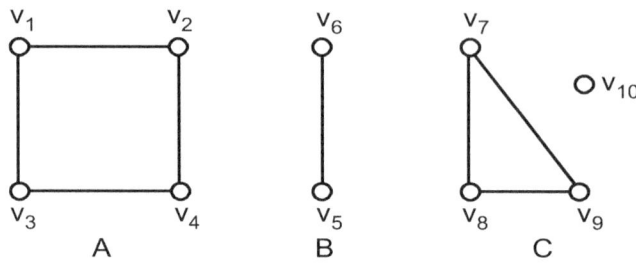

Fig. 4.94

Thus, there are three numbers associated with any graph G :

(i) number of vertices, (ii) number of edges, (iii) number of components.

The number of components in a disconnected graph G is denoted by w (G). If w (G) = 1 then G is a connected graph.

There is another way to interpret the component, which is as follows :

If v is any vertex of the graph G then consider the set H of vertices in G which are connected to v.

$$H = \{w; w \text{ is connected to } v\}$$

Then the subgraph of G induced by H i.e. < H > is a component of G containing the vertex v.

Theorem 2 : A graph G is disconnected if and only if its vertex set V can be partitioned into two non-empty disjoint subsets V_1 and V_2 such that there is no edge in G having one end vertex in V_1 and the other in V_2.

Proof : First Part : Let G be a disconnected graph and u be any vertex in G. Consider the component G_1 containing the vertex u. All vertices in G_1 are connected to u. As G is disconnected, there is a vertex v in G and v is not in G_1.

If V_1 is the set of vertices in G_1 and V_2 is the set of vertices v which are outside G_1, then there is no edge of G joining a vertex of V_1 to the vertex of V_2.

Second Part : Assume that the vertex set V of G can be partitioned into two non-empty disjoint subsets V_1 and V_2 such that there is no edge in G whose one end vertex is in V_1 and the other end vertex is in V_2.

If we choose a vertex u in V_1 and a vertex v in V_2 then by hypothesis, u is not connected to v. Thus, there is at least one pair of vertices of G that is not connected. Hence, G is a disconnected graph.

Theorem 3 : The maximum number of edges in a simple graph with n vertices and k components is $\dfrac{(n-k)(n-k+1)}{2}$.

Proof : Let G be a simple graph with n vertices and k components. If $G_1, G_2, \ldots, G_k$ are k components of G having number of vertices $n_1, n_2, \ldots, n_k$ respectively, then we have

$$n_1 + n_2 + \ldots + n_k = n$$

i.e. $\sum_{i=1}^{k} n_i = n$

As the graph G is simple, each component G_i is also simple. Therefore, maximum number of edges in G_i is $\dfrac{1}{2} n_i (n_i - 1)$. Hence, the total number of edges in G is and we have

$$|E| \leq \sum_{i=1}^{k} \frac{n_i(n_i-1)}{2} = \frac{1}{2} \sum_{i=1}^{k} n_i^2 - \frac{1}{2} \sum_{i=1}^{k} n_i$$

$$= \frac{1}{2} \sum_{i=1}^{k} n_i^2 - \frac{1}{2} n \qquad \ldots (1)$$

But $\left(\sum_{i=1}^{k} (n_i^2 - 1) \right)^2 = (n-k)^2 = n^2 - 2nk + k^2$

$$\sum_{i=1}^{k} (n_i - 1)^2 + 2 \text{ (some non-negative terms)} = n^2 - 2nk + 1$$

$$\therefore \sum_{i=1}^{k} n_i^2 - 2 \sum_{i=1}^{k} n_i + \sum_{i=1}^{k} 1 \leq n^2 - 2nk + k^2$$

$$\therefore \sum_{i=1}^{k} n_i^2 \leq n^2 - 2nk + k + 2nk \qquad \ldots(2)$$

∴ From equations (1) and (2)

∴ $$|E| \leq \frac{1}{2}[n^2 - (k-1)(2n-k)] - \frac{1}{2}n$$

$$= \frac{(n-k)(n-k+1)}{2}.$$

Hence proved.

Corollary : A simple graph with n vertices and more than $\frac{(n-1)(n-2)}{2}$ edges is connected.

Let G be a simple graph with n vertices and more than $\frac{(n-1)(n-2)}{2}$ edges.

∴ If G is disconnected then G has more than 2 or 2 components.

∴ Number of edges $\leq \frac{(n-2)(n-2+1)}{2}$ (by above theorem)

which contradicts to hypothesis that G has more than $\frac{(n-1)(n-2)}{2}$ edges.

∴ G must be connected.

Theorem 4 : Let G(V, E) be a simple graph with n vertices and m edges then $n - k \leq m$ where, k = number of components of graph G.

Proof : Let G be the graph with m edges, n vertices, k components.

We will prove this theorem by induction on m.

Basic step : Let m = 0.

Since, m = 0. Every vertex of a graph G is isolated.

Hence, number of components in G is k = n

Hence, n − k = 0 = m.

Hence, result holds true.

Induction step : Let result be true for any graph with q edges where 0 < q < m.

Let, us remove the edges successively from the graph G until, we get the graph H with k + 1 components.

Let, the number of edges in H = $m_1 \leq m - 1$.

Now by induction hypothesis, $n - (k + 1) \leq m_1$

Hence $n - k - \leq m - 1$

That is $n - k \leq m$. Hence proof.

Distance between two vertices : Let $G(V, E)$ be a connected graph. Let u, v by any two vertices in V. Distance between u and v is denoted by $d(u, v)$ and it is defined by

$$d(u, v) = \text{the minimum of length of } u - v \text{ path in G}$$

Eccentricity of an vertex : Let $G(V, E)$ be a connected graph. Let u be any two vertices in V. Eccentricity of u is denoted by $e(u)$ and it is defined as

$e(u) = \max \{d(u, v) | v \in V \; v \neq u\}$ = It is distance of a vertex farthest from u.

Center of graph : Let $G(V, E)$ be a connected graph. A vertex with minimum eccentricity is known as center of G and that minimum eccentricity is called as radius of the graph G. The max $\{d(u, v) | u, v \in V\}$ is called as diameter of the graph G. That is diameter of a graph means the distance between two farthest points in the graph.

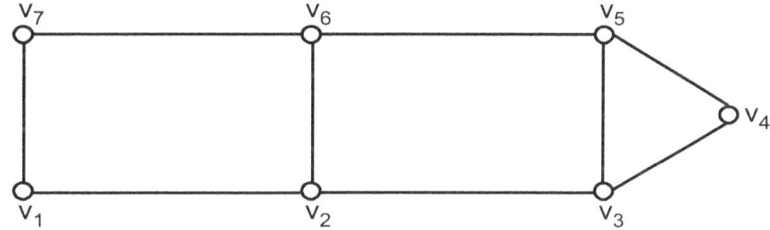

Fig. 4.95

$e(v_1) = 3$, $e(v_2) = 2$, $e(v_3) = 3$, $e(v_4) = 3$, $e(v_5) = 3$, $e(v_6) = 2$, $e(v_7) = 3$

vertices with minimum eccentricity are v_2 and v_6.

∴ $\{v_2 \; v_6\}$ is center of G and G has radius 2.

Also v_1 and v_4 are farthest from each other with distance 4.

∴ Diameter of G = 4.

Theorem 5 : Let $G(V, E)$ be a connected graph.

The function $d(u, v) = $ minimum of length of $u - v$ path, $\forall \; u, v \in V$ satisfies the properties.

(i) $d(u, v) \geq 0$ and $d(u, v) = 0 \Leftrightarrow = u = v$.

(ii) $d(u, v) = d(u, v)$

(iii) Triangle inequality : $d(u, v) \leq d(u, w) + d(w, v)$ for all $u, v, w \in V$.

Proof : Let G(V, E) be a connected graph. Let any three u, v, w ∈ V.

(i) Clearly, d(u, v) = minimum of length of u − v path ≥ 0.

Now d(u, v) = 0

⇒ Minimum of length of u − v path = 0

⇒ u = v.   Otherwise d(u, v) > 0

Also u = v ⇒ d(u, v) = minimum of length of u − v path = 0.

(ii) Clearly u − v path is also an v − u path.

Hence, minimum of length of u − v path = minimum of length of v − u path

d(u, v) = d(v, u)

(iii) By concanating any u − w path P_1 with any w − v path P_2, we get u − v walk P_1P_2.

Now a walk P_1P_2 contains a path u − v path P.

By definition of distance,

d(u, v) ≤ length of P ≤ length of P_1 + length of P_2.

But P_1 is arbitrary u − w path, P_2 is arbitrary w − v path, hence

d(u, v) ≤ inf {length of P_1 | P_1 is u − w path} + inf {length of P_2 | P_2 is w − u path}

That is d(u, v) ≤ d(u, w) + d(w, u)

Theorem 6 : Let G(V, E) be a connected graph. If r = radius and d = diameter of a graph then r ≤ d ≤ 2r.

Proof : Let us take a center v_0 of G.

Now max {d(v, v_0) | v ∈ V} ≤ max {d(v, u) | u, v ∈ V}

Hence r ≤ d .

Also, d = max {d(v, u) | u, v ∈ V}

≤ max {d(v, v_0) + d(v_0, u) | u, v ∈ V}   (by triangle inequality of d)

≤ max {d(v, v_0) | v ∈ V} + max {d(v_0, u) | u ∈ V} = r + r = 2r

Isthmus and Cut Vertex

Consider a graph G in which n is the number of vertices, e the number of edges and w (G) the number of components. In addition to these three numbers, we shall associate two more numbers with G viz. edge connectivity and vertex connectivity of G. The connectivity of a graph tells us about how much the given graph is strong or weak. Let us interpret the vertices of a graph as military stations and edges as the communication lines. In such a graph showing the communication links between various military stations, the main aim of an enemy will be to attack and destroy the weak spots so that after destroying them the communication between the remaining stations fails. As such every country tries to build its communication links in such a way that there will not be any weak spots in the corresponding graph.

The following example will be useful to clear this. Consider two graphs G_1 and G_2 with 6 vertices and 7 edges.

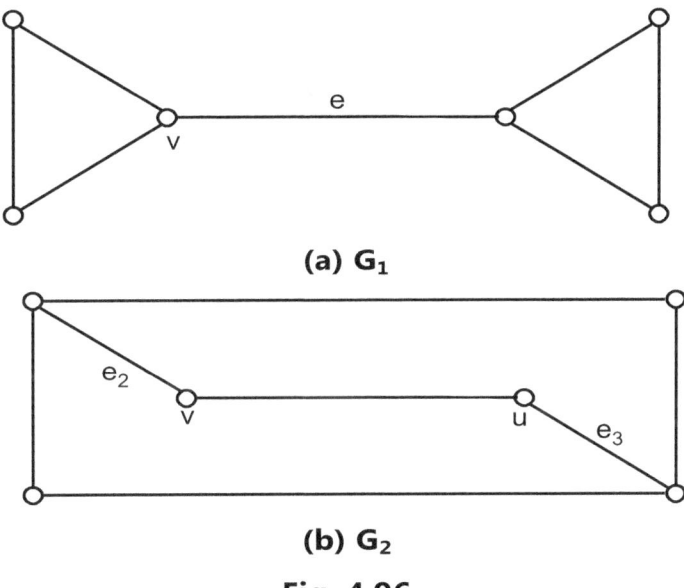

(a) G_1

(b) G_2

Fig. 4.96

The removal of single edge e_1 from G_1 results in a disconnected graph having two components as

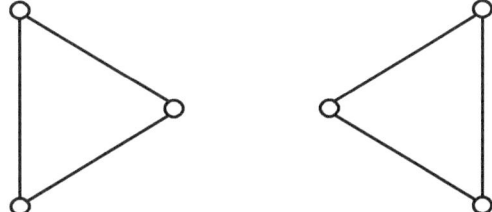

Fig. 4.97

However, after removing any single edge from G_2, the remaining graph is still connected. The enemy will be required to destroy at least two edges say e_2 and e_3 so that after their removal, the remaining graph is disconnected as

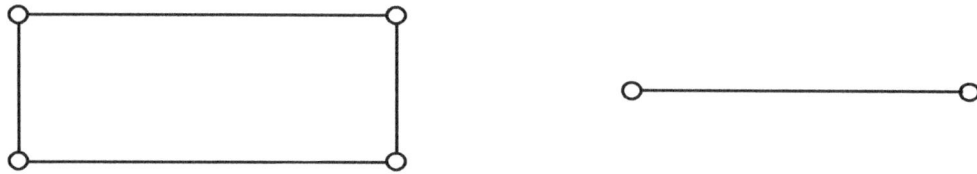

Fig. 4.98

This shows that with same number 6 of vertices and the same number 7 of edges, the graph G_2 is better connected as compared to G_1.

Again in G_1 the removal of a single vertex v results in a disconnected graph as

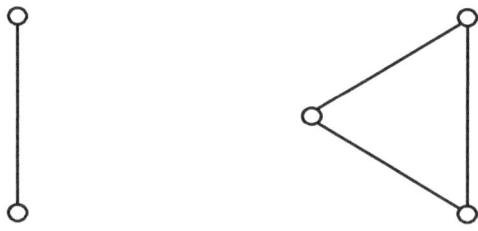

Fig. 4.99

But in the graph G_2 after removing any single vertex, the remaining 5 vertices remain connected and after removing two vertices v and w, the remaining graph is disconnected, the vertex v being isolated.

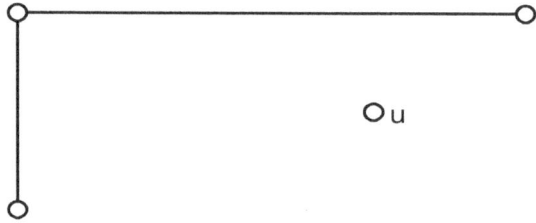

Fig. 4.100

Hence, we see again that the graph G_2 is better connected as compared to graph G_1.

Isthmus : An edge e of a graph G is called an isthmus (or bridge or cutedge) if w (G − e) > w (G) i.e. the number of components in G − e is more than that in G.

In the graph G_1 shown above, the edge e_1 is an isthmus.

We note that the removal of an isthmus from a graph G increases the number of components exactly by one and that the end vertices u and v of isthmus lie in these two different components.

Theorem 7 : The edge e_i of a graph G is an isthmus if and only if e_i does not belong to any circuit in G.

Proof : First Part : In the graph G, let the edge e_i be an isthmus with u and v as its end vertices. Then by definition, G − e consists of two components and the vertices u and v lie in these two components.

We prove that e_i is not in any circuit of G.

If possible, suppose e_i is in the circuit Γ of G.

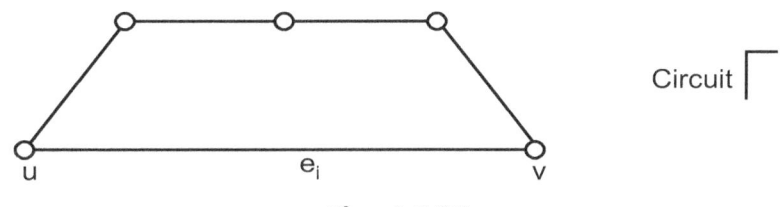

Fig. 4.101

Now by removing e_i from G, the vertices u and v still remain connected through the path p which is a part of circuit Γ. This contradicts to the definition of isthmus.

Hence, e_i cannot lie in any circuit of G.

Second Part : Assume that the edge e_i does not lie in any circuit of the graph G. Therefore, if u and v are two end vertices of e_i then u e_i v is the only path joining them. This implies that after removing the edge e_i from G, the vertices u and v are disconnected.

Hence, e_i is an isthmus.

Cut vertex : Let G (V, E) be a graph. A vertex v ∈ V is called a cut vertex of G if w (G − v) > w (G) i.e. the number of components in the graph G − v is more than that in G. A cut vertex is also called an articulation point.

We know that after removing a bridge (isthmus) from the graph G, the number of components is increased exactly by one. But after removing a cut vertex, the number of components may be increased by more.

Consider the graphs given below.

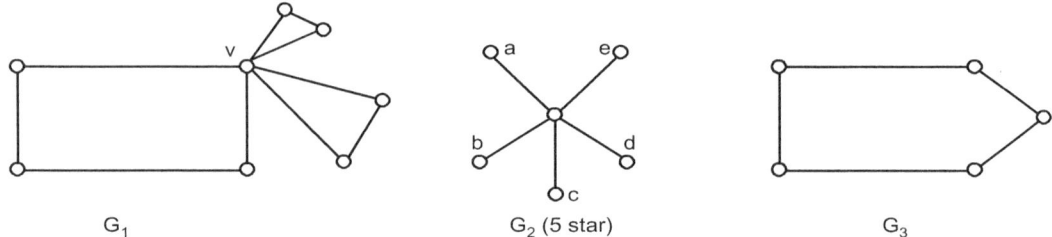

Fig. 4.102

In the graph G_1, the vertex v is a cut vertex. After removing v (and all edges incident on it), the remaining graph is as shown below.

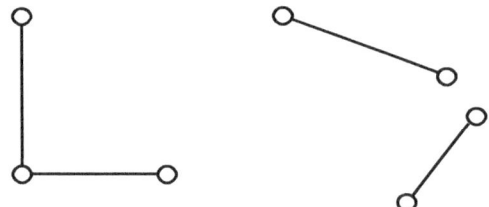

Fig. 4.103

The above graph has three components.

The graph G_2 is a 5-star and u is a cut vertex. The removal of u from G_2 makes all the 5 vertices a, b, c, d, e isolated. The graph G_3 has no cut vertex.

Theorem 8 : In a connected graph G, the vertex v is a cut vertex iff there exist two vertices x and y in G different from v such that every path joining x and y passes through v.

Proof : First Part : Suppose v is a cut vertex in a connected graph G. Then by definition of a cut vertex, the graph G − v is disconnected and has at least two different components. Let G_1 and G_2 be two such components. We choose two vertices x and y such that x is in G_1 and y is in G_2. Initially, there was a path between x and y in the graph G but there is no path between them in the graph G − v. This implies that in the graph G every path between x and y passes through v.

Second Part : Suppose x and y are two vertices in a connected graph G (x ≠ v, y ≠ v) such that every path joining x and y passes through v. If now v is deleted from G then all the paths joining x and y are broken. Thus, in the graph G – v there is no path between x and y. Therefore, G – v is a disconnected graph and the vertices x and y lie in different components. Hence, v is a cut vertex in G.

Theorem 9 : In a connected graph G, the vertex v is a cut vertex iff there exist two or more edges e_i, e_j in G incident on v such that no circuit in G includes both e_i and e_j.

Proof : First Part : Let v be the cut vertex in the connected graph G. Then by definition, G – v is disconnected and has two or more different components. Let G_1 and G_2 be two such components. We choose a vertex x in the component G_1 such that x is adjacent to v in the graph G and e_i be the edge between x and v.

Also we choose a vertex y in the component G_2 such that y is adjacent to v in the graph G and e_j be the edge between y and v. Now e_i and e_j are incident on v in G_2.

Now, we assume that a circuit Γ in G includes both the edges e_i and e_j.

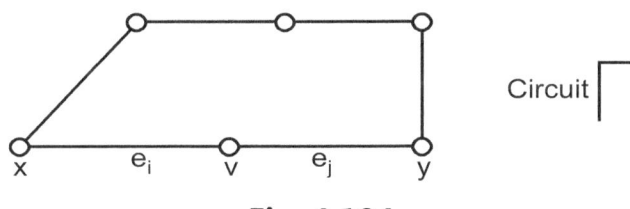

Fig. 4.104

But now we see that after removing the vertex v and edges e_i and e_j, the vertices x and y are still connected through a path which is portion of circuit Γ other than e_i and e_j. This is a contradiction because x and y are not connected in G – v. Hence, any circuit in G will not include both the edges e_i and e_j.

Second Part : Let v be a vertex in a connected graph G and e_i, e_j be two edges incident on v such that any circuit in G does not include both the edges. Let x be the other end vertex of e_i and y be the other end vertex of e_j.

We have to prove that v is a cut vertex. If possible suppose v is not a cut vertex of G. Then the graph G – v is still a connected graph. Therefore, the two vertices x and y are connected in G – v by a path say P_1.

$$P_1 : x\ e_1\ u_1\ e_2\ u_2 \ldots e_k\ y.$$

This path P_1 together with two edges e_i and e_j determine a circuit in G. But this is a contradiction to the hypothesis. Therefore, our assumption is wrong. Hence, v is a cut vertex in G.

Theorem 10 : Let G be a connected graph with at least two vertices. Then there are at least two vertices in G which are not cut vertices.

Proof : Let G be a connected graph with n vertices where $n \geq 2$. We have to prove that in G there are at least two vertices which are not cut vertices. Assume that in G there is at the most one vertex which is not a cut vertex.

Now by connectedness all the vertices of G are connected by paths. Let u and v be two vertices in G which are farthest apart i.e. d (u, v) = diameter of G.

By our assumption one of the two vertices u and v must be a cut vertex. Suppose that v is a cut vertex.

Then G – v is disconnected graph and there exists a vertex w such that u and w are in different components of G – v.

Any path between u and w passes through the vertex v. In particular the shortest path from u to w also passes through v.

This implies that d (u, w) > d (u, v) which contradicts to the hypothesis that u and v are farthest apart. So the assumption made is wrong. Hence, in G there are at least two vertices which are not cut vertices.

Corollary : Let G be a connected graph with n vertices. We have proved in the above theorem that there are at least two vertices in G which are not cut vertices. Therefore, in G the maximum number of cut vertices is n – 2.

Edge connectivity (Definition) : The edge connectivity of a connected graph G is the number of edges in the smallest set of edges whose removal from G leaves a disconnected graph.

We shall denote the edge connectivity of G by $\lambda(G)$.

The edge connectivity of a disconnected graph is defined to be 0. If a connected graph G has an isthmus then obviously $\lambda(G) = 1$.

Consider three graphs G_1, G_2, G_3 given below.

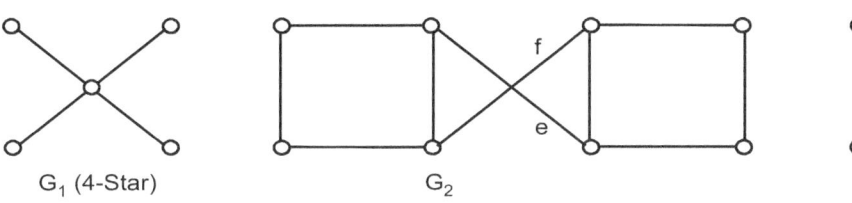

G_1 (4-Star) G_2 G_3 (4-Wheel)

Fig. 4.105

In the graph G_1, which is a 4-star, the removal of any single edge leaves one vertex isolated while the remaining vertices remain connected. Hence $\lambda(G_1) = 1$.

In the graph G_2, the removal of any single edge does not disconnect G_2 but the deletion of two edges e and f disconnects G_2. Therefore $\lambda(G_2) = 2$.

In the graph G_3, the removal of any single edge or the removal of any two edges does not disconnect G_3. However, the removal of three edges e_1, e_2, e_3 results in a disconnected graph leaving the vertex v isolated.

Thus $\lambda(G_3) = 3$.

Theorem 11 : The edge connectivity of a graph G cannot exceed the smallest degree of a vertex in G i.e. if d_{min} denotes the smallest degree of a vertex in G then $\lambda(G) \leq d_{min}$.

Proof : Let G be a connected graph with n vertices $v_1, v_2, v_3, ..., v_n$ whose degrees are $d_1, d_2, ..., d_n$ respectively. Suppose v_1 is the vertex of smallest degree in G.

Therefore $d_{min} = d_1$. Then there are d_1 edges incident on the vertex v_1.

The effect of removal of these d_1 edges (which are incident on v_1) from G results in a disconnected graph leaving the vertex v_1 (of minimum degree) as isolated vertex.

Therefore, $\lambda(G) \leq d_1$

∴ $\lambda(G) \leq d_{min}$

Theorem 12 : Let G be a connected graph with n vertices and e edges.

Then $\lambda(G) \leq \left\lfloor \dfrac{2e}{n} \right\rfloor$, where $\lfloor x \rfloor$ denotes the greatest integer not greater than x.

Proof : G is a connected graph with n vertices and e edges. Let d_{min} be the smallest degree of a vertex in G. Then the degree of each of n vertices is greater than or equal to d_{min}.

∴ Total degree $\geq n\, d_{min}$

∴ $2e \geq n\, d_{min}$

∴ $n\, d_{min} \leq 2e$

∴ $d_{min} \leq \dfrac{2e}{n}$ ... (1)

Also we know that, $\lambda(G) \leq d_{min}$ ... (2)

From (1) and (2) we have,

$$\lambda(G) \leq \dfrac{2e}{n}$$

Now since $\lambda(G)$ must be an integer, we have $\lambda(G) \leq \left\lfloor \dfrac{2e}{n} \right\rfloor$; where $\left\lfloor \dfrac{2e}{n} \right\rfloor$ is the greatest integer not greater than $\dfrac{2e}{n}$.

Vertex Connectivity (Definition) : Let G be a simple graph. Then the vertex connectivity of G is the minimum number of vertices whose removal (deletion) from G leaves either a disconnected graph or K_1 (i.e. a single vertex). The vertex connectivity of a graph G is denoted by K (G).

The vertex connectivity of a disconnected graph is 0.

Consider the two graphs given below.

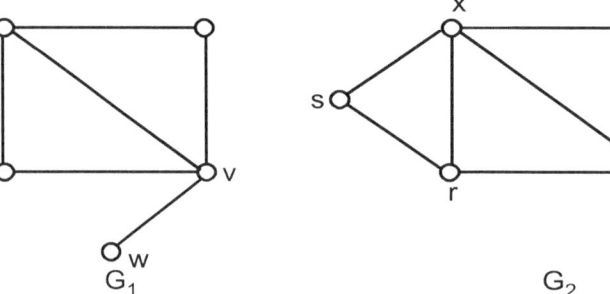

Fig. 4.106

In the graph G_1, the vertex v is a cut vertex and $K(G_1) = 1$.

In the graph G_2, the deletion of any single vertex does not result in a disconnected graph. However, after deleting the two vertices x and y, the remaining graph is disconnected as

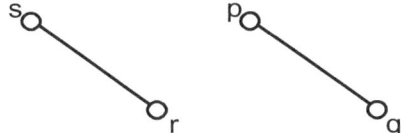

Fig. 4.107

Therefore, $K(G_2) = 2$.

Consider the complete graph K_n ($n \geq 2$) on n vertices. After deleting any one vertex say v_1 from K_1, the n – l edges joining v_1 to $v_2, v_3, ..., v_n$ are also deleted and this leaves a graph K_{n-1}. If we go on deleting in this way the vertices one-by-one, then after deletion of r vertices there will remain a complete graph K_{n-r}. The deletion of n – 1 vertices will leave K_1.

Hence, the vertex connectivity of a complete graph K_n is n – 1.

i.e. $\qquad K(K_n) = n - 1$

Theorem 13 : The vertex connectivity of a graph G cannot exceed the edge connectivity of G

i.e. $K(G) \leq \lambda(G)$.

Proof : Let G be a given graph whose edge connectivity is $\lambda(G) = \alpha$. Therefore, there exists a set of α edges in G whose removal from G leaves the disconnected graph. Suppose that after removing these edges the vertices of G are partitioned into two non-empty disjoint subsets v_1 and v_2. The end vertices of the above α edges in v_1 (or in v_2) are at the most α in number. The effect of removal of α edges from G is achieved by deleting the above end vertices which are less than or equal to α in number.

Hence, the vertex connectivity of G $\leq \alpha$.

$\therefore \qquad K(G) \leq \lambda(G)$. Hence, proved.

By combining the results of the three theorems above regarding the vertex connectivity and edge connectivity of a graph G, we have, vertex connectivity $\leq$ edge connectivity $\leq \left\lfloor \dfrac{2e}{n} \right\rfloor$.

i.e. $K(G) \leq \lambda(G) \leq \left\lfloor \dfrac{2e}{n} \right\rfloor$

In words, the maximum vertex connectivity and edge connectivity that can be achieved with n vertices and e edges is the integral part of $\dfrac{2e}{n}$.

ILLUSTRATIVE EXAMPLES

Example 4.31 : Consider the graph G given below.

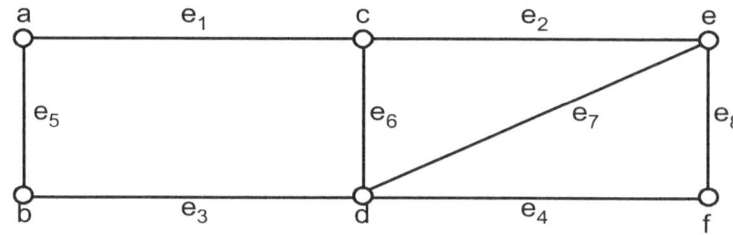

Fig. 4.108

(a) Find all paths joining a to f.

(b) What are the lengths of the paths in (a) ?

(c) Which path is the shortest path ?

(d) What is d(a, f) ?

Solution : (a) The paths joining the two vertices a and f are as follows:

p_1 : $a e_1 c e_2 e e_8 f$
p_2 : $a e_1 c e_2 e e_7 d e_4 f$
p_3 : $a e_1 c e_6 d e_4 f$
p_4 : $a e_1 c e_6 d e_7 e e_8 f$
p_5 : $a e_5 b e_3 d e_4 f$
p_6 : $a e_5 b e_3 d e_7 e e_8 f$
p_7 : $a e_5 b e_3 d e_6 c e_2 e e_8 f$

(b) The path lengths of the 7 paths are 3, 4, 3, 4, 3, 4, 5 respectively.

(c) Among all the paths joining a and f, the paths p_1, p_3, p_5 have minimum length 3. Therefore p_1, p_3, p_5 are shortest paths.

(d) d(a, f) = length of the shortest path. Therefore, d(a, f) = 3.

Example 4.32 : For a given graph G, the graph G^2 is a graph whose vertex set is that of G and u, v are adjacent in G^2 if $1 \leq d(u, v) \leq 2$ in G. For the following graph G, find G^2 and prepare a table of distances in G and G^2 (See Fig. 4.22).

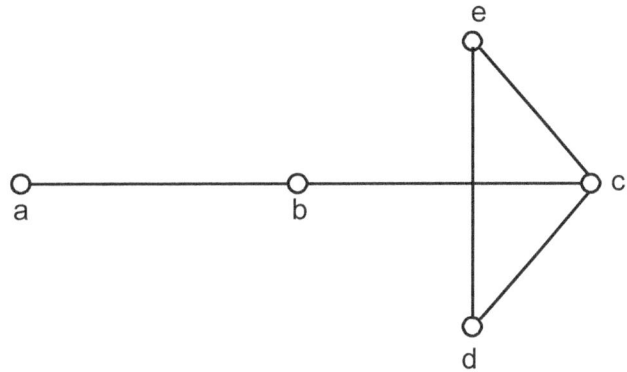

Fig. 4.109

Solution : The table showing the distances in G is as follows :

	a	b	c	d	e
a	0	1	2	3	3
b	1	0	1	2	2
c	2	1	0	1	1
d	3	2	1	0	1
e	3	2	1	1	0

The graph G^2 is as shown below.

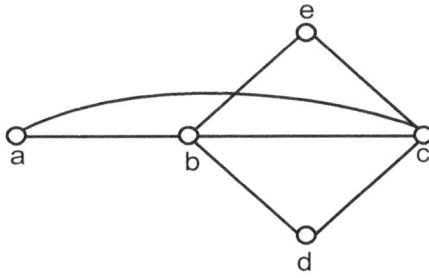

Fig. 4.110

The table showing the distances in G^2 is as follows :

	a	b	c	d	e
a	0	1	1	2	2
b	1	0	1	1	1
c	1	1	0	1	1
d	2	1	1	0	1
e	2	1	1	1	0

Example 4.33 : *Determine whether the following statement is true or false : "Every disconnected graph has an isolated vertex".*

Solution : The given statement is false.

Consider a graph G with 6 vertices a, b, c, d, e, f and 6 edges $e_1, e_2, e_3, e_4, e_5, e_6$.

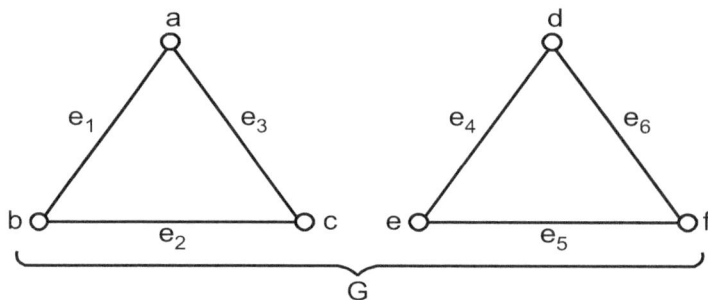

Fig. 4.111

G is a disconnected graph in which there is no isolated vertex.

Example 4.34 : *A simple graph G has vertex set {2, 3, 4, 6, 7, 8, 9, 10, 11, 12}. An edge exists between vertices x and y if x ≠ y and if x divides y or y divides x. Draw the graph G. Is G connected ? What is w (G) ?*

Solution : Under the given condition of divisibility, we see that the vertex pairs like (2, 4), (3, 6) etc. are adjacent. The graph is shown as below.

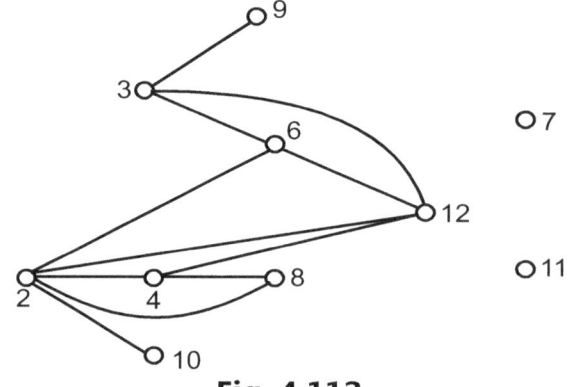

Fig. 4.112

This graph is not connected. It has three components

$$G_1 = \{2, 3, 4, 6, 8, 9, 10\}$$
$$G_2 = \{7\}$$
$$G_3 = \{11\}$$

Example 4.35 : *Find all the bridges in the following graph.*

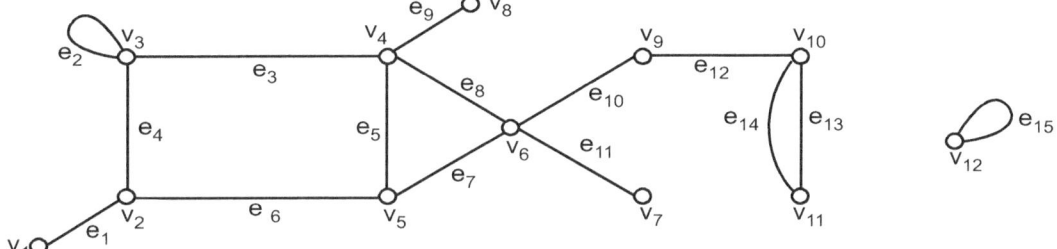

Fig. 4.113

Solution : The bridges (isthmus) in a graph are precisely those edges which does not belong to any circuit of the given graph. In the given graph, the edges $e_1, e_9, e_{10}, e_{11}, e_{12}$ do not belong to any circuit. They are bridges.

Example 4.36 : *Show that if a simple graph G is not connected then its complement $\bar{G}$ is connected. Deduce that if G is a simple connected graph and v is a cut vertex in G then v is not a cut vertex in $\bar{G}$.*

Solution : First Part : Let G be a simple graph which is not connected. Suppose G has two different connected components G_1 and G_2. Consider any two vertices x and y in the complement $\bar{G}$. We shall prove that there exists a path from x to y in $\bar{G}$.

First suppose that the vertices x and y belong to the same component say G_1 of G.

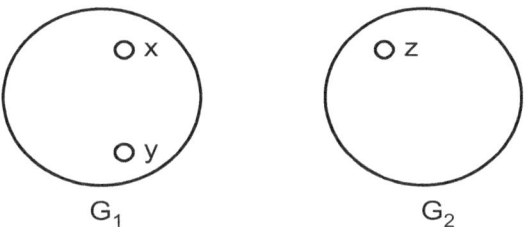

Fig. 4.114

Let z be any vertex in G_2. Then in $\overline{G}$ there exists an edge between x and z, also there exists an edge between y and z. Therefore in $\overline{G}$, x-z-y is a path from x to y. Secondly suppose x and y belong to different components say x in G_1 and y in G_2.

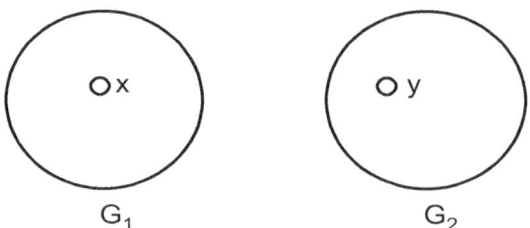

Fig. 4.115

In the graph G, the vertices x and y are not connected. However, in $\overline{G}$ there exists an edge joining x and y. Hence, there is a path from x to y in $\overline{G}$.

Thus, there exists a path between every two vertices in $\overline{G}$. So $\overline{G}$ is connected.

Second Part (Deduction) : Let G be a simple connected graph and v be a cut vertex in G. Then G − v is a simple graph which is disconnected. Therefore, by the first part, $\overline{G-v}$ is connected. But $\overline{G-v} = \overline{G} - v$. Thus, $\overline{G} - v$ is connected. Hence, v is not a cut vertex in $\overline{G}$.

Example 4.37 : *What is the maximum edge connectivity of a connected graph having 5 vertices and 8 edges ? Draw two graphs G_1 and G_2 such that in G_1 the maximum edge connectivity is achieved but in G_2 it is not.*

Solution : A connected graph G has 5 vertices and 8 edges.

∴   n = 5,   e = 8.

Maximum value of edge connectivity is $\left\lfloor \dfrac{2e}{n} \right\rfloor = \left\lfloor \dfrac{(2)(8)}{5} \right\rfloor = \left\lfloor \dfrac{16}{5} \right\rfloor = 3$

(See Fig. 4.116).

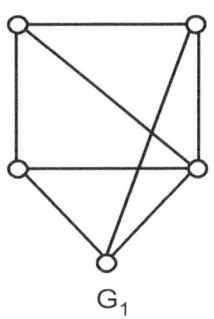
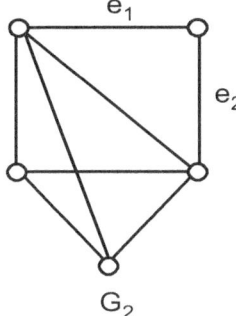

Fig. 4.116

In G_1 the removal of any single edge or any two edges does not disconnect G_1 and $d_{min} = 3$

∴ $\lambda(G_1) = 3$; maximum edge connectivity is achieved.

In G_2 there is no isthmus and the removal of e_1 and e_2 disconnects the graph G_2.

∴ $\lambda(G_2) = 2$; maximum edge connectivity is not achieved.

Example 4.38 : *Prove that a graph with n vertices and vertex connectivity K has at least $\dfrac{K \cdot n}{2}$ edges.*

Solution : We have for any graph G with n vertices and e edges, that

$$\text{vertex connectivity} \leq \text{edge connectivity} \leq \dfrac{2e}{n}.$$

Therefore, by hypothesis,

$$K \leq \dfrac{2e}{n}$$

∴ $\quad \dfrac{2e}{n} \geq K$

∴ $\quad e \geq \dfrac{K \cdot n}{2}$. Hence, proved.

Example 4.39 : *G is a connected graph with at least three vertices. Prove that if G has a bridge then G has a cut vertex.*

Solution : Let G be a connected graph with n vertices where $n \geq 3$. Assume that edge e is a bridge in G with its end vertices x and y. We shall prove that x or y (or both) is a cut vertex.

Suppose x is not a cut vertex. Therefore, G − x is a connected graph. This implies that y is the only vertex in G which is adjacent to x and remaining (at least one) vertices are connected to y. But then we see that G − y is a disconnected graph keeping the vertex x isolated and remaining vertices connected. Hence y is a cut vertex. Similarly, if y is not a cut vertex, then x is a cut vertex.

Further, if n > 3, then out of n − 2 vertices (other than x and y), it is possible that r vertices to x and n − 2 − r vertices are connected to y. In this case, x and y both are cut vertices.

Example 4.40 : *Find the maximum number of edges in a simple bipartite graph with n vertices.*

Solution : Let G is bipartite graph with partition. X and Y with $|X| = r$, $|Y| = s$, with $r + z = n$. It has maximum number of edges iff $G = K_{r,s}$ and in this case G has number of edges equals to $r \times s$.

Now varying cardinality of X and Y, we get different possibilities of $K_{r,s}$.

Now $K_{r,s}$ has maximum number of edges iff $r \times s$ is maximum.

Now we have problem

$$\max z = rs$$

$$\text{subject } r + s = n$$

$$r \geq 0, \ s \geq 0, \ r, \ s \text{ are integers}$$

From calculus, it has solution

$$r = \frac{n}{2}, \ s = \frac{n}{2} \text{ if n is even}$$

$$r = \frac{n-1}{2}, \ s = \frac{n+1}{2} \text{ if n is odd}$$

∴ In these case, we have number of edges equals to $rs = \frac{n^2}{4}$ or $rs = \frac{n^2 - 1}{4}$ respectively.

Example 4.41 : *Let V = {0, 1, 2, ... 20} be a vertex set of a graph G. An edge x and y exists where x − y is divisible by 5. Draw graph G. Explain why G is not connected. What the components of G represent ?*

Solution : Here $x - y \equiv 0 \pmod 5$ on set $\{0, 1, 2, \ldots 20\}$ is equivalence relation.

The components of G represents the equivalence classes of relation $x - y \equiv (0 \bmod 5)$ on set $\{0, 1, 2, \ldots 20\}$.

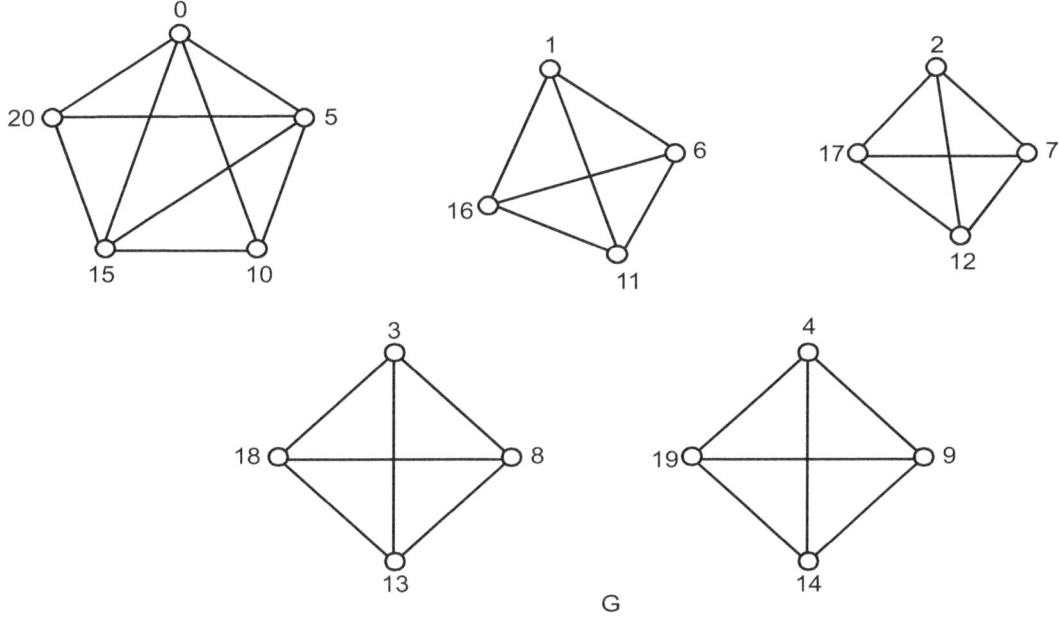

Fig. 4.117

Example 4.42 : *What is the maximum edge connectivity of a connected graph with 5 vertices and 8 edges? Draw two graphs G_1 and G_2 such that G_1 has maximum connectivity is achieved but G_2 it is not.*

Solution : Let G is connected graph with

$$n = \text{number of vertices} = 5$$
$$e = \text{number of edges} = 8$$

$\therefore \quad \lambda(G) \leq \left\lfloor \dfrac{2e}{n} \right\rfloor = \left\lfloor \dfrac{16}{5} \right\rfloor = 3$

$\therefore$ The maximum value of $\lambda(G)$ (edge connectivity) is 3.

Now we will give the examples of graphs G_1 and G_2 as below.

Consider G_1 as

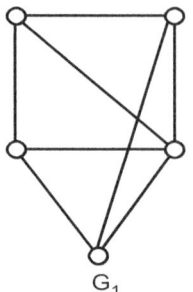

Fig. 4.118

Here removal of any two edges do not disconnect the graph G_1.
But removal of three edges incident on any vertex will disconnect G_1.

∴ $\lambda(G_1) = 3$

Consider graph G_2 as

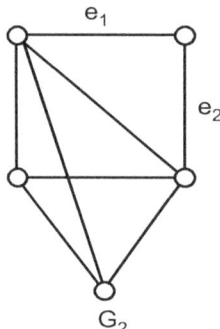

Fig. 4.119

Here removal of any edge do not disconnect G_2.

Also, here removal of e_1, e_2 disconnect G_2 producing components as below.

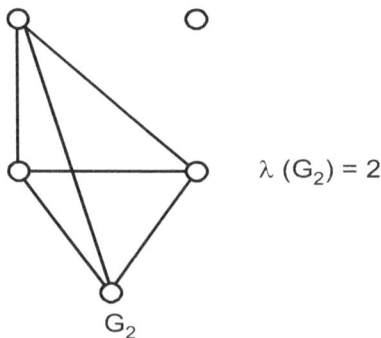

$\lambda(G_2) = 2$

Fig. 4.120

∴ $\lambda(G_2) = 2$

Example 4.43 : *G is a connected graph without least 3 vertices. Prove that if G has a bridge then G has a cut vertex.*

Solution : Let e = xy is bridge in G.

∴ G − e is disconnected graph.

∴ G − e has two components C_x and C_y containing x and y respectively.

Now G has more than two vertices.

∴ Let v ∈ G be a vertex other than x and y.

∴ v ∈ C_x or v ∈ C_y

∴ x is cut vertex or y is cut vertex, because G − x has two components containing v and other containing y or G − y has two components containing v and other containing x.

Example 4.44 : *Find the vertex connectivity K(G) of the following graph.*

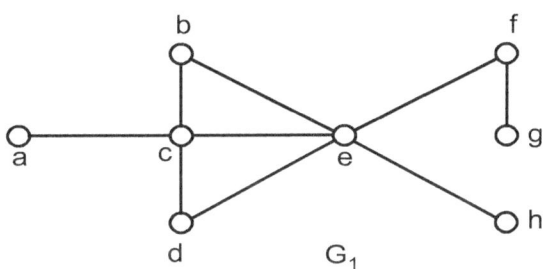

Fig. 4.121

Solution : Removal of single vertex e disconnected the graph G.

∴ K(G) = 1

Example 4.45 : *Find vertex connectivity K(G) of the following graph.*

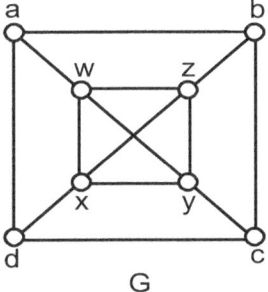

Fig. 4.122

Solution : Removal of any single vertex do not disconnect the graph G.

Also removal of any two vertices do not disconnect the graph G.

Removal of a, c, z disconnects the graph G

∴ $K(G) = 3$.

Example 4.46 : *Find the edge connectivity $\lambda(G)$ of the following graph.*

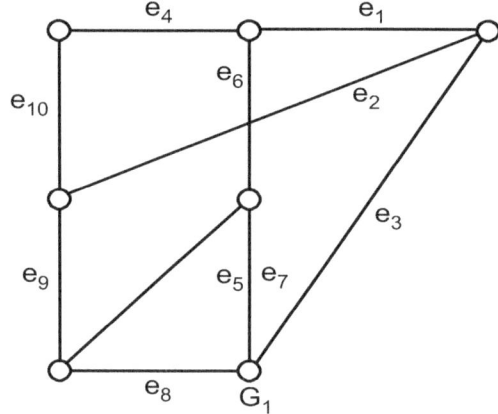

Fig. 4.123

Solution : Removal of any single edge do not disconnect the graph G_1.

Removal of any two edges do not disconnect the graph G_1.

But if we remove e_1, e_2, e_3 the graph is disconnected.

∴ $\lambda(G_1) = 3$

Example 4.47 : *Find the edge connectivity of graph G_2.*

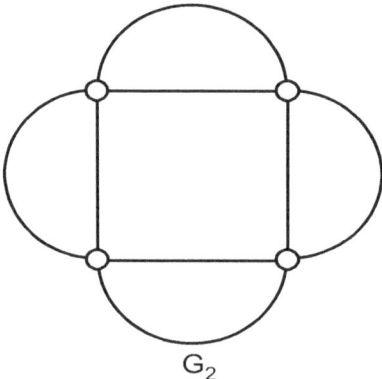

Fig. 4.124

Solution : Removal of any single edge, do not disconnect the graph G_2.

Removal of any two edges do not disconnect the graph G_2.

Removal of any three edges do not disconnect the graph G_2.

Now, if we remove any four edges incident on any vertex leaves a disconnected graph

$$\therefore \quad \lambda(G_2) = 4$$

Example 4.48 : *Prove that in a cubic graph, vertex connectivity equals the edge connectivity.*

Solution :

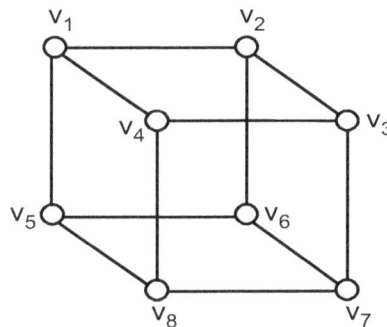

Fig. 4.125

Cubic graph is as shown in Fig. 4.125.

For any graph, we have

$$K(G) \leq \lambda(G) \leq (G)$$

But $\quad \delta(G) = 3$ (minimum vertex degree)

$\therefore \quad K(G) \leq \lambda(G) \leq 3$ ... (*)

Now removal of any single vertex do not disconnect G.

Removal of any two vertices also do not disconnect G.

But removal of v_1, v_3, v_6 leaves G disconnected

$$\therefore \quad K(G) = 3$$

$\therefore$ From (*) $\quad K(G) = \lambda(G) = 3$

Example 4.49 : *Find number of cycles in the following graph.*

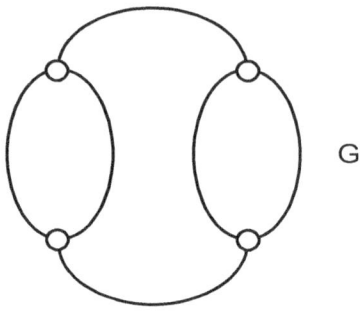

Fig. 4.126

Solution : Cycles of G are listed as below.

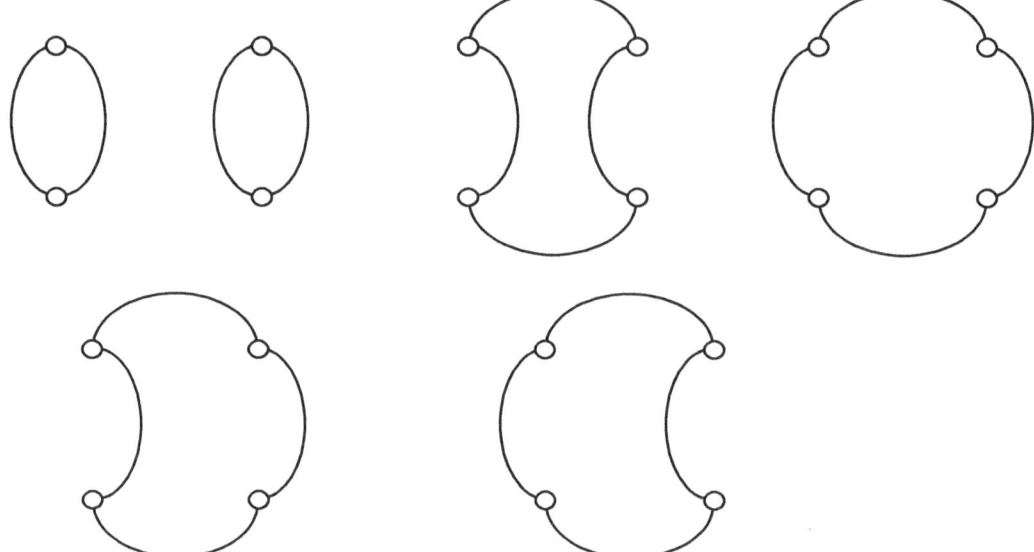

Fig. 4.127

Hence, there are 6 cycles in G.

Note that there are 4 vertices. Since, any cycle in G has atmost length equals to 4.

Example 4.50 : *What is the diameter of Peterson's graph ?*

Solution : Peterson's graph is a graph with vertex set as 2-subsets of {1, 2, 3, 4, 5} and we join any two vertices i.e. 2-subsets if they are disjoint.

Hence, Peterson graph as shown below.

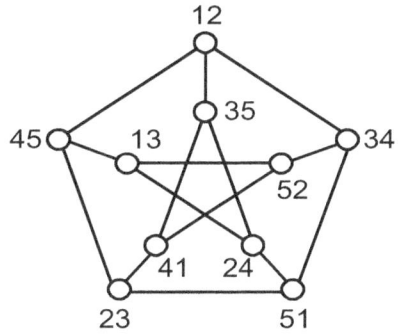

Fig. 4.128

Now we will find diameter of G.

For any two vertices u, v of G, we have

$$d(u, v) \leq 2$$

Also max $\{d(u, v)/u, v \in G\} = 2$

∴ Diameter of G is equal to 2.

EXERCISE 4.3

1. Find the number of cycles in the following two graphs :

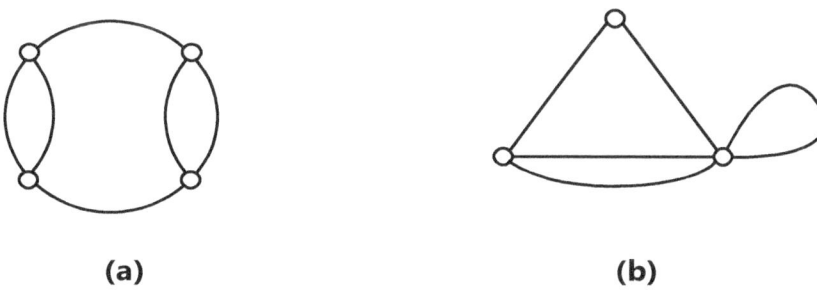

(a)   (b)

Fig. 4.129

2. If an edge e is in a closed trail of a graph G then show that e is in cycle of G.

3. What is the diameter of Peterson's graph ?

4. x, y, z are different vertices in a graph G. Prove that if there is a path from x to y and also a path from y to z then there is a path from x to z.

5. Draw the graphs G_1^2 and G_2^2 where

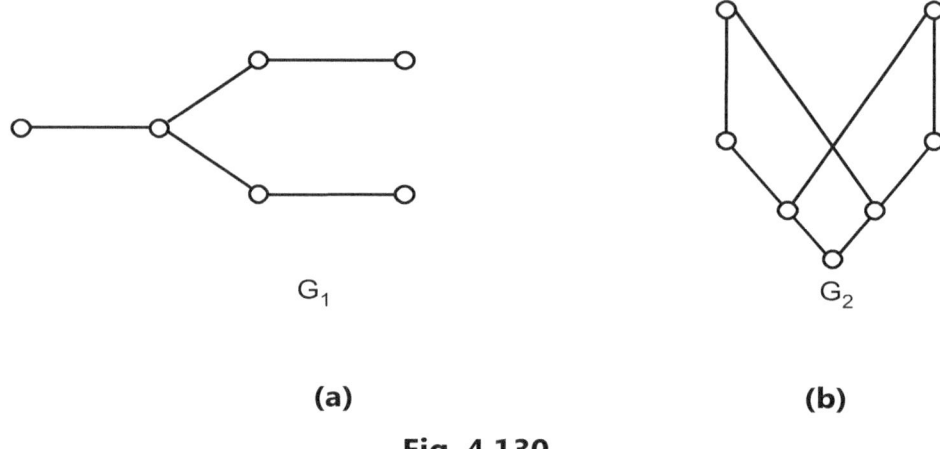

G_1 G_2

(a)   (b)

Fig. 4.130

6. Find (a) the maximum number of edges in a simple disconnected graph with n vertices. (b) The maximum and minimum number of edges in a simple connected graph with n vertices. (c) The maximum number of edges in a simple bipartite graph with n vertices.

7. Let V = {0, 1, 2, ..., 20} be the vertex set of a graph G. An edge between x and y exists when x-y is divisible by 5. Draw a graph G. Explain why G is not connected. What the components of G represent ?

8. Give example of a connected graph such that the removal of any single edge results in a disconnected graph. Show that the number of edges in such a graph is exactly one less than the number of vertices.

9. A graph G has vertices and edges equal in number. Show that G must contain at least one cycle.

10. G is a graph with n vertices and m edges. If $m > {}^{n-1}C_2$ then show that G is connected. For n = 2, 3, 4, draw a disconnected graph satisfying the condition $m = {}^{n-1}C_2$.

11. Prove that in a connected graph G, any two longest paths have a vertex in common.

12. Find all the bridges in the graph.

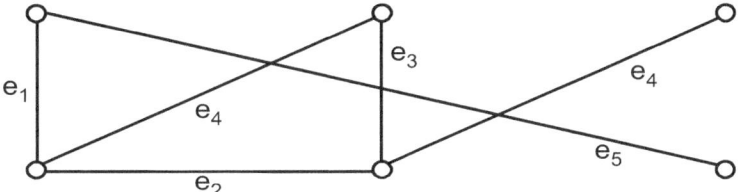

Fig. 4.131

13. What is the edge connectivity of K_n ?
14. Find the vertex connectivity of the following graphs G_1, G_2, G_3.

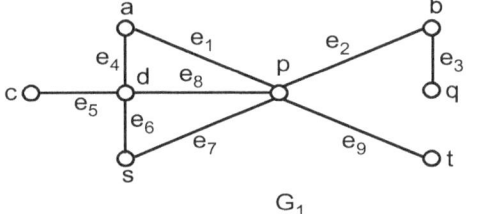 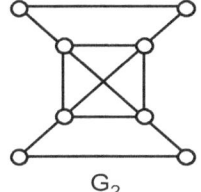 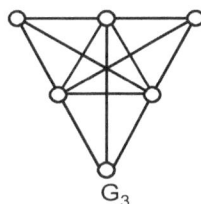

Fig. 4.132

15. Find the edge connectivity of the following graphs G_1 and G_2.

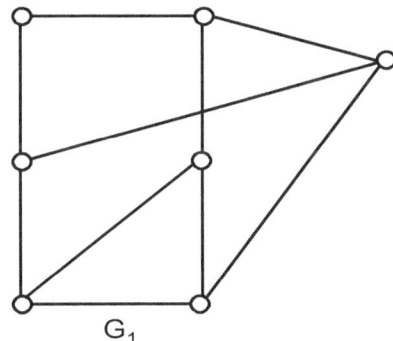 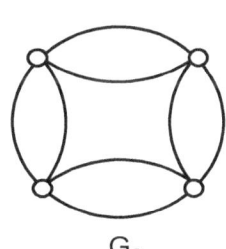

Fig. 4.133

16. A graph is called a cubic graph if it is 3-regular. Prove that a cubic graph as a cut vertex iff it has a bridge.
17. Prove that in a cubic graph, vertex connectivity equals the edge connectivity.
18. Find what maximum vertex connectivity and edge connectivity can be achieved with 8 vertices and 16 edges. Draw a graph showing that they are achieved.

ANSWERS 4.3

1. 6, 4
3. 2
5.

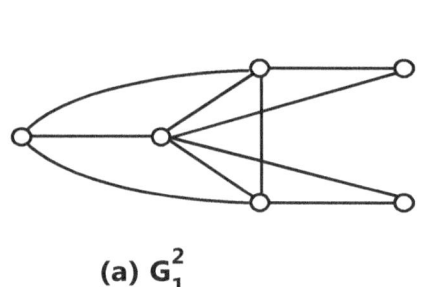

(a) G_1^2 (b) G_2^2

Fig. 4.134

6. (a) $\dfrac{(n-1)(n-2)}{2}$, (b) $\dfrac{n(n-1)}{2}$, $n-1$, (c) $\dfrac{n^2}{4}$.

7.

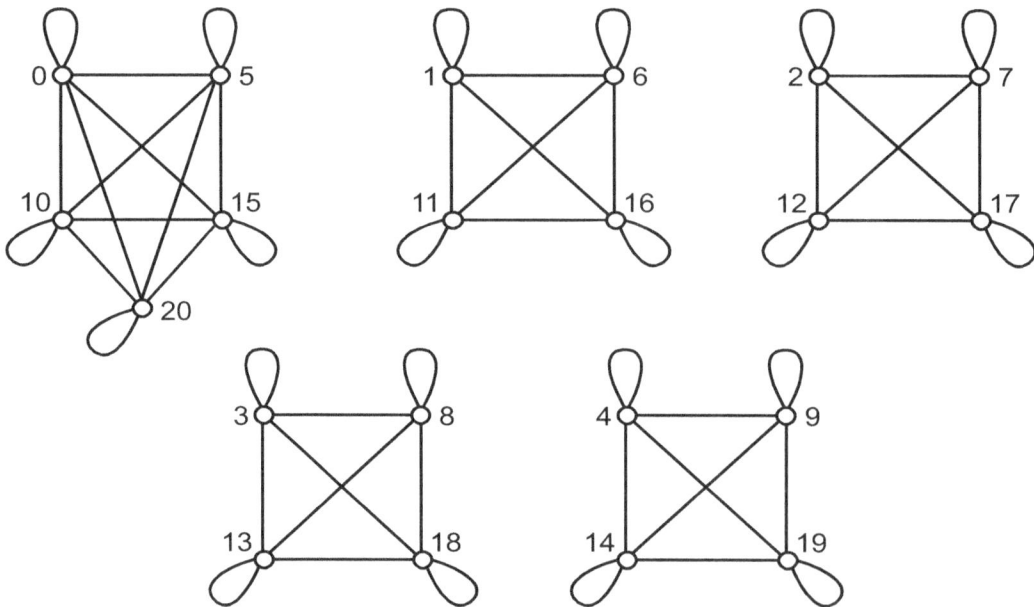

Fig. 4.135

Components are equivalence classes with respect to equivalence relation congruence modulo 5.

1. e_1, e_5, e_6
2. n – 1
3. 1, 2, 3
4. 2, 4
5. 4

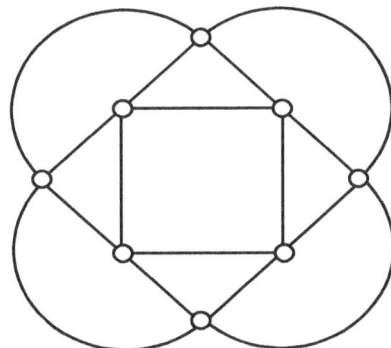

Fig. 4.136

THEORY QUESTIONS

1. What is the difference between operations edge deletion and vertex deletion ?
2. Show that edge disjoint subgraphs need not be disjoint.
3. Show that number of vertices in a self complementary graph is of the type 4k or 4k + 1; where k is an integer.
4. Can we obtain joint of two graphs from their ring sum ? Justify.
5. Can we find number of components in a graph by using fusion of vertices ? Explain by an example.
6. Show that $\bar{\bar{G}} = G$ where – denotes the complement of G.
7. Define spanning subgraph of G with help of an example.
8. Give one application of graph in brief.
9. State and prove handshaking lemma.
10. Prove that any simple graph on n vertices has atmost $\frac{n(n-1)}{2}$ edges.

11. Let G_1 and G_2 be two graphs such that $G_1 \cong G_2$. If G_1 has 20 vertices of degree 4 in G then show that G_2 also has 20 vertices at degree 4.

12. A man has a boat with carrying capacity of two objects only, himself and other. He want to pass a goat, a bundle of grass and tiger from a bank of river to opposite bank of the river through the boat. Show that it is possible for him to do this. Explain this in terms of a graph.

13. Define a complete graph and a regular graph.

14. Define adjacency matrix and incidence matrix of a graph. What is difference between them?

15. Define walk, tour, path cycle in a graph and give difference between them by giving examples.

16. Let G be a graph.

    Let $d(u, v)$ = The minimum of lengths of $u - v$ path $\forall\ u, v \in V$

    where, V = Set of vertices of G

    Prove that d is a metric function on V.

17. Show that maximum number of edges in a simple graph with n vertices and k components is $\dfrac{(n-k)(n-k+1)}{2}$.

18. Let G be a connected graph. Let r and d be radius and diameter of G. Prove that $r \leq d \leq 2r$.

19. Let G be a simple graph with n vertices and m edges. Let k = number of components in G. Show that $n - k \leq m$.

20. Define cut vertex and cut edge. Illustrate these definitions by examples.

21. Let G be a simple graph, show that $k(G) \leq \lambda(G) \leq \delta(G)$

    where, $k(G)$ = vertex connectivity of G

    $\lambda(G)$ = edge connectivity of G

    $\delta(G)$ = the minimum of degrees of vertices in G

MULTIPLE CHOICE QUESTIONS

1. If G is a self complementary graph on n vertices then n takes value possibly
   - (a) 24
   - (b) 22
   - (c) 23
   - (d) 19

2. The graph 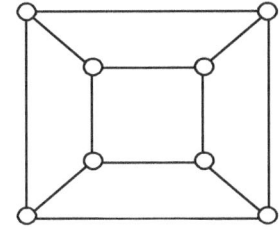 can be decomposed into

   (a) two copies of $K_{1,3}$
   (b) two copies of $K_{1,4}$
   (c) two copies of $K_{1,5}$
   (d) two copies of $K_{1,6}$

3. Complement of graph  is

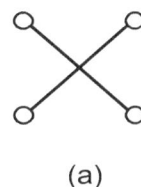 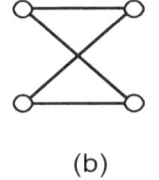 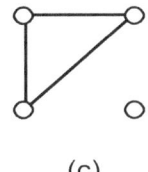 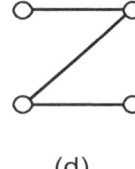

   (a)   (b)   (c)   (d)

4. Consider two graphs

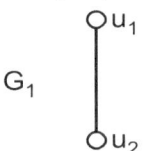 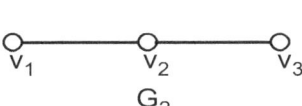

   G_1 G_2

   then $G_1 \times G_2$ is

(a)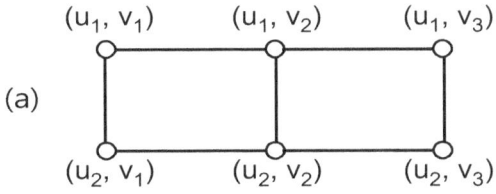

(b)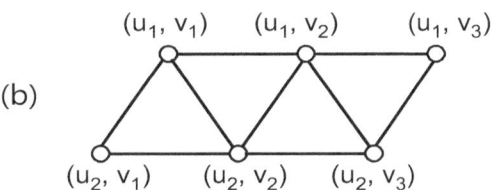

(c)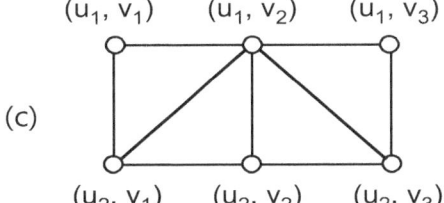

(d)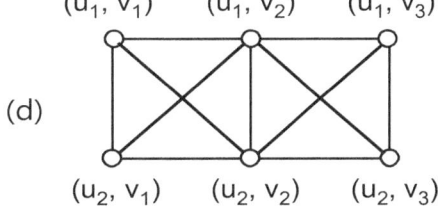

5. Subgraph of the graph

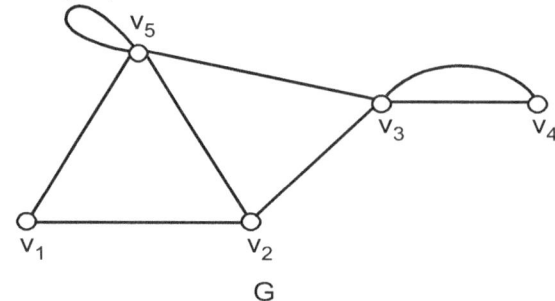

induced by $\{v_1, v_3\}$ is

(a) $\underset{v_1}{\circ}\!\!-\!\!-\!\!-\!\!\underset{v_3}{\circ}$ (b)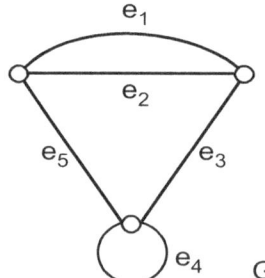

(c) $\underset{v_1}{\circ} \quad \underset{v_3}{\circ}$ (d) None of these

6. Subgraph of the graph

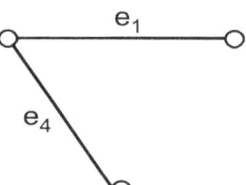

induced by $\{e_1, e_4\}$ is

(a)

(b)

(c)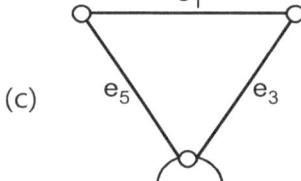

(d) $\circ \quad \circ$

$\circ \quad \circ$

7. For any graph G, which of following is false ?
   (a) $G \cup G = G$
   (b) $G \cap G = G$
   (c) $G \oplus G$ is null graph
   (d) $G_1 \times G_2 = G_2 \times G_1$

8. The underlying graph of the graph $G - \{v_1, v_2\}$.

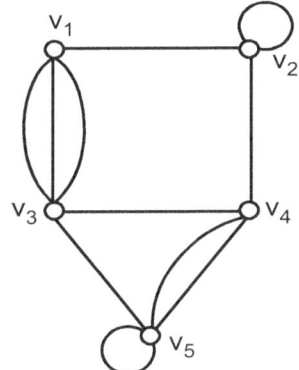

is

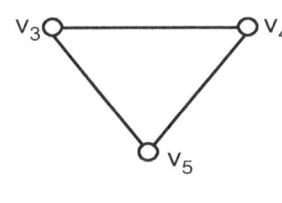 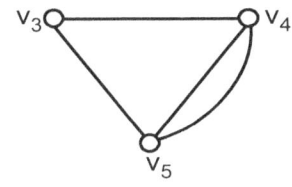

      (a)   (b)

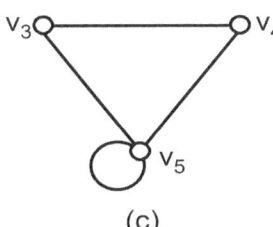 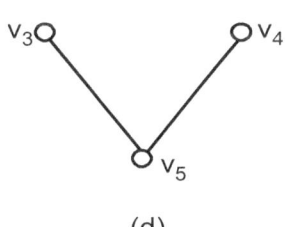

      (c)   (d)

9. Let G be regular graph on odd number of vertices then degree of each vertex in G is possibly
   (a) 21
   (b) 20
   (c) 19
   (d) 17

10. The smallest number of vertices in K_n with 600 edges are
    (a) 35
    (b) 36
    (c) 37
    (d) 38

11. Which of the following are complete graphs ?
    (a) $K_{1,1}$
    (b) $K_{2,1}$
    (c) $K_{1,2}$
    (d) $K_{2,2}$

12. Which of the following is an adjacency matrix of a simple graph ?
    (a) $\begin{bmatrix} 1 & 2 & 3 \\ 4 & 5 & 0 \\ 0 & 0 & 0 \end{bmatrix}$
    (b) $\begin{bmatrix} 1 & 2 & 3 \\ 4 & 5 & 0 \end{bmatrix}$
    (c) $\begin{bmatrix} 0 & 1 & 1 \\ 1 & 0 & 1 \\ 1 & 1 & 0 \end{bmatrix}$
    (d) $\begin{bmatrix} 0 & 1 & 1 \\ 0 & 0 & 1 \\ 1 & 0 & 1 \end{bmatrix}$

13. Let $A(G) = \begin{bmatrix} 1 & 0 & 1 \\ 0 & 1 & 2 \\ 2 & 1 & 0 \end{bmatrix}$ $A(G') = \begin{bmatrix} 0 & 1 & 2 \\ 1 & 0 & 1 \\ 2 & 1 & 0 \end{bmatrix}$
    are adjacency matrices of graphs G and G' then
    (a) $G \cong G'$
    (b) $G \cong G'$
    (c) Sometimes $G \cong G'$ but not always
    (d) $G = G'$

14. Which of the following is an incidence matrix of a simple graph
    (a) $\begin{bmatrix} 1 & 2 & 3 \\ 4 & 5 & 6 \\ 0 & 1 & 2 \end{bmatrix}$
    (b) $\begin{bmatrix} 0 & 1 & 1 \\ 1 & 0 & 1 \\ 1 & 1 & 0 \end{bmatrix}$
    (c) $\begin{bmatrix} 0 & 0 & 1 & 0 & 1 \\ 1 & 0 & 1 & 1 & 1 \\ 1 & 1 & 1 & 1 & 1 \end{bmatrix}$
    (d) $\begin{bmatrix} 0 & 0 & 1 & 0 \\ 0 & 1 & 0 & 1 \\ 0 & 0 & 1 & 1 \end{bmatrix}$

15. Let G be a simple graph with atleast two vertices then
    (a) $G \cong K_3$
    (b) $G \cong K_{2,4}$
    (c) G has atleast two vertices of same degree
    (d) G is null graph

16. Let G be a graph with vertices v_1, v_2, v_3, v_4 then we have possibly.
    (a) $d(v_1) = 1$ $d(v_2) = 2$ $d(v_3) = 3$ $d(v_4) = 5$
    (b) $d(v_1) = 1$ $d(v_2) = 1$ $d(v_3) = 2$ $d(v_4) = 1$
    (c) $d(v_1) = 3$ $d(v_2) = 2$ $d(v_3) = 5$ $d(v_4) = 0$
    (d) $d(v_1) = 0$ $d(v_2) = 2$ $d(v_3) = 2$ $d(v_3) = 3$

17. Let G(V, E) be simple graph with 5 components and $|V| = 10$ then $|E|$ less than or equal to
    (a) 15
    (b) 14
    (c) 13
    (d) 12

18. Let G(V, E) be a simple graph with 5 components and $|V| = 10$ then $|E|$ is greater than or equal to
    (a) 5
    (b) 6
    (c) 7
    (d) 8

19. Let G be a simple graph and K(G), λ(G), δ(G) denotes vertex connectivity, edge connectivity and the minimum vertex degree in G respectively, then
    (a) $K(G) \leq \lambda(G) \leq \delta(G)$
    (b) $\lambda(G) \leq K(G) \leq \delta(G)$
    (c) $\delta(G) \leq \lambda(G) \leq K(G)$
    (d) $K(G) \leq \delta(G) \leq \lambda(G)$

20. Let K_n be a complete graph on n vertices and $K_{m,n}$ be a complete bipartite graph on m + n vertices, then
    (a) $K(K_n) = n - 1$, $\lambda(K_{m,n}) = \min\{m, n\}$
    (b) $\lambda(K_n) = n - 1$, $K(K_{m,n}) = \max\{m, n\}$
    (c) $K(K_n) = 0$, $K(K_{m,n}) = m + n$
    (d) None of these

21. Which of the following graph has a bridge

    (a)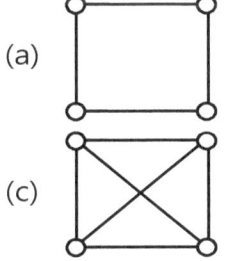
    (b)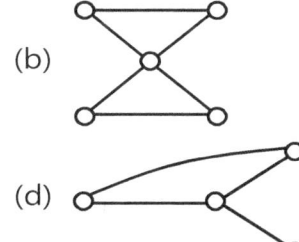
    (c)
    (d)

22. Which of the following graph has a cut vertex

    (a)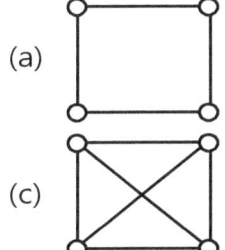
    (b)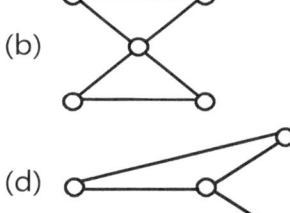
    (c)
    (d)

23. Consider a simple connected graph G with n vertices and n edges (n > 2) then which of the following is true ?
    - (a) G has atleast one cycle
    - (b) G has no cycles
    - (c) The graph obtained by removing any edge from G is not connected
    - (d) G has exactly one cycle

24. Let G be a graph with 100 vertices numbered 1 to 100. Two vertices i and j are adjacent iff $|i - j| = 8$ or $|i - j| = 12$. The number of components in G is
    - (a) 8
    - (b) 12
    - (c) 25
    - (d) 4

25. The minimum number of edges in a connected cyclic graph on n vertices are
    - (a) n − 1
    - (b) n
    - (c) n + 1
    - (d) None of these

Answers

(1) - (a) (2) - (a) (3) - (a) (4) - (a) (5) - (c) (6) - (a) (7) - (d)
(8) - (a) (9) - (b) (10) - (a) (11) - (a) (12) - (c) (13) - (a) (14) - (b)
(15) - (c) (16) - (c) (17) - (a), (18) - (a), (19) - (a), (20) - (a),
(21) - (d), (22) - (d), (23) - (a) (24) - (a), (25) - (b)

SAY TRUE OR FALSE WITH JUSTIFICATION

1. If G is a graph then $G - U = \overline{<U>}$, where U is subset of vertex set of G.
2. Two edges disjoint subgraphs are also vertex disjoint.
3. Any n vertex graph and its complement decomposes K_n.
4. For any three graphs G_1, G_2 and G_3, $(G_1 \cup G_2) \cup G_3 = G_1 \cup (G_2 \cup G_3)$ holds.

5. For any two vertex disjoint graphs G_1 and G_2,
$$G_1 \cup G_2 = G_1 \oplus G_2$$
6. Deletion of central vertex from a wheel graph W_5 leaves null graph.
7. For any two graphs G_1 and G_2,
$$G_1 \oplus (G_2 \cap G_3) = (G_1 \oplus G_2) \cap (G_1 \oplus G_3) \text{ holds.}$$
8. Deletion of two vertices from K_n leaves K_{n-2}.
9. A circle with centre at (2, 3) and radius unity is a graph.
10. There is no simple graph with 10 vertices and 46 edges.
11. There exists a 5-regular graph on 7 vertices.
12. $K_{m, n}$ is regular if m = n.
13. Handshaking lemma is true for multigraph also.
14. There is a group of nine people at a party such that one knows exactly five of the others in the group.
15. There is simple graph with 10 vertices and 46 edges.
16. There is 5 regular graph with 7 vertices.
17. $K_{m, n}$ is regular iff m = n.
18. Adjacency matrix of graph is symmetric matrix.
19. 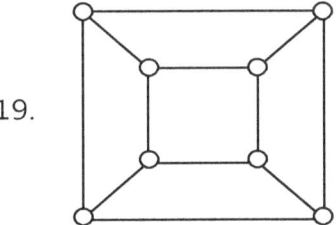 is a bipartite graph
20. Incidence matrix of null graph is zero matrix. But adjacency matrix of null graph is non-zero matrix.
21. Graph has cut vertex of degree 1.
22. Let v be cut vertex of simple graph G then $\overline{G}$ – v is connected.
23. Let G_n be graph whose vertices are the permutations of {1, 2, 3, ... n} with two permutations $a_1, a_2 \ldots a_n$ and $b_1, b_2 \ldots b_n$ adjacent iff they differ by interchanging a pair of adjacent entries. Then G_n is connected.

24. If G is connected graph with atleast three vertices then G has two vertices x, y such that G – {x, y} is connected.

25. If u and v only two vertices of odd degree in a graph G then G has u – v path.

26. Let G be graph with vertex set {1, … 15} in which i and j are adjacent iff their greatest common factor exceeds 1, then diameter of G is 7.

27. The edge set of every closed trail can be partitioned into edge sets of cycle.

28. The longest trail which is not closed then its end points have odd degree.

29. Bipartite graph has unique partition, iff it is connected.

30. Complement of a simple disconnected graph is disconnected.

Answers

(1) False (2) False (3) True (4) True (5) True (6) False (7) True
(8) True (9) False (10) True (11) False (12) True (13) True
(14) False (15) False (16) False (17) True (18) True (19) True
(20) False (21) False (22) True (23) True (24) True (25) True
(26) True (27) True (28) True (29) True (30) False

www.ingramcontent.com/pod-product-compliance
Lightning Source LLC
Chambersburg PA
CBHW080726230426
43665CB00020B/2634